RISING
TIDE

RISING TIDE

The Untold Story of
the Russian Submarines That
Fought the Cold War

GARY E. WEIR AND

WALTER J. BOYNE

BASIC
BOOKS

A Member of the Perseus Books Group

Published by Basic Books,
A Member of the Perseus Books Group

Library of Congress Cataloging-in-Publication Data
Rising tide / by Gary E. Weir and Walter J. Boyne.
p.   cm.
Includes bibliographical references.
ISBN 0-465-09112-1 (alk. paper)
1. Soviet Union. Voenno-Morskoæi Flot—Submarine forces—History.
2. Russia (Federation). Voenno-Morskoæi Flot—Submarine forces—History.
I. Boyne, Walter J. II. Title.
V859.R9W45   2003
359.9'3'094709045—dc22
2003017293

Book design by Jane Raese
This book is set in 10-point Utopia

03 04 05 06 / 10 9 8 7 6 5 4 3 2

For Catherine, the best part of my life

—GEW

For those who fought the Cold War in submarines
deep below the surface of the World Ocean,
both Russian and American

—WJB

CONTENTS

AUTHOR'S NOTE

For those of us who reached maturity in a world without a unified Germany, and who recall exactly how it felt to live with the tensions of the Cold War, the Soviet Union loomed large and far away, but disturbingly able to reach our homes with the ultimate horror of nuclear weapons. We watched Nikita Khrushchev on the television and on advertising billboards vowing to bury the free world, frantically waving his arms while standing at a podium before the General Assembly of the United Nations. The presence of "mutually assured destruction" and the devices and vehicles that would bring that devastation became a constant presence over the course of roughly fifty years. Indeed, our familiarity with them and the official faces behind them became almost normal and comforting in a macabre way. It became a case of "better the devil you know."

But, did we know this devil? Did we ever actually meet this devil? How many Russians did the average American actually know? Did we discuss our mutual anxiety across a table or did we have to settle for watching the May Day parade in Red Square as covered by Walter Cronkite for CBS to see Soviet faces? Our image of the Soviet threat existed as a monolith with a countenance resembling the politician of the moment, but without personality or emotion, and most certainly incapable of communicating that truth that comes from looking another human being in the eye.

In February 2002, as part of the initial stages of this project, I journeyed to Moscow and St. Petersburg in the former Soviet Union to come face to face with the men who went to sea in Soviet submarines and brought the nuclear threat directly to the shores of the United States during the Cold War. In this book, for the first time, the threat assumes an identity, has a personality, becomes human, and relates the daunting and fascinating story of the Cold War through a Soviet periscope. When the United States came closest to nuclear attack, during the Cuban Missile Crisis, the decision to use that weapon rested not only with a Communist Party secretary and a U.S. president, but also with the commanding officer of a Soviet Foxtrot diesel submarine. The scenario many found so sobering in the post–Soviet era Gene Hackman–Denzel Washington film *Crimson Tide* actually took place just off the North American Atlantic coast in 1962. In this case the United States Navy was the potential target and not the fictional Russian fanatic of *Crimson Tide* condemning the United States from far eastern Russia.

In a series of unique and comprehensive oral histories, I sat for hours both in hotel rooms and in homes with senior Soviet submariners and explored their personal origins, families, professional choices, successes, and hardships; making a log of the course taken by each as he rose to the top of his profession and literally navigated the unexplored and explosive waters of the Cold War. The conversations passed from Russian to English and back again through the patience and skill of Iazamir Gotta and Irina Krivaya. Indeed, this project would not have been possible without the vision and effort of Iazamir Gotta and Robert Gottlieb of Trident Media Group.

In Moscow I spoke with the fast attack specialist and Arctic veteran Vice Admiral Anatoli Shevchenko; a witness to the Cuban Missile Crisis, Captain First Rank Nikolai Shumkov; the twins Rear Admiral Oleg

Chefonov and his brother Captain First Rank Igor Chefonov; and the wily intelligence officer Rear Admiral Gleb Kondratiev. In St. Petersburg, the beautiful naval city in the process of celebrating the 300th anniversary of its founding by the father of the Russian Navy, Tsar Peter the Great, I met with Rear Admiral Vladimir Lebedko, a confidant of Admiral Sergei G. Gorshkov who lost a beloved son in the submarine service, and Rear Admiral Lev Chernavin with his vivid memories of the secret Soviet submarine base at Alexandria in Egypt. I also spent hours with Captain First Rank Vladimir Borisov, who trailed the USS *Saratoga*; the expert salvor Captain First Rank Leonid Melodinski; the high-speed Alfa-driver Captain First Rank Boris Kolyada; and the ranking members of the St. Petersburg Submarine Club, Captain First Rank Igor Kurdin and his second, Captain First Rank Igor Kozyr. Sitting down with these people, drinking vodka or sharing a meal, I finally looked the Cold War in the face and discovered the nature of the navy and the people who waged that war at great risk under the ocean.

These former Soviet military men took stock of me as I became acquainted with them. Watching Vice Admiral Shevchenko's deliberately grim determination to maintain constant eye contact with me as he took off his coat at the beginning of our first interview made a lasting impression, as I am sure he intended that it should. When I met in an official capacity with the second-ranking officer of the Russian Navy, Admiral I. V. Kasatonov in Moscow in 1998, I felt that same constant probing across a banquet table, over a rather elegant dinner. I have had the same experience with veteran American submarine drivers. Former chief of the American and NATO Atlantic submarine force, Vice Admiral George Emery, always combines a benign smile with direct and probing eye contact. These submariners immediately take their measure of you, a professional habit and instinct born of experience. The former Soviet officers who contributed to this book always communicated friendliness, sincerity, truth as they saw it, and extreme competence, while also confirming their professional determination, devotion to the Soviet cause, and willingness in years past to use the weapons entrusted to them to defend the interests of the USSR. As Shevchenko occasionally said about Cold War submarine operations and close encounters deep in the ocean with his opposite numbers in the American submarine force, "there were no illusions." As a skeptical historian dreading post-Soviet rationalization and excuses, I found none.

This story also covers a considerable span of time in the history of submarine warfare. In terms of technology, design, and operational capability, Nikolai Shumkov's *B-130*, a veteran of the Cuban Missile Crisis, now seems a relic of the stone age in comparison to Shevchenko's Victor 3 or Kolyada's Alfa. Nuclear propulsion created the true submarine, made long-term submergence possible, and permitted naval architects to design a vessel that would spend nearly all of its time below the surface. In turn, the Cold War competition between the Soviet Union and the United States made the resources available to expand the undersea envelope within which the submarine could operate. Hydrodynamics, screw design, more efficient steam turbines, advanced metallurgy, and a greater attention to acoustics and noise brought the submarine ever closer to fulfilling the holy trinity of undersea warfare: to move faster, operate deeper, and remain quieter than ever.

As advances went to sea on successive generations of quickly produced American, British, and Soviet submarines, the risk increased exponentially in this deep battlespace. Here hostilities take place in three dimensions, against a very quiet adversary you can perceive only via sound and sonar, and must subdue not by hand–eye coordination at the amazing speeds of aerial combat but by the abstract reasoning and mental agility that permits both the encounter and its solution to unfold at a speed faster than that of a jet fighter in the mind of the submarine's commanding officer. Only this kind of talent and skill permitted Rear Admiral Vladimir Lebedko to survive the submerged collision with USS *Gato* that he described for me in the living room of his small St. Petersburg flat below the portrait of his late son. Only this enabled Vice Admiral Shevchenko to pursue an American Sturgeon class fast attack submarine and survive the experience.

More than anything, *Rising Tide* offers an intimate and often frightening oral history of the Cold War Soviet submarine force. I had very little primary Soviet documentation to confirm or challenge the assertions made here. Given the passage of time since the end of the Cold War, documentation has become available in the West to permit a modest critical evaluation of the accounts offered by the officers who met with me in Russia. Unfortunately, the official records of the American and Soviet submarine communities will remain closed and classified. These operators lived and survived by stealth. What they did and how they did it will never completely see the light of day. Nonetheless, this project has endeavored to use a variety of personal primary sources and unclassified documentary sources, both primary and secondary, to place the testimony of these officers in historical context.

Rising Tide is the first of its kind. The bulk of what emerges from this book either appears here in public for the very first time or corrects mistakes or partial accounts appearing in other, earlier works that could not benefit from the access *Rising Tide* had to the men who actually carried out these deeds. Thus, genuine historical efforts, like *Rising Tide,* will come closer than any other endeavor to revealing for public consideration the contributions made by Soviet submariners to the extension of Soviet influence and authority after World War II. Most importantly, *Rising Tide* is a conversation with NATO's Cold War adversaries. They are no longer anonymous or part of a threatening monolith, but rather men with faces, identities, an allegiance, and an amazing story to tell.

Gary E. Weir
Gaithersburg, Maryland
25 May 2003

Introduction

The Soviet commander's sonar suddenly picked up an unwelcome visitor, close aboard. The acoustic signature library identified the contact as an American Sturgeon class nuclear attack submarine. Deciding not to disguise his presence, the commander took the con and swiftly placed his boat immediately behind the American. Captain First Rank Anatoli Shevchenko felt sure that his opposite number had already detected him so he decided to deprive the American of any stealthy illusions he may have had. He also wanted to drive the American away from ongoing Soviet fleet exercises in the area. Suddenly, Shevchenko's opponent decided to lose his pursuer and resume his patrol, so he accelerated away at high speed, doubtless hoping to double back more quietly at some future point without benefit of a Victor class tail. Rather than feeling relief, Shevchenko found only stimulation in the prospect of a high-speed chase. Listening for the sound of the Sturgeon's screws loudly departing at over 24 knots, he waited for the burst of speed to end without accelerating himself. While he waited, his sonar plotted the American's course and speed. When the acoustic signal went quiet, Shevchenko's *K-513* accelerated, along the same bearing and course, for the same amount of time. His boat then slowed down to permit the *513*'s sonar to reacquire the American, who then attempted once again to elude at high speed. While proceeding at an accelerated pace, neither the American nor the Russian could detect his adversary due to the turbulence generated by their high-speed screws, internal machinery sounds, and the increased water flow noises along the outside of the hull. Some of these high-speed bursts lasted for nearly thirty minutes. Like the American, after each prolonged period at high speed, Shevchenko slowed down to 5 knots to give his sonar a chance to reacquire the other submarine. Each time the American realized his effort to elude had failed, and the chase began again.

Since sonar cannot "hear" anything with the boat moving at high speed, the personnel in the sonar room took some time to relax during the accelerations. Many years later, this chase stood out in Shevchenko's memory not only for its speed, daring, and recklessness on both sides, but also for a tradition initiated by the *513*'s political officer. After two hours of chasing had passed, he had the cook reward each hard-working rating in the sonar room for their intense devotion to the chase. While their boat sped after the American and attention to the momentarily deaf passive sonar could relax, the galley provided each sonar technician with a bowl of cream cheese, topped with sour cream, and crowned by a magnificent strawberry! So while the submarine rushed after its adversary, the acoustics team sat back and enjoyed this decadent treat laced with welcome color and vitamin C. As soon as their boat slowed, they went back to work.

≈   ≈   ≈

IN RECENT TIMES, books such as *Blind Man's Bluff, K-19,* and *Hostile Waters* have alerted the public that the submarine forces of the United

States and the Soviet Union had engaged in this kind of potentially world-threatening contest deep below the ocean surface. Films such as *The Hunt for Red October* and *K-19* heightened this awareness, portraying in frightening detail the potential nuclear disaster implicit in the creation of submarine-launched ballistic missiles and the sophisticated submarines that carry them.

Both books and films have attempted to portray the high level of courage and intellect that submariners of both nations needed to carry on their lonely, almost invisible, combat operations that sometimes led to tragic accidents.

The untold story of the Soviet submariners—locked simultaneously in not one but two brutal contests—lies at the heart of all these tales and of this book. The first conflict, in which the U.S. Navy and the Royal Navy served as primary adversaries, will emerge here in a new and revealing way. The second, which pitted Russian submariners against the incredibly mendacious and arbitrary Soviet naval and civil bureaucracy, will appear here in its full and appalling scope. Further, the blame for exposing Soviet seamen to totally unwarranted and unnecessary dangers has never been placed squarely on the man most responsible, Sergei G. Gorshkov, Admiral of the Fleet of the Soviet Union. His unique view of world and naval politics, coupled with the unchallenged authority he had over the destinies of his seamen, led many of those same seamen to die needlessly in fulfilling his goals. And that same unique view concealed a terrible secret, an enormously vulnerable Achilles' heel of which Gorshkov, of all people, must certainly have been aware, but which is explicitly delineated here by his own loyal submariners. The dangerous secret was the incredibly fragile margin of safety in the Soviet submarine nuclear weapon programs.

In the United States, every nuclear weapon program had a built-in system of checks and balances to ensure that nuclear weapons could not be launched by the arbitrary action of some unbalanced aircraft, missile, artillery, or submarine commander. This was reinforced by a strong and effective human factors program that carefully examined those persons who would be placed in control of a nuclear weapons launch. These actions reduced the risk of an unauthorized nuclear attack to a minimum, and were further reinforced by constant monitoring of the individuals involved. As popular an icon of nuclear madness as it became, the film *Fail Safe* portrayed a situation that could never have happened in the U.S. armed services because of these carefully designed procedures.

In stark contrast, this book contains dramatic firsthand, first-person evidence that the final decision to launch a nuclear torpedo or nuclear missile ultimately resided in the hands of individual submarine commanders. The very possibility of a self-determined nuclear launch is frightening enough, but when you add to it the inordinate stresses faced by Soviet submarine commanders, it becomes truly horrifying.

Previous books and films on the admittedly brave and patriotic Soviet submariners have portrayed them as basically identical to their American counterparts in terms of personality, motivation, and skill levels. This derives in part from good storytelling and from the common post–World War II nostalgia phenomenon in which veterans of the Luftwaffe meet and socialize with their former U.S. Army Air Forces opponents, or British Desert Rats drink with their former *Afrika Korps* enemies in Munich beer halls. One prescribed conclusion is that the men on each side were in fact professionally similar.

This is a comfortable approach to take for the Cold War submarine conflict, for it then becomes more understandable, almost sporting. But it is basically incorrect. The Cold War Soviet submariners had totally different personal frames of reference upon which to base their decisions, far different pressures to respond to, and much inferior training. This becomes obvious from the frightening specifics provided by these Russian warriors who, in their own words, allowed us to plumb their psychological depths. The startlingly severe background of the underwater war is revealed in first-person narratives that provide intimate insight into the individual submarine officers.

As vital as the human element is in submarine warfare, success, particularly in submarine versus submarine action, ultimately depends upon technological superiority. Fortunately for the West, the United States, and to a lesser degree the United Kingdom, were able to maintain a decisive technological superiority over the Soviet Union. This superiority added immeasurably to the burden of Soviet submariners, and in some instances pushed them closer to the nuclear brink than their adversaries ever intended. There is no little irony in the fact that the great efforts made by the Soviet Union to catch up in the naval race as it had done in the aeronautic, missile, and space arenas may well have been the final defense burden straw that broke the economic back of the Soviet Union, plunging it into financial chaos and eventual dissolution on December 25, 1991.

An analysis of the thinking and philosophies of the Soviet submariners helps explain their sometime inexplicable reactions to emergency situations (which occurred far too often) and to their own bureaucracies. The foundation for understanding this analysis is realizing just how little value was placed on human life in the Soviet Union, even that of a highly trained military man, and how that small value was further depreciated by Stalin's cruel and vicious rule.

It is one thing to say that a tyrant regards a human life as of little worth; it is another, larger thing to say that the bureaucracy the tyrant rules does the same. But it is an enormous thing to say that a malignant bureaucracy has so traumatized its nation that generations of individuals place similar small values on their *own* lives. The pervasive conviction that a soulless life lost means nothing—not even to the person whose life is sacrificed—trickled down to individual actions, and in many cases had the effect of turning the gold of heroism into the base metal of robotic indoctrination.

A brief synthesis of the naval history of Russia and the Soviet Union is necessary to make the naval experience understandable in terms of national needs, its geographical scope, and its past successes and failures. This background is particularly important when we examine the effect that Admiral Gorshkov had upon the modern Soviet Navy, as found in Appendix 1. But first, a recounting of the history of Russian and Soviet submarine forces will allow us to assess the individual actions of the submarine officers whose stories are related here. Any objective evaluation of this history requires, in turn, that a comparative analysis be made of the contemporary submarine forces of other nations, those of Germany and the United States in particular. Without this, the relative success or failure of Soviet submarines in the Cold War would be difficult to measure.

1

STALIN'S GRAND PLAN

———————

The Soviets had a penchant for claiming that many inventions originated with Russian scientists. They dismissed Thomas Edison as a latecomer, for the Russian inventor Paul Jablochkoff had created a small arc light "candle" that was a commercial success in 1887, when eighty of them were installed in the Grands Magasins du Louvre in Paris.[1] The Wright brothers are given similar short shrift thanks to the brief, ramp-assisted hops of Alexander Feodorovitch Mozhaiski's steam-powered monoplane in 1884. And under the impetus of Peter the Great's belief that Russia would not survive without a navy, Yefim Nikonov created the prototype of the modern midget commando submarine in 1720.[2] This antedated by more than fifty years David Bushnell's more famous egg-shaped *Turtle*, which was employed in three (unsuccessful) submarine attacks against the Royal Navy in New York Harbor in 1775 and 1776, and which Americans have always considered the first submarine.[3]

Nikonov's submarine was more conventional than the *Turtle* in appearance. The torpedo-shaped, oak-planked hull was covered with oil-soaked animal skins for waterproofing. The vessel was to be armed with rockets fired from tubes—an uncanny forecast of the nuclear future. Propelled by oars, an order was placed for a number of vessels, along with the rockets to arm them. This was the peak of Nikonov's progress, however, for no successful production followed, and interest lapsed with the death of Peter I in 1725.

Notwithstanding Nikonov's disappointment, later Russian patriots developed submarines of various types. The first one constructed of iron appeared in 1834. Designed by Karl Andreyevich Shil'der, it was tested extensively. Propulsion was by manpower, using fin-like vanes. Armament again included rockets, but also featured mines. A second version successfully destroyed a target ship by the use of mines.

Further designs followed during the Crimean War of 1853–1856, elicited by the Russian need to offset the crippling Anglo-French naval advantage. One of these was by an experienced German submarine practitioner, Wilhelm Bauer. Named *Le Diable Marin*, it was the most successful submarine to date, despite still being powered by men straining on treadmills that looked strangely like modern exercise equipment. *Le Diable Marin* made 133 successful dives, but encountered trouble on September 6, 1856, when on its 134th dive underwater growth prevented its propeller from turning. Had the government bureaucracy functioned better, Bauer's designs could have been improved upon, but as was so often the case in Imperial Russia, the project was dropped and Bauer returned to Germany.

Halfway around the world, another disadvantaged naval power, the Confederate States of America, also attempted submarine warfare on a minor scale. Two submarines, both named *Pioneer*, were tested unsuccessfully. The third was the CSS *H. L. Hunley*, which began an inauspicious career by sinking twice, with a loss of life each time. The desperate Confederates raised it on both occasions. It sank for the last time on its February 17, 1864, attack on the USS *Housitanic*. This was the first successful submarine attack against an enemy warship, and the *Housitanic* sank with a loss of five lives. The ill-fated *Hunley* went down for the third time, taking its crew with it. Unlike the South, the *Hunley* would rise again: It was lifted from the Atlantic waters outside Charleston harbor on August 7, 2000, at the conclusion of a $17 million recovery effort.[4]

In Russia, Major General Konstantin Borisovitch Gern created an advanced submarine design incorporating a self-propelled torpedo in 1867. More notably, Gern's submarine was steam-powered, with compressed air furnishing the necessary oxygen for combustion when submerged. Successfully tested, it also ran aground on bureaucratic indifference, and development ceased—new rather than proven projects seemed to excite the Russian Navy procurement offices.

Ivan Fedorovich Alexandrovsky designed the largest of the nineteenth-century Russian submarines. An artist and photographer, he created a 355-ton iron monster powered by compressed air engines that had some initial success, but dived too deep in 1871 and was crushed by the pressure. This implacable phenomenon, the incredible pressures exerted by the weight of water twisting a sturdy iron or steel hull into a tortured mass of compressed metal, would haunt submarine designers and crews forever.

In 1865, Alexandrovsky submitted a design to the Naval Technical Committee for a "self-propelled mine"—a torpedo. (Mines were often called torpedoes during this period, and the United States' first admiral, David S. Farragut, was referring to tethered mines when he gave his famous August 5, 1864, order in Mobile Bay, Alabama: "Damn the torpedoes, full speed ahead.")

The Russians brought their concept of scale to the world of submarines for the first time in 1879, when Tsar Alexander III witnessed the trials of the second submarine built by Stefan Karlovitch Dzhevesky. The trials were so successful that a total of fifty of his submarines were ordered and built as the Type III. Thirty-four of these were assigned to Sevastopol in the Crimea and sixteen to the base at Kronstadt in the Baltic. While all fifty were pedal-powered craft, one of the sixteen assigned to Kronstadt was modified to hold storage batteries and an electric motor—the world's first submarine so powered.

Although no other submarines by Dzhevesky were electric-powered, electricity was clearly the motive power of the future, and was incorporated into the designs of submarines of other nations. This propulsion development was complemented by the advent of dependable self-propelled torpedoes, the combination of which gave the submarine a chance to become an effective weapon. England's Robert Whitehead was the first to produce a self-propelled torpedo. Powered by a compressed air engine, Whitehead's 1870 torpedo carried 18 pounds of dynamite as its warhead, and featured a self-regulating device that kept the torpedo at a constant preset depth—thus starting the trend to what would be called "smart weapons." The torpedo became instantly popular, for small torpedo boats were seen as an inexpensive antidote to the increasingly costly large capital ships. By 1881 Whitehead's torpedoes were in general use in Britain, which purchased 254, Russia (250), France (218), Germany (203), Denmark (83), Italy (70), Greece (70), Portugal (50), Argentina (40), and Belgium (40).[5]

Ironically, after all of its own excellent research and design, Russia turned to foreign countries for further submarine purchases. The first of these was designed by the Swede Torsten Nordenfeldt and built in Great Britain. With a submerged displacement of 230 tons, the *Nordenfeldt* was powered by a 1,000-horsepower steam engine on the surface. Pressurized steam provided underwater propulsion, and was good for about twenty miles at five knots. Unfortunately, the *Nordenfeldt* was lost at sea en route to Russia.[6]

In 1901, the *Petr Koshka* was created in the Kronstadt shipyard. A small vessel of some twenty tons, it was designed to be carried on board a larger warship, and launched at sea to attack the enemy. The first series of modern Russian submarines were built under the leadership of Ivan Grigorevich Bubnov, who would effectively be the superintendent of submarine construction until the Russian Revolution in 1917.

Under Bubnov, both indigenous and foreign designs were studied, and an initial prototype, the *Delfin,* the first true combat submarine of the Russian Navy, was built at the famed Baltic Works in St. Petersburg. The *Delfin* was followed by a construction program of the larger 140-ton Kasatka class. Six of these were completed and five sent to the Far East in November 1904.

Given the Cold War that lay in the future, it is ironic that the next series of Russian submarine efforts centered on boats developed in the

United States by rivals John P. Holland and Simon Lake. The advent of the Russo–Japanese War in 1904 increased the Russian Navy's already keen interest in submarines, and they secured rights to manufacture both Holland and Lake submarines. They obtained examples of both types clandestinely, since the United States government had prohibited the sale of arms to either opponent in the Russo–Japanese War.[7]

Russia's geography created difficulties in acquiring a fleet of submarines for use against Japan. Submarines from the United States and Germany, as well as those built by Russia, had to be laboriously transported by rail to Vladivostok on the Sea of Japan.[8] To do so, they had to be disassembled, shipped, and reassembled. The Trans-Siberian Railroad tracks were hardly smooth, and the more than five thousand miles of jolting damaged components that were of course held together with nuts and bolts. The bumpy ride shook many of the fasteners loose so that they later admitted salt water and made the boats very vulnerable to corrosion.

Thirteen submarines—a mixture of Kasatka class boats with Holland and Lake types—were operational by 1906, months after the end of the Russo–Japanese War. Seven other submarines were operating at other locations, and seven more were being built. In the succeeding years, enthusiasm for submarines would have to buck budget realities, and while the total number of submarines planned for the Russian Navy varied from over one hundred and fifty to as few as thirty-eight, only about thirty were available for operations in the last full year of peace, 1913.

These early submarines would sortie out as far as one hundred and fifty miles from port, maintaining station for as long as two weeks. This was a remarkable performance for the time, and one must admire the hardiness of the crews, given the extremely primitive conditions on board the boats. In a typical submarine, more than twenty crewmen were jammed into a cylinder about seventy feet long and twelve feet wide at the broadest point of its beam. With no refrigeration and a minimum capability to cook, food was unpalatable while the drinking water quickly became rank. The interior was always dark, wet, and cold, filled with either the fumes of an early gasoline engine or the bitter acrid smell of overworked storage batteries. The gasoline fumes represented a far greater hazard than a bad odor, for any break in a fuel line or

puncture of a tank could result in a spill that would create a catastrophic explosion from vapors set off by any of the thousands of available electrical sparks on board.

But above all there was the omnipresent sense of impending danger,
for any crewmember could make a mistake that would result in the
deaths of all: a single valve thrown the wrong way, a single hatch left
open, or a careless hand at the controls. Each could mean a fatal plunge
to the bottom of the sea.

Despite these hazards, which would remain as a permanent feature
of submarine duty, there was no shortage of volunteers, and some remarkable voyages were made, including the first underwater explo-
ration of an oceanic ice field in December 1908. This chilling look into
the future was carried out by the *Kefal,* a Simon Lake–designed and
–built boat under the command of Lieutenant V. A. Merkushev, who
cruised for one hour and thirty-two minutes (a distance of four miles)
under the ice in Ussuriy Bay near Vladivostok.

The Imperial Russian Navy was in the same relative state of disarray
as the Imperial Russian Army when the First World War began in August
1914. The Russian naval forces in the Baltic vastly outnumbered the opposing German fleet, especially in capital ships. Despite this, the Russians elected to adopt a defensive attitude, depending upon minefields,
shore fortifications, and the big guns of its ships to hold the enemy at
the entrance to the Gulf of Finland, well away from St. Petersburg.

But by 1914, Germany's U-boat fleet—its impressive *Unterseeboote*
craft—had surpassed that of Russia in both numbers and technology.
The *U-26* sank the Russian cruiser *Pallada* on October 11, 1914, with a
single torpedo. It was the first sinking of a Russian boat by a German
submarine, and the start of a three-decade long interval during which
Germany would hold a psychological edge over Russia in submarine
warfare. The balance would not change until the waning months of the
Second World War in 1945.

To offset the combat deficiencies of Russian submarines, British submarines were sent to the Baltic, working in cooperation with the Imperial Russian Navy. The British enjoyed relative success, forcing the
Germans to direct more ships to the area and to lay many more mines,
but the Russian submarines were for the most part ineffective—they

fired fifty torpedoes during 1915 without achieving a single hit.[9] Three ships did fall to Russian deck-guns, however. The continued lack of success, along with generally declining morale, did not bode well for the Russian submarine force in the Baltic. It became almost useless, with its boats either scuttled to avoid advancing German forces, or transferred by inland waterways to Kronstadt.

Russian submarines did considerably better in the Black Sea, where the enemy was less formidable, and (after 1916) the leadership of forty-one-year-old Rear Admiral Alexander Vasilevich Kolchak would make a difference. (Kolchak would remain loyal to Imperial Russia, and head a White Russian Siberian government formed in early 1918, with its capital at Omsk. His forces were a mixed bag of loyalist Russians and the Czech Legion. Most of Siberia was in White hands by late 1918, and Kolchak claimed to be the ruler of all Russia, but Tsar Nicholas II and his family were murdered by the Bolsheviks at Yekaterinburg, formerly Sverdlovsk, that year. Early in 1920, Admiral Kolchak's government collapsed, and he was executed.[10])

Under Kolchak, the submarines of the Black Sea Fleet conducted relatively low level but successful operations against coal shipping that was vitally needed by both Germany and Turkey. His leadership extended until he was deposed by a new phenomenon in Russia—a delegate assembly of sailors and soldiers. It was the writing on the wall, for on November 8, 1917, the Bolshevik takeover of power turned control of the Black Sea Fleet to the local revolutionary councils—the Imperial Russian Navy was no more.

The general lack of success of the Russian submarine force stands in marked contrast to the nearly war-winning efforts of the German Imperial Navy's *Unterseeboote*.

The German U-boats had proved to be deadly, as Great Britain's shipping losses were already exceeding its shipbuilding capacity by August 1915.[11] By the end of 1915, 640 ships totaling 1,189,031 tons had been sunk at a cost of twenty U-boats. Germany had averaged only ten U-boats at sea at any one time in 1915. This was lifted to thirty by the end of 1916, and that year's campaign would see the destroyed tonnage nearly doubled, with 1,301 ships totaling 2,194,420 tons sunk. (This is merchant shipping only, and excludes warships.) By the end of 1917, the number of sinkings rose to an intolerable 3,170 ships, comprising almost 6,000,000 tons. Convoys reduced this to a still crippling 1,280 ships totaling 2,625,000 tons in 1918.

Despite its terrible effectiveness, the massive German submarine effort was to no avail; Germany was exhausted by almost four years of war on two fronts, and when its last great series of offensives on the Western Front ended in failure in the late summer of 1918, enough Americans had already arrived in France to turn the tide. Yet by any analysis, the German submarine war had been a successful, even brilliant, campaign. Submarines had cost the Allies more than 18 million tons of shipping, of which almost 11,000,000 tons were British, at the cost of 178 U-boats lost in action. The ratio of ships to submarines sunk was about 31 to 1.[12]

The marked contrast in operational effectiveness between the German and Russian submarine efforts in both the First and Second World Wars explains many of the problems the Soviets had to contend with during the Cold War in terms of tradition, doctrine, interservice rivalry, and developing leaders.

GERMAN AND SOVIET SUBMARINES IN WORLD WAR II

On September 3, 1939, the signal "Commence hostilities against England immediately" was sent to all U-boats. Within an hour, a second message followed, defining the five categories of shipping that could be attacked without warning. These included warships, ships known to be carrying war goods, ships engaged in military activity (e.g., resupplying a warship), cargo ships sailing with a warship escort or in convoy, and armed merchant ships or troopships. The entire German war plan was based on finishing the Poland campaign quickly, and then coming to terms with Great Britain and France.

The German submarine force went to war with a total of fifty-six U-boats, about one-sixth of the number that Admiral Doenitz thought was necessary. Of these, thirty were the small 250-ton coastal submarines that were called "Baltic ducks" and, while useful for coastal operations, were best suited for training. Eighteen were the excellent Type VII 500-

ton boats for use in the Atlantic. They were very similar to the submarines used by Germany in the First World War, but improved by the introduction of "wakeless" electrically propelled and magnetically fused torpedoes. As an initial surge, some thirty-nine submarines put to sea. But the wear and tear of combat operations was staggering, and the U-boats had to return to rearm and refit more swiftly than they could be replaced on stations. In December 1939, so few were at sea that only four ships averaging 4,000 tons each were sunk.[13] The first months of the war were not impressive, as U-boats sank only 103,544 gross register tons (GRT) in 1939 and 525,000 during the first five months of 1940.[14]

The situation changed dramatically after the fall of France in June 1940. By then, Hitler controlled more than 3,000 miles of coastline that stretched from Norway along the coasts of Denmark, Holland, Belgium, and France. Vast bases, which were later equipped with virtually bombproof submarine pens, sprouted up at Brest, Lorient, La Pallice, and St. Nazaire. This improved tactical situation was reinforced by Hitler's August 17, 1940, decision to conduct unrestricted submarine warfare.[15] The new bases made it possible for Doenitz to put more submarines at sea for longer periods of time. They also made it much more difficult for the Allies to counter with anti-submarine patrols.

Doenitz used his submarines as a matador used a cape and sword, directing their movement from one part of the ocean to the next so that they could always operate where the targets were most numerous and most valuable. When Hitler declared war on the United States on December 8, 1941, Doenitz immediately dispatched submarines to operate against the easy pickings of American coastal shipping. The American ships were perfect targets. They sailed individually on regular routes, sometimes with full running lights, but in any event silhouetted against the bright lights of the American coast.

Allied shipping losses continued to soar during the following year, despite inadequate cooperation by the Luftwaffe and the unproductive diversion of German submarines to the Mediterranean. A total of 1,662 ships were sunk, 1,006 of them in the Atlantic. Total tonnage reached 7.8 million tons. Submarine losses had increased to eighty-six, an average of 7.2 per month at a time when twenty new submarines per month were entering service. And the pickings were so good that submarine commanders could elect not to attack a ship riding high in the water, on the basis that it carried no cargo, and knowing that a cargo-laden ship would be along to sink in short order.

At his headquarters in France, Doenitz did some straight-line projections of the number of submarines that would be available to him in 1943, and the trend lines led him to believe that sinkings would reach 800,000 tons per month. This was the figure that he had long ago picked as the tonnage necessary to defeat Great Britain. After another ineffective surface fleet action, Admiral Raeder was forced to resign. Doenitz became a Grand Admiral and commander in chief of the Navy on January 30, 1943. This, along with the remarkable string of U-boat successes, went to his head, and he openly claimed that his submarines were about to win the war in the Atlantic. Hitler listened to him gladly, having just gone through the agony of the defeat at Stalingrad. Yet it was pure hubris on Doenitz's part, for while the first three months of 1943 yielded another 151 ships and a further 476,390 tons sunk, U-boat losses had reached forty. Doenitz had the cup of victory snatched from his lips before he could drink, for from this point on, the confluence of Allied technology, tactics, and intelligence services completely reversed the course of the submarine war.

It had been fortunate for the free world that Nazi Germany had not given submarines the early priority that would have simply prolonged the conflict. During the three years that it took to build up U-boat forces to the level Doenitz knew he needed, the Allies had not been idle. Both the Royal Navy and the U.S. Navy had used the time to develop anti-submarine forces in great quantity. Brilliant combat leaders, such as the famous Commander "Johnnie" Walker, emerged. They perfected tactics that tripled the effectiveness of convoy escort groups. These had greatly increased in size, and, in addition, often had an independent hunter-killer group composed of small ships and, if possible, an escort carrier attached to seek out and suppress enemy submarines. By 1943, the Allies were able to attach rescue trawlers to convoys to pick up the precious merchant crews whose ships had been sunk.

The capability of the escort groups was vastly enhanced by new technology that included high-frequency direction-finding equipment (called Huff-Duff), which used triangulation to pinpoint a submarine after it had transmitted its message to Doenitz.[16] (Just as the Luftwaffe was noted for its garrulous voice communications, so did the submariners engage in too many transmissions.) Radar, rare at first, eventually became standard equipment on virtually every Allied ship, and by 1943 it was widely used in aircraft. Using the Air-to-Surface Vessel (ASV) radar enabled planes to pick up submarines at distances of twelve miles and more at night and in bad weather. For visual identification, Leigh Lights were installed in aircraft. These large, high-intensity searchlights were automatically controlled by the radar. The aircraft could approach stealthily, then bathe the target in a brilliant white light and drop depth charges before it could submerge.

But the most unanswerable Allied arrow in the anti-submarine warfare quiver was the prodigious increase in the production of ships. Doenitz had labored under the illusion that the maximum combined U.S. and British ship production would total no more than 1.2 million tons per year. He, like other German leaders, vastly underestimated American production capability. The United States built eighteen new shipyards in 1941, and produced 6.1 million tons of shipping in 1942. Great Britain reached 1.8 million in the same year. In 1943, the combined U.S./UK production was an incredible 14.6 million tons. The modular Liberty ships were being built at the rate of three per day, and one was rushed from keel-laying to launch in an unbelievable *four days.*[17]

Of course the Germans took countermeasures wherever possible. Their major effort was in the increased production of U-boats, and despite bombing efforts, Doenitz had a fleet of 365 U-boats by October, 1941, of which as many as 196 were operational at one time.

After mid-1943, Allied bombing of shipyards forced the German Navy to supplement the traditional methods of building submarines with widespread prefabrication. The major components of submarines were built in thirty-two widely separated locations, then transported by barge to sixteen main locations where the internal components were installed. The three sections were then delivered to three seaside shipyards where they were welded together and launched. (The dispersal of manufacture due to bombing was successful until Allied fighter-bombers began the systematic destruction of the German transportation system (rail, road, and canals) in late 1944 and early 1945.)

By the end of 1943, the U-boat fleet reached its peak number with 442 operational boats. But Allied countermeasures had effectively defeated the U-boats by May 1943. On the 31st of the month, Doenitz had to go personally to Hitler and report that instead of the Battle of the Atlantic being won—it was lost "temporarily." In the next six months, 167 German U-boats were lost, and only fifty-seven Allied merchant ships were sunk.

During 1944, U-boat losses reached 264, while only 230 new boats entered service. The size of the operational force began to decline in December 1944, for the first time since September 1939. When the war ended on May 8, 1945, there were 360 boats still operational, many of a very advanced type, as discussed below. Some 230 of the surviving U-boats were scuttled by their crews, while the Allies received the surrender of about one hundred.[18]

To recap, during the ten years from 1935 to 1945, the German U-boat fleet had about 1,162 operational boats. Of these, 920 carried out an estimated 3,000 war patrols, sinking 150 warships and 2,840 merchant ships totaling more than 14,000,000 tons. No less than 1,060 U-boats were lost in action or were scuttled after the surrender. Of some 36,000 wartime submarine crewmembers, 27,491 were listed as dead or missing in action, and another 5,000 were captured.[19]

The Germans also achieved major technological advances, many of which would be adopted by other navies in the years to come. The Soviet Navy would benefit most of all from the German advances. Among the first of these was the snorkel, a 1933 Dutch invention that was basically an air tube that could be extended and retracted like a periscope, and through which air could be drawn for underwater diesel engine operation and the diesel exhaust could be directed. Snorkel operation was hard on the crews, but added greatly to their safety by reducing the radar signature of the submarine. Some snorkels and periscopes had radar-absorbent material (buna) applied to them, in the same manner that stealth bombers do today—and for the same reason.[20]

Another 1933 invention was the fish-shaped, single propulsion U-boat that had been advocated by Dr. Hellmuth Walter, who had developed a hydrogen peroxide closed-cycle engine system. These boats proved to be too difficult to realize, and were supplanted by the

"Electro" boat, the Type XXI submarine advocated by Drs. Friedrich Schuerer and Hermann Broecking in November 1942.

The Type XXI used an extremely advanced hull design combined with the same reliable MAN diesel engines of older submarines.[21] The most significant internal change was the substitution of huge electric motors (4,200 horsepower surfaced, 800 hp submerged) that were more powerful than the 4,000-horsepower diesel engines. A small 225-hp electric motor was used for silent running at very slow or "patrol quiet" speed. The Type XXI could run submerged at 16 knots for an hour, although using a snorkel while submerged would reduce the speed by 1 or 2 knots and the surface conditions of the ocean driven by the weather would slow a snorkeling boat still further. For many commanders, the ability to recharge their batteries while hidden just below the surface justified the temporary loss of a knot or two. Unfortunately for them the noise of the diesels running while the boat was submerged made them easier targets for increasingly effective sonar.

In 1944, Doenitz turned to the Type XXI as Germany's last chance, and 200 were ordered initially; this was soon increased to a total of 1,300. Unlike earlier models, in which all amenities were sacrificed to reduce weight and size, the Type XXI was large and comfortable, with private quarters for officers and even a deep freeze for food. As a result, cruises were programmed for five months. The Type XXI was by far the most advanced submarine in the world in terms of performance (depth capability, underwater speed, and endurance) and electronic equipment. It featured the group-listening apparatus sonar, so accurate that the periscope did not have to be raised for an attack. The Type XXI was also designed for increased stealth, having a special synthetic rubber material on the hull to reduce detection from sonar and on the snorkel head to reduce detection from radar.[22]

By the end of the war, Germany had produced 117 Type XXI's; of these only thirteen were surrendered to the Allies, the rest being scuttled. But their influence on submarine design would be felt in countries around the world for years to come. The much smaller but technologically similar Type XXIII was also quite successful. Some sixty-two entered service, and one, *U-2336*, sank two British merchantmen on May 7, 1945, the last sinkings to be claimed by a German U-boat.

The Battle of the Atlantic had characteristics later found in the contest between Western and Soviet submarine forces in the Cold War. In both situations the Western Allies were outnumbered by their opponent in total number of submarines, but ultimately gained a decisive technological superiority. And in both cases, the Western Allies saw that superiority diminish over time and, in some instances, be completely outdistanced by their opponent. Fortunately, the late-blooming technical superiority in submarine weaponry of both Nazi Germany and the Soviet Union could not overcome the enormous advantage of the Western Allies in resources and productivity.

UNITED STATES SUBMARINES IN THE FIRST AND SECOND WORLD WARS

Just as America had begun the air age with the Wright Flyer, then allowed many foreign countries to surpass it in airpower by 1914, so had it done with the submarine age. The work of John Holland and Simon Lake had inspired foreign navies, particularly Russia's, but although Congress had funded a 300-ship Navy, the third largest in the world after Great Britain and Germany, insufficient money had been spent on the development of submarines. When war came in April 1917, no one knew whether or not U.S. submarines were capable of crossing the Atlantic under their own power to engage the enemy. Four of the primitive K-series boats were dispatched for duty in the Mediterranean, one leaving under tow of the submarine escort tender *Bushnell*. All reached Point Delgada in the Azores, where they remained for the rest of the war.

Seven of the larger and relatively more modern L-class boats also crossed the Atlantic, where they took up station at Bantry Bay in Ireland, conducting patrols there until the end of the war.[23] Later another eight O-class submarines crossed the Atlantic, with the tender *Savannah*, but did not reach the Azores until after the November 11, 1918, Armistice was signed.[24] American submarines did not have much to do during World War I, German merchant shipping being almost entirely suppressed, and it was fortunate that this was so.

Despite the inadequate efforts, the United States Navy had the good fortune to have assigned a young officer from Texas to the submarine program. Lieutenant Chester W. Nimitz was assigned to the USS *Plunger,* then commanded the USS *Snapper,* USS *Narwal,* and USS *Skipjack* until 1912. In 1913 he began studying the use of diesel engines in submarines, and went to Germany and Belgium for information on the latest types. All of this experience would stand him in good stead during the Second World War, when he would send his submarines to wreak havoc upon the Japanese.

When the United States received six German U-boats as war prizes in 1919, the Navy was appalled to find how superior they were in every respect to American submarines. There followed several series of American boats that failed to match the German World War I craft in performance. It was not until 1933, with the arrival of a new class of "fleet boats," that American submarines began to equal German submarines of the First World War.

The United States had taken some emergency actions after war broke out and recommissioned some obsolete O-class boats for use in training, while commencing an intensive building program. The result was that it possessed about 111 submarines of varying age and capability in service on December 7, 1941. Most of these were the R- and S-class boats built during and after World War I, but about 40 were "fleet boats," and these became the nucleus of a larger, more capable fleet that would dominate the war in the Pacific.

The prewar submarine warfare doctrines of Imperial Japan and the United States were very similar. In both navies, the submarine was intended to operate as an adjunct of the fleet, and reduce the enemy's strength by attrition, so that when the great fleet engagement that both navies foresaw was fought, some of the principal ships would already have been disposed of.

Both navies also created submarines of a generally similar size and appearance, but with each modified to specific missions. A typical Japanese submarine, like the *I-19* (which sank the aircraft carrier USS *Wasp*), was 365 feet long, displaced 3,654 tons submerged, had a crew of 94, and carried seventeen torpedoes. The *I-19* had a 16-knot cruising speed and could submerge to a depth of 330 feet.

The American equivalent, one of the Gato class, was 311 feet long, displaced 2,424 tons submerged, had a crew of 85, and carried twenty-four torpedoes. The Gato (that name would become familiar to the Soviets during the Cold War) also had a 16-knot cruising speed and a nominal submergence limit of 300 feet. The Gato class was far more comfortably outfitted for its crew than its Japanese counterparts, which was the case in every class of vessel in the war.

The greatest difference for the first eighteen months of World War II lay in the effectiveness and reliability of the torpedoes. The Japanese torpedoes were far superior in performance. The American MK XIV steam torpedo was equipped with an "influence exploder" (MK-6)—a magnetic pistol to detonate the warhead. This top-secret device was intended to let the torpedo explode as it passed under the keel of an enemy ship, thus "breaking its back." The device was so secret that testing was held to a minimum—no test was ever conducted with a live torpedo, for they were considered too expensive to be used in this way. Torpedo production was very low—only 720 were built in 1941 and 2,382 in 1942—and submarine commanders were urged to be frugal in their use of torpedoes, and only 2,010 were expended in 1942.[25]

When war came, there was a terrible shortage of torpedoes, and those that were available did not work in the majority of cases. Submarine skippers made attack after attack in which the torpedoes bounced off the side of an enemy ship. When complaints were sent to the Bureau of Ordnance, they were rejected, and the crews were accused of not using the weapon system properly.[26] Only when Vice Admiral Charles A. Lockwood took it upon himself to test torpedoes were a whole series of problems discovered and eventually rectified over time. Production of improved torpedoes was increased, and submarine commanders were urged to be liberal rather than frugal in the use of torpedoes.

Immediately after the outbreak of war, the order was sent to the U.S. submarine fleet to begin unrestricted submarine warfare against Japan. Curiously enough, the Japanese submarine fleet tried to adhere to its prewar doctrine, and sought to attack American warships. American submarines, on the other hand, while more than happy to attack warships, concentrated on destroying Japan's merchant marine, and did so with a vengeance after the torpedo problems had been cured.

Japan began the war with about 6,000,000 tons of "steel" shipping, that is, ships made of steel and displacing over 500 tons. It added another 800,000 tons through capture of enemy shipping, and built a further 3.2 million tons in the course of the war. It thus had a total of about 10,000,000 tons of shipping as targets for the American submariners, who used 288 submarines and 15,000 torpedoes to sink 1,150 ships totaling 4.9 million tons. Aircraft sank 750 ships of 2.5 million tons, while mines accounted for 210 ships of almost 400,000 tons. This massive destruction deprived Japan of ninety percent of its merchant fleet, and reduced its imports from over 22 million tons annually in 1940 to the starvation level of 2.7 million tons in 1945.

American submarines also sank 214 Japanese naval vessels, totaling almost 600,000 tons. One of these was HIJMS *Shinano*, the world's largest carrier, on its maiden voyage on November 28, 1944.[27] When, at the end of 1944, large targets had become scarce, U.S. submarines cruised on the surface to attack and sink thousands of barges, sampans, smaller steel ships, and fishing vessels. It was an essential, if ungallant, way to wage war for Japan had come to depend upon these small boats to sustain life at a minimum level. The loss of these vessels, combined with a disastrous rice crop, meant that there would have been a ghastly famine in an already malnourished Japan by the spring of 1946. It was perhaps the supreme irony of the war that the atomic bombs that forced surrender saved many millions of Japanese from starvation.

In retrospect, it is easy to see that Japan had inadvertently and inexplicably made one of the most impressive and least commented on military blunders in history. The island empire, so totally dependent upon merchant shipping for imports and exports, had neglected to create an effective anti-submarine warfare arm in their navy that would safeguard the transit of merchant ships. It was not until November 1943 that it had its first dedicated "Escort Command" of anti-submarine warfare ships, and even then it was a low-priority mission.[28] The reason lay in the traditional warrior mentality of Japanese leaders, who regarded defensive measures as cowardly. Just as with aircraft, the Japanese planned to be the only ones doing the shooting, and defensive measures were therefore not considered. (The strong American emphasis on rescue efforts was inexplicable to the Japanese, who could never understand how the United States could "waste" submarines by using them to rescue downed aviators. The U.S. submarine rescue efforts were highly successful, rescuing 540 flyers, among them future president George Herbert Walker Bush.)

The overwhelming success of the American submarine fleet, which constituted only two percent of American naval personnel strength while inflicting more than sixty-three percent of Japan's merchant shipping losses, contrasted markedly with the efforts of the Japanese submarines. The Japanese, while well trained and well equipped, concentrated on attacking American warships, which were protected by excellent anti-submarine escorts. But Japanese tactics were rigid. In one instance, Japanese submarines were deployed on tripwire duty in advance of a Japanese naval operation. They lined up in parade ground fashion, so that when one submarine was found, the positions of the rest could be easily determined. These dispositions permitted the destroyer escort USS *England* single-handedly to find and sink six submarines in a twelve-day period.

The offensive-minded Japanese submarine commanders virtually ignored the vast number of U.S. supply ships that eventually roamed the Pacific by the thousands, and that would have been relatively easy targets. When it at last became obvious to the Japanese Navy that submarines could be employed more profitably against merchant and supply ships than against warships, it was already too late. The tide of war had turned, and the Japanese submarines were assigned to military tasks that included the most humbling of all, supplying sacks of rice to Japanese garrisons starving to death on bypassed islands as the Americans leapfrogged toward Japan itself.

Japan was even more predisposed than Nazi Germany to building suicide weapons, and they built "pocket submarines" and human torpedoes. The most predominant type, the *kaiten,* was designed to be carried by mother submarines and then launched to attack enemy ships. Crewmen were given treatment equivalent to that given the more famous kamikaze (meaning "divine wind") pilots. While several thousand were built, and many were employed, they too were largely ineffective, thanks primarily to a lack of training and a difficulty in maneuvering.[29]

When the war ended, there were many of these suicide weapons left, along with surface suicide boats—a demeaning end to a fleet that had once boasted the *Yamato,* the largest battleship in history.[30]

Thus it was that while German U-boats brought Britain to the brink, the United States, with fewer and less capable submarines, was able to achieve "silent" victory in the Pacific. The difference lay in part in the quality of the opponents, for while Germany faced Great Britain and the United States, with all of their technical and productive prowess, the United States faced Japan, which badly misused its ASW capabilities. It was just as well, for even with Japan's inferior performance in anti-submarine warfare, the United States Navy lost 52 submarines, 374 officers, and 3,132 enlisted men in the Pacific War, a shockingly large percentage of all U.S. Navy casualties in World War II.[31] Submarine service was not a suicide mission, but its proportion of casualties was higher than those of the surface navy.

THE SOVIET SUBMARINE FORCE IN WORLD WAR II

The early Soviet Navy had to build from a very shattered base, for after the revolution and the bitter civil war that followed, the once powerful Imperial Navy had been reduced to a fraction of its former size. Further, while the proficiency of the Russian Navy had not been great for decades, it was so diminished now that former Tsarist officers were drafted into service as "naval technicians," and one can only guess what their relations were with the very crews that had not only mutinied, but led the revolution that destroyed their world.

Yet mutiny was still in the air, and, angry with the terrible food and living conditions, the Baltic Fleet at Kronstadt revolted against their new Bolshevik masters on February 28, 1921. No one knew better than the still tiny Bolshevik party the danger implicit in a naval revolt, and a decision was made to crush it with whatever violence and bloodshed was necessary. The uneven battle lasted for twenty-eight days of bitter fighting. More than 6,000 of the dissidents were killed immediately, and many more were subsequently executed.[32] When the Red troops finally conquered the "counterrevolutionaries," a decision was made to disestablish the navy as an independent force. It became instead the "Naval Force of the Red Army," and would not be independent again until December 30, 1937.

The "counterrevolution" had a profound effect upon the future Soviet Navy, because for many years the principal efforts at reconstructing it were political rather than technical. The *Komsomol*—the Young Communist League—became the major source for officer personnel to ensure that a future Red Navy would be politically sound.

The Japanese were the last of the foreign countries to pull their troops out of the Soviet Union, leaving in August 1922. From that point on, there were several efforts to rebuild the Soviet Navy, each with emphasis on the importance of the submarine fleet. Things moved slowly, however, and by 1930 there were still only fourteen Soviet submarines in commission.

In the following years, successive Five Year Plans and, more importantly, dictator Joseph Stalin's direct interest established a sizeable submarine building program. By 1939, the Soviet Union had the largest submarine fleet in the world, with one hundred fifty submarines in commission. Of these, as many as seventy-five percent were smaller, coastal boats, but they were suitable for the defensive purposes intended.

Unfortunately for the morale and the training of the force, however, the Soviet Navy had been devastated by the Stalinist purge of officers that had begun on June 11, 1937. Among the first to be executed was Stalin's finest soldier, Marshal of the Soviet Union Mikhail N. Tukachevsky, along with the naval commissar, V. M. Orlov. Among the many bogus charges leveled at them was their opposition to a powerful Soviet surface fleet. All eight admirals (known, in Soviet parlance, as "flagmen") of the navy were executed in the purge.

On June 22, 1941, when Nazi Germany invaded the Soviet Union, there were 218 submarines in the Red Navy, spread out among the Baltic, Black Sea, Arctic, and Pacific Fleets. The submarines were for the most part modern, but the crews lacked training and the initiative of the commanders was still stunted by the ferocity of Stalin's purges. While a submarine commander could be executed for any reason, including not doing anything, he was far more likely to be executed for doing something that was unsuccessful or that resulted in damage to his boat.

The Germans, working in concert with the Finns, executed 103 mine-laying operations to bottle up the Baltic Fleet in the Leningrad/Kronstadt area. (Both sides made impressive and effective use of minefields.) German airpower was also very effective in the Baltic, in both offensive operations and anti-submarine warfare. Soviet submarines would occasionally break out of the minefields and elude the German anti-submarine flotillas, but with minimum effect. German naval vessels had escorted some 1,900 merchant ships, of an aggregate 5.6 million tons during 1942, and lost only 20 ships totaling 40,000 tons—less than one percent of the total.[33]

The Soviet Union regained a presence in the Baltic in the late summer of 1944. The Red Army reached Riga in August, and the Finns surrendered on September 4. Hitler insisted that the remaining German bridgeheads in the Baltic be held as long as possible, but by the end of 1944 it was obvious that some 2,000,000 troops and refugees had to be evacuated.

The German Navy began a massive evacuation attempt that, despite all the difficulties, was tremendously successful, with ninety-nine percent of those slated for evacuation reaching Germany. Those who did not make it included the victims of the greatest sea disasters in history—disasters that also represented the greatest successes of Soviet submarines.

On January 30, 1945, the 25,484-ton *Wilhelm Gustloff* sailed from Pillau, near Danzig, with some 6,100 people on board, including soldiers, sailors, technicians, and civilian refugees. Captain Third Rank A. I. Marinesko, commanding the Soviet *S-13*, fired a spread of four torpedoes, three of which struck the *Gustloff*. It sank in a little over one hour, taking some 4,000 people with it.

On February 10, Marinesko would score again, this time against the 14,600-ton *General Steuben*, carrying 3,000 wounded soldiers and its crew. Of these, only 300 were saved.

Both ships were legitimate targets, and Marinesko was awarded the title Hero of the Soviet Union. But the very fact that these two sinkings were the most noteworthy of all the Soviet submarine activity in the Baltic during World War II is an indication of the relative ineffectiveness of their very large submarine fleet.

Soviet submarines in other areas did not have any more success. The submarines of the Northern Fleet were perhaps the most helpful of all, since they supported the defense of the land areas around Murmansk. The Black Sea Fleet was rendered ineffective early on by German airpower and the swift advance of enemy ground forces. The Pacific Fleet made its greatest contribution by sending some of its submarines all the way around the world to reinforce the Northern Fleet. (One of these was lost off the northwest coast of the United States, sunk by the *I-25*, a Japanese submarine. Besides sinking some merchant shipping, the *I-25* conducted the only bombing raids on U.S. soil, launching a Yokosuka E14Y in two attacks on the wooded Oregon coast, where it dropped a total of four 76-kg incendiary bombs.[34])

Thus the Great Patriotic War, as the Soviet Union, with justifiable pride, termed the Second World War, ended for the Soviet Navy on an unimpressive note. While the Red Army had distinguished itself in the most titanic battles in history, and the Red Air Force had provided close air support for the Army, the Navy had not distinguished itself. The surface navy (even where numerically superior, as it was in the Baltic) had not engaged the enemy in any fleet actions, and the level of effort of the submarines was, as noted, unremarkable. The Red Navy had done well in coastal defense efforts, in riverine warfare, and in amphibious landings. Rear Admiral Gorshkov, a future four star admiral, architect of the Cold War Soviet Navy, and its commander in chief, had distinguished himself in all three of these efforts, and had also proved himself to be politically adept.

Born in 1910, Sergei Gorshkov emerged from the Frunze Higher Naval School in 1931. He spent much of his early career in the Black Sea and Pacific Fleets accumulating experience in navigation and ship operations, mostly in destroyers. By 1939 Stalin's purges had taken their toll on the naval officer corps and the potential German threat created fast-track opportunities for junior officers. In that year Gorshkov returned to the Black Sea Fleet and successfully completed the senior officer's course at the Viroshilov Naval Academy. He had command of a cruiser squadron in the Black Sea when the Germans invaded the Soviet Union in 1941. Active in combined operations designed to protect Odessa early in the war, Gorshkov became a rear admiral and received command of the Azov Flotilla in October of 1941, only ten years after receiving his commission in the Soviet Navy. As the Germans penetrated his homeland he played a pivotal role in the amphibious landings at Kerch in December 1941, designed to relieve Sevastopol, and as the deputy naval commander in operations designed to protect Novorossisk, the latter bringing him to the attention of the future minister of defense General A. A. Grechko. Gorshkov ended the war directing the naval operations of the Danube Flotilla in support of the Army's effort against the Germans in the Ukraine and in the Balkans. By 1951, now Vice Admiral Gorshkov became commander in chief of the Black Sea Fleet. He took up residence in Moscow in 1955 as first deputy commander in chief of the Soviet Navy under Admiral N. G. Kuznetsov, and with the assistance of a rising political star, Nikita Khrushchev, he replaced Kuznetsov as commander in chief in 1956. He held that post until his retirement in 1985.[35]

The Soviet Navy Gorshkov knew was in a very difficult way in 1945, despite a profession by Joseph Stalin that the Soviet people "wanted to see their Navy still stronger and more powerful." Stalin envisioned Hitler's dream—a titanic struggle between the Soviet Union against the Western powers—as taking place by 1960 at the latest, and he planned to have the most powerful army, air force, and navy in the world, able to take on Great Britain and the United States in combination.

One of the great ironies of Stalin's vision was the fact that as he flogged Soviet industry mercilessly to rearm at the expense of civilian consumption, his putative enemies were disarming at a frantic rate and jump-starting their consumer industries to provide basic items that were always luxuries in the Soviet Union, and luxury items that would never be available. It was the ultimate triumph of Rockefeller and Ford over Marx and Lenin that the buildup of consumer industries continually strengthened the economies of the Western powers, while the efforts of Stalin and his successors in establishing a huge military economy ultimately brought about the demise of the Soviet Union.

The decade that followed saw the Soviet Union in Stalin's iron grip for eight years, during which he followed through by establishing a shipbuilding program of colossal proportions. Had it been fulfilled to the letter, the Soviet Navy would have possessed four aircraft carriers, ten battle cruisers, twenty-four cruisers, and an incredible 1,244 sub-marines, along with all of the other ship classes pertinent to a first-class navy.

The time had passed for such a formidable navy, but no one was going to inform Stalin of that fact. Ironically, the paranoia that drove him to the many purges of leadership caused political shake-ups that damaged the operation of the Soviet Navy. He abolished the Navy Commissariat, and placed the navy under the People's Commissariat of Defense, later designated the Ministry of the Armed Forces in March 1946. Then, he turned on Admiral Kuznetsov, as he had earlier turned on Marshal Tukachevsky, Marshal Georgi Zhukov, the aircraft designer Andrei Tupolev, and many others. Kuznetsov was court-martialed and dismissed as commander in chief of the navy on the customary charge of treason. In February 1950, he was recalled as Commander in Chief of the Pacific Fleet Navy. The new commander in chief of the navy as a whole was Admiral I. S. Yumashev, but his tenure would be short, for Kuznetsov would once more resume that role in 1951.[36]

Given the damage done to the Soviet Union by Germany, and the immense amount of resources that had been poured into the war, it was impossible to provide the industrial resources necessary for the creation of such a gargantuan fleet. Instead, the Soviet Navy leadership tried to complete the twenty-four big cruisers of the Sverdlov class.[37] The main concern of the top admirals was not so much to have dominating firepower at sea as to create vessels in which crews would learn the trade of being sailors before being trained to fight.

Much of the momentum to acquire a large surface fleet died with Stalin in 1953. His death was followed by the usual Kremlin infighting, and when First Secretary Nikita Khrushchev denounced Stalin and the "cult of the person of Stalin" in his February 1956 speech to the 20th Congress of the Soviet Union, it was evident that there was a new power source, one to which Admiral Gorshkov immediately gravitated. (It would not be until 1958 that Khrushchev assumed the post of premier, and became head of both state and party.)

Thus it was in 1956, eleven years after the Great Patriotic War ended, that Gorshkov was given command of the Red Navy. He immediately paid lip service to Khrushchev's policy that large surface ships were obsolete and that missiles and submarines were the weapons of the future. He also supported Khrushchev's view that the Red Navy was an important element of foreign policy and supervised the provision of surface ships, submarines, personnel, and materials for mine warfare to countries the Soviet Union wished to influence.

Gorshkov sanctioned the huge Soviet submarine construction program that was bringing new boats into service at the rate of eighty per year. Their purpose was to defeat the enemy by disrupting naval and sea communications. The United States and the North Atlantic Treaty Organization (NATO) nations were seen as the principal enemy, and if a conventional war were fought, the Soviet Union believed that between eighty and one hundred large transports would be arriving at European ports daily, with as many as 2,000 vessels en route simultaneously. Such a massive effort could only be defeated by a massive submarine force.

Yet both the United States and the Soviet Union had moved forward with nuclear weapons and missiles. If the war turned out not to be conventional, but rather nuclear, submarines would be needed to launch nuclear missiles against enemy carrier groups, and against the enemy coast.

Gorshkov was thus faced with enormous opportunities and challenges. On the one hand, under his guidance, the Soviet Navy had to be swiftly elevated in quality and capability to undertake the missions that Khrushchev envisioned. On the other, he did not have a large share of the military budget nor, more importantly, a broad base of personnel upon whom to draw to command and man his ships.

It would be his most important task to see that the best possible candidates were selected to command submarines and be responsible for nuclear weapons. (Nuclear-powered submarines were just visible on the horizon.) To achieve this Gorshkov had to create the doctrine and supervise the training of the Soviet Navy, which lacked all the components of naval experience and confidence that are so vital in wartime. At the same time, he had to elevate the stature of the navy within the military complex of the USSR, so that it would receive a fair and adequate share of the military budget. Finally, he had to attend to the myriad other details of building and running a huge navy, while still nourishing his private dream of creating a large and balanced surface fleet.

There are many ways to evaluate Gorshkov's relative success or failure. One of these is to examine the growth of what came to be the principal weapon of the Soviet Navy, its submarine force, by examining the types of submarines, the quantities in which they were built, and the methods by which they were employed. To assist in this, a brief summary of Soviet submarines, along with comparisons with their United States counterparts, may be found in Appendix 2. Readers already knowledgeable about Soviet submarines and their designations, and their counterparts in the U.S. Navy, may not need to consult this material, but a reader less familiar with the subject matter may wish to bookmark this appendix for easy reference.

A second and perhaps more interesting way to measure Gorshkov's relative success or failure is to listen to the words of his own submarine commanders. In the following chapters, Soviet submarine personnel will recount their adventures—and misadventures—as Gorshkov's greyhounds of the sea.

2

CRUISES AND TROUBLES

In the immediate post–World War II days, the Soviet submarine force was numerically the strongest in the world, but suffered from a plethora of variant models, a few of them dating from World War I. In practical terms, it had 229 submarines, 86 of which were intended for coastal work.[1] Intended primarily as defensive weapons, the smaller coastal submarines were also the type with which most Soviet submariner crews were familiar.

Yet Stalin's dictum called for an oceangoing fleet, and while the Soviet Navy possessed 124 nominally oceangoing submarines, only six of these were the advanced ex-German Type VIIc and Type IXc boats.[2] There were many submariners who were familiar with coastal operations, but the war had not provided extensive experience in long-range oceangoing operations.

The United States recognized the implicit threat of the Soviet submarine fleet and respected the Soviet ability to mass-produce weapons of high quality when it was moved to do so. The T-34 tank, the Ilyushin Il-II *Shturmovik* attack plane, and the endless batteries of excellent artillery attested to Soviet scientific and industrial prowess. All were built in quantities unheard of in the West or in Germany (over 100,000 T-34 tanks, 33,000 *Shturmovik*s, and hundreds of thousands of artillery pieces and rocket batteries), and all were excellent at their assigned missions.

The initial estimates of Soviet submarine strength grew from a potential 300 oceangoing submarines in 1950 to as many as 2,000 submarines only a few years later.[3] The rapidly expanding political and scientific successes of the Soviet Union made these estimates seem valid. Politically, the Soviet Union had extended its Iron Curtain all across middle and eastern Europe by 1948, engulfing Estonia, Latvia, Lithuania, Poland, Bulgaria, Rumania, Yugoslavia, Albania, Czechoslovakia, and East Germany. In Asia, the Communist forces of Mao Zedong had come to the fore and would defeat the Nationalist Chinese in 1949. North Korea had fallen under Communist domination, and by 1950 Ho Chi Minh would proclaim the Democratic Republic of Vietnam to be the legal (and Communist) government of that country.

This was a time when the Soviet Union had succeeded in creating an atomic bomb by 1949 and a thermonuclear bomb by 1954 (admittedly with the help of a magnificent combination of spies and traitors). It had reverse-engineered interned Boeing B-29's to create a fleet of Tupolev Tu-4 bombers with the capacity to make a one-way raid on the United States with nuclear weapons. Just as the United States had done, the Soviets had plunged into the science of missiles, building on German experience, and using German scientists and technicians.

The Soviet Union had also imported the most advanced German submarine technology on a wholesale basis, raiding captured German shipyards for completed vessels, components, tools, drawings, and, just as with the missile program, engineers and technicians.

All of this gave credence to the concerns of the United States, which had just proved the effectiveness of submarine warfare against the Japanese in the Pacific while learning at the same time how difficult anti-submarine warfare was against the Germans in the Atlantic. Given the drawdown of U.S. naval forces, particularly in the very small ships that would be required for anti-submarine warfare, the threat of 300 Soviet submarines (modern types, based on the German Type XXI[4]) was more than it could handle. A threat of 300 submarines at sea at one time (implying a total fleet of 1,200) was an impossible situation that could not be addressed by any foreseeable means other than nuclear retaliation.

There was also a nuclear threat. Soviet nuclear technology was rightfully presumed to be behind that of the United States, so it was assumed during the early 1950s that the Soviets might create a "nuclear torpedo," essentially a remote-controlled 400-ton submarine that would carry an atom bomb and be positioned in some vital target such as the Suez Canal or New York Harbor, where it would be detonated. (It is a sad commentary on humanity's moral, scientific, and political development that the world faces the same sort of threat today from terrorists outfitting canister ships with primitive nuclear dirty bombs, probable derivatives of sophisticated Soviet suitcase-bomb technology.)

The U.S. Navy made anti-submarine warfare (ASW) a priority because of its estimate of the devastating effect the Type XXI boats would have if the Russians could mass-manufacture them. This estimate appeared in the then-classified ("SECRET") Low Report of 1950, commissioned one year earlier by the American Chief of Naval Operations, Admiral Forrest Sherman. The hundreds of Soviet coastal submarines did not factor into the decision at all save for the obvious basic capacity to build boats. Rather, a Soviet Union capable of mass-producing Type XXI clones with the potential of successfully challenging the best NATO ASW countermeasures proved more than sufficient to kick off United States naval interest in anti-submarine warfare at a new and aggressive level that has echoed down through the Cold War to the present day. For the same reason, in 1950, the U.S. Navy began work on the important and unique seafloor Sound Surveillance System (SOSUS), an acoustic network designed to gather information on Soviet submarine characteristics and operations. Thus began a complex international underwater dance, in which the submarine and anti-submarine forces of the West would be pitted against those of the Soviet Union in unending simulated warfare. This hazardous exercise, conducted for more than fifty years and still ongoing, if at a reduced rate, implicitly carried with it the risk, at the least, of catastrophic nuclear accident, or, at the worst, of an unauthorized nuclear exchange.

The Soviet naval high command could look to the mighty Soviet industry to fulfill its quotas and generate as many submarines as Stalin and his successors required. The submarines, however apportioned among the Baltic, Black Sea, Northern, and Pacific Fleets, would require a tremendous construction program, followed by even more difficult to sustain logistic and maintenance programs. Each of these programs—construction, logistics, and training—would vie with the actual operation of the submarines for qualified personnel, and each would demand massive and continuing training efforts. (This was perhaps doubly difficult for the Soviet Union, for the technical training had to be supplemented by political training to ensure that the Soviet Navy adhered to the official Communist political line.) The heart of the Soviet naval command's problem was to find men for the challenging task of commanding and operating the submarines as they were built.

Of course, Soviet society was very different from that of the United States. All Soviet citizens were expected to be preoccupied with societal goals, and those in the workplace, particularly in the military services, were considered public figures in a sense, and therefore accountable for their actions. Stalinist philosophy, which prevailed for many years after his death, regarded the individual as a servant of the state. But in the post-Stalin period a new sense of self-worth appeared among Soviet citizens, one based on an inherent flaw in the Soviet system. People found that hard work for official goals was not nearly so rewarding as using a public position for personal interests. Life was so difficult that they began to devote more and more time to improving their lives by means regarded as illegal by the state. They were, in effect, imposing a limited market economy on the Soviet Union by private means. This naturally resulted in a decline in the growth rate of the Soviet economy, a slackening of its technological progress, and a decrease in the standards of quality of both goods and services.[5]

Essentially, corruption made it impossible for the "good Soviet citizen" to do as well as the citizen who carried on some form of illegal activity, be it bribing officials, pilfering state goods or materials, entering into private commercial transactions, or doing services such as repairing a toilet in an apartment for pay, rather than doing an assigned job. Stealing from the state was so common that in 1986 Mikhail Gorbachev mentioned it in his report to the twenty-seventh party congress.[6] Given the depressing conditions under which most citizens lived—two families crammed into a tiny apartment, food stores poorly stocked with inferior goods, a waiting time of years for a refrigerator or telephone service—it is not surprising that those who "got ahead" by such illegal means were more highly regarded than people who conscientiously fulfilled their prescribed Soviet duties.

In a country whose economy was based on agriculture and heavy industry, fewer and fewer people wished to take part in either, although it was extremely difficult to change social status or careers. Obtaining a higher education became a primary goal in order to achieve party membership and a slight advance in social status.

Oddly enough, social factors such as these worked to the advantage of the Soviet Navy in personnel matters, but to its terrible disadvantage in achieving the level of quality necessary in its ships, particularly its submarines. In personnel matters, the navy, as services do the world over, "looked after its own." Sons of naval officers were given the opportunity to enter the appropriate schools, such as the Nakhimov secondary school in Leningrad.[7] There they received their last two years of secondary education, and, if qualified, were able to go on to higher naval schools where they could specialize. For example, those who were interested in submarines (or were perceived by their instructors as good submarine material) were assigned to the Higher Naval School in Leningrad. A naval career was prestigious; those who became naval officers formed an elite group that enjoyed privileges beyond the ken of ordinary Soviet citizens.

Vladimir Lebedko

A committee chaired by Rear Admiral Francis Low of the wartime American Tenth Fleet anti-submarine intelligence group studied the potential Russian maritime challenge in 1949 at the behest of then Chief of Naval Operations Admiral Forrest Sherman. His group defined a Soviet

submarine fleet modeled on captured German Type XXI U-boat technology as the most dangerous maritime threat to American shores. The
Low Committee Report appeared in a classified form in 1950 and
helped drive the priorities of American submariners over the next half
century. During that same period, the Russian submarine community
fulfilled Low's greatest fears, growing in numbers, professionalism,
technical sophistication, and experience.

Vladimir Lebedko's own career offers an excellent case in point, an
insight into the growth of a professional war-fighting community.
American submariners came from the Naval Academy in Annapolis,
various university Reserve Officer Training (ROTC) programs, the cream
of a very carefully composed recruitment campaign, and Admiral Hyman Rickover's nuclear power school. Vladimir Lebedko and his comrades came from a very different world.

Born in 1932, Lebedko endured with his family the Great Patriotic
War against Nazi Germany. As that conflict ended, he found himself settled in Sevastopol in the southern Soviet Union and, along with many of
his friends, very much in love with sailing and the sea. With his family's
approval, he entered the Baku Naval School on the Caspian Sea as soon
as he successfully emerged from the Soviet equivalent of the twelfth
grade. Shortly after his entrance, the navy uprooted the entire school
and its teaching staff, moving it to Kaliningrad on the Baltic Sea.
Lebedko finished the course at the new institution, now called the Second Baltic Advanced Naval School, and then traveled to Leningrad, the
former St. Petersburg, to spend eighteen months at the First Baltic Advanced Naval School.[8]

As the Soviet Union recovered from the war and the early signs of
Cold War manifested themselves, even this institution underwent significant changes. Lebedko's tenure as a student witnessed the conversion of his institution into the Soviet Union's Advanced Submarine
School. He had entered naval school with an inclination toward mine
warfare, but emerged as a qualified submariner.

That change in career direction came as a surprise in his last year at
the school. In the United States, individuals volunteered for submarine
duty, went through a series of intellectual and physical tests, and knew
full well what lay ahead. As Lebedko and his fellow students began

going to courses on submarine navigation, theory, tactics, engineering, and design, as well as weaponry, they accepted the new direction as "fate." Six months after graduation, he found himself a lieutenant in Sevastopol and assigned to a group of Whiskey class diesel submarines.[9] Due to the terrible shortage of qualified submarine officers, promotion from ensign to lieutenant came very quickly, as did substantial responsibility. He took over the mine-laying department on one boat, the weapons department on another, and served in the demanding position of commanding officer's assistant on a third.

The rapid changes in the Soviet submarine force, their drive to educate more officers, and the pressure to expand their operations on a global scale emerged from the determination and vision of one man, Admiral Sergei Gorshkov. Lebedko recalled meeting the admiral first while on duty in Sevastopol in the mid-1950s. He realized at once that Gorshkov supplied the vision, the political clout, and the administrative savvy that had given birth to global Soviet naval power. The submarine force formed a critical pillar of his carefully planned design. Lebedko would have regular access to Gorshkov over the years for a variety of personal and professional reasons. When they first met, Gorshkov had come to Sevastopol to welcome new submariners to the service, encourage them in their effort, and instill in them his vision of the future. A stocky man of modest height, the admiral wore glasses in his later years, but they did not hide the ability of his clear hazel eyes to arrest an individual and command his attention. He received the respect and fierce loyalty of Soviet naval officers. Gorshkov's efforts brought him world recognition as well as a commodity considered priceless among Soviet officers: true respect from friend and foe alike.

Lebedko's career in Gorshkov's navy, like that of many Soviet naval officers, would take him to many places and put him through numerous trials completely beyond the ken of his primary adversary in the great Cold War contest. His early assignment as the commander's assistant on board the Whiskey class diesel-powered *S-91* gave him his first experience both at a shipyard and with the difficult process of delivering a new boat to its operational command without leaving the confined world of the Soviet Union or the Soviet sphere of influence.

S-91 emerged from the shipyard in Nikolaev City on the Black Sea in

December 1953, and became a commissioned vessel of the Soviet Navy on August 20, 1954. As number fifty-six in the long construction run of the Whiskey class since 1951, this boat formed part of an effort to supply the navy with sound, flexible, long-range submarines that would make them competitive in the grand undersea contest. One hundred and thirty-eight more of this class would join the fleet before its retirement in 1955.[10] With *S-91* in the Black Sea, Lebedko experienced everything from a near sinking due to technical malfunction while submerging to training for clandestine operations.

He also helped deliver the *S-91* to the Northern Fleet by making an amazing journey that his American colleagues fortunately did not have to duplicate. Even in the early 1950s, the Soviets rarely risked their submarines and crews in an open-ocean journey to the northern and far eastern fleet bases. A boat in the Black Sea ordered to join the Northern Fleet would face a Mediterranean transit and a journey along the western European coast to the Kola Peninsula, in full view of NATO forces. This seemed too great a risk given the alternatives. The intricate internal river and waterway system within the Soviet Union permitted Whiskey class boats to make the journey from the Black Sea to the Northern Fleet bases near Polyarni without running the NATO gauntlet.

In the summer of 1954, Lieutenant Lebedko helped take the *S-91* first to the Northern Fleet and then, almost immediately, across the northern edge of the Soviet Union to the Pacific. Only by listening to Soviet submariners recount this experience does the overpowering size and the varying weather and sea conditions of the Cold War Soviet domain become comprehensible. Lebedko recalled sailing past Crimean shores on his way to the first leg of the journey.

> At night the submarine was passing the southern coast of Crimea glittered with thousands of lights. Wind would bring the fantastic fragrance of the Crimean flowers. Some of us were leaving Crimea, the pearl of the Black Sea coast, forever and some just for several years.[11]

When the submarine arrived at Zhdanov City on the Sea of Azov, *S-91* had to play piggyback. She slipped into a floating dry dock, the doors closed behind her, and the pumps expelled the water. Once secured in the dry dock's bay and covered with tarps, both for protection and to hide it from prying eyes, a tugboat towed the floating dock slowly toward the River Don. The entire trip would take fifty-one days.

Some days treated the crew to boring routine, others to farm fields, ancient structures, and churches that stood along the Don River canal long before the Bolshevik Revolution of 1917, and still others to life-threatening encounters. In one case, as the tugboat and its submarine cargo reached Rostov, the dry dock collided with a railway bridge. The commanding officer of the boat ordered Lebedko to get back into the submarine when all of his colleagues scrambled out of the hatch, afraid that the boat would roll over. They had reason for concern because at one point shortly after the collision, S-91's instruments showed a 32-degree roll to port. A light seemed to dawn as Lebedko remained in the submarine while the others ran for safety: His captain was teaching him to define problems rather than run from them. Repairs to the floating dry dock took two days.

Moving through the Volga–Don Canal, S-91 took advantage of the largest waterway in the western Soviet Union. The tug and towed dock increased their pace on the Volga, which permitted them to make time against the possibility of becoming trapped as the rivers of Kareliya began to freeze. Only the nineteenth-century Mariinsky Canals presented a true problem. Too shallow and too old, they often required the crew to pull the dock along and at the locks old women and pack animals pitched in to force the old controls to do the job.

The tugboat and the floating dry dock discharged their burden at Lake Onezhskoe. S-91 then entered the modern, nineteen-gate White Sea canal and, in spite of some ice, crossed it quickly. Lebedko and his comrades tied up at the White Sea port of Belomorsk on the fifty-first day of their journey. A few days later they braved the storms and snowdrifts of the Barents Sea, arriving at Polyarni on November 7.

Within two months S-91 received orders to join the Pacific Fleet. Unlike Americans operating out of New London, Norfolk, Charleston, San Diego, or Pearl Harbor, Soviet submariners spent most of their careers near or above the Arctic Circle. Like the transit from the Black Sea to Polyarni, the fleet command preferred an internal route to the Pacific in spite of the treacherous ice conditions and the brief window of opportunity afforded by the seasons. Most Soviet diesel submarines destined for service in the Pacific continued to make this journey on the surface well into the 1960s with the Foxtrot class. The *S-91* would make its trip in a 46-vessel convoy under the direction of Vice Admiral Rossokho. The staff at Polyarni fitted all ten of the convoy's submarines with wooden and metal barriers, which would protect them against the ice and permit icebreakers to tow the submarines with minimal damage.

Within three days of the convoy's July 7, 1955, departure the ships found themselves surrounded by extremely dense and dangerous ice formations that would haunt them until they reached the Bering Strait. *Lenin* and the grand old man of the Russian icebreaking fleet, *Ermak,* led the way from the departure point in the western Arctic. They would later hand the convoy off to the eastern Arctic icebreakers, *Mikoyan* and *Kaganovich.* If the constant presence of thick fog did not lead to collisions with the ice, then the floes seemed determined to squeeze the vessels into pulp along the way. The density of the ice in the Laptev Sea and Vilkitski Strait swiftly increased to four times that seen by the departing convoy.[12] The intense ice conditions made it necessary for reconnaissance aircraft to stay with the convoy as long as possible to locate fissures that the icebreakers might exploit to make the voyage easier.

On August 17, the convoy broke into the clear water of the Chukchi Sea after covering 850 miles in 39 days. All the ships made it through successfully in spite of the seeming determination of Arctic ice floes to capture and hold them fast. Looking farther east as they passed through the Bering Strait, the coast of Alaska loomed in the distance. The new submarine base at Provideniya Bay, an inlet of the Bering Sea on the southeast margin of the Chukotski Peninsula, provided all of the first aid needed to remedy minor damage inflicted by the ice on some submarine propellers. They would linger for only a short time at Provideniya Bay, preparing for a journey under their own power south to Kamchatka, site of the submarine base prepared for them near Petropavlovsk-Kamchatsky. Lebedko and his messmates celebrated the end of this arduous journey, one that took them close to the Americans and new challenges, but far away from the sweet aromas of home and the Black Sea flowers.

≈ ≈ ≈

BY 1956 THE NAVAL HIGH COMMAND determined that the submarine fleet needed to begin long-range patrols that would establish a Russian blue water presence around the globe. These deployments marked
the Soviet Submarine Force's coming of age and some of the first open
challenges to the United States Navy in the relatively new Cold War. *S-91*
made the voyage across the Soviet Union's northern borders to provide
a Pacific component for this early effort to establish a Soviet presence in
the deep ocean. Autonomous Pacific Ocean deployments provided the
first real chance to take stock of the submarine's physical integrity, the
stamina of the crew, the boat's true operating environment, and the activities of American anti-submarine forces. Admiral Gorshkov knew his
crews lacked experience. They could not yet compare to an American
undersea fleet seasoned by World War II. However, he would change all
of that.

In 1956, *S-91* and two other Pacific-based submarines became the
first to initiate long-range reconnaissance patrols. After the journey to
Polyarni and the transit across the ice-laden north, the *S-91*'s Black Sea
sailors considered themselves seasoned as their commander prepared
them for a seminal journey.

They left Kamchatka on August 21, 1956, and turned south. As part of
their training, the crew initially stood at a high level of readiness the Soviets called N-1, announced by an alarm and requiring the commander
to remain at his post. A less intense N-2 schedule later divided the crew
into a watchbill of three four-hour shifts. Those off duty at any given
point would sleep, study, perform maintenance, and do other work in
accordance with their daily responsibilities.

Captain Third Rank Milovanov took *S-91* to sea, assisted by the executive officer Captain-Lieutenant Stepochkin and the commander's assistant, Lieutenant Lebedko. Responding to the boat's secret task,
technicians at the base painted out the hull number, the external lights
remained dark, and the flag never appeared. The vessel had orders to go
deep immediately upon detecting ships, planes, or any active sonar signals. While the sun remained high she proceeded submerged at 210–270

feet, breaking the surface occasionally with her instrument masts to establish a link with the naval command or to obtain navigational information and celestial fixes. *S-91* would come to the surface only at night to recharge her battery.

As determined by the general headquarters in Moscow, the voyage plan took the crew to the Sea of Okhotsk and then permitted them to visit the port of Korsakov, on Sakhalin Island. *S-91* would then cruise through the western Pacific Ocean to Midway Atoll, and then back to Kamchatka.

The boat wound its way in and out of the Kuril Islands, first in the Sea of Okhotsk for three days and then back into the Pacific Ocean. The commander submerged, sure that their passage had gone undetected by either the Japanese or their own Soviet coastal forces. *S-91* moved back into the Sea of Okhotsk on August 30. At Sakhalin Island, the watch exchanged call signs with the port authority, raised the Soviet flag, entered the harbor, and tied up at Korsakov.

The few days in port began with a welcome change of cuisine and fresh supplies from the many Korean merchants and grocers in port, and ended with freshwater baths for the crew as well as supplies of bread, meat, and cabbage. September 1 found the boat sailing away from Sakhalin into water that would permit an average cruising depth of 300 feet.

Lebedko's fervent admiration for his Captain Milovanov had begun to diminish. Milovanov was a truly unusual personality to be qualified for submarine command. He befriended the crew, never failed to find the best joke for any situation, and eloquently and regularly addressed Communist Party meetings. However, he rarely handled the submarine himself. He surrendered that job to his assistants, who did most things for him. He did not punish anyone, but never stood up for anyone either. Lebedko at last realized that Milovanov was a terribly weak-willed person who drank every day. As a joke he had taken on the nickname "Valya," short for Valentin, but also a girl's name. There was no question of the captain's masculinity—he was not homosexual. But the crew began to use his nickname freely, and this undermined discipline.

Unfortunately for *S-91*, it had another unusual leader, the new executive officer Captain-Lieutenant Stepochkin. He was a very interesting and sociable person who had a tendency to crack lewd jokes at the most inappropriate times, did not care for submarines, and never learned the intricacies of the boat as he should have.

Lebedko's first confrontation came as the *S-91* lay on the bottom at 300 feet during a pause for repairs when "Valya" opened the hatch of compartment two and stumbled through, obviously drunk and holding a cup of vodka in his hand. Apparently ready for a party, he approached Lebedko, looking for company.

"Vladimir Georgievich, let's drink to the health of the submariners!" he said.

Lebedko flinched. "Comrade commander, I'm on watch. Share this with the navigator," pointing him to Lieutenant Malko, who was enjoying a nap, completely oblivious to the events transpiring around him.

The two officers shared the vodka and kissed and hugged each other in Russian style. Next Milovanov left to go aft. The men in compartment five were working on the batteries, and had the deck plates pulled up to permit access to the battery spaces beneath. Entering compartment five, Milovanov fell into the void and tore his calf muscles down to the bone.

Fortunately, *S-91* had a doctor on board. Lieutenant Azarov, who had joined the submarine at Sevastopol, treated Milovanov and sent him to his cabin to recover. The episode concluded the captain's active participation in the mission. He could not walk to the control room or make the climb to the bridge. He never reported the matter to higher authority while still on patrol, would not request permission to return to base, and ordered Stepochkin and Lebedko to cover his watch. From that point on, each had to stand daily eight-hour command watches while Milovanov recuperated in his sea cabin.

S-91 continued its mission into the Pacific Ocean. Frequently maneuvering submerged through groups of commercial ships and fishing vessels, she passed Japan's Hokkaido Island, moving south and then east.

During nocturnal breaks on the surface to recharge the batteries, the crew would lift the injured "Valya girl" up to the conning tower bridge with ropes to enjoy both a cigarette and the cooler night air. While the captain blew smoke rings, Lebedko and the navigator would take star sightings, plot their position, and fill in details about bottom topography, coastal geography, and strategic points observed that their charts lacked.

As *S-91* approached 30° north latitude, the crew suffered as internal ship temperatures occasionally reached 105 degrees. Whiskey class boats did not have air conditioning, having been designed primarily for operations in the far north. Lebedko frequently thought that Gorshkov would have to rethink this one if he planned more patrols into warmer climes.

The climate on board occasionally led even the most responsible members of the crew to make some ill-considered choices. In one instance, *S-91* had just surfaced and both Lebedko and Stepochkin went to the bridge. The former had the first watch. The ocean did not present any threat; Lebedko scanned a calm sea with his binoculars and found no menacing ships or planes. Putting his binoculars down for a moment he suddenly could not locate Stepochkin. Calling his name produced no result. Out of instinct, the junior officer immediately looked over the side, to both starboard and port. Lebedko shouted, "Man overboard," as he found the truant Stepochkin, laughing, floating, and holding the sub's hull with one hand while waving with the other. Some of the men pulled Stepochkin back on board. As a lesson, Lebedko called for the crew to dump the rubbish overboard. It was contained in special zinc-coated boxes to ensure they would go to the bottom, but killer whales or sharks made a feast of the trash, as he knew they would. Stepochkin watched the drama and admitted his foolishness.

Lebedko worried that too many days at 105-degree temperatures would affect an officer's ability to make sound judgments and would severely reduce the combat readiness of the crew. With Milovanov useless and Stepochkin weak, Lebedko had to assume more responsibility than he wanted on his first Pacific voyage.

While the boat's orders for this cruise emphasized testing the range and endurance of the boat, it also called for careful reconnaissance and checking the validity of their charts. Soviet charts for these waters frequently lacked the latest information on obstacles to navigation, bathymetry, and depth soundings.

As *S-91* set its return course for Kamchatka on September 13, the boat began a routine dive and the navigator switched on the fathometer.

Looking at the first acoustic readings, he experienced an unwelcome rush of adrenaline and shouted, "36 feet under the keel!" The captain ordered the boat to surface, and they realized that they had nearly crashed into a submerged mountain that did not appear on the official naval charts. Instead of the four-mile depths that the charts indicated, a quick fathometer survey of the region revealed depths of 420 feet, 525 feet, and 1,140 feet.

The navigator's attention to duty had saved the boat. For submarines, catastrophe frequently lurked just beneath the surface, even when the navigation charts said otherwise. Impressed, Lebedko realized more strongly than ever that nothing could replace watchful officers, good instruments, and an alert crew. But this was not to be his last lesson on the voyage—one on survival technique lay ahead.

After some terrible weather encountered on the patrol's final leg, S-91 sighted Kamchatka on September 20, tying up at the base at roughly 2230 hours. Captain Milovanov reported to Rear Admiral Paramoshkin on the survey and reconnaissance results of the S-91's patrol. When asked, he claimed that his injury resulted from a fall during the violent storm encountered on the return journey. The crew and junior officers supported his claim and let the episode pass. On the whole, the S-91 received very high marks. The admiral decorated the captain, and both Lebedko and Stepochkin thanked God that they were not punished. In the early Cold War Soviet Navy, a pragmatic officer quietly accepted "the absence of punishment" as an important and significant reward.

≈   ≈   ≈

REGARDLESS OF the S-91's difficulties, the Soviet naval command considered the submarines stationed at Kamchatka as deployable assets in case of a national emergency. The cost to the crewmembers in discomfort and danger were ignored, for human life simply did not enter into the calculations of the naval high command.

As a veteran of the first deep-ocean patrols conducted by Soviet submarines in the Pacific, Lebedko realized the limitations of the navy's technology and the need to train crews and to improve habitability on board. If significant improvements did not come, the boats and the crews could not hope to perform to expectation. Regardless of their shortcomings, vessels like the *S-91* remained on 24-hour call. They lived on the razor's edge. Lebedko did not know it, but shortly after returning from the *S-91* patrol, doing a favor for a friend would turn into a white-knuckle Cold War experience.

The base to which *S-91* returned had yet to acquire the human touches that would turn wilderness and a very inhospitable environment into something of a welcoming home for the submariners stationed there. Only in 1956 did the submarine base get an officers' club, where the men could watch films, play pool, have a cup of coffee, and talk. Visiting the club on November 6, Lieutenant Lebedko encountered a good friend, the executive officer of the Whiskey class boat *S-178*, Captain-Lieutenant Valentin Bez. A very literate and strong-willed officer, Bez would eventually rise to flag rank. Among his accomplishments was establishing the most remote Pacific submarine base at Bechevinka Harbor in Kamchatka.

Bez had a favor to ask. Since the commanding authorities considered the *S-178* well prepared for patrol, she was on emergency duty. This meant that she would remain prepared to deploy on a moment's notice at any hour in case of an alert. Bez had important command business to conduct that day in Petropavlovsk. He hoped that Lebedko would cover for him on board *S-178* so he could attend to the command's business in the city. Sensing a fairly light and routine task, Lebedko had no trouble helping a friend in need. Besides, it would only last for a few days and might prove interesting.

Later in the day Lebedko ironed his suit, put on a new shirt, donned a fresh jacket, and took a packet of cigarettes with him, planning to return to the club. He never made it, as a breathless seaman found him and reported that the *S-178* had orders to go on combat alert as of 1740 as a measure against the heightening world crisis.

In October and November of 1956, the world's attention was focused on the Middle East and Eastern Europe. France, Great Britain, and Israel had allied themselves against Egypt in a violent encounter that combined Israel's security ambitions in the region with Western Europe's objection to President Nasser's decision to nationalize the Suez Canal. At the same time, the Hungarian rebellion was under way, trying to divorce the country from the Communist sphere of influence in Eastern Europe. The Hungarian revolt was crushed by the Red Army, despite condemnation by the United Nations and the United States.

These almost simultaneous crises increased tension between the United States and the Soviet Union. On the very day Bez asked his favor, President Eisenhower placed the American armed forces on full alert in response to the possibility that the Soviet Union might use its armed might to assist the Egyptians under attack at Suez.[13]

Lebedko had other concerns; 1956 had witnessed the loss of at least three submarines. A raging fire had started in the closed-cycle diesel compartment and swept through the Quebec class *M-256,* destroying her structural integrity and causing her to sink in the Baltic with forty of her crew, including her captain. (The Quebec class was so fire-prone that they were known as "cigarette lighters" by Soviet navy personnel.) Only seven men survived, purely by luck and the fact that the accident took place close to their home base at Tallinn. The tragedy of the situation was that another submarine, *M-200,* was nearby and its commander, Captain Kolpakov, began preparations to rescue any survivors above the crippled *M-256.* However, his orders were countermanded by fleet headquarters, which, in essence, told him to concentrate not on saving submariners, but on salvaging the submarine. Lebedko tried to understand the logic behind such orders, telling himself that perhaps the Cold War danger was so great that submarines were considered more irreplaceable than crews. But in his heart he knew—and every submariner knew—that the men should come first and the equipment after.

The *M-200* itself would not survive long. It collided with a destroyer near Tallinn, Estonia, experienced a fire ignited by liquid oxygen, then exploded and sank. Twenty-eight crewmen died; only seven were saved.

Like every other Soviet sailor, Lebedko had no choice but to shrug off these disasters and concentrate on the current crisis. As far as the events of the Middle East were from Kamchatka, he recognized the need for the Pacific alert, for it marked the transition of the Soviet submarine force from being just a regional force to one that would play an important role in the Cold War. As time passed, it was evident that Admiral Gorshkov's navy would play on a global scale, regardless of its state of preparation. Officers, ratings, ships, submarines, weapons, and technology would have to measure up to new demands. United States naval power now exerted almost complete authority in the Pacific; the Soviet submarine force was determined to change this, no matter what the cost.

As he walked toward the pier and the waiting *S-178*, Lebedko initially dismissed the alert as a test. He would make sure that *S-178* measured up, but he knew, he prayed, that they faced only a test. With both diesels fired up and functioning well, the crew made preparations to get underway. The vessel's commander, Captain Third Rank Sorokin, held in his hand the envelope he could open only when the boat entered the Avachinskaya Firth, well out to sea. Like Lebedko, he hoped a test lay ahead.

It was not a test. It was real.

Opening the classified envelope, the captain discovered that they had to navigate directly into harm's way and reach their station at sea—a set of coordinates out in the open ocean—by November 9. Sorokin opened up his diesels to their maximum and for the better part of two days raced through the northern Pacific on the surface to his station.

The order to reconnoiter the region did not bother him. Both he and Lebedko had already done that since the submarine fleet began the first long-range patrols many months earlier. However, the other instructions in the envelope disturbed him greatly. They ordered him to make all preparations to attack and destroy the surface ships and vessels of "the adversary." The instructions carried a red stamp and the signature of the commander of the Soviet Pacific Fleet. The adversary was not mentioned explicitly—again a means by which headquarters could avoid responsibility in the event of a mistake—but he understood too well the identity of the intended target.

The orders stunned the *S-178*'s officers. The commander, executive officer, and the political officer signed the envelope according to standard procedure to confirm their understanding of the mission. The sky grew dark as *S-178* left the firth into the path of a growing storm. The captain and Lieutenant Lebedko took the first watch.

Valentin Bez returned to the base two days later with his mission completed to find seamen dragging the water for a body. When he asked what was going on, he found that the command had initiated a search for Lebedko, who had suddenly gone missing. They assumed he had drowned by falling into the harbor waters overnight. The search ceased when Bez discovered that *S-178* had sortied in response to alert orders. He hoped that his friend's fate would not turn out worse than simple death by drowning.

On November 9, right on schedule, Lebedko and his messmates arrived at a location 240 miles away from their base and 262 miles from Paramishura in the Kuril Islands. They sat at the crossroads that American forces from Alaska or Hawaii might use if headed for the northwest Pacific and the route that the U.S. Navy might take if they emerged from their naval base at Yokosuka, Japan. Sorokin's patrol orders also mentioned another, even more forward station close to the Gulf of Alaska.

The following day the weather turned angry. A violent storm created immense waves that drove the turbulence very deep. Instead of finding the usual safe haven well below the surface, the boat's instruments registered 10-degree rolls as far down as 300 feet. While rolling and pitching, another major threat to their survival surfaced: They were desperately short of fresh water. Lieutenant Svyatez, the submarine's doctor, informed Lebedko that the crew had just about exhausted the small amount of fresh water on board the vessel. A Whiskey class diesel submarine had three fresh water tanks, located in compartments one, three, and seven. As the doctor and Lieutenant Lebedko assessed the situation, the worst possible scenario emerged. The main water tank in compartment three was almost empty; the water in the other two tanks had spoiled badly.

Lebedko cursed the inefficient logistic support that the bases supplied the submarines; not having fresh water was intolerable—there was no excuse. Yet if the mission were aborted because of the deficiency, the heads that would roll would be those of the crewmembers, not the supply people on shore.

They were more than 300 miles out to sea with orders to possibly engage the Americans, and the crew's basic health was threatened by spoiled water. The commander turned down a recommendation to request permission to return to base. Instead he told the doctor to "clean the water."

Over the next few days the vapors from boiling, foul water augmented the diesel and personal odors seizing the vessel's atmosphere. The cooks and the doctor repeatedly brought the water to a rapid boil and passed it through a filter, using the still tainted fluid to make dense, thick coffee. The crew choked it down, joking about the "super-vomiting soup of the day."

The weather remained violent for several days. Fires broke out when water streamed in, shorting out the main electric distributor. When Lebedko went on watch duty on the bridge, he tied himself to the base of the bridge compass within striking distance of the communication pipe. Later he wrote:

> The submarine would dive to the ocean or rise to the sky. Most of the time I couldn't see the sky. Churning and raving water was all around. When a wave was just about to cover the submarine I would inhale, but the water wouldn't soon disappear and it felt as though I wouldn't have enough air in my lungs to breathe. I had never experienced anything like this before. At one point, when a wave was covering me, I saw a big black ship above me with her lights on, I rushed to the communication pipe and screamed, "Left the helm," but nobody could hear me. I thought, "This is the end," and I closed my eyes. Luckily our vessels missed each other. The wave raised the submarine on a crest and the unknown ship fell down into a trough. I didn't see that ship anymore. I thought to myself, in cases like this, the voice of one man is the voice of no man.

By November 12 the storms had ripped the conning tower railing to pieces and damaged the tower door, ensuring that those in this portion of the submarine would stand in water up to their knees. Eventually, the conning tower hatch could not keep a watertight seal and constantly leaked, placing the stability of the boat in danger. The pumps worked overtime expelling the water and the crew worked to repair the hatch.

The order to return to base came on November 17, but the ocean did not stop pounding them until the volcanoes of Kamchatka came into view. They tied up on November 19, and the commander toasted the officers and crew. No one greeted them or thanked them for a job well done.

After a good night's sleep, Lebedko examined the damaged exterior of *S-178* and felt fortunate to be alive. He had a very long and energetic conversation with Valentin Bez about making sure the supply organization supplied enough water to keep his fresh water stores in order. It took the crew the better part of two months to get the stench out of the boat and their nostrils.

Lebedko was heartened to learn of an incident that had happened in May, for it boded well for the entire submarine service, even though a submarine, *S-99*, the *Golden Fish*, had suffered an emergency and almost sank. Fortunately, the submarine salvage ship *Pulkovo* had been nearby, and had given the *S-99* enough assistance that it could limp back to its base at Libava, where it began to sink at its mooring. It was near a crane that attached slings to it, however, keeping it afloat long enough to get the crew out. It would have been tragic to have lost them at the pier in their home base. Best of all, the incident produced reports that a new rescue detachment was being established with a new salvage vessel, the *SS-30*, that could take divers down as deep as 200 meters below the surface to rescue submariners. The *SS-30* was so sophisticated that besides the essential emergency air and power sources, it also carried a sonic connection device to furnish music and radio messages to the crew.

≈   ≈   ≈

IN AN EFFORT TO EXPAND both Soviet influence and the reach of the navy, Moscow decided to befriend the Sukarno regime in Indonesia in 1959. In return for a few Whiskey class submarines and a training program that would provide an undersea capability, the Russians secured a supply base in the southern Pacific and a welcome in that area of the world for their submarine fleet. In the spring preparations began in Vladivostok for the transfer of *S-91* and *S-79* to the Indonesian Navy.

Lebedko and the crew of the *S-91* found themselves demonstrating the capabilities of their submarines sooner than expected. Khrushchev permitted the navy to sell a license to build Whiskey class submarines to the Chinese and a high-level delegation came to Vladivostok to examine the boats. With preparations for the transfer to Indonesia nearly complete, *S-79* and *S-91* emerged as the obvious candidates for the important show-and-tell.

The Chinese delegation arrived at Vladivostok in early July. Rumors circulated at the base that the group, generals all, would include North Korean marshal Pan Dakhuai. Lieutenant Alexander Gavrilchenko of the *S-79* received orders to conduct a tour of his vessel at the pier, providing an introduction and basic technical details. Lebedko and *S-91* would take the delegation to sea. The commander of the cruiser detachment, Rear Admiral Boris Petrovich Lamm, went along as commanding officer. Lebedko handled the boat and Lamm assumed the ultimate responsibility for the safety of the delegation.

The next morning *S-91* played host to a group of eight Chinese. The crew found their behavior parochial and a bit arrogant, always looking at things carefully and knowingly while listening to the interpreter. The *S-91* took their Chinese guests to a test site. They demonstrated firing the 25-mm deck gun and diving procedures, along with full-speed operation both on the surface and submerged. Then the crew went to battle stations and simulated torpedo attacks. When Lebedko took the submarine into shallow water to simulate close-range attack or intelligence-gathering techniques, the Chinese officers were particularly impressed.

The galley later served dinner, giving all of the guests, including Rear Admiral Lamm, their first experience eating while submerged. Wine formed part of the table fare, but the Chinese proposed no toasts. For Russian naval officers, heartfelt toasts rank in importance with the main course. One part of the meal cannot exist or satisfy without the other. When he could no longer stand the absence of this all-important part of the meal, Admiral Lamm diplomatically offered a toast "to Soviet–Chinese friendship" and added, "I've been serving the navy all my life but it is my first time aboard a submarine. I have never seen a crew operate in such harmony. These aren't just seamen, they are real professionals. To the health of the submariners!" The generals nodded and joined the salute to the crew.

When the submarine returned to Vladivostok, Lebedko and Gavrilchenko received the delegation's thanks and a medal called the Star of the 1st of August, named for the anniversary of the creation of the Chinese Army. These red stars set in a golden frame and decorated in the middle with a golden character looked very handsome on their black naval uniforms.

Soon thereafter Captain Second Rank Susoev and Captain Third Rank Fedor Volovik took over the Indonesia-bound submarines. Volovik assumed command of *S-91* and proved to be all that Milovanov was not: professional, gregarious, and a future friend to many of the officers and men. As the boat underwent final preparation, he encouraged the crew to study the South Pacific region, South Asia, and their primary naval adversary in the area. The officers worked with the ratings to elevate everyone's understanding of English. In addition, the habits and capabilities of American anti-submarine forces became part of daily conversation and official training.

As the sun rose on August 8, 1959, the crew bade farewell to their families at the pier and brigade commander Captain Peter Vosmak gave a parting speech. In the Russian tradition, he hugged the commanding officers and wished them well.

S-91 tied up for a short time at Zolotoi Rog harbor to pick up an Indonesian submarine commander, Major Purnamo, and his torpedo officer Captain Sugito. Admiral Vitali Alexeevitch Fokin arrived to offer his best wishes and to witness the departure. At 7 P.M. the two submarines and the tanker *Polyarnik* got underway.

They had unwelcome company from the beginning. While *S-91* endured a force five sea and 30-degree rolls on their first day out, they were constantly monitored by American Lockheed P-2V Neptune ASW aircraft. At times the pilots flew no more than 100 to 150 yards above the Soviet ships. This close surveillance continued for the entire voyage, with Neptunes and Grumman Albatross amphibians sharing the task. In one incident an Albatross passed over the surfaced *S-91* only twenty yards above the bridge. In each case, the aircraft kept their intelligence-gathering cameras rolling without pause. This worried the Indonesians so much that Major Purnamo would hide inside the submarine or cover himself to avoid American spying. The major hailed from the aristocratic family of an Indonesian diplomat. Educated as a naval officer, he spoke fluent French, English, and Dutch, and understood orders in Russian and Polish. To the Russian officers he seemed approachable and interesting.

On August 11 the small convoy maneuvered past Tsushima Strait, site of one of the most significant battles of world history during the Russian–Japanese War at the turn of the century. The next day the tanker *Arkhangelsk* relieved *Polyarnik,* permitting the latter to return to base, and both submarines made trim dives after refueling to evaluate the boats' handling and buoyancy and to calibrate instruments. The latter activity worried the American onlookers, who wanted to monitor the entire process.

Inside *S-91* the heat began to build, with on-board temperatures of better than 120 degrees as the group approached the equator. Working conditions deteriorated, many men became lethargic and felt sick, and still others fainted. Eighty-five percent humidity reduced the reliability of the radio, the torpedo firing mechanisms, and the propulsion diesels. In the galley, the refrigeration failed and the fresh food began to rot, treating the entire crew to the expected potent aroma.

During the second week of August, the Pacific treated the boats to storms at force seven just as storm damage caused the diesels to shut down. Quick and intense repair efforts took place submerged while the typhoon passed overhead, tearing up the surface of the ocean, but barely detectable a few hundred feet below.

Carrying out Gorshkov's desires to expand Soviet influence in the Pacific at the expense of the United States, the officers and crew of both submarines found their passage close to the Philippines both significant and ominous, especially when placed in the context of the constant American P-2V overflights. The *S-79* and *S-91* navigated near Mindanao and the sites of American World War II battles with the Japanese at Samar and Leyte.

The U.S. Navy's historical presence soon turned into menacing reality. As *S-91*'s navigator took out his photocopies of British Royal Navy South Pacific charts to guide the boat into the Celebes Sea, two unknown submarines surfaced and then quickly submerged again. American ships and aircraft promptly disappeared, suggesting that they were now being monitored by submarines, an even more disturbing surveillance alternative.

On August 25 the Soviet submarines arrived at Surabaya on the island of Java, moving to the naval base the next day. The role played by the Soviet naval officers in Indonesia placed them in an awkward situation. A domestic insurgency challenged the Sukarno regime's authority, and even friends of the new government had reservations about the Soviet presence. Still others wondered about the purchase of these submarines.

The navy base culture demonstrated the odd confluence of Russian, eastern bloc, and Asian eccentricities. The prospective Indonesian commander of *S-79*, Major Kuusno, owned some pubs on base that provided Czech beer to the submariners in the evening and would then offer it for sale in the morning immediately next to the crew's shore accommodations. For many of the Russian officers, the beer flowed too freely and often proved too expensive. Then there was the sacred status of the Indonesian 11:00 A.M. coffee break. Lebedko later recalled:

> The flag would be raised at 8:00 A.M. Then at 11:00 A.M. there would be so-called "coffee-time" which was something holy on the base. Once I saw a destroyer lifting a motorboat and suddenly the 11:00 A.M. bell rang, so the destroyer stopped dead in the water and the motorboat went on hanging on the hawsers until the break ended.

The Soviets helped their Indonesian colleagues learn submarine operation and maintenance. The Russian operators carefully reviewed with the Indonesians everything they had absorbed earlier in Poland at a special course on the Whiskey class boats. It took until early September 1959 for the two submarines to complete their at-sea tests with new Indonesian officers and ratings. Before the month concluded, the Indonesian Navy had two submarines and the Russian submariners returned to Vladivostok, spending fifteen days steaming north on board the Russian surface ship *Tobolsk*. Many years later they learned to their regret that both the *S-91* and *S-79* had sunk while under Indonesian command.

Such idle days were few and far between for Russian submariners, and they relished the time off. For almost all of them, the future held a continuing series of cruises from northern ports, where wives held families together despite months of bad weather, poor accommodations, and bad rations. The sailor's return was always joyous, his departure always sad. Yet life aboard a submarine had an attraction of its own, particularly as it moved forward into an age of first nuclear weapons and then nuclear power.

3

"UNDERWAY ON NUCLEAR POWER"

Interest in nuclear propulsion began in both the U.S. and Soviet Navies before World War II, but the pressures of that conflict prevented any specialized development until after its conclusion. When peace came, however, both navies began to pursue the use of nuclear power plants with ever-increasing vigor.

The Soviet effort reflected Joseph Stalin's determination to create a navy second to none, and it was natural, given the Soviet wartime experience and the wealth of material captured from Nazi Germany, that the submarine fleet would be vastly expanded. The captures included finished submarines, shipyards, unfinished submarines, their components, and a host of scientists and technicians. The initial Soviet expansion was in submarines of the traditional diesel-electric type, and this was sustained even after nuclear-powered submarines were introduced into the fleet. (This may have occurred because some sort of widespread failure in nuclear propulsion had been feared, so a large conventional force was retained as a safety measure, or it may have been an effort to keep Soviet industrial capacity working at its maximum at a time when nuclear power plants were not being built in quantity.) This dual track in submarines was in clear contrast to the United States Navy, which directed all of its efforts to nuclear-powered submarines after initial experiments had proved them to be successful.

While the U.S. Navy had begun research into nuclear propulsion on a limited basis in 1939, it would not be until chance had provided a most unlikely candidate to lead, guide, push, prod, goad, and flog the program that it would gain the solid momentum that continues to the very present.

That unlikely candidate was Hyman G. Rickover (1898–1986), born in Makow, a small town fifty miles from Warsaw. He migrated to the United States with his mother and sister in 1904, and entered the United States Naval Academy in 1918. (It is worth speculating about how the shape of world navies might have been changed if Rickover had remained in his native Poland and gone, as he might have during those turbulent times, to a Russian naval academy. Given his intellect, his drive, and his absolute determination to succeed, he might well have come to direct the Soviet nuclear submarine effort.)

Rickover graduated 107th out of 540 in his Class of 1922, eventually earning a master's degree in electrical engineering at the Naval Postgraduate School. He made a reputation for himself as head of the Electrical Section of the Bureau of Ships during World War Two and truly came into his own during his postwar assignment at Clinton National Laboratories at Oak Ridge, Tennessee. The assistant chief of the Bureau of Ships, Vice Admiral Earle Mills, selected Rickover as the future head of the Navy's nuclear program for the Oak Ridge job because of the captain's organizational ability, his eye for engineering talent, and his reluctance to walk away from institutional or bureaucratic fights. Rickover hated losing and Mills wanted that kind of man in the inevitable fray over the navy's desire to enter the nuclear world. While Mills did not place the other naval offices at the Oak Ridge program directly under Rickover's authority, the army officer assigned to write their fitness reports delegated that task to Rickover as the senior naval officer present. If he was to write their fitness reports, all of the naval officers knew that he was in charge. Mills was not alone in his appreciation of Rickover the organizer and fighter. Even Dr. Edward Teller recognized Rickover's ability. In his letter of August 19, 1947, to Dr. Lawrence R. Hafstadt, the executive secretary of the Joint (Defense) Research and Development Board, Teller advocated nuclear ship propulsion and mentioned that he was very much impressed by Captain Rickover.

At the conclusion of his tour of duty, Rickover sought and gained assignment as Special Assistant for Nuclear Matters to the Chief of the Bureau of Ships. He and many others in the navy recognized this post as a portal on the future, an exciting future worth the fight. Rickover also saw, correctly, that through this position he could control the navy's entry into the age of nuclear propulsion. To do so, he became an adept politician with Congress, a task he found easier to accomplish when he received a parallel posting to the Atomic Energy Commission (AEC), which reported to the Congressional Joint Committee on Atomic Energy (JCAE). The AEC wanted to monitor the development of naval nuclear propulsion as part of its congressionally mandated authority over all nuclear matters. Thus, Rickover found himself wearing two hats, one naval and the other civilian. Over time, he would use his civilian status repeatedly to sidestep or challenge the naval chain of command. It also enabled him to resolve most AEC/U.S. Navy issues in the manner he desired.

Rickover had a difficult personality, disregarded formal channels whenever it was convenient, and was anti-social in the sense that he abjured the Officer's Club and other naval niceties. These failings, when combined with a jarring arrogance, alienated many inside the navy and out. Rickover was smart, knew what he wanted and how to get it, and was determined despite all opposition to provide the navy with nuclear power plants and a nuclear submarine built to his demanding standards.

All of this combined to deny him promotion to flag rank. He was passed over for promotion to admiral twice, both times because he was not liked—he did not fit the mold at a time when many regular naval officers, combat veterans, were being forced to retire. The official rationale was that promotions were not for what an officer had done, but for what he was capable of doing in the future—and they obviously did not believe Rickover was capable of doing much. It seemed certain to the naval brass that so disliked him that regulations would now take their course and the gadfly Rickover would be retired after thirty years of service.

They misjudged their man, who had so solidly established relations with Congress that the Senate held up the promotion of thirty-nine others and threatened to require the participation of civilians on naval promotion selection boards if Rickover was not promoted. The navy promptly folded, and Rickover's promotion to rear admiral was announced by President Eisenhower in July 1953. The abrasive admiral would use basically the same technique to solidify his control as Director of Naval Reactors, rising to four star rank, and retiring only when finally forced to do so in 1982, at the age of 82 (if you believe his application to the Naval Academy) or 84 (if you believe the records of his grade school in Poland). He died in 1986.[1]

The basic interaction between Rickover and the navy is encapsulated in his three-line quote from the July 1958 *Reader's Digest*. In it he says, "One of the most wonderful things that happened in our Nautilus program was that everybody knew it was going to fail—so they left us completely alone so we were able to do the job."[2]

Rickover's 1953 promotion granted him great freedom of action. The first nuclear submarine, *Nautilus* (SSN-571), became a budget item in the FY 1952 program, and despite its obviously highly experimental nature, a decision was made to arm it with torpedo tubes. The hull was modified over time to adapt to the changing design of the reactor, and it included—as backup—advanced batteries and four 420-bhp diesel engines. One of the decisions he had made as a captain was that the navy should make the pressurized-water thermal reactor its nuclear power plant. It would be called the standard submarine thermal reactor (STR). His selection was made on the basis of the navy's experimental experience with the type, and the fact that it was inherently safer than the contemporary alternative type that used liquid metal (either sodium or sodium–potassium alloy) for heat transfer.

The fission of uranium atoms produces heat in a nuclear reactor, which is perfect for a submarine as there is no combustion and no oxygen is required. The reactor heat is transferred via a primary coolant to a steam generator, which creates steam to drive the turbines to turn the propeller shafts.

The difference in safety between the systems revolved around the fact that in the STR, pure water running through the hot core of the power plant became only minimally radioactive. The water both cooled and moderated the reactor, and if for any reason the water drained out, the reactor would shut down. In the liquid-metal coolant reactor, there was a tremendous hazard of seawater accidentally flooding the reactor and reacting violently with the sodium. In addition, the liquid metal remained radioactive at a very dangerous level for decades after use. This made all sorts of repairs and regular maintenance difficult and the potential for exposure to lethal doses of radiation much more likely.[3]

Despite the known hazards, a second nuclear-propelled submarine, the USS *Seawolf* (SSN-575),[4] was built and tested with a sodium-cooled power plant. Difficulties in service led to it being retrofitted with an STR.

All of Rickover's past efforts were now justified and his future efforts ensured when at 11:00 A.M. on January 17, 1954, the *Nautilus* got underway under the command of Commander Eugene Wilkinson, who, in the best naval tradition, made history by issuing the laconic but forever memorable statement, "UNDERWAY ON NUCLEAR POWER." The *Nautilus* was officially launched on January 21, 1954, christened by First Lady Mamie Eisenhower.[5] It was commissioned on September 30, 1954.

The roughly $100 million *Nautilus* was 320 feet long, displaced 3,530 tons on the surface, and could achieve 23 knots when submerged. Its "shake-down" cruises went well, including the first, a 1,381-mile trip to Puerto Rico, entirely underwater, in ninety-one hours. Although touted by the unknowing as having "unlimited range," the *Nautilus* was first refueled in February 1957 after twenty-six months in service. In more than sixty-two thousand operational miles the radical new boat had been "attacked" in friendly anti-submarine warfare exercises some five thousand times—but only three of these were judged successful.[6]

The safe and reliable *Nautilus* would reach the North Pole under the ice on August 3, 1958. The *Nautilus* was the first of the earliest group of five types of U.S. nuclear submarines. These totaled only thirteen submarines, four of the Skate[7] class and six of the Skipjack[8] class. These nuclear submarines represented both the dawn of a new era and the death knell of the diesel submarine in U.S. Navy service.

≈   ≈   ≈

THE SOVIET NUCLEAR PROGRAM was led by a few key scientists, including Igor V. Kurchatov and Anatoliy Petrovich Aleksandrov, all under the kindly paternal political hand of Lavrenti Beria. A major submarine designer, B. M. Malinin, advocated nuclear submarines, as did one of his key protégés, Engineer Captain First Rank Vladimir N. Peregudov, who became the chief designer of the first series of Soviet nuclear submarines. So ambitious was the Soviet nuclear submarine program that lead units of three classes of nuclear submarines were commissioned between 1958 and 1960. These classes were given the NATO code names November, Hotel, and Echo I and II. Two pressurized-water nuclear reactors powered all three submarine types, known collectively to NATO as the HEN class (Hotel, Echo, November).

Work began on the November class in 1954 under the direction of Peregudov. The first ship was placed in commission on April 8, 1958, and twelve more joined the fleet by the end of 1963. Yet the November class as a whole was ill-starred, thanks to production speedups, design insufficiencies, and a lack of quality control.

Despite the Soviet predilection for long production runs, Hotel boats were caught in a shift in defense planning and only six were built. The Hotel was the world's first nuclear-powered ballistic missile submarine, with the first one completed in 1959, slightly ahead of the U.S. Polaris-carrying *George Washington,* but capable of only surface missile launching. Hotels made their way to patrol off both the east and west coasts of the United States, presenting a threat to Strategic Air Command bomber bases, which were within an eight-minute flight of this vessel's submarine-launched ballistic missiles (SLBMs). The first of the Hotel class was the infamous *K-19*.

The Echo I and Echo II class cruise missile submarines were also starcrossed, being powered by the very dangerous VM-A reactor, which caused several accidents, becoming involved in no less than four "midwater" collisions. Fortunately, no boats were lost as a result of these mishaps, but reactor problems were so great that by 1989 all HEN-reactor-powered boats were withdrawn from service.

The vast resources poured into the Soviet submarine program gave it a glamour that was enhanced by the operation of nuclear boats equipped with guided or ballistic missiles. Just as in the U.S. Navy, the Soviet nuclear submarine arm became a beacon for the best and the brightest officers and men in the Soviet Navy.

An inside view of the early Soviet effort is best provided through the eyes of Captain First Rank Vladimir S. Borisov, now retired. Borisov, a true patriot and an extremely able submarine commander, makes an astute assessment of early Soviet nuclear submarine problems and gives a detailed record of their achievements. Borisov is not entirely free of Soviet polemic, but he is for the most part admirably objective.

According to Borisov, the Soviet Union recognized that the submarines it built after World War II were not sophisticated underwater vessels and could not effectively counteract the continually improving anti-submarine forces of the Western allies. The Soviets, like the United States, had several options in the choice of reactor type, but Aleksandrov and Dollezhal, both "academicians," a title akin to that employed by a Western university professor, decided in the fall of 1953 that the Soviets would follow the American example and adopt nuclear reactors of the pressurized water type. The general designer of the underwater nuclear vessel was Peregudov. His assistant was P. Degtyaroev, while Aleksandrov supervised scientific research. Aleksandrov subsequently became the president of the Soviet Academy of Science. Having decided on the reactor, the Soviet government approved the building of its first nuclear submarine, the ill-fated *K-3*, which was later named *Leninsky Komsomol*. In the early stages the project was so secret that not even naval specialists were involved in any consultations. Only after Admiral

Kuznetsov appealed directly to the defense minister were naval experts allowed on the panel. Headed by Rear Admiral A. Orel, the naval members of the panel soon discovered many significant problems. Among other things, they required a redesign of both the submarine's hull and bow. The submarine (just as the CIA had believed) had originally been designed to carry a single enormous torpedo rather than the usual complement of more than twenty.

Captain Second Rank Leonid Osipenko, an experienced officer with World War II experience aboard the submarines of the Black Sea Fleet, took command of *K-3* after its launching on August 9, 1957, three and a half years after the American *571* boat. He was an experienced commander of diesel submarines and, with a willing crew, quickly learned to command the first Soviet nuclear submarine. In the process, the submarine and its crew had several successful cruises, including one under the Arctic ice. Its main mission, however, was to test the reactor.

So successful was the *K-3* in its early years that Captain Osipenko was awarded the title Hero of the Soviet Union, while Aleksandrov and Peregudov became Heroes of Socialistic Labor.

Unfortunately, the early days of the Soviet nuclear propulsion program did not proceed as smoothly as its American counterpart. As much as the navy headquarters tried to suppress information on accidents from the outside world, it was inevitable that within the Soviet Navy, any accident or even incident quickly became known throughout the fleet. When, as in 1961, there were no fewer than twelve instances where nuclear submarines had to return to base because of accidents, the rash of rumors was staggering. On balance, the Soviet Union would have served its own interests better had the information been freely and openly disseminated, for over the years many of the accidents had a harrowing similarity that might not have been the case if there had been more open analysis of the problems by the people primarily concerned—other Soviet submariners.

An internal investigation of these accidents by the Northern Fleet Command revealed the following disturbing similarities:

1. Most fires occurred while subs were returning from patrol, and still submerged.

2. When the emergency was discovered, an order was given to surface, while emergency repairs were undertaken at the same time.
3. In all cases, water entered the hull, due to either a rupture caused by fire or explosion, or the improper operation of certain valves and hatches.
4. Within a short period of time, electrical shorts deprived the command post of control over the submarine's important systems, including the communication systems.
5. With the loss of forward motion and the intake of water, buoyancy and stability were soon lost.
6. The ultimate result was often capsizing, or sinking.[9]

Had this study been made early on and disseminated throughout the engineering and operational establishments, procedures might have been developed to lessen the effect of an on-board fire and emergency.

The *K-3*, the famous *Leninsky Komsomol*, the first Soviet nuclear submarine, experienced a minor accident in 1960 that was a hint of what the future might hold. Assigned to cruise under the Arctic ice, the *K-3* broke her periscope when she surfaced and had to return to base—unlike diesel submarines, the November class boats had just one periscope. But breaking the periscope turned out to be fortunate, for on the way back a leak occurred in the steam generator and cracks appeared in the nuclear fuel elements.

K-3 immediately reported the propulsion plant problem to the Northern Fleet and the boat's proximity to base permitted help to arrive promptly and prevented a possibly catastrophic accident. The incident was really a metaphor for the problems of the entire Soviet system, for over time the leak from the steam generator killed more than a dozen crewmembers via radiation sickness. The navy suppressed news of this incident for years after the event. *K-3* spent long months in shipyard overhaul, having the steam generator problem and fuel-element cracks corrected.

The *K-8* replaced the *K-3* on its Arctic mission, the former commanded by Captain Second Rank V. Shumakov. His boat entered the Arctic Ocean on October 13, 1960, submerging at 10:02 A.M. Seven hours later, at 5:00 P.M., the starboard reactor water tank began leaking badly, an ominous sign, but the crew reacted quickly and seemed to stop the leak. At 7:00 P.M., the pressure fell to a critical level in the portside reactor.

The *K-8* surfaced immediately, stopping both reactors while all the radiation counters went crazy with high readings. It was obvious that the portside steam generator had leaked. If this continued the reactor's uranium rods would overheat, leading to a catastrophic meltdown. Captain Shumakov ordered the men to leave the reactor and turbine compartments, knowing that they had already received dangerous doses of radiation.

Thirty minutes of frantic effort by other crewmen managed to stop the leak in the steam generator, and a pipeline was made to carry fresh water to cool the reactor. Large amounts of radioactive gases spread throughout the boat, contaminating everything. In the meantime, the *K-8* cruised slowly toward home base, using only her electric motors. At 11:30 P.M. she moored at the pier, with thirteen crewmen already suffering from terrible headaches and vomiting. Later investigation would show that the shipbuilders had left a plug in the pipeline, put there for testing how airtight the lines were—and forgetting to remove it. Still later, examinations of forty-two of the *K-8* crewmembers showed that they had received radiation doses equal to those of the people who had been assigned to clean up the Chernobyl power station after the accident there in 1986. (Fate would reach out again to the *K-8* only ten years later, with even graver results.)

The year 1961 got off to a disastrous start on January 27, when the experimental diesel-powered submarine *S-80*, specifically designed to test cruise missiles, went down in 600 feet of water off the Kola Peninsula. Nothing was known of the event save for the loss of it and all sixty-eight of its crew. (Six years later, the *S-80* would be salvaged; the bodies of all sixty-eight crewmembers were found on board. Investigation showed that a faulty valve in the snorkel had admitted an unstoppable flow of water.)

The *K-3*, *K-8*, and *S-80* were but preludes to what became perhaps the most notorious submarine accident of all time, that of the infamous nuclear-powered, missile-carrying *K-19*, known forever afterward as "the widow-maker" or "Hiroshima."

In their internal documents, the Soviet Navy drew a distinction between a nuclear accident (in which no one died) and a nuclear catastrophe (which caused deaths). The *K-19* experienced the first nuclear catastrophe in Soviet history, and came to be regarded as a cursed boat, for it encountered two more serious incidents in its naval career.

To be only thirty-three years old and in command of the most advanced warship in the world, carrying the most advanced weapons, is a heady prospect, and Captain First Rank Nikolai Zateyev was well aware of the honor being accorded him when he became captain of the *K-19* in October 1959.[10] He was also aware that his every action would be under the microscopic examination of his naval superiors, who would be slow to praise but quick to find fault.

The constant vigilance of critical observers was a characteristic of the Soviet Union from its first days, and it led to a very rigid bureaucracy in which conformance was prized over initiative. It also led to a system in which an individual's primary concern often came to be hiding all mistakes, whether it was in an attendance report or in the inspection of a critical weld on a nuclear reactor.

Soviet submarine commanders such as Zateyev had a dual problem. They were subject to the informal bureaucratic rules that required them to be on the defensive and continually protect themselves, but they could not conduct the operation of such a miracle of technology as the *K-19* without taking chances on the people they selected as crewmembers. Each new man was implicitly a gamble, and no matter how well you knew him, or how well you trained him, there was always the possibility that he might not attend to duty conscientiously, or, in the worst case, might fail to perform properly in an emergency.

The problem was compounded by the fact that both officers and crewmembers were in critically short supply for two reasons. The first was the rapid expansion of the Soviet submarine fleet, which soaked up personnel faster than they could be recruited. The second was the high level of mental and physical ability required of any crewmember on a nuclear submarine. Not many candidates could meet the standards of performance required, and even fewer had the psychological wherewithal to endure the unique combination of boredom and terror that was the lot of the submariner.

There was particular pressure on Zateyev and the *K-19* to perform, as Soviet Premier Nikita Khrushchev was throwing down the gauntlet to the West. He wished to use the R-13 nuclear missiles of the *K-19* to emphasize the power and flexibility of the Soviet Navy. Thus it was that in early July 1961 Zateyev and his crew were participating in a well-advertised maneuver in which the conventional submarines of the Soviet Navy would attempt to track and hunt down the *K-19*, as the NATO naval forces might have to do some day. In the Soviet scenario—and, as it proved, in reality—the *K-19* was easily able to evade detection and attack, and was preparing to surface and fire the dummy R-13 missile it carried to a target on the Soviet missile range. The other two missiles it carried were the genuine article—nuclear armed and ready for war.

At 4:15 A.M. on July 4, 1961, the *K-19* was about 1,500 miles from its home base, submerged at 150 feet in waters about 100 miles away from the Norwegian island of Jan Mayen, just above Iceland. It was at that moment that the boat's radiation detection equipment began sounding its raucous, terrifying call. At that same moment the lives of many of its crewmembers began to be measured in days and their health in roentgens.[11]

In a Soviet nuclear submarine of that period, the single worst accident that could occur was a rupture of a primary cooling circuit that carried heat from the reactor core. If that line burst, there was nothing to cool the chain reaction of the nuclear power plant. The uranium rods would heat up until they melted through the hardened steel of the reactor, ultimately reaching the point where a nuclear meltdown and an environmental catastrophe became inevitable.

As soon as he diagnosed the emergency, Zateyev recognized the seriousness of the problem and ordered the *K-19* to surface and send an emergency message back to base. The radio man reported that this was impossible; the long-range antenna had flooded and was out of operation—another failure of the shipyard.

In a relatively brief conversation, the propulsion engineers devised an emergency system that could be rigged and would supply the reactor with cooling water from the thirty tons of drinking water available in the ship. The implacable, unspeakable reality was that the men who volunteered for the task were also volunteering to die. They would have to go to work in the nuclear reactor compartment itself. They knew that within minutes their bodies would be saturated with such an intense dosage of radiation that they would inevitably die within days.[12]

For these brave young men the decision was quite simple. If no one volunteered, everyone would die in a rush of heat and radiation that would destroy the submarine and send more contaminated material into the environment than later occurred at Chernobyl. If a team volunteered, they would certainly die, but they would save the others in the crew, and the submarine as well. But it took a nobility of character and a brave heart to make the decision to be a sacrificial victim, and it speaks well for the Soviet Navy and Captain Zateyev that there were willing volunteers.

Eight men, led by Lieutenant Boris Korchilov, picked up their pipes, pumps, and welding equipment and stepped to their deaths in the hot glowing atmosphere of the reactor. The effects were not subtle; they knew immediately that they were receiving a lethal dose of radiation, but they worked steadily for two hours, welding the pipes, routing them between the reactor and the water tank, and installing the valves. As they worked Zateyev and his officers kept an anxious eye on the reactor's temperature, which continued to climb toward the critical point while the crew made the necessary alterations to the water circulation system at the cost of their lives.

After two hours that seemed like two years to the men watching and two centuries to the men inside the nuclear power plant, the valiant team staggered out through the reactor door. As they pulled their respirator masks off, they began vomiting, the first symptom of radiation poisoning. Some collapsed immediately, others were barely able to walk. Their fate was sealed, for they had received more than one hundred times the dose known to be lethal. They knew it, and so did the other crewmembers, who quickly carried them, as heroes, forward for medical treatment.

Unfortunately, the jury-rigged emergency system that they had sacrificed their lives for failed almost immediately. They needed another volunteer to fix it, and this would be a man who had seen death mask faces when the original team of eight had emerged. Undaunted, Chief Petty Officer Ivan Kulakov volunteered to enter the tiny chamber to repair the system. There he found water hot in both temperature and radiation covering the floor, while the metal of the pipes and the valves was almost too hot to touch. Kulakov methodically went through the repair he knew he had to make, and left the chamber. As he began stripping himself out of his clothing, the word came—another valve had failed. Already nauseated and dying from the radiation, and fully aware that his body could not keep this up for long, he forced himself back into the compartment to replace the failed valve. When he emerged a second time, the crew carried him to sickbay and made him as comfortable as possible. The gauges on the control panel told the tale. The rate of temperature rise began to slow, and just as it reached 1,470 degrees—frighteningly close to the point where a massive nuclear meltdown could occur—the temperature steadied and then began to decline. The jury-rigged emergency piping and valves had held; drinking water was flowing in to cool the nuclear reactor.[13]

With the immediate danger of overheating postponed, Zateyev now had to make another decision. The K-19 could make only about 10 knots on the surface, meaning it would take five or six days to travel the 1,500 miles back to base. The radiation level on board the K-19 was so high that all aboard would receive a lethal dose in that time. He knew that he had to get the crew off the ship to save them. One alternative, preferred by some of a crew driven by fear and anger to a near mutiny, was to ground the K-19 on the beach of the near island of Jan Mayen. The second, far more risky, but kinder to the environment, was to turn in the direction opposite of home and hope to find a Soviet vessel to take the crew off, and tow the K-19 home.

Zateyev opted for the more dangerous choice, and for ten long hours it seemed that he had made a mistake, for no Soviet ships or submarines appeared, and the low-frequency radio that they were able to rig received no signals. But the K-19's luck, if not turned, had at least improved, for the Soviet submarine S-270 appeared.[14] The two boats maneuvered so that the K-19's crew could be removed. The most seriously ill were transferred first, their clothing and their bodies so radioactive that they quickly contaminated the compartment on the S-270 where they were accommodated. Then the remainder of the crew was taken off, and the K-19 taken under tow.

Fleet headquarters at last rolled into action and another submarine, *S-268*, and a destroyer, the *Byvaly*, were dispatched to render assistance. Three days later the *K-19* crewmembers were home, beginning a fateful period in which the most heavily radiated members of the crew—the volunteers who saved the *K-19* and the world from an uncontrolled nuclear explosion—started to die.

Even as death from radiation sickness took its toll, the typical Soviet reaction began; *K-19* crewmembers, despite the stress of the accident and their exposure to radiation, were subjected to a relentless grilling intended to prove that Captain Zateyev had somehow failed to follow regulations and could thus be blamed for the accident. Zateyev, ill himself, wondered if he would change directly from his hospital uniform into a prison uniform.

In Zateyev's memoirs, he sadly notes that the experience gained from treating (or, in some instances, maltreating) the victims of the *K-19* nuclear accident was ignored, and did not play the role it should have in the treatment of victims of the Chernobyl tragedy that would occur twenty-four years later.[15]

Soviet bureaucratic politics displayed its most vicious side in the final report of a military commission that examined the survivors, and found them to be diagnosed as suffering from "asthenic vegetative syndrome"—a cobbled term that hints at mental illness but does not relate to radiation sickness in anyway.

Even abandoned by its crew and towed into harbor, the *K-19* still had malice to inflict. As it floated at the pier, three compartments filled with radioactive water and its ventilation systems kept running, spewing out contaminants that blighted everything within a half-mile radius. The naval headquarters had decided to scuttle the ship when misplaced sentiment among crewmembers called for it to be instead washed clean of radiation, have new nuclear reactors installed, and be put into service once again. It was a dreadful mistake, for every crew that served in it subsequently knew the story of the boat called "Hiroshima," and there would be two more accidents before it was finally decommissioned in 1991.

Many years after the catastrophe, Captain First Rank Zateyev made a speech:

The first nuclear submarines were accepted by the navy from factories with bad defects. Serious disadvantages were revealed during tests of the reactor of the *K-19*. Worse, the submarine was
noisy when cruising under water. I informed the factory heads
and submarine detachment commanders on this fact. I also told
them that I wasn't going to sign the acceptance act on readiness of
the submarine for active service. But in accordance with the order
of the naval commander-in-chief Admiral Sergei Gorshkov, I had
to sign the acceptance act. Most of the first generation torpedo
nuclear submarines were accepted with the same defects.

The rush both to compete with the United States and to develop a
navy whose global reach would enhance Soviet power and confirm the
validity of Russian communist dogma led to shortcuts, flawed plans,
dangerously accelerated technological development, and the priority of
politics over safety and lives. Russian naval personnel and their families
paid dearly to confirm the validity of an empty Soviet dream.

4

THE CUBAN
MISSILE CRISIS

———————

Perhaps the most amazing thing about the Cold War—except for its surprisingly peaceful denouement—was that the truly vital events that shaped the destinies of both the United States and the Soviet Union (and thus, implicitly, the world) came down to the intelligence, drive, leadership, and persistence of individual human beings.

In the United States, a small team led by J. Robert Oppenheimer, Major General Leslie Groves, and a handful of others succeeded in creating the atomic bomb that would be so influential in ending World War II, and then, ironically, in maintaining the peace. Their work was also appreciated and used in the Soviet Union, which had so penetrated the

American scientific establishment that Stalin was far more well informed of progress on the atomic bomb than the then vice president of the United States, Harry S. Truman. The espionage work of Julius and Ethel Rosenberg and Klaus Fuch was so systematically thorough that the capable Soviet scientific community was able to telescope years of research into months. The Soviet Union exploded an atomic bomb at 6:00 A.M. on August 29, 1949, under the supervision of scientific director Igor Kurchatov.

The Soviet Union had a rather different approach to security and to incentive systems. Lavrenti Beria, the much-feared head of the KGB, went to the Soviet test sites to inspect the bombs personally, and hugged Kurchatov upon its success. Two months later he superintended the awards given to the Soviet scientists participating in the tests, and his rule was this: Those scientists who would have been shot had the test failed became Heroes of the Soviet Union. Those who would only have been imprisoned were given the lesser Order of Lenin. It may be an apocryphal story, but it is illustrative of the climate of Soviet atomic research.

The shock effect of the Soviet atomic explosion went far beyond the effective radius of the bomb, for it shook political and military leaders in the United States to the core. They had not anticipated a successful Soviet test for several more years, and Stalin's possession of nuclear weapons, the Tupolev Tu-4 delivery aircraft, and the largest army in the world changed all the strategic equations.

One direct result of this startling upset in planning was that Dr. Edward Teller was authorized to proceed with development of the hydrogen bomb. Teller, who was both praised and damned as the "father of the H-bomb," led, with Ernst Lawrence, a group that simultaneously ratcheted the world one step closer to total destruction even as it increased the probability of peace because of the terrible nature of the weapon.

Teller had no illusions that the security efforts put into effect by the United States as a result of the revelations in the Rosenberg and Fuchs spy cases would deter friend or foe from making a similar hydrogen bomb. He fully expected the USSR to follow in relatively short order with a successful test. Teller and his group succeeded on November 1,

1952, when they detonated "Mike," the first hydrogen device in history, at Eniwetok Atoll in the Marshall Islands.

In the Soviet Union, Andrei Sakharov and Igor Tamm were the individual counterparts to Teller and Lawrence, and they detonated the first Soviet thermonuclear weapon (unofficially called "Sakharov's Layer Cake") on November 3, 1953. This rapid closure on American scientific leadership again startled the United States—but still not enough to jar it from a comfortable complacency.

That task was reserved for the October 4, 1957, debut of the Earth-orbiting satellite *Sputnik*. The name meant "Fellow Traveler," meaning a companion to the Earth, but having a sinister connotation in the United States for its meaning as Communist sympathizer. *Sputnik* weighed only 184 pounds, but the little satellite seemed gigantic to American scientists who knew they had no rocket capable of placing such a satellite into orbit.

The implications of *Sputnik* were tremendous, for if the Soviets could place a satellite in orbit, they could also place a missile targeted at the United States, a point that the increasingly belligerent Soviet premier, Nikita Khrushchev, made on several occasions.

The combination of Soviet nuclear and rocket advances completely changed the complexion of American politics, and of American public opinion on defense spending. The United States had almost completely disarmed after the Second World War, counting upon an illusion of atomic capability to keep the Soviet Union in check. Curiously enough, Stalin was also well informed of the inadequate state of the American nuclear stockpile, and was not deterred by the threat of American nuclear weapons.

The mere detonation of an atomic or thermonuclear device did not mean that a nation automatically possessed a weapon. To develop weapons that could be safely manufactured, stored, and deployed before use was a tremendous research task in itself. As other nations entered the nuclear weapons club, the USSR began a flurry of testing, dropping bombs from aircraft, and as time marched on and weapons became smaller, adapting them to missiles and to torpedoes.

The nuclear torpedo was particularly attractive to the planners in the Soviet Navy, for it offered the only practical means available to counter the powerful American carrier task forces that dominated the oceans. Bombers could of course deliver an atomic weapon, but the fighters operating off American aircraft carriers were so effective that the chance of a Tupolev Tu-4 bomber breaking through to drop a bomb were slim. Submarines, however, had the advantage of stealth, and a 10-kiloton blast from a submarine would effectively destroy the heart of a carrier task force.

The Soviet Navy sought to develop a nuclear weapon to use, exactly as the U.S. Navy had. The first of these was the T-5 nuclear torpedo. This weapon had trouble early in conventional performance trials as the detonator tended to go off prematurely due to the effect of ocean turbulence on the torpedo passing through the water. Nonetheless, after the warhead was successfully detonated at the Novaya Zemlya nuclear test center, a trial-firing of the T-5 at the same location in 1957 by *S-144* under the command of Captain Second Rank G. V. Lasarev resulted in a 10-kiloton nuclear explosion that destroyed a half dozen target ships. The results pleased the naval high command and provided them with a capability that enormously enhanced the potential effectiveness of their still largely conventional submarine fleet. Between 1957 and 1961, Soviet scientists and engineers rendered the warhead independent, so it could ride with any torpedo then in the navy's submarine arsenal. Lavrenti Beria, who was also the head of the nuclear industry in the Soviet Union at the time, reportedly referred to the weapon as RDS, an acronym for "Stalin's Revenge." (Stalin had died in 1953.) By early 1961 only a final test of the new weapon remained.

To many of the Soviet submariners, proceeding with the tests of nuclear weapons was premature, given that there were already deadly serious problems with Soviet submarines, both diesel-powered and nuclear.

The horrifying rate of Soviet submarine accidents did nothing to slow the command emphasis on nuclear weapons development even though it sometimes slowed or halted the actual tests themselves. The Foxtrot[1] submarine *B-37* received the initial assignment to perform the final tests of the T-5 torpedo, which the Soviet Navy counted on to be able to defeat American aircraft carrier task forces. The *B-37* was commanded by thirty-five-year-old Captain Second Rank A. S. Begeba, who seemed a good choice based upon his experience and the respect he received from his crew and colleagues. Shortly before the test date, early in the morning as the crew brought the boat's systems on line, *B-37* experienced a catastrophic explosion while resting at the pier. Eyewitnesses saw flame surge out of the snorkel pipe just before the entire bow exploded. Hydrogen accumulation had likely caused an explosion when the electrical systems came alive and the resulting fire detonated some of the torpedoes. The explosion killed fifty-nine *B-37* crewmen, nineteen men aboard adjacent submarines, and fifty-four more on shore. The force of the blast propelled the vessel's anchor to the shore 1.2 miles away from the dock. The Northern Fleet now needed another candidate to perform the nuclear tests.

That replacement was Captain Second Rank Nikolai Shumkov's *B-130* Foxtrot. In October 1961, Shumkov received orders at the Polyarni submarine base to test the torpedo above the Arctic Circle at Novaya Zemlya's twelve-kilometer firing range. The experimental team governing the test asked the fleet meteorologists for a day that might provide winds blowing toward the North Pole. They wanted to divert the nuclear cloud both for reasons of safety and to avoid any NATO attempts to guess their purpose by means of air sampling. The army's nuclear weapons program would also mask their event by testing a much more powerful 30-megaton warhead at a site in the eastern Soviet Union.

Shumkov received instructions to aim the torpedo toward the end of the test range at a specific location that would place the warhead in proximity to data collection devices operating for only a few seconds as the explosion took place. The torpedo would detonate by means of a time fuse and not on contact with any test ship or landmass. Just before departing Polyarni, Shumkov had minor difficulties with his vessel's compass and did not completely trust the device for this sobering and dangerous business. Instead he used his periscope and visual reckoning to make the shot. To assist the commander of the test boat, the staff at Novaya Zemlya placed a huge wooden visual targeting aid at the point where the detonation should take place.

Accompanied by a minesweeper as a monitoring ship, *B-130* carried two nuclear torpedoes to the test site through some very rough seas on the morning of October 23. Shumkov had already decided that while he would fire and report as ordered, he would also move his vessel out of line with the target as fast as he possibly could after launch. He did not relish the idea of the shock wave and the deadly nuclear cloud.

Between four and five o'clock on the afternoon of October 23, 1961, *B-130* launched the new torpedo and Shumkov briefly experienced the blinding flash of the detonation through his periscope. As he maneuvered his boat to place part of an island between it and the blast, the shock wave struck. The force of the blast transmitted through the water tossed his boat around like a toy. Barely able to keep control, Shumkov felt relieved that at least the ocean would protect his crew to some degree from the resulting fallout. The detonation came in at 10 kilotons, the same as the earlier test with the T-5 prototype.

Four days later *B-130* returned to the test site to repeat the process. The first test torpedo exploded well below the surface, providing data on a detonation in the submarine's natural environment. In this second test, the staff at Novaya Zemlya set the weapon to run and explode at shallow depth, making the blast more of a surface effect than a submerged test. Shumkov did not envy the ground crew at the site charged with cleaning up the first effort and placing a new targeting aid in place for the next test shot. No precautions were taken to protect them from the radioactive fallout. In essence, they sacrificed themselves, whether they knew it or not at the time, to the best interests of the Soviet system.[2] The second shot went as well as the first.

Shumkov's effort won the applause of admirals and test staff alike. Rear Admiral Yamshikov asked him to prepare a list of those personnel critical to his success because they certainly deserved recognition. The *B-130*'s commander had the feeling that the admiral had already composed his own list and made the request as a formality. Regardless of the decorations destined for the crew, three months later Shumkov received the Order of Lenin, the highest award then available to a naval officer. This precious symbol of achievement complemented the Ushakov Medal he received from the submarine force after bringing *B-130* back to Polyarni. Yet he felt better about having ensured the safety of his boat and crew than receiving the medals and orders resting on his chest. He did not know that the accolades would bring him and his crew a new and even more responsible assignment within the year.

≈ ≈ ≈

ONCE AGAIN EVENTS WOULD BE DETERMINED by individuals. In this instance, the tension of the Cold War was escalating because of the growing ego of the Premier Khrushchev, and his contempt for American politicians, including the newly elected president of the United States, forty-four-year-old John F. Kennedy. Khrushchev was promising his people not only that they would surpass the United States militarily, but that they would also surpass the United States in terms of its living standards.

Khrushchev was understandably distressed that the United States had installed nuclear missiles in Turkey, which was considered an eternal enemy of Russia. These intermediate-range missiles could strike Moscow in eight minutes and were a powerful deterrent to war.

Meanwhile, Fidel Castro had seized power in Cuba, appointing himself premier on February 16, 1959, and from that point on he gravitated ever closer to Moscow politically, and declared in August of 1960 that he would look to the Soviet Union for military support. The United States responded by imposing an embargo on Cuban sugar and breaking off diplomatic relations on January 3, 1961. In March 1960 President Dwight D. Eisenhower had authorized the development of a Central Intelligence Agency plan to train 1,500 Cuban refugees and sponsor their invasion of Cuba. Kennedy approved the plan, and the infamous Bay of Pigs invasion took place on April 17, 1961. It was a complete fiasco, humiliating Kennedy and making Castro a hero in the eyes of many. It also convinced Khrushchev that his initial opinion of Kennedy as "weak" was correct.

He therefore felt positive about the June 1962 suggestion of Fidel Castro's brother, Raul, that the Soviet Union should move intermediate-range ballistic missiles into Cuba to act as a deterrent to any further invasion attempt.

The Soviet Union developed Operation Anadyr to secretly install missiles—and other weapons—in Cuba without the United States becoming aware of it until it was "too late." The operation was successful, and more than 42,000 Soviet troops, as well as the material and equipment necessary to create missile sites, were brought in unnoticed over the next few months.

Colonel General Semyon Ivanov, chief of the General Staff's Chief Operations Directorate, was in overall charge of Operation Anadyr,[3] and part of his plan was for Soviet submarines to proceed to Cuba to cope, if necessary, with any American naval forces dispatched to prevent the increase of Soviet power in Cuba.

Captain Shumkov and his *B-130* formed part of the Soviet preparation to deal with the expected political and military storm the Cuban operation might cause. Admiral Vitali Fokin, deputy to the commander in chief of the Soviet Navy, and Admiral Rossokho, commander of the headquarters of the Northern Fleet, along with several other flag officers, gave Shumkov and the commanders of three other Foxtrot submarines a detailed briefing on the deployment of Soviet naval forces to the Caribbean as a part of Operation Anadyr. The briefing took place at the headquarters in Gadzhievo, the base near Polyarni.

As the admirals explained it, the Soviet naval high command in Moscow had decided to establish a submarine base on the island of Cuba, less than one hundred miles off the American coast. Shumkov and his three Foxtrot shipmates were to set their course for the port of Mariel on the northwest Cuban coast.[4] Technicians and support personnel from the Northern Fleet submarine base at Polyarni awaited them there, having made the trip earlier on Soviet cargo ships. Those same cargo ships carried missiles capable of sending nuclear warheads on their way toward American cities.

Seven Golf[5] ballistic missile submarines, each with three R-13 ballistic missiles equipped with 3.5-megaton warheads, were the second submarine force in Anadyr, and were to follow Shumkov's group. One of the Golf submarines, *K-153,* was commanded by Captain Second Rank Vladimir Lebedko, Shumkov's friend.

The briefing contained precise instructions on how the submarines would proceed, what their courses would be, and when and how they would report. In addition, the admirals added more general information that included both wisdom and warnings. They would fulfill their part in Operation Anadyr by proceeding secretly to the Caribbean, carrying the formidable torpedoes that Shumkov had tested only the year before.

Aware of the enormous responsibility of using a nuclear weapon in warfare, Shumkov asked the assembled flag officers the key question: What were the rules of engagement for use of the torpedo, especially in unexpected or unusual situations? As he had expected, their replies were cryptic and foreboding. One of the flag admirals said, "Once your face has been slapped, don't let them hit your face one more time."[6] The assembled admirals nodded approvingly, for this simple Delphic statement slipped the awesome responsibility of perhaps starting World War III from their shoulders directly onto those of Shumkov and his fellow submarine commanders, a technique designed to blur the direct line of responsibility, common in the Soviet Union since the days of Joseph Stalin. It was an unconscionable act of bureaucratic and personal cowardice, and it was fraught with hazard for the world, for the decision to use a nuclear weapon in warfare now rested on each of the four commanders individually, admirable officers to be sure, but never tested or evaluated as to their capacity to make decisions of this literally Earth-shaking gravity.

All four submarines departed their base on October 1, 1962, at thirty-minute intervals, passing through the towering cliffs that flanked the entrance to the bay, with Shumkov's *B-130* leaving last. He and his shipmates rounded the North Cape separating the stormy snow squalls of the Barents Sea from the Atlantic Ocean. Aware of the general tensions between the two countries, the captain knew that both his mission and the device resting in his forward torpedo room could push the world over the brink if intelligence and restraint did not prevail in the halls of power.

As he watched the intricate operations of his well-trained crew, Shumkov realized that his superiors had selected *B-130* for Anadyr because of his success with testing the nuclear torpedo they now carried toward Cuba. They had fired it successfully in peacetime; they could be expected to fire it successfully if war came. He would be ready, despite knowing that the havoc his 10-kiloton warhead would cause would almost certainly engulf his beloved *B-130*. Each of the four submarines in the Anadyr detachment carried twenty-two torpedoes, nearly half of which were loaded into ten tubes at the base, six in the bow, and four aft. This permitted the balance to rest on racks in the respective torpedo rooms. In each submarine, one of the torpedoes resting in a forward tube carried a 10-kiloton nuclear warhead. Shumkov knew that the other three captains did not have the benefit of his experience; he wondered if they might use the new weapon with less restraint than he.

Looking through his periscope into the storm that welcomed them into the Norwegian Sea, Shumkov briefly surveyed a vessel his sonarman had detected, then waited for the unwelcome representative of the Royal Navy to pass. The slightest mistake would mean detection. Then a Royal Air Force Avro Shackelton anti-submarine aircraft would drop sonobuoys, followed by one of Her Majesty's ships literally sitting on top of him for hours. There was no time for that; pressing matters awaited Shumkov at his destination.

A man of stocky build and obvious physical strength, Shumkov held himself erect in the control room of his boat with a customary, but barely detectable, stoop. This manifested itself more out of habit than anything else, but this time he physically felt the weight of his mission on his shoulders, a burden he knew would grow. The British ship ran without lights perpendicular to his submarine's course. Thanks to the terrible weather, the British submarine hunters would find him hard to detect, but it also made it difficult for him to track their vessel.[7]

Morale had not yet reached that normal high that occurs some days after departure. His officers and crew were still subdued, depressed from having taken premature leave of their families. The families were not permitted to know that their men had to spend a few days in secret briefings and preparation before going to sea, nor, of course, how serious their mission was. Now the crew faced anti-submarine warfare patrols and a sea-state nine that made them hold on every moment of the day as the boat rolled and pitched as much as 40 degrees in the shallow ocean layers near the surface.

While only two days had actually passed, the time since departure seemed like an eternity. Shumkov ordered his executive officer to reduce the speed of *B-130*. He shrugged off the appearance of the British and the possibility of Norwegian surveillance. All Soviet submariners expected to encounter these hurdles when making a transit into the North Atlantic. After emerging from the base shielded by the Kola Peninsula, passages into the North Atlantic were few and narrow. The Americans referred to the region between the Norwegian Sea and the Atlantic as the Greenland–Iceland–United Kingdom "gap," or simply the GIUK gap. Most frequently Soviet submarines would use the Iceland–Faeroes passage on the eastern side of the gap to gain access to the Atlantic. He ran the risk of detection regardless of the route he chose and not all of the hunters took the form of ships and aircraft. Shumkov knew of the new American underwater submarine sound surveillance system (SOSUS) but had very few details about its capability. He worried far more about the more familiar British anti-submarine vessels and the aircraft that might detect him with sonar or spot him on the surface recharging his batteries. As always, taking advantage of night and the weather, and running as quietly as possible, seemed his best options.

Unfortunately Shumkov could use none of these options with any regularity. From the beginning he felt uncomfortable with the guidance he had received at Gadzhievo and the restrictions placed upon his flexibility as commander. Since the four Foxtrots participating in this operation could not maintain regular contact with one another, the Northern Fleet command had assigned a strict course to each submarine and limited the freedom of the commander to deviate from a specific geographic corridor en route to Cuba. At any point along its corridor a submarine could only maneuver in a navigational circle with a thirty-mile radius. Each commander also had to maintain an average speed of nine knots and report by radio to Moscow at preset points along the route.

While the orders seemed rational enough on paper, in practice they took on both a tragic and comic aspect for the four submarine commanders. Remaining in the prescribed corridor prevented any collisions between the submarines as they progressed through American anti-submarine barriers on their way to Cuba. Unfortunately, professional rationality ended there. On any combat deployment, Soviet designers anticipated that the Foxtrot type could sustain a combined submerged and surface average daily speed of five to six knots, not the nine knots expected on this trip. In addition, Shumkov realized only after going to sea that his boat's batteries would not hold a charge as long as they should. As was customary in the Soviet Navy, the overhaul and inspection of the B-130 had been criminally inadequate, and the batteries' critical flaw had been ignored. He had asked for new batteries months before their deployment, but the yard claimed not to have them and then told him "not to look for ways of avoiding the mission ahead, but rather for ways to accomplish it." It was an easy answer for anyone who did not have to go to sea to fight.

Thus handicapped, Shumkov had to surface with greater frequency, using his diesels to recharge the boat's batteries. Under normal conditions, he could use his snorkel, the device perfected by the Germans during World War II to permit a submarine to expel exhaust and take in air to run the diesels while submerged, avoiding exposure on the surface. But the weather facing *B-130* on the surface ruled out regular snorkeling as it subjected the boat to turbulence that made the entire crew long for the depths.

As he mulled over the dilemma, Shumkov shook his head. With all their accumulated wisdom, the navy leaders in Moscow should have expected difficult weather, knowing that as *B-130* approached the shipping lanes along the American east coast she would be sailing right into the hurricane season. This lack of forethought spelled potential disaster for all four Soviet Foxtrot crews.

Not allowed to deviate from his orders and preset course, Shumkov crossed paths very early with Hurricane Ella. With winds clocked at eighty miles per hour it became a category one hurricane on October 17 and began moving north into the path of the approaching Foxtrots. It soon gained in speed and ferocity, sustaining a category three rating through October 19 and 20 with winds measured at 115 miles per hour. Downgraded to a tropical storm on October 23, Ella still packed winds and turbulence at seventy miles per hour, affecting the approach to the American coast for hundreds of miles around. Clearly, no one in Moscow had anticipated hurricanes, despite their being a common phenomenon in the area.

At this point the absurdity of their departure instructions assumed a tragic aspect. Shumkov could do nothing to avoid colliding with this force of nature. He had to surface to recharge batteries far too often in the middle of the storm and then repeat the process later to report to fleet headquarters at the prescribed times. Keeping the boat dry proved impossible. Furthermore, while Moscow received his long-range reports under cover of darkness, *B-130*'s position made it necessary for

Shumkov to approach the surface and extend his radio antenna in virtually transparent tropical waters, very early in the afternoon, and either in the middle of a violent storm or in bright sunshine and clear skies. Thus he either fell victim to the weather or openly risked detection by the ever vigilant American Navy. To this experienced submarine officer, it seemed incredible that a government that could create a submarine as formidable as the *B-130* and arm it with a nuclear weapon could be so ignorant in its employment.[8]

In the meanwhile, the average nine-knot speed requirement began to take its toll. His batteries held their charge for shorter and shorter intervals. Needing to so frequently leave the relative peace and smoothness of submerged operation to recharge or report to the Northern Fleet came very near to destroying *B-130*'s ability to carry out its mission.

In the rough tropical weather on the surface, Shumkov's crew lived with constant seasickness. The endless vomiting combined with the usual potent stench of a Soviet submarine was made even worse by the absence of air conditioning, a convenience never needed in the icy waters of the north. Often the watch officer had to be chained to the bridge so as not to lose him overboard. Once submerged two hundred feet below the surface, though, most turbulence disappeared.

Shumkov considered his crew "men of iron," but he wondered how long they could endure all of this and remain battle ready. His mechanical wizard, engineer Victor Parshin, found no time to sleep amid the constant flow of damaged machinery reports. Parshin cursed the overhaul yard constantly for the poor battery performance. He supervised the recharging of antiquated batteries while the submarine maneuvered through waters that varied from 77 to 82 degrees near the surface. With these temperatures, the recharging batteries would quickly approach 117 degrees, the point where they could explode unless the charging process was stopped. Without a battery cooling system, the temperature in the boat sometimes rose to 140 degrees, with a humidity of 90 percent. It became intolerable for the crew, and men fainted or collapsed with heatstroke, presenting serious problems for the medical corpsman on board.

To compensate for being able to make only six to eight knots while submerged, Shumkov had to drive his diesels at a maximum speed on the surface to keep the nine-knot average required by his mission orders. The surface turbulence created a variety of physical stresses on the boat and crew that the builders never intended. The hurricane's waves would cause the boat's propellers to emerge from the water and spin in the air, causing the diesels to race wildly and making the submarine difficult to control. Violent movement on the surface also caused serious crew injuries and structural damage, wreaking havoc on the piping systems carrying air, water, hydraulic fluid, and fuel oil. The fuel stench, which permeated the clothing and the soul of every diesel submariner, became nearly intolerable as the boat's already inadequate ventilation system was damaged. *B-130*'s poor water distillation system could not keep up with the crew's needs and everyone went on water rationing. None of the officers or men even thought of cooking in this environment. Cold, pickled vegetables took over the daily menu, and eating without becoming ill was difficult.

≈   ≈   ≈

AS SHUMKOV'S SUBMARINE PLOWED through the storms, geopolitical tensions continued to rise. On October 1, 1962, American Secretary of State Dean Rusk had warned the Soviets that the Kennedy administration would not make a deal over Cuba to ease the current tension between the opposing Cold War forces in Berlin. On October 4 the administration imposed a policy of banning from American ports those countries supplying arms to Cuba. Secretary Rusk also worked with the Latin American foreign ministers to compose a public censure of Fidel Castro. On October 6, the American Congress approved restrictions on foreign aid to any country shipping military or strategic supplies to Castro's island.

In the United States the evidence of the extent of the Soviet incursion grew. The advanced optics on board U-2 reconnaissance aircraft revealed Komar class Soviet patrol boats off Mariel as well as the presence of MiG-21 fighters on the island farther to the east. U-2 surveys of Soviet cargo ships en route to Cuba, their configuration, and the freight containers lashed to their decks also led the Central Intelligence Agency to conclude that some of the latter contained the fuselages of Ilyushin Il-28 bombers, capable of carrying 6,500 pounds of nuclear or conventional weapons to a range of 750 miles. While profoundly disturbing, these pieces of evidence did not conclusively demonstrate the presence of long-range offensive capability on the island, and both Soviet diplomats and their leadership in Moscow made that very plain to the international community. Kennedy also decided to suspend U-2 overflights for a time to avoid having one of the aircraft fall victim to a surface-to-air missile.[9]

At the same time, Kennedy's State Department moved quickly to persuade Latin American leaders to join the administration in condemning the introduction of Soviet military forces in Cuba. Clearly, any diplomatic measures against the Soviets on the world stage would prove impractical without a consensus in the Western Hemisphere. The Americans had to characterize the course adopted by Khrushchev and Castro as dangerous and provocative.

The U.S. Navy concentrated its forces in the Caribbean area both to conduct normal peacetime exercises and to act swiftly if the president called. To stay abreast of constantly changing events, Kennedy ordered the resumption of U-2 flights over Cuba in spite of the risk. Unfortunately, a quick U-2 "milk run" by Air Force Major Richard J. Heyser on October 14 returned photographic intelligence that precipitated a potentially deadly crisis. The CIA's National Photographic Interpretation Center discovered among the U-2 photos a new missile site designed to accommodate Soviet SS-4 "Scandal" medium-range ballistic missiles. This vehicle routinely carried 2- or 3-megaton nuclear warheads. Fired from Soviet territory, the SS-4's 1,020-mile range endangered only a few American targets, but Cuba lay only ninety miles off the Florida coast. The entire southeastern United States, including Washington, D.C., suddenly came within range, as did the Panama Canal and many critical locations in Latin America. To make matters worse, U-2 missions flown on October 17 betrayed the presence of additional missile sites just west of Havana. The Soviet specialists built these facilities to accommodate the far more powerful and accurate SS-5 "Skean" intermediate-range ballistic missile, capable of twice the SS-4's range. Shortly thereafter, low-level reconnaissance specialists from the Navy's VFP-52 squadron confirmed the U-2 findings.

On October 20, President Kennedy and his advisors concluded that the Soviets had crossed the line; the nuclear offensive capability obviously resident in Cuba had to go. After listening to advice from all sources, Kennedy decided to address Soviet action with a blockade. Publicly, the administration used the word "quarantine" to describe the American reaction. Kennedy would employ a peaceful and almost clinical prescription to combat what the Americans perceived as a hostile and intrusive policy executed in a deceptive manner. Naval forces moved quickly to establish a "quarantine line" as an anti-submarine barrier to protect the American coast. Drawing this line well south of the position normally taken to cover the GIUK gap, American naval leaders concentrated their forces to provide the president with greater power and flexibility.

Responding to orders, American anti-submarine warfare (ASW) forces manned a 600-mile line from Cape Race, Newfoundland, to a point 300 miles northwest of the Azores. The rest of the fleet began planning the more intricate blockade that the president would initiate on October 24. For the entire week before the quarantine date, a massive American military buildup took place in southern Florida between Miami and Key West. The American public, informed by television and print media, watched as war seemed once again to raise its ugly head.

B-130's first encounter with the American Navy came on October 20, the same day on which Kennedy made the decision that the Soviets had gone too far. The crew expected some anti-submarine action against them—not because of any overt act, but because of something truly unusual. On that day, the commercial programs and daily banter on American coastal radio, monitored for information and entertainment, suddenly began to disappear. The frequencies available to *B-130* became disturbingly quiet. Shumkov and his shipmates guessed that some change in the political situation and their presence off the coast might have contributed to the unusual American quiet.

Years later Shumkov decided that SOSUS had probably detected him first. He knew his position and the fact that among the deployed Soviet submarines this area belonged to him alone. Monitoring naval radio from Roosevelt Roads and Bermuda, his radioman heard a plain language transmission made by a ground station to a Navy Lockheed P-2V Neptune ASW aircraft that provided *B-130*'s coordinates with disturbing accuracy. It seemed that some shore-based detection system had authorized the aircraft to prosecute a contact.

The probability of misinterpreting intercepted enemy communications made the failure of the Soviet Navy commanders to give guidance to the Anadyr group even more reprehensible. Most U.S. communications were encrypted, but even when given in the clear, the Soviet submariners were not expert enough in English to understand exactly what was meant.

Shumkov's anxiety intensified. He did not quite believe his radioman's first warning that the Americans had authorized the aircraft to use its weapons after establishing the submarine's exact position, but it could not be discounted. Shortly thereafter the *B-130* visually detected the approaching aircraft while on the surface during one of the increasingly frequent battery charges. At that point, the radio officer announced that he had made a mistake—the American Neptune had received orders to use its cameras, not its weapons.

Vastly relieved, Shumkov ordered his crew to dive the boat to 375 feet with a 90-degree change in course to port. He realized that *B-130* would soon find herself facing American surface forces and, given the condition of his submarine, it would prove difficult if not impossible to evade them. In conformity with his orders, he reported the Neptune contact and remained on course to Cuba.

Unaware of the larger events taking place on the surface, and still following his orders, Shumkov had already taken *B-130* and its nuclear torpedo across the American quarantine line.

Two days later, President Kennedy addressed a national television audience showing no sign of the light-hearted and elegant manner that so endeared him to the American public. A determined commander in chief revealed the presence of Soviet intermediate-range nuclear missiles in Cuba and the administration's plans to arrest the buildup and reverse the process through a naval quarantine and international pressure. He made it clear that he would employ the massive nuclear firepower at his disposal against the Soviet Union and Eastern Europe at the first sign of offensive action against either the United States or its allies. Kennedy's message informed not only his fellow citizens, but also the rest of the world. The headlines printed by the *Washington Post* the next morning announced the quarantine, but used the more aggressive term "blockade." It also emphasized in its third bold headline just above a picture of Kennedy in the oval office that "U.S. Will Sink Defiant Arms Ships." The following evening the president announced that the quarantine would take effect at 10 A.M. eastern daylight time on October 24, exactly one year and one day after Shumkov witnessed the blinding flash of a nuclear explosion through his periscope.

Early in the afternoon of the quarantine's first day the president's strategy began to bear fruit. Six Soviet cargo ships turned away from the line, inspiring Attorney General Robert Kennedy's comment that Khrushchev had finally blinked in their eye-to-eye confrontation. Sixteen other Soviet cargo ships in the Atlantic had stopped dead in the water or had come about and set a course for home. While others ships continued to approach, Kennedy felt more positive than he had for many days.

The next day international focus shifted for a moment to the United Nations. On October 25 Adlai Stevenson had his now-famous confrontation with the Soviet Union in the Security Council. Asking his Russian counterpart Valerian Zorin to deny that his government had placed nuclear-capable missiles in Cuba, Stevenson shouted out that Zorin should not wait for the translation, but respond immediately. The Russian refused. The American ambassador then proceeded to display for the stunned Security Council the photo reconnaissance evidence that had convinced Kennedy.

While Stevenson and Zorin verbally battled in the Security Council chamber in New York City, Shumkov and *B-130*, still on course, surfaced once again for a battery recharge. The American secretary of defense Robert McNamara had already announced that the U.S. Navy would use the commonly recognized wartime method of three grenade explosions to invite any foreign submarines in the area to surface before using force against them. As the advantage in the geopolitical standoff passed to the Americans, submarine hunting became much more intense. Shumkov would not have long to wait.

Almost as soon as the boat began recharging, *B-130*'s radar operator detected a group of several large ships forming a barrier directly across their prescribed course, an American aircraft carrier and its escort ships. To make matters worse, Parshin, the chief engineer, soon reported that the recharge might prove problematic, since two of the storm-tossed diesels ceased operation and could not be repaired at sea. *B-130* now had one diesel left and batteries barely able to hold a charge. Shumkov knew that he had little choice but to keep charging as best he could; one hour, two hours, how long? As his sonar operator reported the approaching sound of ship's propellers, the commanding officer of *B-130* decided not to dive, but to remain on the surface recharging his depleted batteries until visual contact with American forces. Then he would dive, hoping that his ship-handling skills would pull them through this precarious situation. He suddenly became very conscious of the nuclear torpedo resting in one of his forward tubes and the power of the approaching ASW group.

Shumkov recalled years later that the Americans behaved very strangely as they approached. They stopped, proceeded for a time, and then stopped again. They were obviously reducing their own noise emissions to make detecting *B-130* in the warm and tropical waters a bit easier for the sonar operators on the escorting destroyers. When they came within four miles of *B-130*, Shumkov ordered his executive officer to dive the boat, shutting down the noisy diesels, shifting to electric motors, and sliding below the surface.

Instead of providing a measure of security and the promise of possibly evading the approaching Americans, technical problems continued to haunt him. Nearing forty feet, Shumkov's diving officer reported that the boat's forward dive planes would not deploy. These control surfaces, one each mounted on the port and starboard, worked with a similar set at the stern, permitting the vessel to alter depth swiftly while submerged. While not absolutely necessary on a long, relatively straight, high-speed run, these planes would provide critical assistance in the close maneuvering that evasion demanded. As he considered ways of eluding the American task group with this new handicap, his sonarman reported a series of three quick explosions just above and to the starboard of their position; three grenades used as a signal. The USS *Essex* (*CVS-9*) and her entire antisubmarine group now took up station at his position, roughly thirty feet above his head.

≈   ≈   ≈

THE AMERICAN CARRIER USS *Essex*, a battle veteran of World War II and Korea, emerged from the New York Navy Yard in Brooklyn in the summer of 1962 as the navy's most modern ASW support carrier. She now possessed the bow-mounted SQS-23 sonar, an entire array of the latest electronic and physical countermeasures, and the new iconorama tactical display, part of the postwar evolution of the on-board combat information center for surface ships.

It was about 8 o'clock on the morning of October 26. Soviet navigators Lubichev and Tronza examined their position and compared the data with the information provided by the sonar. *B-130* had an American carrier and four destroyers just overhead.

As Shumkov continued to dive through 300 feet, members of the crew managed to rig out the truant dive planes by using a manual mechanical technique, bypassing the automatic controls. As they did so the triple explosion took place again: Mr. McNamara's international signal for a submarine to surface. The Americans seemed determined to have their way. Shumkov had no intention of complying unless his boat failed and saving his crew required it. He would soon need to contact Moscow and to report his predicament. Successfully making that report would present quite a problem given his present situation. He also wondered what sort of instructions he would receive regarding the rules of engagement. He did not know how the confrontation between the Soviet Union and the United States had evolved over the past few days. His masters in Moscow might have decided on a stand to protect the reputation of the USSR and its valued strategic ally in Cuba. For a split second, he recalled the blinding flash of the nuclear torpedo at Novaya

Zemlya almost exactly one year earlier. This situation seemed as close to hell as any he had imagined.

He leveled the boat at 450 feet and rigged for silent running.

Unfortunately, the technical plague continued. Compartment six, his propulsion room, reported that a cooling line designed to draw water from the ocean to reduce the temperature of the propulsion system had developed a major leak. Seawater surged into the compartment under increasing pressure as the boat went deeper. When *B-130* leveled at 450 feet, she was still taking water. Shumkov immediately sounded the alarm and had his crew go to their emergency stations, naturally contemplating an immediate trip to the surface to ensure the boat's safety. He dreaded surfacing with an entire ASW task force just above. The risk of hitting one of the American ships as he rose made that choice very hazardous, while the accumulating water in compartment six made it necessary.

The propulsion spaces filled with steam as the cooling pipe, wrapped around the diesels, spilled water on engine surfaces still hot from surface operations. Two alert crewmen quickly closed the safety valve for that pipe and the leak ceased in a now nearly uninhabitable compartment. With news of the temporary repair, Shumkov elected not to surface but to maneuver out from under the *Essex* task force; all the while damage reports from his crew seemed to provide an odd lyric to the constant rhythmic pinging of the American active sonar against the boat's hull. American ASW forces had his position. *B-130* had lost its second most important weapon, stealth.

Shumkov desperately wanted to disappear. With the leak under control, and at a patrol-quiet speed of between two and three knots, he began moving in a very wide circle and coming shallow. He wanted to use the warm water near the surface to confuse the American sonar. He hoped his course would prove just as confusing. It worked. The *130* disappeared from the American sonar. The task force commander immediately assumed that the Russian would try to move toward the open ocean in an effort both to evade and find deep sanctuary. As he changed depth, the behavior of the surface ships raised Shumkov's hopes that he might get away. While the Americans moved away into deeper waters, he took his boat not toward the open sea but closer to the American coast and in the direction of Cuba and his destination at Mariel.

B-130 could not move fast enough to make the momentary respite from American surveillance last for more than a few hours. Frustrated in their effort to regain contact, the *Essex* ASW task group returned to the point at which Shumkov evaporated from their sonar and began a systematic search. The *B-130*'s sonar operator could hear the destroyers pinging and the search beginning. Well aware of his boat's limitations, Shumkov knew that his moments of freedom would soon come to an end. The Americans would occasionally stop to permit one of the destroyers to listen carefully before resuming with their active sonar. At sea for nearly twenty-six days, he had come to within 400 miles of Mariel but he now knew that the Americans would have him before he could reach Cuba. They came closer as each moment passed.

Shumkov decided to surface. The relentless submerged chase had to stop. Besides, he needed to recharge his flawed battery and to improve the conditions inside the boat for his crew. With the ASW group close, but no longer directly above him, he reached periscope depth without any danger of collision only to discover that his pursuers had already made up for lost time. Looking through his periscope, Captain Shumkov saw USS *Blandy* not more than 45 feet away.

He surfaced to find the Americans filming the proceedings, but this did not bother him. Gathering intelligence in these circumstances seemed natural, and given a reversal of roles he would do precisely the same thing. Immediately after he broke the surface he ordered his radio operator to report their predicament to Moscow. On the seventeenth try, the signal made it through: ". . . forced to surface after pursuit, battery low, drinking water nearly gone, two of three diesels disabled, surrounded by four American warships, awaiting instructions." While those instructions, with a closer definition of the current rules of engagement, would certainly come, Shumkov relied on his own appreciation of the circumstances to govern his actions.

The Soviet Union and the United States were not at war. His expertise did not lead him to diminish the danger and consequence of this confrontation over the Soviet–Cuban alliance, but at that moment the rules of war did not apply. He did not expect his opposite numbers on the

American ASW vessels to use their weapons. At most he anticipated that an overzealous commander might ram him, sending the *B-130* and its crew to the bottom in a politically motivated "accident." If the Americans did use their weapons, he would know that the war was no longer cold and act accordingly. He knew that *B-130* possessed a weapon that could consume the entire *Essex* task group, just as he knew that at the present range, he and his crew would almost certainly perish as well, but they would do their duty and follow orders. While the missiles destined for Cuba might never make it to the launch pad, his nuclear weapon lay primed and ready in a tube in the forward torpedo room. In addition, unlike the other Foxtrot commanders, he had once used this weapon.

Moscow merely acknowledged receipt of his message. The naval command did not offer any solutions to his predicament and made it clear that he had to extricate himself from the situation and return to base as best he could. While not a comforting instruction, neither did it suggest that the nuclear confrontation should shift from potential on land in Cuba to reality at sea off the southeastern coast of the United States.

Following these orders proved very difficult and humiliating given *B-130*'s position and limitations. The *Essex* ASW task group followed Shumkov's submarine for five days as he moved out into the open Atlantic. They harassed the Soviet vessel by various means, knowing that its battery condition would prevent prolonged submergence or any attempt at a high-speed escape. USS *Barry* would frequently position itself roughly 300 yards from the submarine and then rapidly close as if to ram. Each time, at a distance of 100 yards, the destroyer suddenly turned and took up position parallel to *B-130*'s course. After Shumkov suggested via semaphore that the American commander cease playing his dangerous and provocative game, the situation settled into a matter of routine escort, as *B-130* set off toward deep water and her home base at Polyarni. The Americans shadowed Shumkov closely until she met with a Soviet Navy tender not far from the Azores.

Restraint and careful definition of the rules of engagement permitted the United States and the Soviet Union to avoid a potential nuclear exchange. While everyone focused on Fidel Castro and Cuba, the more immediate danger, which rested in the hands of an experienced submarine commander from Siberia and his three fellow Foxtrot commanders, went unnoticed. Professionalism, not emotion, ruled the day.

Shumkov learned later that the other Foxtrot submarines of his Anadyr group had not fared any better than *B-130*. Captain Second Rank Alexey Dubivko of *B-36* experienced most of the same misfortunes that befell Shumkov, with a few unique events thrown in for good measure. The *B-36* sonar-officer Peter Pankov came down with appendicitis, making an operation necessary 330 feet down, while Hurricane Ella whipped the ocean surface to sea-state nine. The crew cleaned the officers' wardroom with alcohol and Doctor Victor Ivanovitch Buinevich performed the procedure successfully, assisted by a seaman instead of a nurse.

The experience of Captain Second Rank Valentin Savitsky in *B-59* came closest to the purgatory suffered by Shumkov and the *130*. Hurricane Ella damaged his snorkel, the boat's rubber hatch seals cracked, and the diesel cooling systems became covered in salt from seawater, causing the diesel engines and electric compressors to take turns malfunctioning. This crew also experienced stifling hot conditions averaging between 122 and 140 degrees. Moreover, the carrier USS *Randolph*, leading Hunter-Killer Task Group 83.2 (Task Group Alpha), pursued *B-59* as relentlessly as the *Essex* group did the *B-130*.

≈   ≈   ≈

ON BOARD *B-59* was a twenty-five-year-old radio surveillance officer, Vadim P. Orlov, who would retire as a Captain, Second Rank. His first-person view of *B-59* is both chilling and revealing.

When the four Foxtrot submarines went to Cuba, he was assigned to the *B-59* as the head of an OSNAZ group of ten highly qualified radio officers distributed among the four Mariel-bound submarines. They would take care of transmission with Moscow and the Northern Fleet during Operation Anadyr; interboat communication if that became necessary; radio transmission surveillance of the American forces at sea; radar detection; the surveillance of American commercial radio; and intelligence derived from high-frequency direction finding. The men assigned to his group had both submarine experience and prior service on board surveillance trawlers.[10] By comparison, the communications officers already assigned as a regular part of each boat's crew had only a one-month internship in radio surveillance before leaving for Cuba.

The OSNAZ group went with the Anadyr mission particularly to intercept data on American preparation, on deployment plans broadcast by NATO and the United States Navy, including valuable shortwave transmissions difficult to pick up via land units or trawlers. As the 1950s concluded, the Soviet Union already had a very capable radio surveillance center in Cuba equipped with the latest surveillance equipment, radars, an antenna field, and about 170 experienced maintenance and analysis personnel.

The importance of SIGINT, or signals intelligence, made this kind of facility a common occurrence during the Cold War, and most NATO and Warsaw Pact countries had them in strategic locations. The United States and NATO had a similar close surveillance facility in Norway, monitoring the USSR's Globus-encrypted communication system. Globus provided a guide and encryption key to all sensitive naval radio networks and frequencies. When carried on board, Globus looked like a big book sheathed in a lead cover. Each surface ship and submarine had one aboard. The lead cover ensured that the book would either sink when hurled overboard or go to the bottom with lost vessels.

Years after the Cuban missile crisis, the Navy and the CIA, in conjunction with Howard Hughes' company, Global Marine, tried to salvage the lost Golf class missile submarine *K-129*. After that boat went down for the last time in the Pacific on March 11, 1968, the CIA's Operation Jennifer retrieved the submarine's bow, which contained a copy of Globus as well as Akula system cryptographic equipment that could send and receive high-speed encrypted radio transmissions.

It took about one year for the Soviets to realize the Americans had compromised their codes. As a result, the USSR quickly changed the entire naval communication system as well as all cryptographic gear deployed at sea. They also had to take considerable time and trouble to find out the kind and amount of information the Americans discovered while the code permitted them extraordinary access to Soviet communication. It took three months to assess the damage and put controls in place. In the process they abolished the Akula cryptographic system and replaced it with the much more sophisticated Integral system.

Before their departure for Cuba, the OSNAZ officers received a detailed briefing on their mission complete with frequencies to monitor and a special communication and listening schedule. They learned that the Foxtrot boats would remain in Cuba to conduct submerged espionage and surveillance and they would have completely outfitted accommodations in Havana. Their luggage and other personal items would travel to the Caribbean on a cargo vessel before the four Foxtrots ever embarked on Anadyr.[11]

As Shumkov's crew would also discover with *B-130*, accommodations on board the submarines proved woefully inadequate. On *B-59*, Captain Savitsky had to order some of his warrant officers out of their compartment to give Orlov and his SIGINT people space for their work. Having to make this accommodation did not make him happy. The confines of his boat would barely permit his crew to fulfill their tasks and to maintain readiness. His first reaction upon meeting Orlov has remained vivid in the latter's memory over the years: "What the hell are you and this OSNAZ group doing aboard my sub?"

The OSNAZ officers worked in shifts lasting at least four hours, but sometimes ten or twelve. They worked and slept in the same room, forbidden by their orders from helping with the cleaning and cooking aboard the submarine. This irritated the crew all the more. They also suspected that the SIGINT team actually belonged to the KGB and not the GRU, which made the crew nervous and conscious of their every word and action.

Orlov gave orders to have the radio surveillance gear installed in a fifteen-square-meter compartment. The group kept their surveillance results, cryptographic codes, maps, and other essentials in an adjacent space. Only Orlov could give permission to enter. Not even the boat's commander had free access to these spaces, documents, and papers. As the head of the radio surveillance group Orlov knew all Soviet surface ship and submarine frequencies and he alone could provide the information his group needed to carry out their surveillance effort. He tasked his men to intercept signals at different frequencies when the submarine changed its location and he helped his men distinguish between American and Soviet military transmission frequencies. As OS-NAZ group leader he also analyzed surveillance data, prepared surveillance summaries, reported to the submarine commander every four hours, and sent intelligence data back to base every day.

The on-board OSNAZ effort constantly amazed and annoyed Captain Savitsky. On one occasion, early in the voyage to Mariel, Orlov reported the approach of a NATO surveillance aircraft and the vulnerability of *B-59* to aerial ASW techniques as it navigated the Norwegian Sea. He warned the captain of the plane's approach with a ten-minute margin to spare. Orlov suggested that the boat go deep to avoid detection. Savitsky replied, "How the hell do you know?" Orlov seemed too young and inexperienced to possess this kind of information and to use his equipment so well that he could make predictions with such precision. Savitsky also suggested strongly that the choice of how to evade belonged to him. When the aircraft actually arrived, Savitsky dived the boat. Orlov could not tell him how he knew the aircraft would intersect their course because the captain did not need to know. After that event it took only four or five days for Savitsky to adjust to the presence of Orlov's group, which continued to amaze him with information derived from their work.

The crew knew that *B-59* carried a nuclear torpedo carefully monitored by a KGB officer and initially wondered about both the advanced weaponry and the level of secrecy surrounding OSNAZ activities. After they passed through the GIUK gap, Savitsky announced that their course would take them to Mariel in Cuba and he kept them apprised of changes in the political situation based on reports from fleet headquarters and SIGINT interceptions.

As far as Orlov could tell, the submarine managed to pass the GUIK gap undetected and moved into the Atlantic Ocean.[12] The OSNAZ group listened carefully for aircraft and surface ASW forces. Savitsky would surface his diesel-powered Foxtrot at night to recharge the batteries, remaining submerged during the day with both snorkel and antenna up, to renew the air, recharge if necessary, and maintain communications.

As they approached the eastern coast of the United States, Orlov's group concluded from their intercepts that the U.S. Navy had initiated an alert and four aircraft carrier task groups would address any ASW challenge. They informed both Savitsky and Northern Fleet headquarters. The latter reacted by confirming their orders to Mariel.

An American aircraft carrier ASW group detected *B-59* on October 19, 1962. Savitsky found himself in water about 1,800 feet deep and far too warm for comfort. The tropics began to have their effect and the necessity to remain submerged quickly rendered the air hot and stale. At about 2300 hours, Savitsky's efforts to elude began to fail in the face of overwhelming force. He found himself at 450 feet with an eight-ship American task group just above. The destroyers rattled them with active sonar pings and the customary three-grenade explosion signal ordering them to surface. The crew did not know what would happen, tension grew, the air became more stale, and blue indicator lights illuminated the propulsion compartment indicating that the batteries needed a recharge. Extremely angry at his situation and the behavior of the Americans, Savitsky ordered the nuclear torpedo placed in the tube in the forward torpedo room just before surfacing. He did not know what to expect and would take no chances.

The captain began signaling his intention to surface with his active sonar in conformity with international rules. He surfaced at 1600 on October 20th into a whirlwind of dazzling lights, a near circle of surface ships, and a helicopter hovering about ninety feet above his head. The sudden surge of fresh air made Savitsky, his political officer, the watch officer, the signalman, and Orlov feel drunk as they filled their lungs on ascending to the sail bridge. As these senior officers watched the circus on the surface, Orlov's people worked furiously to communicate with the Northern Fleet. It took them a while to get through, but when they did it took Gorshkov only twenty minutes to respond. The admiral ordered them to escape, evade, and head for Bermuda. He advised them that no war had begun, so they should avoid starting one at all costs.

Knowing that it would take Savitsky eighteen hours to recharge his batteries completely before any attempt to follow Gorshkov's instruction, Orlov ordered his men to get to work. He put up the antenna and started to intercept hoards of signals: from the aircraft carrier group, from Norfolk, and on dozens of frequencies. As he later recalled:

There were so many frequencies, the air was filled with talking and signals. My men worked like dogs and I didn't have time to analyze all the data! But we worked and worked, listened and listened! It was like during a war—there were no codes, all messages were clear. There were too many frequencies, I didn't have enough equipment and enough men to listen to all this!

The OSNAZ team found the frequency of the aircraft carrier ASW group and discovered that USS *Randolph* (*CVS-15*) and her escorts, ten ships in all, had *B-59* in their sights. Orlov also learned that the Americans assumed that nuclear power rather than diesels drove *B-59*. American naval command tasked the *Randolph* group with tracking Savitsky's boat and ASW aircraft dropped scores of sonobuoys to keep track of the *59*'s movements. While he charged his batteries, Savitsky permitted his crew to come topside in small groups to provide direct access to fresh air.

Orlov found the entire experience humiliating. The American crew played Yankee Doodle, danced, and tossed both bottles of Coca-Cola and packs of cigarettes down to the Russians. The Soviet crew realized how dirty and sweaty they looked in comparison to the American officers wearing summer trousers, blue shirts, and white hats. They consumed cooled drinks and seemed to smile while watching the *B-59* crew as if they belonged in a zoo. In spite of intense irritation and real concern, no war had started and it did not seem as if one would. The captain ordered the forward torpedo room to remove the nuclear torpedo and place it back on its reserve rack. Orlov felt physically relieved, because Savitsky's manner had already convinced many of the crew that he would not have waited for a special order to launch the torpedo. He would have acted on his own initiative.

When Savitsky ordered the torpedo loaded only hours before the crew remained calm and followed orders. Three officers aboard the boat held the keys necessary to use the weapon—the commander, the executive officer, and the political officer. A KGB officer on board guarded the torpedo and never left it, sleeping next to the device in what could often become the coldest compartment on the boat. Orlov's relief at the captain's decision to remove the nuclear device from its tube stemmed from a knowledge of submarines, crews, and the realities on board:

> The crew perceived their commander as a god, so they would have followed his order to launch the nuclear torpedo. Neither the executive officer nor political officer would have voiced objections to the commander regarding the torpedo launch. In case of a war, Savitsky wouldn't allow the belligerent to seize the submarine, he would have rather scuttled the sub or blown the sub up than be captured by the enemy.

Orlov saw Savitsky as the kind of commander who would not mind taking a few enemies with him if he had to destroy his own boat.

When the battery recharge concluded, *B-59* began moving slowly on the surface toward Bermuda. The OSNAZ group intercepted communication indicating that the carrier would soon withdraw, leaving four surface ships from its escort contingent to track the submarine, with a surveillance aircraft overflight every fifteen minutes. He also intercepted a transmission indicating the current level of international political tension and that, in the midst of it all, the Americans had forced two other Foxtrots to surface.

At midnight, between regular floodlight illuminations from the escort ships, Savitsky took his boat down to 450 feet, changed course by 180 degrees, and made revolutions for 14 knots. As Orlov remembers it, it took the Americans fifteen minutes to realize the boat had vanished. *B-59* surfaced at 0300 and informed the Northern Fleet of its escape now that Savitsky had placed fifty miles between himself and the Americans. In the morning *B-59* received an order to return home. Savitsky chose to remain on the surface for the return leg. Like Shumkov and his other comrades, he had little left to hide.

Had Savitsky—or any of the other three Foxtrot submarines—elected to do so, the Cuban missile crisis could have become World War III in an instant. This lack of command and control over nuclear weapons would haunt the fears of both Soviet and American leaders for the entire Cold War—and it may well still be a threat.

The commander of *B-4*, Captain Second Rank Rurik Ketov, Shumkov's good friend, had the least distressing trip, despite suffering major flooding that could have been disastrous. Still, the *B-4* managed to avoid the larger American task groups, and became the only Mariel-bound Foxtrot not forced to the surface during the crisis.

All during the return trip, Shumkov mulled over the problems they had encountered. He knew very well that the inexperience of the Soviet submariners, the inflated expectations of the naval command, and the determined American ASW forces had spoiled the transit of four Foxtrots to Mariel. What he did not know was that the failure of the Foxtrots had led to the cancellation of the follow-up mission for the seven Golf missile boats. In addition, Shumkov had to face further operational problems on the return leg, eventually requiring the towing services of the salvage ship *Pamirs* near the Azores. The *B-130* arrived back at her base in late November 1962. The last to set out in October, she completed the journey first. The other three returned in mid-December.

At their home base, they received a less than enthusiastic reception. Shumkov recalled that, "there were no festive greetings and friendly handshakes from the headquarters."

The final piece of the confusing puzzle fell into place in January, when the four Foxtrot commanders were sent to Moscow to explain their failure to the First Deputy Minister of Defense Marshal Andrei Grechko, a close friend of Admiral Gorshkov. Grechko, believing that the navy had dispatched four of the much faster November[13] class nuclear boats to Mariel, flew into a rage demanding to know why they ever considered surfacing in front of the Americans! When Marshal Zakharov very tactfully informed Grechko that the mission had been assigned to Foxtrot class diesel boats, the storm subsided a bit, only to break out again over the humiliation of the American tactical victory. All of the Foxtrot commanders received withering reprimands for the Anadyr mission and its failure.

Like a good Soviet officer, Shumkov took the reprimand silently, noting to himself the irony of the situation. The Soviet headquarters had ignored Hurricane Ella and somehow believed that they had sent nuclear boats. And in typical Soviet fashion, the reprimands were soon forgotten—submarine commanders were in too short supply, and the fleet was increasing every month. Within a year all four officers of the Operation Anadyr Foxtrot submarines received new commands, three in nuclear boats and one in a new diesel. Fortunately for the navy, the misplaced official outrage and the commanders' performance as professionals were two very different things.

5

An Uncertain
Nuclear Beginning

Despite a number of successful patrols, the Soviet Navy never managed to eliminate all the technical problems aboard the nuclear subs. The nuclear pioneers encountered a number of difficulties because of construction faults and inadequate equipment. One of the main problems was failure of the steam generators, which would often result in high radioactivity in the submarines. The causes proved far more complex and idiosyncratic than conditions in the United States program.

Soviet shipyard budgets and production schedules regularly fell victim to priorities driven by personal ambition, politically driven large-scale economic programs, or ideological priorities. Thus shipyards often built submarines at a pace dictated by state priorities frequently beyond the navy's control, a haphazard system made even more complex by the perpetually erratic flow of appropriated funds. The latter often caused the yards to accelerate their work at the end of the year both to take advantage of late-arriving funds and to meet politically imposed deadlines, which only occasionally served the navy's operational needs. Quality control took second place and a prescribed political rigidity prevailed in the relationship between naval personnel and the yards, which led directly to many accidents and catastrophes at sea, some of which have already been described.

Northern Fleet commander Admiral Chabanenko corroborated Vladimir Borisov's views on construction inadequacies when he said, in December 1959 that the Northern Fleet received the three first nuclear submarines as part of project 627A, and the boats proved unsatisfactory, "the commander in chief ordered us to accept them . . . they needed the act of acceptance for bonuses, orders, and golden stars."[1] These circumstances became a perpetual plague for Soviet submariners for the duration of the Cold War.

The first Soviet nuclear sub, the *K-3*, now commanded by Captain Second Rank Y. Stepanov, ran into trouble again in September 1967 in the Norwegian Sea. A fire started in the hold of compartment one when hydraulic oil was ignited. The flames immediately enveloped the entire compartment, where twenty-eight men served. The fire spread to compartment two when the hatch was opened, lasting about two minutes but killing another ten sailors. The entire crew of compartment three, except for one man, Boatswain Lun, had passed out from fumes. The executive officer of the *K-3* recalled:

> Later on it would be found that most of the dead submariners were next to the hatch of compartment three. They could not get through because the compartment two officer, Captain-Lieutenant Malyar, was lying on the hatch to prevent his submariners from opening it. He knew that if it were opened, the central compartment would be set aflame, and the boat would be lost. The fire in

compartment one died out before any of the twenty torpedoes (including two that were nuclear tipped) could explode.

Boatswain Lun managed to blow the main ballast tanks and the submarine surfaced. With great effort he opened the conning tower hatches and carried Stepanov to the bridge, where he regained consciousness. Of the seventeen men in the central compartment, fourteen were made ill by the fumes, and one died.

Fifteen minutes later, Stepanov ordered that a radiogram be sent to fleet headquarters telling of the accident, saying, "39 men died aboard the K-3, 24 men are in need of urgent medical help." The coordinates of K-3's location were sent, and amidst a severe storm, four submarines and the salvage ship Beshtau, along with many other surface ships, were sent to the accident area to rescue the submarine. Among those on board Beshtau were Captain First Rank Borisov and a relief crew for K-3 (many, but not all, Soviet boats had second crews; this was the case for all of the missile boats).

Despite the severe storm and the rolling decks of the ships, they managed to transfer the injured crewmen and rush them to a hospital. The entire incident was hushed up, and the story of K-3 was not known generally for many years. The Soviet Navy took K-3 out of service in 1991 and currently there are plans to convert her to a museum ship if the resources become available.

On March 8, 1968, the Soviet submarine fleet suffered a loss that would have widespread tactical and political implications. The importance of the ballistic missile submarine was so great that each of the contending superpowers had to closely monitor those of its opponents. Enemy ballistic missile submarines were tracked and followed continuously, so that in the event of war they could be attacked and disposed of before they could fire their lethal missiles. There thus began an international game of cat and mouse in which one submarine would stalk another, frequently engaging in provocative tactics that precipitated the occasional collision.

According to Soviet sources, the diesel-powered K-129, commanded by Captain V. Kobzar, was about 750 miles northwest of the island of

Oahu, Hawaii, en route to its Pacific patrol station. The *K-129* was a modernized Golf-2 class boat and the first with a ballistic missile complex capable of underwater launches. It was for this reason that the experienced Kobzar was selected to command it. The missile had a range of almost 900 miles and was extremely accurate.

The Soviets argued that an American submarine trailing *K-129* struck the Soviet boat's keel while both were at a depth of about 150 feet. The Soviet submarine struggled to the surface, then sank, the noise of its imploding compartments illuminating U.S. passive sonar systems as the helpless hull plunged to a depth of more than three miles before reaching the ocean floor. There were no survivors.

The official view from American sources was that the *K-129* must have suffered an internal explosion—hydrogen from the batteries, or perhaps a torpedo—and that there was no collision. Soviet sources deny the possibility, and point instead to the fact that the American submarine *Swordfish* later pulled into Yokosuka harbor in Japan for secret repairs to its conning tower (sail) and periscope.

Though the U.S. Navy knew of the exact location of the *K-129*'s hulk, it did not reveal it to the Soviet Union, which launched an extensive but unsuccessful search for the sunken submarine. The Soviets placed four submarines in a line, ten miles apart, to search the ocean where the *K-129* was presumed to have sunk.

Four months after the sinking, the special-purpose boat USS *Halibut* took photographs of the wreckage and even retrieved some items from the hull. Again according to Soviet sources, the photographs support the theory that the bottom of the *K-129* had been slashed by the sail of a submarine, presumably that of the *Swordfish*. In 1974, a unique salvage operation using Howard Hughes' *Glomar Explorer* succeeded in raising about one-third of the forward portion of the *K-129*. The hulk was closely examined, and American investigators were appalled at the crude construction of the hull and the obvious signs of the poor quality control of maintenance efforts. The remains of six crewmembers were found. They were carefully handled and given a dignified burial at sea with full military honors.

A more catastrophic accident took place on April 11, 1970, when tragedy struck the unlucky *K-8* again. It would eventually sink with twenty-two men, including the sub's commander, Captain Second Rank Bessonov. Fire was again the culprit, with flames raging in compartments eight and nine. The fire spread rapidly via the ventilation system and electrical cables. The reactor scrammed (shut down) immediately and the turbine engines stopped, leaving the boat dead in the water.

The deputy detachment commander, Captain First Rank Kashirsky, was on board, and he later described the tragedy:

> When the fire started the crew was given the alarm. Bessonov ordered the boat to surface, and everyone put on their life-masks as the central compartment filled with smoke and toxic fumes. It was impossible to move aft until after the submarine surfaced. The commander opened the conning tower hatch and crewmen were evacuated to the bridge. The captain ordered some across the hot deck to the stern escape trunk. A few hours later they descended into the after portions of the submarine only to find that all of their shipmates there had been asphyxiated.

A Bulgarian cargo ship arrived the following morning and took off forty-three men from the K-8. Bessonov sent a message to Moscow, informing headquarters of the catastrophe. The cruiser *Murmansk*, ten surface ships, three subs, and the floating base *Volga* were dispatched, along with a second crew to replace the main crew aboard the K-8.

The searing heat of the fire had warped the submarine's hull and it began to take on water. By the end of the third day the K-8 had no high-pressure air, so the crew, near exhaustion now, could not blow the main ballast tanks. As the submarine slowly sank, the storm got ever more severe. The submarine could not be towed, as the tow-lines snapped like thread, and it was extremely difficult to remove the crew to the rescue ships.

The K-8 sank on the morning of April 12, 1970, into 4,125 meters of water. Sadly, it took twenty-two men, including Captain Bessonov and the executive officer, V. Tkachev, with her. The rescuers managed to save only Captain Third Rank V. Rubenko. For six months the Soviet ships patrolled the region where the submarine sank. In July 1970 the Soviet government awarded the crew of the K-8 with orders and medals for their courage and valor. The families of the lost sailors were not told the truth about the accident until thirty years later, a typical example of the hard-hearted preference for rigid security and ideological denial.

Only two months after the loss of the *K-8*, the specter of dangerous underwater dogfights rose again outside Petropavlovsk, the huge Soviet missile submarine base on the Kamchatka Peninsula. There the American submarine *Tautog*, captained by Commander Buele G. Balderston, was about to add to the laurels he and his crew had gained the previous year for monitoring the test of a new Soviet cruise missile. This time their task was tracking an Echo II class submarine. The demanding process had brought the two boats closer and closer together in an underwater minuet that ended with the *K-108*, known as "Black Lila," driving its belly through the *Tautog*'s sail, leaving a big portion of one of its propellers in the conning tower. The unthinkable had happened—two nuclear submarines, each one equipped with nuclear-tipped missiles, had collided beneath the surface.

As the *Tautog* moved away, the sonar men could hear what appeared to be the sounds of their opponent sinking. Fortunately, the *K-108* was captained by an unusually adroit submariner, Captain Boris Bagdasaryan, who gave the exactly correct order "reverse engines" at the exactly correct time, reversing the Black Lila's seemingly inevitable plunge to the ocean bottom into a champagne bubble ride to the surface. Both ships then limped home in utter secrecy, the *Tautog* to Hawaii, the *K-108* back to Petropavlovsk. Both crews were sworn to secrecy, both captains correctly assumed their careers had been damaged forever, but there were no casualties—a blessed relief from the pattern of most submarine accidents.

≈   ≈   ≈

DESPITE THE FACT that the reactors and other equipment were not reliable, Gorshkov kept pushing for more patrols, ignoring the repeated accidents and malfunctioning systems. He particularly wanted to emulate the cruise of the American *Nautilus* under the Arctic ice, and his nuclear submarines gave him the opportunity to do so. At the end of 1962 the nuclear attack submarine *K-21,* commanded by Captain Second Rank Vladimir Chernavin, who would eventually rise to become the commander in chief of the Soviet Navy, cruised under ice for 50 days. The crew practiced methods of maneuvering under thick ice and surfacing in *polinyas* (large areas of thin ice).

In 1963, four years before its unfortunate episode in the Norwegian Sea, *K-3* was ordered to prepare for a cruise to the North Pole. At the time, it was commanded by Captain Second Rank L. Zhiltsov, who took it to the vicinity of the North Pole but did not immediately find a *polinya* for surfacing. On its third try, on July 17, the *K-3* surfaced near the North Pole, winning prestigious awards for its crew.

Year by year, Gorshkov's submariners fanned out, exploring more oceans and making their presence felt around the world. One highlight of these adventures took place in September 1963, when the nuclear attack submarine *K-181,* commanded by Captain Second Rank Y. Sisoev, had a successful cruise under the Arctic ice. As Sisoev described it:

> The *K-181* left the base at the scheduled time on the 29th of September in 1963 and maneuvered towards the North Pole. It was about 6 P.M. when the navigator B. Khramtsov reported, "One mile to the Pole. . . . The submarine is cruising across the Pole!" At this time the devices detected a big polinya covered with thin ice. Then the fleet commander gave permission to surface in the polinya. The submarine maneuvered and stopped right beneath it, and smoothly reached the ice. The conning tower broke the brittle ice and the submarine surfaced. I quickly went to the upper conning tower hatch, opened it, and went to the bridge, which was a responsibility and a prerogative of the sub's commander.

The submariners raised both the Soviet flag and the naval flag and took pictures before submerging again and completing its other tasks.

Sisoev's great success allowed him to enroll at the Academy of the General Headquarters, and Captain First Rank Borisov was appointed to succeed him as commander of the *K-181.* Borisov's first task was a daunting one, for in December 1965 he was ordered to patrol the eastern coast of the United States, to the south from Bermuda, to study the American underwater surveillance system.

Borisov's noisy submarine was very quickly detected by the very sound system he was supposed to study. His submarine came to the attention of an American command that went by the acronym COSL. Commander Ocean Systems Atlantic, based in Norfolk, Virginia, controlled the relatively new SOSUS surveillance grid off the east coast of North America and the Caribbean. In the process of making his dash to the south, Borisov took *K-181* across the entire detection network.

An explanation of the American SOSUS system is in order here, even though it requires a chronological digression. In the early 1950s, the typical range of a sonar system was slightly less than one mile. With the advent of the U.S. Navy's SQS-4 system, the range increased to almost three miles, and more under optimum conditions. In 1950, the navy began development of a long-range, fixed sound-surveillance system called SOSUS, the result of intense research. Before World War II oceanographers discovered that the ocean layer in which the most dramatic temperature change occurred, called the thermocline, would often reflect active sonar signals back to the surface. Other, more shallow layers could bend the sound signal in the water and redirect it, like a prism, to the surface or into the depths according to temperature and increasing pressure. The latter factors would themselves vary according to geographic location and season. Submarines could hide from intrusive sonar waves by lurking below the thermocline or other layers exhibiting dramatic temperature change. American submarines detected variations in temperature versus depth by means of an instrument developed at the opening of World War II called the bathythermograph.

They made other similar discoveries, including natural ocean conditions that extended the sonar's range. The deep sound channel, discovered in 1937, for example, provided an avenue for sound over hundreds, sometimes thousand of miles. SOSUS involved arrays of passive receivers or hydrophones that were positioned on the seabed near routes that Soviet submarines would have to take on their sorties. The data traveled to shore stations via cable for analysis, and were sent to Atlantic Fleet headquarters. SOSUS corresponded, in a way, to the Chain Home

Zapadnaya Litsa was one of the most important Cold War Soviet submarine bases
on the Kola Peninsula, serving the Northern Fleet submarines and their crews.
(Courtesy of Vice Admiral Anatoli I. Shevchenko)

The transit from the Northern Fleet to the Pacific Fleet across the northern seaboard
of the USSR posed a great threat to the boat and crew. This old photo taken during one of
those transits gives an idea of the conditions braved by the Soviet submariners who did
this on a regular basis before nuclear power enabled them to pass under the ice.
(Courtesy of Rear Admiral Oleg G. Chefonov)

The view from the conning tower forward as a Foxtrot plows
through the ocean on the surface.
(Courtesy of Rear Admiral Lev D. Chernavin)

This close-up catches
Lev Chernavin on the bridge
of his Foxtrot class boat on the way
to the Mediterranean in the
late 1960s. *(Courtesy of
Rear Admiral Lev D. Chernavin)*

Another shot of Chernavin, as
usual the tallest man in the
photo, in Alexandria, Egypt,
site of a secret Soviet
submarine base, wearing his
tropical white uniform in the
company of two shipmates.
*(Courtesy of Rear Admiral
Lev D. Chernavin)*

Rear Admiral Lebedko is pictured here (upper left) at a public function
in Moscow as part of Admiral Gorshkov's immediate entourage. As Admiral
of the Fleet of the Soviet Union from 1956 to 1985, Sergei Gorshkov (center)
is widely regarded as the father of global Soviet naval power.
(Courtesy of Rear Admiral Vladimir G. Lebedko)

The man who went to sea and sailed
into the Cuban missile crisis in his
Foxtrot class *B-130,* Nikolai Shumkov.
(Courtesy of First Rank Nikolai A. Shumkov)

A posed photo of *K-181* and its crew a few months after they trailed the USS *Saratoga* on an Atlantic Ocean transit. *(Courtesy of First Rank Vladimir Borisov)*

The American SSBN USS *James Madison* submerges to begin the process of test-firing the first Poseidon submarine-launched ballistic missile in the summer of 1970. Under Kondratiev's orders the surveillance trawler *Khariton Laptev (SSV-503)* photographed the event. *(Courtesy of Rear Admiral Gleb P. Kondratiev)*

USS *James Madison* left some debris from the launch, which was quickly retrieved by the *Khariton Laptev* for intelligence evaluation. *(Courtesy of Rear Admiral Gleb P. Kondratiev)*

The Russians retrieved this telemetry buoy from the test area in which
USS *James Madison* fired the first Poseidon submarine-launched ballistic missile
in a test off Cape Canaveral in the late summer of 1970.
(Courtesy of Rear Admiral Gleb P. Kondratiev)

The crew of the USS *Calcaterra* watched as Soviet retrieval teams raced to pick up
Poseidon launch debris and telemetry devices after the launch.
(Courtesy of Rear Admiral Gleb P. Kondratiev)

Here Anatoli Shevchenko poses with his Victor 2 class attack submarine in the early 1980s. *(Courtesy of Vice Admiral Anatoli I. Shevchenko)*

This is a Victor 3 class boat leaving the Kola Peninsula for a deployment at sea. Shevchenko drove this kind of submarine later in his career. The distinctive pod containing the cable spool for the new towed-array sonar rests at the top of the vertical stabilizer. *(Courtesy of Vice Admiral Anatoli I. Shevchenko)*

radar system used by Great Britain in the Battle of Britain. As data were gathered, analyzed, and stored, it was possible by the use of electronic spectrum analysis to identify submarines at great distances and determine not only their speed, course, and type, but even their individual identity.

Under the code name Project Caesar, the U.S. Navy and the Western Electric arm of AT&T began the preparations for SOSUS as early as 1950. The first Caesar station, Charlie, built in 1954 at Ramey Air Force Base ninety miles west of San Juan, Puerto Rico, began effective listening in February 1955 via hydrophone arrays mounted on the ocean bottom. By the end of that year the Americans had nine operational Caesar surveillance stations.

Few of the listening stations were exactly alike. The type of installation varied according to surface and ocean bottom conditions, and the same criteria determined cable lengths for the arrays. Bell Laboratories tuned these hydrophone arrays resting on the ocean bottom to the very low frequencies of the 5- to 150-Hz bandwidth, passing on any signals detected to shore-based consoles that recorded the contact by means of a continually moving stylus placing horizontal strokes across a moving track of electrosensitive paper.

Early SOSUS grew swiftly into a system of eighteen deep-water arrays. The navy and Bell Telephone later added ten more shallow-water arrays. In 1959 the American naval–industrial collaboration further upgraded the system, adding digital spectrum analyzers and new display consoles to multiply the low-frequency ranges covered by the system. Altogether the United States expended roughly $51 million on acoustic detection research during the first SOSUS decade, with an additional $375 million to actually create the network. This very expensive American ASW asset listened carefully while Borisov raced to capture the elusive prize assigned to him in the autumn of 1966: an aircraft carrier.[2]

In September of that year *K-181* left its base and was in the Atlantic Ocean when Borisov received a radiogram with an order "to trail the U.S. aircraft carrier as soon as we detect her."

Trailing the carrier would be no problem. Detecting her was the hard part. There followed a series of orders and counterorders that proved the value of the Soviet nuclear submarine beyond all doubt. Orders streamed from Moscow, sending the *K-181* to "occupy the quest region in the north-western part of the Atlantic Ocean." The navigator, Captain-Lieutenant Kaspert-Ust, completed the estimates. The submarine started moving at full speed. Two days later another order came, this time saying that *K-181* "would maneuver to the region situated at the entrance to the Caribbean Sea from where the American aircraft carrier *America* was expected to leave for the Atlantic Ocean."

Now the submarine turned back and steamed to the south at full speed. Then, at last, Borisov received the final, more detailed order, "The aircraft carrier task group is expected to leave the Mediterranean Sea. Maneuver towards the Gibraltar, detect the aircraft carrier, and trail her." The order was signed by the commander of the Northern Fleet, Admiral Semeon Michailovitch Lobov.

The submarine started steaming toward the Mediterranean at top speed. Borisov was worried that he would not be on time to catch the task group leaving the Mediterranean. When the submarine got the last order she was 2,400 miles away from the presumed meeting point with the aircraft carrier task group. They had to steam through the ocean for four days at full speed. Borisov coaxed every knot of speed from *K-181* by retracting the bow dive planes, reducing hydrodynamic drag, and not increasing the reactor's power, but still coaxing an extra three knots from her. Now the submarine moved at 27 knots underwater on 60 percent of the reactor's power.

Three days later the fleet commanding unit informed them that an aircraft carrier escorted by five ships had left the Mediterranean Sea and was moving at 22-knot speed into the Atlantic Ocean, but failed to say anything about the aircraft carrier's general course. The *K-181* had covered 2,000 miles by that time, and that night its sensitive instruments picked up the low-frequency sounds of the carrier's escort ships.

K-181 closed with the carrier task group, then slowed to the lowest speed. Diving low, Borisov carefully took his boat into the middle of the American formation, right between two escorting ships. The submarine moved next to the aircraft carrier, recording the roars of her turbines until morning. Then the submarine surfaced to periscope depth to observe the members of the task group and to confirm the name of the carrier. The task group consisted of the aircraft carrier *Saratoga*, the cruiser *Cleveland,* and four frigates. It was a considerable triumph to put *K-181* within killing distance of the aircraft carrier, and Borisov was happy to report his feat to the fleet headquarters.

Borisov's passive sonar could pick up the task group's activities, and he would occasionally rise to periscope depth to view the proceedings from a distance. He saw the *Saratoga* refueling the escorting ships, under cover of a smoke screen laid down by aircraft. At the end of the day, the *Saratoga,* escorted by three frigates, maneuvered south toward the Azores.

The *K-181* had to move at full speed, bypassing the Azores and avoiding U.S. territorial waters, to detect the aircraft carrier again. It took a full day to catch up with the *Saratoga,* moving into the middle of the group and masking herself with the noise of the carrier's turbines. Borisov ordered that photographs be taken of the task group at periscope depth.

Every time the submarine came shallow to periscope depth, Borisov very carefully assumed a position at the stern of the carrier so the action of the great ship's screws would mask the noise generated by his boat. He used his sonar only when the frigates' sonar was operating as well.

When the aircraft carrier passed Bermuda, the *Saratoga* participated in scheduled American naval exercises. During the day on October 21, the Soviet boat observed the carrier refueling some of the escorts. The officers on board watched as *Saratoga*'s aircraft partially obscured the scene with smoke devices, but Borisov thought nothing of it at the time. Personnel on board the *181* boat took turns photographing their mark in this submarine "sting" operation. All of their attention focused on the collection of intelligence, avoiding collisions during necessary communication with fleet command, and maintaining speed and contact. The *181* used radar and radio only when the Americans did. Otherwise Borisov kept his boat below the task group and in the wake of the great ship's screws.

The young commander did not realize it, but on the next day the Americans began to observe him as he focused on his quarry. On October 23, *K-181* appeared on the Flag Plot of the American Chief of Naval Operations. The plot provided the senior officer of the U.S. Navy with a comprehensive naval synopsis of the situation in the oceans of the world. The commander of the ASW Force Atlantic reported that SOSUS picked up the contact just after four in the afternoon on October 22. SO-SUS held the contact and the next day P-3 surveillance aircraft dropped sonobuoys and detected Borisov's boat roughly 600 miles east of Bermuda making 18 knots in the wake of the carrier.[3]

When ASW aircraft activity increased around the task group in the immediate vicinity of Bermuda, Borisov felt that wisdom dictated leaving the area. When he reported the American anti-submarine activity to fleet command, they responded with curt instructions "to stop the trail and maneuver back to base."

As it passed homeward bound through the Greenland–Iceland–United Kingdom gap, K-181 hit a net and entwined a steel hawser around the right propeller. "One-legged," the submarine had to keep moving, but now only at 16-knot speed. Despite this, it arrived at the Za-padnaya Litsa base on November 7, 1966. The weather was terrible: fog, snowdrifts, and freezing cold. With great effort the submarine moored to the pier, where the head of fleet headquarters, Vice Admiral G. Egorov, was waiting with the flotilla commanders to meet the crew. After presenting a detailed report, Borisov gave Admiral Egorov an album with photographs of the Saratoga and the escorting ships.

But Borisov had far more than photographs to report. In trailing the aircraft task groups the submarine had made nine simulated conventional torpedo attacks on the aircraft carrier, from different directions and distances, and sent twenty radiograms on the task group actions to the fleet headquarters. The K-181's expert radiomen recorded the sound of the aircraft carrier's turbines at different depths, invaluable information for another cruise.

Years later, Borisov learned that the United States had made a decision to attack any Soviet submarine that was detected submerged or surfaced in a 100-mile radius from U.S. aircraft carriers in peacetime. A North Atlantic Treaty Organization (NATO) regulation called for warning unknown submarines with small explosions to signal that it should identify itself. If he had not broken off contact when he did, the Americans would have soon instructed him with small grenade explosions to surface or face destruction. He left for home just in time.

In July 1967 Borisov was appointed as the head of the nuclear submarine Detachment 3. The experienced Captain Second Rank N. Sokolov, who in 1963 had participated in the cruise to the North Pole aboard the *K-3* as her executive officer, was appointed as commander of the *K-181*. The *K-181* was named one of the best submarines of the Northern Fleet and was awarded with the Red Flag Order on the day of the 50th birthday of the armed forces on the 23rd of February in 1968.

Borisov's colleague, Vladimir Lebedko, who ultimately rose to the rank of admiral, reflected years later on the early trials and successes of the Soviet Union's nuclear submarine fleet. He suspected that only Lewis Carroll could have written in a fantasy the parallel events that often took place off the coast of the United States while Americans went about their daily business. He remembers that:

> The submarine was equipped with a navigation and guidance system that required a long cruise along a regular route to obtain the more detailed coordinates required for missile trajectories. We considered Washington as the most probable target. During the patrol I would imagine Washington (the city was not far from us) in the evening where people were getting back home from work or going out, people were going to the theaters or concerts. Life was in its full swing and nobody even thought that there was a stealthy submarine just to the east collecting data for a missile launch. At the same time there could have been somebody trailing us, waiting for us to start moving towards our target to catch us in time. We were fighting for the right to exist, the cornerstone of the concept put forth by Charles Darwin. But his concept dealt with animals. We were human beings, conscious creatures who should be able to curb our instincts and do one's best to collaborate with each other to make people happy.
>
> Nevertheless, had I received an order to launch the missiles, no nerve or muscle of mine would have shaken and I would have done it. That was how we were brought up.[4]

The American submariners patrolling the GIUK gap and the Barents Sea would have understood and reacted in the same way if so ordered. Many of them would have also suggested that the acronym for the dominant Cold War strategic principle of mutually assured destruction, or MAD, described the situation very well.

≈   ≈   ≈

BORISOV KNEW that if the Soviet Union wished to continue operations like that conducted against *Saratoga,* they would need bases for logistical support much closer to operational areas. Gorshkov could not fulfill his ambitions close to home and, thwarted from placing a submarine base in Cuba, he actively sought suitable naval support facilities in the warmer seas of the world.

With this in mind, surface ships and submarines surveyed parts of the Atlantic Ocean in 1967 and the Indian Ocean in 1968 and 1969. These two navy-sponsored scientific expeditions explored strategic ocean areas to extend both scientific knowledge and the reach of the Soviet submarine force.

In the Atlantic Ocean the operation took the code name Priliv-1, and included the nuclear submarine *K-128,* diesel boats *B-21* and *B-36,* the submarine tender *Tobol,* the floating maintenance base *PM-93,* and the oceanographic ship *Polus.* The tankers *Lena* and *Koida* and two other vessels also participated in the expedition, for a total of ten ships manned by 1,315 men.

In addition to oceanographic research, the Russians experimented with the positioning of submarine replenishment bases at sea. These remote sites provided a location to anchor both a tender and a floating dock. Securely attached to an anchor cable, these facilities would give logistical support to Soviet submarines on extended patrols or long-range missions.

Unfortunately, during the eight months of the expedition from March through October 1967, violent storms and force ten squalls tossed the ships and crews around like so many toys. Tied up to the experimental dock anchored by cable and weights, both *B-21* and *B-36* sustained considerable damage from the waves and wind that constantly battered them against their moorings. At times, repair and replenishment work proved physically impossible and the submarines had to withdraw, keeping their distance from the tender and dock. Twenty-one times the ocean washed members of the crew overboard, only to have alert shipmates save them just in time.

In spite of these dismal circumstances, Soviet planners felt that the idea still had potential. Reality challenged their assumptions, and conditions at sea demonstrated the need for closer examination of the concept. *Polus* installed deep-water anchor barrels on the ocean bottom at roughly 4,260 feet to secure both the tender and dock, only to discover that, in spite of their great weight, the anchors and cables traveled across the ocean bottom with the strong currents.

The entire project provided quite a show for the American intelligence community. Within the range of American Lockheed P-3 Orion aircraft for 114 days, the Soviet expedition experienced 78 overflights complete with air-dropped sonobuoy surveillance. Expedition participants actually retrieved some of the buoys after the P-3's had passed.

Priliv-1 kept the submarine crews and support personnel working on remote repair and replenishment for a record time. *B-21* remained at sea for a total of 87 days and the *B-36* for 69 days. This project demonstrated the possibility of maintaining nuclear and diesel submarines at sea in southern latitudes, performing tasks such as general repair, loading torpedoes and missiles, transferring crews, and supplying the boats with fuel, water, and provisions. However, the atmospheric turbulence of the southern latitudes made this type of logistics effort a truly dangerous task.[5]

Hoping to employ lessons learned from the Atlantic experience to increase their prospect of success, the navy's oceanographic expedition Priliv-2 journeyed to the Indian Ocean in 1968 to pursue a similar scientific and logistical mission. This time the heavy-lift salvage ship *Kil-21* joined the expedition, bringing with her many of the capabilities found only in ports and shipyards. The expedition also brought rubber and other protective materials to insulate the submarine hulls from the damage sustained from banging against the floating docks.

On November 26, *Polus*, with the commanding officer of the expedition Admiral Lev Vladimirsky on board as well as the mission's senior submarine advisor, Borisov, arrived at the rendezvous north of Madagascar.

Conditions in the Indian Ocean and naval experience in that region promised the kind of success on this second mission that Mother Nature had denied on the first one. Unlike the Atlantic, the Indian Ocean provided shallow-water banks in zones of comparative meteorological calm. These natural advantages made locations such as Fortune Bank (chosen for the first installation) especially suitable for remote replenishment sites.

Few people other than oceanographers, geophysicists, and submariners realize that the ocean hides most of the taller mountains that mark the Earth's surface. Volcanic action pushed Fortune Bank up from the ocean bottom before recorded history to an altitude of approximately nine thousand feet. Over the centuries, the action of currents and waves near the surface flattened the top of this imposing peak. The weather is often moderate at Fortune Bank, while just a few miles away, in deeper water, conditions are impossible.

The submarine *K-21* installed the anchors for the remote site at Fortune Bank in early December. Six anchor barrels carrying the legend "Property of the U.S.S.R." in both Russian and English went into the ocean to serve as a firm, fixed point for the cables that would hold the floating dock and tender in place. During the installation the crews experienced waves of only twelve feet during passing storms, while ships out to sea endured much more severe conditions.

On a regular 24-hour schedule, the meteorology laboratory on board *Polus* launched instruments to measure temperature, humidity, and pressure distribution in the atmosphere. Climate data served not only to predict the weather that would affect their present work but also future submarine replenishment missions conducted at the new remote site.

In the process the laboratory staff frequently found things in the atmosphere that their instruments could not measure. American P-3 Orion surveillance aircraft regularly kept tabs on the activities of the task group at Fortune Bank, in one instance flying very low and slow to launch ten sonobuoys in a single pass. The Japanese also monitored the Soviet activity at Fortune Bank, sending their reconnaissance ship *Kai-Maru* from Shimonoseki to observe the remote site installation.

For the leadership of the Soviet Navy, the importance of this mission went beyond the immediate task of establishing a remote replenishment site at a strategic location for their submarines. *Polus*'s presence in the region provided an opportunity to show the flag, to demonstrate Soviet naval range and expertise, to provide officers with a controlled experience abroad, and to accomplish something that the Russians had not yet achieved in the Soviet era.

In February 1969, after a very successful port call to Karachi, Pakistan, Admiral Vladimirsky received an order from Moscow to pay an official port visit to Colombo, Sri Lanka, and then to return home via Valparaiso, Chile, orders that would make *Polus* the first Soviet ship to circumnavigate the Earth—above the surface! (The nuclear attack submarine *K-133* and nuclear missile submarine *K-116* had joined the rather exclusive club of those who had circumnavigated the world while submerged. The submarines were escorted by the salvage ship that had the second crew under the command of Captain Second Rank Y. Druzhinin. The ship and submarines cruised through March 26, steaming for 25,000 miles underwater without surfacing.)

Polus had logged more than 44,000 miles while completing the remote site installation at Fortune Bank, all the planned oceanographic work in the Atlantic, Indian, and Pacific Oceans, and successfully navigating Patagonia as well as the Straits of Torres and Magellan.

After visiting Tangier in Morocco, the ship refueled from a tanker and headed north. On July 16, 1969, *Polus* tied up in Leningrad as an orchestra played for them from the pier. The commander of the Leningrad naval district, Admiral Baikov, met the ship and congratulated the crew and the expedition officers.

Polus had cruised 49,927 miles in nine months. The ship worked for seven months in the tropics, passing through three oceans in the process. It was obvious that Gorshkov's navy intended to be seen and to pursue any other ships of any class or nationality, anywhere in the world.[6]

Admiral Gorshkov also intended to overcome the mechanical and engineering difficulties that had plagued the early Soviet nuclear submarines by launching several new classes of nuclear boats that would soon rival, and in some instances surpass, their American counterparts.

6

DEATH

IN THE DEPTHS

The submarine's chronometer read 0700. The aroma of the morning meal drifted through the open hatch leading to compartment number two as the cooks in the mess began their morning routine. Captain First Rank Vladimir G. Lebedko, now at the helm of *K-19*, ordered a change in depth from 120 to 180 feet while the boat maintained a 90° course at five knots. The sonar station quickly reported no contacts at the new depth, the horizon was clear.

As he moved about the control room, Lebedko reviewed his plans for the day. In roughly one hour he would put this new crew and their commander through a tough training schedule that would call for their best effort. With this in mind, he had sent the commander to his bunk three hours earlier to get some needed rest. He did not expect him back in the control room until 0800. Lebedko had prepared well and he hoped the crew and their officers had done the same. He would accept nothing short of excellence. For a brief moment he noted the activity in the galley and began thinking of his empty stomach.

Then it happened.

At 0712 on the morning of November 15, 1969, he felt a terrible dual-impact, the entire boat shook, and then *K-19* came to a complete halt, as if a giant hand had grabbed the bow and held it fast. Everything went black. He suddenly had a very strong feeling that breakfast would have to wait.[1]

As superstitious as navy personnel of all nations are, it is almost inconceivable that the *K-19* would have been rebuilt after its disastrous nuclear accident in 1961. Yet she was towed to the shipyard in Severodvinsk and there had the entire reactor room, the radiation-laden compartment six, cut out of the hull and replaced with two new reactors. The entire submarine was decontaminated (although those who sailed on her never felt at ease about this) and returned to routine service in January 1964. In December 1968, she was back at the shipyards again, this time for the conversion of her missile batteries to allow underwater launches.

Lebedko, an experienced submariner and confidant to the father of the Soviet Navy, Admiral Sergei Gorshkov, had joined the *K-19* shortly before its departure from Zapadnaya Litsa, the Soviet nuclear base near Polyarni. Although not a terribly desirable seagoing command, the boat was serving as a training and exercise platform for the new crew of *K-40* and its rather inexperienced commander, Captain Second Rank Valentin Shabanov. As a senior trainer and supervisor, Lebedko would put the *K-40* crew through their paces on board "Hiroshima." He particularly wanted to evaluate the ability of their captain to perform his duties. *K-19* left the base on November 14, 1969, en route to an exercise area not far from Kola Bay.

Lebedko had no warning of possible disaster on November 15. The sonar had not detected any landmass, guyot (a flat-topped seamount), submerged mountain, or submarine in the area. Thus, on their second

day at sea, reality suddenly confronted him with a test far more demanding and dangerous than that he had prepared for Shabanov and
his new crew.

As he felt the collision, experience took over like a reflex action. In
these situations you did not survive by careful planning but rather by
professional instinct, the ultimate tool of the experienced submariner.
Shortly after the control room illumination died, the emergency lights
came on automatically to reveal that *K-19* had a 3-degree down angle
and her depth had already increased. Lebedko immediately ordered the
central ballast tanks blown and the speed increased. If this partial alter-
ation of ballast worked to even a small degree it would demonstrate the
relative location of the object hit and whether his boat had become attached to something as a result of the collision. If the boat's speed actually increased, he could eliminate geography and topography as his
nemesis. Mountains did not move for submarines. His predeparture
briefings assured him that no other Soviet boat occupied the test area
designated for *K-19*. At sea, his sonar had revealed nothing. Therefore, if
the sub could dislodge itself, the possibility increased that it had come
hull-to-hull with the U.S. Navy.

Captain Third Rank Pervenuk quickly responded to Lebedko's orders
in the command center of *K-19*, blew the central ballast, and signaled
for an increase in the vessel's speed. The down angle had already increased to 4 degrees and the depth to 195 feet. As the compressed air
forced the ballast water out of the tanks, the boat began to rise very
slowly and its speed increased to three knots. Lebedko then realized
that his partner in the collision lay slightly below and parallel to the
bow. His boat could never have begun its ascent otherwise. With the
roles reversed, *K-19*'s opposite number would have held the Soviet boat
down with its considerable bulk. The Russian's forward motion also indicated that a moveable American submarine sat at the far end of his
severely damaged forward sonar array. He ordered a further increase in
speed, a sharp upward angle on the dive planes, and a general emergency ballast blow. As the boat began to respond, the crew felt *K-19* literally tear away from the other vessel with bone-chilling metallic
squeals. Lebedko's instruments now showed a 25-degree up angle as the
boat raced for the surface like a tiny bubble in a glass of champagne.

Roughly fifteen minutes had passed since the collision. As the boat ascended a bewildering variety of objects continued to fall aft and *K-19* kept taking water in its damaged forward compartment. Lebedko eased the angle of his ascent to 23 degrees, his speed increased to eight knots, and the boat soon broke the surface, assuming a 5-degree list to port as she settled. He brought the *K-19* crew to safety at chart position 69°32.8' north, 35°56.8' east, in the northern reaches of the Barents Sea, just south and east of Edge Island, part of the Norwegian Spitzbergen group. Years later he recalled:

> As [the submarine] slowed down, the standard lighting returned. I could see the faces of the crewmen. They were impossible to recognize: white, pale and sort of gray. I must have looked the same. I went to the bridge where Shabanov already was. I didn't see any visible damage, scanned the horizon and soon ordered the commander to move to the collision area to observe the water surface. I went below decks to compartment one; there was still some water. I must say [nervously] that there were torpedoes in all the bow torpedo tubes.
>
> At 0850 I ordered the commander to maneuver back to the base and, tired, I fell down on the sofa in the navigator's tower. I analyzed the situation and deduced that had *K-19* maneuvered backwards she would have ended up underneath the "unknown object," which would have eventually driven the submarine's bow into the seabed [at 618 feet]. I didn't want to imagine what would have happened then. If the "unknown object" didn't surface, that meant that it had sunk. I went on thinking "perhaps it wasn't a sub, otherwise we would have heard her."[2]

The commanding officer of USS *Gato* would not have agreed. Although he could only have his logical suspicions, in November 1969 Lebedko actually collided with this American Thresher class submarine, one of a series that represented the cutting edge of quiet submerged operation. Having achieved extraordinary submerged speed with USS *Skipjack* and its sisters as the 1960s began, the U.S. Navy spent the rest of that decade trying to improve in each category of the holy trinity of submarine warfare: depth, speed, and quiet operation. A variety of classified engineering and architectural advances produced USS *Thresher,* a vessel destined for a sad end in April 1963, as one of only two American nuclear submarines lost during the Cold War. In spite of the fatal accident, *Thresher* represented a leap forward in quiet submarine operation.[3] If *Gato* remained still, neutrally buoyant, or proceeded at a patrol-quiet speed, *K-19* would have had a very difficult time detecting her passively on that Arctic November morning in 1969.

Although the collision with USS *Gato* was a frightening close call for the *K-19,* it wasn't the worst accident it would experience. The real disaster came on February 24, 1972, as the *K-19* came home from yet another Atlantic patrol. A hydraulic fire erupted in compartment nine and spread rapidly through the *K-19* as it tried to surface. The commander, Captain Second Rank Viktor Kulibaba, sent out an emergency signal as soon as the submarine surfaced. Rescue appeared in the form of the missile cruiser *Vice Admiral Drozd,* which took off those of the surviving crew who could be spared. An eighteen-man party was left on board the *K-19,* along with twelve men who were trapped aft, in compartment ten. The *K-19* was taken under tow, but a vicious winter storm of almost hurricane force arose, persisting for three weeks. All that time, the dozen sailors trapped aboard the *K-19* lived in pitch-black darkness, surviving on canned food and the water that condensed on the dull steel walls of the ever-rocking hull. All twelve men, truly iron men in an iron ship, survived the exhausting ordeal. A total of twenty-eight crewmen died in this accident.

The *K-19* was patched up once again, and in 1976 was given yet another missile upgrade, only to have an explosion and fire in a reactor compartment while in port. Repaired once again, and redesignated *KS-19,* the unlucky boat did not have its next fire until 1988. This was apparently enough even for the Soviet Navy, and it was taken out of service and decommissioned in 1991. But like some black albatross of doom, the *K-19* still floats, moored to an abandoned pier in Polyarni, no doubt waiting for one more disaster.

Admiral Gorshkov reacted to the difficulties encountered with the *K-19* and other boats with typical Russian resolve. The admiral resolved to deploy his submarine force against the United States in the full knowledge that he was putting his crews at risk in boats with inherent flaws and carrying nuclear weapons that also had inherent flaws. The dangers to the environment implicit in a nuclear accident were less well known to him, and a lesser concern in any case. His biggest concern must inevitably have been a nuclear accident that might be misinterpreted as a hostile Soviet act by the United States, one that would bring retaliation. Against these worries, he balanced his concept of the national security of the Soviet Union. He must have concluded that the risk of attack from the United States was greater than the risk of a nuclear catastrophe, and therefore insisted that his nuclear submarines be deployed.

Gorshkov also spurred the development of new submarines that would better serve the three most essential elements of submarine warfare: stealth (which usually meant noise reduction), speed, and the ability to dive to great depths.

One of the most advanced of these attempts was Project 705, which NATO referred to by the code name Alfa. The Alfa was a truly remarkable boat, innovative in almost every way. It had two very powerful liquid-metal-cooled reactors, capable of generating an enormous 45,000 shp and applying it to a single propeller. The beautifully shaped hull was made of titanium, an expensive metal that is extremely difficult to work with, but of enormous strength, enabling it to dive as deep as 2,460 feet before reaching its "crush depth," that terrible depth at which a submarine hull implodes from the pressure of the overlying water.

Only 267 feet long, the Alfa could reach a speed of 45 knots submerged. Although highly maneuverable, it had one drawback—its considerable noise, which made it easily detectable by NATO forces.

Yet the Alfa represented more than a technical advance to the Russian submariners; it was an answer to the Americans whose superior anti-submarine warfare equipment and admittedly superior submarines had made the developing undersea contest seem one-sided at times.

One such submariner is Captain First Rank Boris Kolyada. Retired now, he lives in one of the cold, gray, anonymous apartment complexes that were provided for naval officers as a particular perk.

The Soviet Navy had placed its mark on Kolyada from birth. Born in Kiev on March 15, 1948, his father served as a naval officer in virtually every major base on the rim of the Soviet Union. With a command in the Black Sea Fleet at the time of his son's birth, the senior Kolyada specialized in mine warfare, a field that had produced important results against the Nazis during the Great Patriotic War. From his earliest days, Boris Kolyada knew the naval bases, saw the ships, met the officers who drove the Soviet fleet, and watched his father.

Following a family destiny that he saw as less of a responsibility than a pleasure, the young Kolyada entered Frunze Naval College in Leningrad in 1966 with the intent of becoming a mine warfare officer. At Frunze he followed a course of study that included mines, but led to a specialty in anti-submarine warfare. Although he expected assignment to a surface ship upon graduation in 1971, Kolyada's orders sent him instead to the Northern Fleet at Polyarni. He would practice ASW, but not from the surface.

Kolyada displayed early on an ability to master complex systems. Initially awed by the intricacy of the internal systems of the Foxtrot class diesel submarines and the daunting task of having to master every system to qualify in submarines, he put his mind to the task and passed his examination in less than one month. Years later he still felt that training in diesel submarines constituted the only "real" submarine school. Yet nuclear boats made other, unique demands. That dangerous technology required great care, knowledge, and discipline, but the systems did not present the young officer with the sheer complexity characteristic of a diesel boat. He finished his training at Polyarni in August 1971 and went to sea the following April.

His first experience gave Kolyada a taste of the complete Cold War menu. He formed part of a Foxtrot crew joining a small fleet of submarines and surface ships en route to the Mediterranean Sea. Commanded by Captain First Rank Lev Chernavin, this group consisted of ten submarines, including eight Foxtrot diesels and two Juliett class missile boats. Chernavin took these boats south both for training and for the vital face-to-face contact with NATO that would make more proficient submariners of the men on board. The new Russian support base and training center in Alexandria, Egypt, would provide a remote home, an opportunity for any required repair or upgrade, and tactical instruction in one of the most intense areas in the world for the submerged game of cat and mouse: the Mediterranean. The British Royal Navy and the American Sixth Fleet awaited their arrival.

Kolyada did not have to pass Gibraltar before witnessing the welcome the British and Americans had in store. The latter had observed their passage earlier through the Norwegian Sea with Lockheed P-2V Neptune surveillance aircraft. As the Chernavin group passed the coast of northern Spain, the Royal Navy took over, surveying their movements with Nimrod surveillance jets. In years past, NATO had not witnessed Russian submarines moving into the Mediterranean in these numbers. Now the Russian submarine force had come to stay, and training in this environment would both enhance their ability and demonstrate their shortcomings. Admiral Gorshkov wanted to show them off and educate them at the same time.

Kolyada spent the next eight months learning his craft in the sea once dominated by truly ancient mariners like the Phoenicians and Carthaginians. Conventional training could not beat this experience. While Soviet forces still lagged behind the United States in submarine capability and ASW technology, for the new officers on board Chernavin's school of boats, this kind of experience proved priceless. In some cases, it took the Soviet boats the best part of two days to evade, even for a short time, the American and British forces hunting them. Other times during the eight-month deployment, NATO forces forced one of the Soviet boats to surface or caught them already on the surface during a battery recharge. In any case, the experience helped the officers and crews grow as professionals. Every experience proved important, right down to wearing the new white cotton uniforms in the warm climate and enduring Foxtrots not yet equipped with air conditioning.[4]

For the most part, U.S. naval assets became the targets of Soviet tactical exercises, especially the carriers and American submarines. While a noisy Foxtrot would have a hard time trailing an American Thresher[5] or Sturgeon[6] class submarine, reaching for the prize would and did improve their skills.

In his eight months on the job in the Mediterranean, Kolyada demonstrated a level of technical competence that pleased his superiors. Upon promotion to senior lieutenant in 1977 he seemed a likely candidate for executive officer on board a diesel destined for combat patrol, but instead he received orders to proceed to the Kronstadt Naval Base on the Gulf of Finland to join the crew of a nuclear boat—an Alfa— still under construction farther north at the Sudomekh Shipyard. Kolyada moved his wife and daughter from Polyarni to Leningrad, and proceeded to Kronstadt to see what the Soviet Navy had for him there.

The boat he saw being built at the shipyard immediately aroused his interest, for it was like nothing he had ever seen. The titanium hull had a cigarlike appearance, with the sail sleekly faired into the hull surface to reduce hydrodynamic resistance at speed. The vessel looked like a work of art, a sculpture, rather than the product of a shipyard.

When he joined the rest of the crew to undergo nuclear training he realized that the submarine's company numbered only thirty-one, including himself; less than half the normal complement. While this alone seemed extraordinary, the absence of the regular enlisted ratings made the circumstances even more peculiar. He sat in nuclear propulsion class and worked in practical settings with thirty commissioned and warrant officers. This amazing submarine would carry no more. Each and every member of the crew had a commission, a college degree in a technical field, or its equivalent in technical training. The cutting edge engineering, the level of automation, and the widespread application of advanced computer technology warmed his technical heart. As he recalled years later, "I felt as if I had just discarded my tractor and boarded a spaceship."

He had a great deal to learn. Senior Lieutenant Kolyada was responsible for the entire weapons suite—on an American submarine, he would have had the nickname "Weps." All of the men assigned to caring for and launching the weapons would respond to his instructions. Compared to his experience on diesel boats, the Alfa seemed completely empty, the passageways oddly vacant, lacking the familiar congestion. As weapons officer, he would check the automated systems, do his rounds to certify all of the automated controls, and then return to the central command station from which he and the other officers would respond to the commander's instructions while at sea.

The Alfa's performance amazed him; it could dive very quickly to nearly 3,000 feet and accelerate from 6 to 42 knots in two minutes. The Alfa could move faster and dive deeper than almost any other submarine.[7]

Kolyada and the thirty other crewmembers worked with the vessel and the shipyard for a full year before taking her out for a shakedown and trials in the White Sea in December of 1978. Even though it was still in need of some repairs and the resolution of technical problems, the commander nonetheless formally accepted the boat on Christmas Day. The shipyard workers needed their money and the state authorities would not pay until the navy took responsibility for the submarine. This was one of the major faults in the Soviet system, a rigid adherence to bureaucratic procedure rather than focusing on the needs of the weapon system. In the Soviet Union, the consequences of December 31 production deadlines often assumed terrible forms, sending many of the early Soviet nuclear boats to sea with defects. Taking over an Alfa still in need of some refinement demonstrated to the commander and crew that they had to live with bureaucratically imposed risks.

After a relatively successful shakedown run, Kolyada took over the weapons division on board as the boat headed for its operational base, arriving at the nuclear attack submarine base at Zapadnaya Litsa in the Bolshaya Litsa Fjord on December 31, 1978. Kolyada had free rein of the weapons system, and his ASW specialty training at Frunze soon made him an expert at submerged detection of other submarines.

Submerged and still, or moving at a reduced, patrol-quiet speed of roughly six knots, the sophisticated sonars carried by Soviet Alfa class and American Los Angeles[8] class attack submarines were not troubled by surface turbulence or significant radiated self-noise. A submarine hunting another submarine would use sonar to target an enemy, and then attack with wire-guided torpedoes capable of 50 knots and armed with both active and passive acoustic sensors. In the 1950s, Russian designers conceived the submarine that eventually became the Alfa with this ASW function in mind. The vessel might serve many purposes, employing torpedoes or SS-N-15 missiles to subdue its targets, but its designers primarily intended it for submarine hunting. Kolyada could not have asked for a better assignment. As he pointed out:

It was much more interesting to be on patrol with this submarine. Detection . . . that was my "hobby"; how to get at them, how to find them. There were many nuances for the commander to eval-uate, many parameters to consider: water, ice, weather condi-tions, hydro-acoustics. So many elements had to be integrated to arrive at an accurate detection.[9]

Boris Kolyada served on three different Alfas on his way from Cap-tain-Lieutenant to Captain First Rank. By the time he accepted com-mand of his own boat, he had an appreciation of what it took to lead and wage war under the sea. When he began his tour as executive offi-cer, and soon afterward as a commander, Kolyada recalled having trou-ble sleeping, knowing that the crew's welfare and the success of the boat rested on his shoulders. Captain First Rank Baranov went to sea with him soon after Kolyada first received command of an Alfa from his superiors in the Northern Fleet. Fortunately, Kolyada could talk to Baranov, who came along to guide him. He could discuss with this expe-rienced officer the problems and demands of command and find posi-tive reinforcement during a challenging time of transition. All of this took place in one of the most technologically intense environments possible and with the knowledge that as they hunted, so the American adversary hunted them.

As it was for so many of his Russian and American colleagues, the hunt was the most exciting thing in his life. All of the factors—acoustics, ocean bathymetry, navigation, torpedo capability, sonar information, the readiness of the crew, and the challenge of both evading and detect-ing American Los Angeles class submarines—had to be integrated in his mind and translated into decisive action. In the Cold War–simulated combats, both sides knew that their adversary would probably not launch his weapons; but after the encounter both sides knew which of them had won.

Occasionally Kolyada would discover a Los Angeles class boat on his tail. They usually made no secret about their approach, falling in behind him to see how Kolyada would evade. After a short joust, which would frequently bring both submarines disturbingly close to each other,

Kolyada would accelerate and go deep. His titanium submarine, capable of diving to 3,000 feet, could ultimately go where only American sonar or SOSUS could follow. If he slowed to a patrol-quiet six knots or less at great depth, finding him could well prove impossible. For a Soviet submariner, part of a community so long in the shadow of the American submarine force, the Alfa brought them near equality and technical superiority. No wonder Gorshkov loved them so, cherished their highly trained crews, and spent so much money building them that they became known as the "golden fish."

At first sight it would seem natural to conclude that this submarine had truly emerged from a science fiction thriller with all of the antiseptic and alien qualities commonly thought to characterize the unearthly. Looking at the faces of the people who served on these unique boats would change that impression immediately. Kolyada and his fellow officers, like many of their American adversaries during those years, discovered that the emotional, physical, and intellectual effects of the technology and the performance flexibility it promised came on them in a rush, like a shot of adrenaline, and constituted the second best physical thrill in a man's existence. They could perform in amazing ways, not overtly and loudly, with public display, like their colleagues in aviation, but silently, blindly, and with subtlety, deep in the submariner's natural environment.

Decades later, in his study in St. Petersburg with a professionally rendered model of his Alfa in hand, Kolyada mentioned that as a commander of one of these vessels he could dive very quietly to nearly 3,000 feet and accelerate from 6 to 42 knots in two minutes. Just recalling these details made his eyes widen and a sudden, subtle smile appear on his face; he resembled a satisfied gambler looking at his adversaries across both a rich pot and a winning hand. The great game did not get any better than this. The Alfa made an ace look weak. It came very close to fulfilling completely the holy trinity of submarine warfare. In an Alfa, Kolyada and his shipmates could move faster, dive deeper, and do it more silently than almost any submarine on the planet. Holding the model in his hand, with his memories and imagination deep in the Cold War North Atlantic, it quickly became apparent that he loved his country, adored his wife, *but this was his boat.* An American "sub driver" would understand.

TRAGEDY STRIKES AGAIN

While Kolyada was pushing the envelope of submarine performance with his Alfa, tragedy stalked other boats in the relentless activity of the Cold War. The *K-429* was a Project 670 "Skat" boat, termed Charlie class by NATO. A relatively small boat, the Charlie class was designed for mass production at relatively low cost. It was the first Soviet boat with the capability to fire anti-ship missiles while still submerged. *K-429* proved to be a particularly unfortunate Charlie, for it sank in Sarannaya Bay, bordering the Bering Sea, on June 23, 1983. The entire crew was lost. In an unusual move, the Soviet Navy salvaged the *K-429* and returned it to service. But, perhaps as cursed as the *K-19* or the *K-8,* the *K-429* sank at the pier at its home base on September 13, 1983, killing sixteen crewmembers. The *K-429*'s captain was imprisoned as a result of this accident, but the submarine went on to yet another career: Raised a second time, she was leased to India, where she served till 1991 as the *Chakra.*

A much more dramatic sinking occurred on October 6, 1986, when the Yankee class *K-219* sank in the Atlantic, 680 miles northeast of Bermuda. Its story is told at length in *Hostile Waters*[10] and reveals not only the heroism of the submarine's officers and crew, but also the brutal disregard for human life by the Soviet naval bureaucracy.

The well-respected Captain Igor Britanov commanded the *K-219.* He was all too aware of the dangers implicit in any Soviet nuclear submarine, particularly one as old as the *K-219,* and especially one carrying the dangerous liquid-fueled RSM-25 missiles. Two liquid fuels, nitrogen tetroxide and hydrazine, normally propelled the weapon. They would explode on contact with each other when introduced into the rocket engine. Nitrogen tetroxide proved the greatest hazard because it could also explode on contact with ordinary seawater. In an old Soviet submarine, some 300 feet beneath the surface, bending and flexing to the pressure of the water and the drive of the steam turbines, seawater was not an unusual visitor.

K-219 had already experienced an extremely dangerous incident on an earlier patrol. One of the sixteen missile silos had experienced a leak of nitrogen tetroxide, seawater had intruded, and an explosion had ripped the tube open, killing a sailor and allowing water to flood in. Only decisive action on the part of the captain had saved the *K-219*, and after repairs it sailed again with the defective missile silo welded shut.

On October 3, 1986, while engaged in the routine but always deadly excitement of dueling with an American submarine, the USS *Augusta*, seawater intruded into missile silo six, and the RSM-25 missile suddenly became more dangerous to the *K-219* than the American cities upon which it was targeted. Toxic gas began to fill the area around the silo.

Britanov attempted to prevent the explosion by venting the silo to the sea, but a massive explosion rocked the *K-219* and sent it plunging toward the ocean's bottom, water roaring in through the ruptured hull. By pouring on full power and blowing all his tanks, Britanov reversed the process, sending the *K-219* bounding to the surface in a colossal spray. The boat shuddered, rolled, then began to bob softly, safe from the crushing power of the depths, but still vulnerable to the fire, toxic gas, and flooding that now imperiled it and, Britanov knew, could interrupt the cooling of one or both of the reactors, sending them out of control.

After radioing his emergency message to the Northern Fleet, Britanov took stock. Three men were dead, and more were threatened from the deadly gases that roiled through the ship, spreading from compartment to compartment. As he calculated his next move, the reactor overheat alarm went off—the worst possible sound at the worst possible time.

Sheer bravery on the part of seaman Sergei Preminin, a member of the reactor team, saved the ship and the world from a nuclear explosion. Preminin secured the reactors, but, weakened by the gases and the effort, was unable to remove the exit hatch and leave. He died at his post, aware that he was giving his life for his comrades.

The reactors were shut down, but there was no stopping the poisonous gas filling the ship, and the captain finally had to order everyone to evacuate the boat, sealing the compartments behind them as they left.

Help was supposedly on the way; a freighter, the *Fyodor Bredkin*, was due to arrive in less than an hour's time. Evacuation meant one thing: lining up on the *K-219*'s rolling deck, already hot as a frying pan from the fires raging below, and trying to keep those already prostrate from gas poisoning and placed in stretchers from being washed overboard.

When the *Fyodor Bredkin* arrived, the sick and injured men were taken aboard first, followed by the majority of the *K-219*'s crew. Britanov and a few others remained behind as the *Fyodor Bredkin* began an agonizing and ultimately futile effort to take it under tow. Tortured by the fire, the *K-219* took on more and more water until it slipped beneath the surface on October 6; Captain Britanov, clutching the Soviet flag, was rescued just before the unlucky boat started its 18,000-foot plunge to the ocean floor.

Britanov was of course charged with crimes against the state; he was found guilty, but before sentencing was pronounced, the charges were dropped by Mikhail Gorbachev.

Despite the sad catalog of bureaucratic failure that the *K-219* represented, work on developing newer and better submarines continued.

≈   ≈   ≈

THE ALFA AND THE SIERRA[11] types demonstrated the importance of speed and deep diving. The Soviet Navy of the 1980s wanted to develop these vessels further, generating more numbers with even greater weapons and detection capability. The Mike class became the next step in this effort. The design went into production in 1978 and joined the fleet in December 1984. These new boats, 354 feet long and 34.5 feet wide, displaced 8,500 tons when submerged, and could dive to 3,200 feet.

In 1984, the first units of the Mike class joined an ASW squadron of the Northern Fleet consisting mostly of Alfas and Sierras. Originally conceived as a test platform for detection systems of greater range, more potent weapons, and extended operations at maximum depth, Mike failed to meet expectations. The detection capability fell far short of the promised range, and the policy of Perestroika dramatically reduced funding for advanced systems. The navy altered the vessels for multipurpose work, accepted their shortcomings, and sent them to sea.

By that time, Boris Kolyada had completed his command tour on board an Alfa and, as a Captain First Rank, assumed control of a Northern Fleet attack submarine squadron. In January 1989, Rear Admiral Fhkiryatov assigned him to the Mike class submarine *Komsomolets, K-278,* as the senior commander. The boat's new commanding officer was Captain Second Rank Evgeni Vanin, a veteran of five years commanding submarines. The former Alfa commander would now instruct Vanin in much the same way that Baranov had taken him in hand years earlier. Vanin worked at the base for months to properly train his crew, but Kolyada was forced to report that they had not yet achieved the desired level of performance. Yet Kolyada knew that Vanin was effective, firm with the crew but not capricious, tactful, assertive, hardworking, and capable of prompt decisions under stress. All he and his crew needed was some practical experience with *K-278* to bring them together as a cohesive unit. *K-278* sortied on February 28, 1989, expecting to return on May 30.

Kolyada would make it back to base; Vanin would not.

Komsomolets's orders took her to sea for three months to hunt for American surface ships and submarines. Her captain and crew remained on alert and on call around the clock. Ignoring none of the targets detected by his sonar, Vanin ran torpedo drills on every detected vessel. A fishing ship in the Norwegian Sea became the first object to provide training for the crew on this outing. During these practice sessions, the crew would plot the target's course and speed, choose the weapons and the best attack solution, and then the computer would feed the proper information to the fire control system. These practice drills would not require the captain or crew to arm the weapons or perform any elaborate technical preparations. Running drills with the fishing boat as the target, the *278* lingered in the vicinity of Bear Island, not far from North Cape. Norwegian submarines and ASW aircraft infested the entire area.

Its deployment orders sent *Komsomolets* right into the middle of a NATO exercise in the Norwegian Sea called "Northern Wedding." The Russians did not appreciate the presence of American carrier battle groups that far north, so *278* joined an advanced attack force tasked with catching the carrier USS *America* as she carefully approached West-Fjord on the Norwegian coast at 68° north latitude.

Given the roles assigned to American submarines providing ASW protection during the exercise, the encounter quickly became exciting. As *Komsomolets* approached the Americans, Vanin's sonar picked up a submerged American target. He quietly slid in behind the contact, hoping to trail the American as long as possible. Unfortunately, the effort backfired. The American skipper quickly detected *278* and each commander tried to take up station behind the other, both to hide in the noise of his opponent's screws and to assume the best torpedo-firing position. Kolyada recalled that the encounter "became a dogfight lasting some minutes, reminiscent of three-dimensional aerial combat during the Great War."

Vanin reported the detection as well as the deep dogfight to Northern Fleet headquarters. He included sonar confirmation of the target as a Los Angeles class submarine. Vanin ordered the crew to battle stations and initiated preparation for torpedo attack. All of this, including the frantic submerged maneuvering, took too much time. The American's proximity and aggressiveness did not permit an easy or safe firing solution and the possibility of an accident or an incident grew with every minute. After ninety minutes of submerged dancing, Vanin chose to break off the contact and resume his progress south.

The very next day another Los Angeles class boat showed itself. Evidently laying in wait for the approaching *K-278*, the American accelerated and deliberately moved into a position that permitted its detection. Each submarine maneuvered to assume the desired trailing position, with the American moving, by increments, dangerously close to *Komsomolets*. Commander Vanin did not care for the dangerous jousting and, on Kolyada's advice, went deep to 2,100 feet, where the *K-278* could stand the crushing ocean pressure—and the American could not. The Los Angeles–type submarine remained directly above Vanin for a time, keeping track of *K-278* by sonar. Wanting to keep to the schedule and tasks in his orders, Vanin "kissed the American goodbye with a torpedo drill simulating an attack" and then went on his way south, remaining at depth as he left the scene.[12]

Kolyada concluded that the occasional high-speed bursts employed by Vanin to evade gave hostile sonar a good target. The surface groups involved in "Northern Wedding" brought with them a full complement of ASW forces armed with the best detection and attack technology available. Vanin proceeded to follow his orders, which took him away from the site of his dogfight to a region just north of the Shetland Islands. His superiors wanted him to linger in that location to confirm the presence of an American aircraft carrier. With the density of opposing forces and the sheer numbers of submarines in that portion of the GIUK gap, the situation grew more dangerous by the hour.

The move gave them a short respite from submarine detection, only to have another threat emerge. The sonar supervisor reported intense active sonar signals from surface vessels close aboard. In the control room, Vanin consulted first with his executive officer Oleg Avanesov and then his navigator Michael Smirnoff. Studying the charts, they chose a new course for the boat just in time. The active sonar "pings" grew even stronger, requiring the *Komsomolets* to evade. When the signals again began to increase in strength three hours later, Vanin estimated the distance to the surface vessels and, satisfied with the margin of safety, decided to take a look. He came shallow and broke the surface with his periscope to more precisely determine his location and to record the radio signals of the pursuing ship. His crew went to battle stations in response to the general alarm and Vanin placed his pursuer in the periscope crosshairs. Increased magnification revealed the persistent American as one of the U.S. Navy's Stalwart class. Vanin realized that this specialized vessel carried the U.S. Navy's most advanced, surface-deployed, towed array sonar, called SURTASS. Vanin ordered a dive to evade.

Komsomolets remained on patrol, following an ever-expanding circular search for American submarines operating in the approaches to Soviet home waters. Then Vanin received an ominous message: A Soviet diesel submarine had experienced a fire costing one of the crew his life. Vanin ordered a complete inspection of all electrical systems. The next day, April 5, the propulsion officer, Captain Second Rank Valentin Babenko, reported the inspection complete and everything in order.

Despite this, the patrol took a quick and fatal turn. On April 7,

Komsomolets began the thirty-eighth day of its deployment, proceeding on course, 74 miles west of Jan Mayen Island in the Norwegian Sea at a depth of roughly 1,100 feet. The sonar reported no contacts, the horizon was clear.

At 1103 engineer Captain Third Rank Vyacheslav Udin yelled "Alarm!" through the control room loudspeaker. Fire had broken out in a compartment where there was no crewman stationed. Vanin saw that the indicator lights showed that the temperature in compartment seven was higher than 150°F. Pulled out of a sound sleep by the staccato noise of the alarm, Kolyada slid out of his rack, pulled on his pants, and struggled to put on his jacket and respiratory mask as he ran to the control room. The entire boat knew the danger posed by an on-board fire while submerged, and the crew immediately went to their assigned stations.

In the control room, Vanin and his propulsion officer, Captain Second Rank Valentin Babenko, listened to senior seaman Nadari Bukhnikashvili report over the internal communication circuits on the situation in compartment seven, only to have his transmission cut short.

Kolyada just then entered the control room and immediately asked, "Are there any men still in that compartment?"

Babenko replied, "Senior seaman Bukhnikashvili, but I can't raise him on the communications link."

Kolyada and Vanin realized that the fire-extinguishing system in compartment seven would kill Bukhnikashvili. Tragically, his time and breathable air had run out. They could not communicate with him and they knew that he understood the measures open to them. Only seconds remained, if that.

Kolyada ordered Vanin, "Commander, supply extinguishing foam to compartment seven."

Vanin immediately complied, calling for extinguishing foam to compartment seven and an ascent to 120 feet.

Babenko now ordered Warrant Officer Vladimir Kolotilin to compartment six to see if he needed to activate the extinguishing system in that compartment to contain the situation.

The control room panel for compartment seven lit up, indicating entry of chlorofluorocarbons (CFCs) into that space to fight the fire. At

1109 Kolotilin reported from outside compartment six, "CFCs vented to compartment seven; I sealed hatch. Some smoke leaked from the hatch seal, but I effected repairs."

The growing feeling that the situation had come under control suddenly evaporated in a volatile and fatal mist. Given his location, Kolotilin might have seen the lubricating oil spraying out of a ruptured line in his compartment, but he would have had no time to take any action. The aerosol fuel, momentarily suspended in the air as a heavy vapor, ignited and instantly killed him in a blinding sheet of flame. Then all communication with the stern compartments and the submarine's loudspeakers went dead.

Men from compartment five moved forward and reported on a fire in their spaces over one of the emergency phones. The pressure from the fires in compartments six and seven kept growing, driving the disaster through the boat.

Valentin Babenko, *278's* propulsion officer, ordered the right turbogenerator stopped just as the left one stopped itself. Given the situation, the reactor immediately shut down and the rising *Komsomolets* lost all forward momentum at a depth of 480 feet. The helm stopped responding at roughly the same time. The control room indicator panels lit up with countless short circuits throughout the boat.

Dead in the water at 480 feet, without forward momentum to maintain trim and lacking the most basic attitude control, *Komsomolets* began a slow descent. Vanin ordered, "Blow the middle tanks!"

The reactor officer quickly turned the proper key on the panel, and high-pressure air surged into the main tanks, expelling the ballast. *K-278* stopped its descent and slowly began to rise, breaking the surface at 1116. The weather was abysmal, with snow-filled winds of more than 100 miles per hour from the north, the vicious sea raging, and the temperature at four degrees below zero.

As watch officer on the bridge, Captain-Lieutenant Alexander Verezgov reported the surface conditions to Vanin and observed that the heat had peeled off the acoustic tiles covering the boat in the vicinity of compartments five, six, and seven. The superheated after sections of the boat boiled the water around them.

At 1121, only eighteen minutes after the alarm, the fire moved into compartment four and the primary reactor cooling pump began sparking and smoldering. Further forward, smoke began seeping out of the helmsman's control panel in the central control room and the entire space began to fill with smoke. By 1127 the officers and crew in the control room had to use extinguishers to keep the fire under control in their spaces, wearing respirators to breathe.

Tragically, the system of breathable-air pipes that supplied the portable respirators began to kill rather than save. A fire in a contained space can quickly consume the air and generate dark, thick, and deadly smoke. In each crewman's fire kit was a face mask with both an air-filtering unit and a small breathable-air source. The *K-278* had pipe-mounted ports on the ceiling of each compartment into which a sailor can briefly plug a hose attached to his mask for a quick series of breaths before detaching and moving on to escape. But in the *K-278* fire, the pipelines became filled with smoke under intense pressure, and breathing through the mask was a death sentence.

At 1140 Captain Vanin sent a distress signal to Northern Fleet command. By that point, the diesel generator had stopped and the cooling system failed, but fortunately the nuclear plant was already shut down.

At 1158 Vanin ordered, "Everyone who is able, please communicate with the control room." He needed to know who remained alive and the extent of his ability to communicate through the smoldering submarine. Less than an hour had passed since the alarm.

By noon, the situation seemed nearly impossible as the emergency breathing system now fed the fire with air, driving the temperature in the stern compartments to as high as 1,832°F.

Vanin decided to begin moving aft as soon as possible. He ordered propulsion officer Babenko to prepare a rescue party to open compartment four, to check on the reactor.

Captain Third Rank Udin and Lieutenant Anatoli Tretyakov entered the compartment first. Their flashlights could barely pierce the black smoke. In the sealed room above the reactor, they found Lieutenant Andrew Makhota and Warrant Officer Michael Valyavin barely able to breathe; working quickly, they carried the two half-conscious officers to the control room in compartment three. Babenko and his rescue party began ventilating the compartment in an effort to reach compartment five. Outside the submarine, smoke rose above the sail as the ventilators forced fresh air into compartment four.

Udin led the rescue party into compartment five, nearly tripping over men lying on the floor. Captain-Lieutenant Sergey Dvorov managed to rise to his feet. Others followed, despite having most of their clothes and hair burned off. Burned skin hung like rags from their scorched limbs and the expression on their faces revealed their extreme pain.

Babenko's team evacuated first those who could still walk. They all went to the bridge, where the medical officer Doctor Leonid Zayats awaited them. Dvorov and Valyavin then put on their respirators, went further into the compartment, and carried the unconscious bodies of Warrant Officer Sergey Bondar and Seaman Vladimir Kulapin through a maze of wires and pipelines to medical assistance. Doctor Zayats began treating them on the bridge. When they arrived neither man showed any sign of life and the best efforts of the doctor and his assistant could not revive them. An entry in the boat's log noted: "Bondar and Kulapin died; confirmed by doctor." Two others were already dead.

Working in shifts, rescue teams labored constantly in compartments four and five assisted by a recently repaired diesel generator and cooling system. In addition, Captain-Lieutenant Igor Orlov managed to completely secure the reactor, rendering it entirely safe and sparing the crew any chance of radiation exposure. After several hours of leading the firefighting effort in compartment five, Sergey Dvorov fainted from fatigue, heat, and smoke. After the doctor revived him, Dvorov headed right back to the fire only to find Vyacheslav Udin standing in his way. Udin ordered the exhausted officer up the escape trunk to the sail bridge to get some fresh air into his lungs.

As the quality of the air in compartment five improved, Valentin Babenko asked his commanding officer for permission to open compartment six. At 1346 Vanin gave the order and the propulsion officer sent two teams into the compartment. Before entering, Babenko used the pumps to move water out of the spaces, enabling them to open the hatch. Shortly thereafter, they walked into a wall of fire.

≈   ≈   ≈

A SOVIET IL-38 AIRCRAFT passed over the bridge at 1420, the first sign of possible assistance. The entire Soviet submarine force rescue fleet sortied as soon as Vanin's distress call arrived, but Major Gennadi Petrogradskikh and his aircrew flew over the crippled submarine first. His orders obliged him to search for the boat near Bear Island, contact its crew, and report Vanin's estimate of the situation and his rescue needs.

Petrogradskikh left his base at 1243 and less than two hours later sighted the *278*. Vanin replied to the pilot's questions and asserted that the crew could control the fire. The pilot, receiving no particular requests, left briefly to lead the rescue ships to *278*'s position. As the *Il-38* flew past *Komsomolets* at 1440, the pilot and crew saw the water next to the hull aft of the sail boiling and foaming, as well as light smoke coming from the bridge hatch.

At Kolyada's suggestion, Vanin ordered his officers to collect all essential documents including the ship's log. He also told the engineer Babenko to compose a report on the submarine's condition as a basis for further planning. When he finished his evaluation, the engineer informed his commander that, "Due to the fire, compartments seven and six are no longer water-tight. They will fill with water and it is possible that the submarine will sink." He knew that he had understated the situation. At the current rate of flooding, the *278* might remain on the surface for two days or, in a worst case scenario, for a day and a half. He knew that if the Northern Fleet did not act, they would all be dead by 0300 on April 9.

Vanin thanked his engineer and assumed the worst case situation. He and Kolyada planned for the arrival of the rescue team and with them the additional fire-fighting chemicals that would quench the blaze in compartments six and seven. They would then authorize a small contingent from the crew to stay behind to manage the towing from on board *278*. The rest of the crew would evacuate to the rescue ships. As they consulted, the bulkhead temperature between compartments five and six rose to roughly 196°F and fires continued in compartments six and seven.

At 1645 the sub's hull shook under the force of three detonations in quick succession. Warrant Officer Kadantsev returned to the bridge from compartment five to report that explosions took place behind the compartment five bulkhead. Then another explosion rocked the ship. The rubber acoustic hull coating fell off the stern section of the boat completely and floated next to the vessel in a huge sheet. *Komsomolets* also took on a more profound list to starboard and began sinking by the stern. Vanin ordered adjustment of the stern ballast to keep the boat afloat, but the control panel did not respond. Either the power had failed or the compressed air flasks, among other things in the compartment five bulkhead, accounted for the explosions.[13] In any case, *278* was sinking much faster than Babenko had estimated. Kolyada now stepped in and ordered the entire crew topside. He shouted to Vanin, "Order everyone to the upper decks and set the life-boats."

Kolyada knew the boat could not survive the explosions. He looked at Vanin and ordered, "Evgeni Alekseevich, it is time, let's go."

"Boris Grigorievich, you go," Vanin replied, "I want to make sure that everyone has left the boat, and then I'll go as well."

The vessel's stern began to sink, lifting the bow up out of the water. Kolyada later recalled the bow and the forward dive planes rising above the horizon: "It was the first time in my life I saw such a sight." The crew struggled to remain on the deck and wrestled with rusted brass couplings and washers that made opening the life raft containers nearly impossible. Kolyada instructed Warrant Officer Semyon Grigoryan to extract the rafts from their containers through the upper lid alone. It took three men to pull the huge inflatable raft out of its container through the small opening. Finally successful, and with the *278* shifting under their feet, they threw the raft onto the water surface only to watch it inflate and immediately turn keel up in the turbulent water. Terrific wind and waves tossed the raft over the bow to the starboard side, with its keel still pointing toward an unfriendly sky.

Warrant Officer Grigoryan tried to catch the raft just as the water approached the sail hatch. Kolyada left the boat for the raft as the water reached him. He did not need to jump into the sea, for the ocean lifted him off the sinking deck and he tried to swim. Warrant Officer Kopeika locked the conning tower hatch with his foot to avoid quicker flooding in accordance with Babenko's orders. Kolyada remembers that as the last act he witnessed on board *Komsomolets*. The next moment, he and most of the crew turned their attention to surviving in the icy water.

Kolyada later commented that,

> Strangely enough the water didn't shock me with its cold tempera-
> ture. I'm not sure whether my body expected the water to be cold
> or the wind cooled my body so that it was even warmer in the wa-
> ter, but I didn't feel cold at all. However, the waves kept stopping
> me. I also wasn't getting enough air. More often than not I would
> inhale water with air. Some of the men had already turned the raft
> over and it wasn't far from the submarine so I quickly reached for
> it. I grabbed the rubber edge only to discover that I did not have
> the strength to pull myself in. Talant Burkulakov was already in
> the boat so he helped me. Then Warrant Officer Grigoryan got into
> the boat. Other submariners swam next to the raft holding its
> edges. Just then I turned round and saw the submarine standing
> almost vertically and slowly sinking. In a few moments the waves
> calmly closed above her. It was 1708.[14]

All of those in and around the raft tried to help others struggling to reach safety. Kolyada knew that the rescue ships could not arrive until 1800 and that the raft could not accommodate all of the survivors. Men rode in the raft while others surrounded it, grabbing the sides, knowing that many would not last until the rescue fleet arrived.

Major Petrogradskikh and his Il-38 stayed with them the entire time but could render only minor assistance. At the same time a Norwegian patrol aircraft appeared and occasionally interfered with the major's attempts to accurately drop some survival gear containers. Some of those still in the water also experienced a very powerful explosion just under them from the ocean depths, probably the detonation of the *278*'s tor-pedoes.[15]

The snow and freezing spray combined with the force of the waves to destroy hope, energy, and life. For some, death was insidious, coming over them gradually and rendering them slowly helpless. Kolyada re-marked on it as an experience he would like to forget, but cannot.

I have read about people freezing in snow and ice. When I was aboard the raft I went through it myself. First I didn't feel my fingers and hands, then the numbness extended down my arms to my elbows and from my feet to my ankles. Things were getting worse every minute. My head was getting heavy, waves rocked me, I felt queasy, my eyes were closing although I didn't want them to; gradually indifference was overwhelming me. The men on board first tried to make jokes, then they sang the Varyag Song but everyone was near exhaustion. The waves would pass over the boat and each time washed someone away. I thought that I must keep moving, otherwise I could freeze. I turned back and saw Talant Burkulakov reclining, he felt really bad. I was slowly falling asleep. Suddenly Lieutenant Fedotkin shouted that he saw a ship and kept shouting to let everyone know. He aroused everyone, giving them new strength.[16]

The fishing trawler *Aleksey Khlobistov* served numerous smaller fishing boats as a floating base and processing facility near the site of the *Komsomolets* disaster. At 1315 she ceased operation to respond to Vanin's distress call. The captain hauled in his lines, pulled up his sea anchor, and ordered his engineer to make turns for 14 knots. His navigator had already plotted the course to intercept. Once the *Khlobistov* came within striking distance, the rescue aircraft led him to the site of the sinking submarine and the life rafts floating in the ocean loaded with desperate men. The captain quickly made the following entries in his log:

1500. Found two rafts (one of them had men aboard) in a four mile path along the prescribed course.

1520. Crew launched the motorboats. There was a raft with two men (one of them had life-jacket on) floating next to it off the beam, 0.3 nautical miles from the *Aleksey Khlobistov*. There were two rafts in all, one of them had men aboard, approximately 0.3 nautical miles away. At 6:35 the motor boats cruised from this ship to rescue the men.

An orange motor boat approached the *278*'s life rafts and took the survivors on board. Kolyada was near death, having used every spare ounce of energy to stay in the raft. Yet the tragedy was still unfolding.

≈   ≈   ≈

Komsomolets took six men down with her. These included Vanin, Udin, propulsion engineer Captain Third Rank Anatoli Ispenkov, and warrant officers Alexander Krasnobaev, Sergey Chernikov, and Victor Slusarenko.

When the submarine vanished from the surface, Vanin, Udin, Krasnobaev, Chernikov, and Slusarenko knew where to go. Her designers had equipped each Mike boat with a capsule that would permit men to escape if the vessel could not rise to the surface. These five tried to escape in the capsule. Their shipmate Ispenkov went far below decks as the *278* sank, trying to supply some power to the boat by keeping the diesel generator on line. When that proved fruitless, he could not get back to the upper decks and died at his post.

The bad luck followed them as the boat plunged to the ocean depths. Bulkheads began to collapse and internal systems came loose from their mountings as the *278* picked up speed in her death descent. Amid the shrieking noise and mounting fear, Warrant Officer Chernikov read the instructions on the use of the chamber out loud to Udin and Slusarenko, who worked frantically to follow the procedures. Having reached the last step in the instructions, the men discovered that the lock holding the chamber in place would not release—the chamber could not leave the boat.

Udin ordered all of them to put on their respirators as the smoke from the fire enveloped them. Slusarenko and Chernikov quickly complied. Waiting for the others to begin breathing safely, Udin hesitated for a moment before donning his own, a fatal mistake, for he, Vanin, and Krasnobaev died from the highly concentrated poisonous gases forced from the stern compartments by air and water pressure into the forward compartments. Slusarenko and Chernikov climbed into the rescue chamber. As *Komsomolets* hit the ocean floor, the chamber suddenly separated and immediately shot to the surface, rocketing Slusarenko and Chernikov toward safety. As they rose, some of the boat's torpedoes detonated on the bottom below them. The ascent went by in a flash and the capsule broke the surface, bobbing on the waves like a cork.

The high-pressure atmosphere inside the chamber necessary for survival in the deep ocean greatly exceeded the pressure of one atmosphere on the surface. In their frantic effort to escape confinement and survive, Chernikov and Slusarenko immediately opened the capsule without taking the time to equalize the pressure. Chernikov released the hatch and the difference in pressure shot him out of the chamber like a projectile; he was killed when he struck the surface of the ocean. Slusarenko also rose out of the capsule, but only to his waist, the force ripping the respirator from his face. As the open capsule filled with water and began to sink, Slusarenko pushed himself out and swam toward the raft. He joined the other survivors floating on one of the rafts until the motorboat evacuated them.

The rescue was difficult. Few of the victims had any strength left; some were immobile. Those in the water held on to the rafts in a desperate death grip. If they could not use their frozen hands, they held the raft fast with their teeth. Pulling them aboard the motorboat was an exercise in both rescue and persuasion. The rescue crew had to convince these men that their luck had turned.

At 1925 the motorboats brought the rescued submariners back to the *Aleksey Khlobistov*. The waves and poor weather conditions forced the motorboats to circle the ship until an opportunity to move close presented itself. The survivors boarded the fishing trawler, taking with them the bodies of less fortunate shipmates. The *Khlobistov* crew provided food and warm clothing.

Between the growing assistance provided by the fleet and the medical personnel on board the trawler, eight doctors tended to a decimated crew. The physician of the *Aleksey Khlobistov*, Doctor Shabasov, later recalled the frantic effort to save as many of the severely exposed crew as possible.

The trawler's medical spaces could accommodate only 13 men at a time. However we prepared to receive the survivors. They were treated with all possible means, medication, drugs, intensive thermal therapy, and artificial respiration. Captain-Lieutenant Orlov and seaman Kozlov arrived in extremely poor condition. Orlov was brought back from clinical death three times. There were almost thirty submariners. Many of them weren't showing any signs of life. We literally had to run from one man to another. . . . Veins of some submariners became so narrow that injections proved nearly impossible. It was agony to realize that, in some cases, you could do nothing when one of them was dying.[17]

No therapeutic alternative went untried. Crewmembers rubbed the survivors' skin with alcohol, vodka, cologne, and other liquids. When the circulation improved, the submariners went into a hot water bath to complete the process. Many of the *278* crew reacted physically and psychologically to their traumatic experiences. In the midst of their treatment some would stand up suddenly, raving and wildly gesticulating. The medical team and crewmen from the *Khlobistov* had to restrain them. Some of the survivors did not immediately understand where they were or how they got there. For those who could recover, only time and rest would help.[18]

The *K-278* went down 112 nautical miles southeast of Bear Island off the Norwegian coast in roughly 5,000 feet of water. Of the sixty-nine officers and crew who sortied with *Komsomolets* on February 28, 1989, only twenty-seven returned alive.[19]

The *Komsomolets* tragedy symbolized how deadly the undeclared Cold War could be at so many levels—in space, in the air, on land, on and under the sea. But the most crucial level would prove to be in intelligence gathering, for which the Soviet Union and the United States had very different techniques. Both sides would develop those techniques to the highest levels, and in many ways, the outcome of the Cold War depended upon their relative success.

7

A Variety of
Intelligence Gathering
Methods

———————

Shots rang out as the car sped away into the night. Turning a corner the driver realized that one slug had found its mark. The Americans could shoot far better than he expected. A bullet pierced the rear window, passed through the seat, and into the back of the rear admiral dressed in civilian clothes who rested far too calmly behind him. When he glanced back, the driver saw a small, solid man with a benign face, sharp nose, and large probing eyes. He did not slump over or lose consciousness, but quickly and economically issued orders not to stop. This passenger had no desire to explain his wound to the West German police or the NATO military authorities. They had to make it across a border checkpoint into the German Democratic Republic, the DDR, and the drive would take time. It was 1974 and the very hot Cold War still raged, painfully illustrated for everyone by a Germany torn between east and west.

They drove through the night from the scene of the gunfire to the DDR border, blending in with the busy West German highway traffic as they went. The occupant of the back seat had successfully penetrated a NATO nuclear facility south of the federal capital of Bonn and, upon exiting, encountered some American military police who dramatically demonstrated their displeasure with his efforts as the car pulled away into the dark night. A secure military hospital lay just beyond the border crossing chosen by the admiral. Treatment there would come without question and Rear Admiral Gleb Kondratiev could make sure the information he risked so much to obtain would find its way to Moscow and then to the Kola Peninsula in the frozen north, home to the submarines of the Soviet Northern Fleet.

They had no trouble at the border. Kondratiev's position as a senior naval intelligence officer and the deputy head of the general headquarters of the Northern Fleet permitted him smooth passage through the checkpoint. Handing his treasure off to a subordinate before the doctor insisted on surgery, Kondratiev could not help but think that all of this seemed very far indeed from a small village outside Poltava in the Ukraine where he had come into the world in 1924 and a universe away from the sugar beets and cattle that provided the backdrop to his childhood.

In spite of the evening's events, he had no desire to go back. Why would he? Like Anatoli Shevchenko and the crew of *K-513*, his superiors gave him the opportunity to match his considerable wits against the best. In spite of the obvious risk, could it get much better than this? He doubted it. Just before the hospital anesthetist worked his magic, he thought he saw the admiral smile, an expression at once comforting and disturbing. He had only seen it once before, in a textbook picture of a sculpture bust placed in a position of prominence in a small chateau in southern France. The artist had rendered the face and smile of Voltaire, the penetrating eighteenth-century observer of the human condition. Kondratiev's smile had a disturbing similarity. At once it set you at ease and then suggested that he knew far more about you than you could possibly imagine.[1]

≈   ≈   ≈

BY THE MID-1950S, the world recognized that the two superpowers, the United States and the Soviet Union, were fairly equally matched in military power. The Soviet Union had a much larger army, with many more tanks and artillery pieces, while the United States had an obviously more dominant navy, with its aircraft carriers projecting power around the world. Both sides were building increasingly capable undersea fleets that included both attack and missile-carrying submarines. The United States had a superior bomber fleet and an adequate radar warning system, but only a small, if very efficient, force of interceptors. The Soviet Union had fewer and less effective bombers, but the most comprehensive defense system in the world, with hundreds of radar systems, thousands of surface-to-air missiles, and thousands of interceptors. Both sides had fielded brilliant intercontinental ballistic missile systems, increasingly sophisticated, and with a mutual capability to destroy not only each other, but the world's environment in the process. Both superpowers had allies and client states of varying degrees of loyalty, power, and efficiency.

This tricky balancing of unthinkable might fostered an uneasy peace resting on the fragile premise of MAD, mutually assured destruction. For the concept of mutually assured destruction to work, each side had to assume that the other had rational leaders, and events proved that this was in fact the case.

But there was one area in which the two sides were totally mismatched, and that was in the gathering of intelligence. The USSR had for years fueled its scientific and military communities with information gained from spies placed at every level in the scientific, political, intelligence, and military organizations of the United States, Great

Britain, and in other states. In contrast, the two great Allies had very little success in penetrating the Soviet Union, and the information they did receive was often planted "disinformation."

This was due in part to another great difference: The United States and Great Britain were open societies where visitors could come and go without restrictions, and where the media continuously printed scientific and military information as soon as it was available officially or was leaked unofficially. The exact opposite was true in the Soviet Union. Foreigners were admitted only grudgingly and were kept under close surveillance during their visits. Secrecy was tightly maintained in the media, and any transgressions were summarily punished. Soviet citizens were kept under similar grim observation, and any contact with Westerners was immediately suspect.

The vast size of the USSR, the traditional secretive Russian mind-set, and the brutally effective Soviet counterintelligence methods left the United States virtually void of information at the most critical point in its history, when, for the first time since 1812, it was vulnerable to an attack. Some of the early Allied attempts to gather intelligence were almost laughably primitive, and serve more to illustrate the desperate straits in which the United States found itself than anything else. Project GENETRIX began in January 1956, and resembled the desperate attempts by the Japanese to use prevailing winds to carry balloons with incendiary bombs across the Pacific to the United States. In GENETRIX, camera-carrying balloons were launched from Turkey and drifted across the Soviet Union at altitudes of up to 40,000 feet taking photographs. They were recovered in midair over the Pacific, and the photographs were useful for improving maps of the Soviet Union.

The United States and Great Britain had made a number of overflights, using North American RB-45 and Boeing B-47 bombers to penetrate Soviet territory and bring back desperately needed information, some so critical that the decision whether or not to go to war depended upon it. This was hazardous in the extreme to the crews involved, and presented a real danger to international relations. The Soviets had reacted strongly wherever they could, for they well remembered that Germany had made similar overflights in the months leading up to their June 22, 1941, invasion.

Growing concerns about the strengths of the Soviet bomber and intercontinental ballistic missile (ICBM) forces made it evident to U.S. planners that despite the risks, a new aircraft capable of photographing key areas in the USSR was absolutely necessary. The combination of a specially designed aircraft, high-resolution cameras developed by Dr. Edwin Land (of Polaroid fame), new lenses from the Hycon Corporation, and new Mylar-based film from Eastman Kodak made such a mission feasible.

By the time Gary Powers' U-2 was brought down by a surface-to-air missile in May, 1960, the United States was already investing massive amounts of time, money, and effort in a follow-on program to the U-2's that operated under the code name Discoverer for the public, but was known as CORONA in secret. Just as technical developments had made the U-2 feasible, so did other advances enable CORONA—the first successful spy satellite—to operate. In August 1960, the satellite *Discoverer XIV* made seventeen orbits around the Earth, then ejected twenty pounds of film in its capsule. The tracked capsule was then snatched out of the air by a Fairchild C-119 aircraft. When the film was analyzed, it showed areas of the Soviet Union never before photographed, and contained more information than had been gathered in all previous photographic missions over the USSR.

From this point on, the Soviet Union became almost an open book to the United States. Ironically, the most important result of the Discoverer missions was that the United States now had enough information to prevent it from making a fatal miscalculation about Soviet intentions. It was thus of almost equal benefit to the United States and to the Soviet Union. By the time the CORONA program was concluded thirteen years later, it had imaged all of the Soviet missile complexes, the deployment of every class of submarine, discovered the Soviet anti-ballistic missile program, identified Chinese missile-launching sites, pinpointed Soviet surface-to-air missile sites, identified Soviet command and control installations, and much more. It was a revolutionary program, and may very well have been the key element that kept MAD from fruition.

The United States also employed acoustic ASW techniques that were far more sophisticated than aircraft or orbiting satellites, and, for the time, produced superior results. By the 1970s, the undersea surveillance system, SOSUS, had a global reach, covering all those points through which Soviet submarines would pass. SOSUS fixed, ocean-bottom acoustic arrays were supplemented in the mid-1980s by towed-array technology, then called the Surface Towed-Array Sensor System (SUR-TASS). This new development uses U.S. Navy ships as part of a worldwide network of ship and shore systems conducting underwater surveillance.

The Soviet Union countered U.S. intelligence efforts in many ways; one of the least expensive and most productive was to bribe traitors to provide information. From the early days of the Cold War, when spies like Julius Rosenberg and Klaus Fuchs handed the Soviets key intelligence about the United States, to later traitors such as John Walker and his family, Aldrich Ames, and Robert Hanssen, Russian and Soviet intelligence has often relied on Americans who were willing to hand over secrets for a price.

The Soviet Union soon created its own fleet of spy satellites, but much of the information flowing to the Soviet Navy came the old-fashioned way, gathered by individual ships and submarines in its sometimes technologically unequal contest with the U.S. Navy and its allies.

≈   ≈   ≈

ONE PRINCIPAL PRACTITIONER of gathering information by ships was Rear Admiral Gleb Kondratiev. His Ukrainian birthplace was near the site of Peter the Great's victory over Charles XII of Sweden in the eighteenth century, as well as the base to which U.S. bombers flew on shuttle bombing raids over Germany during World War II. He came into the Soviet Navy the hard way, as his father was forced to move often in his career. As a result, Kondratiev had to attend no less than eleven schools before graduating with a gold medal at the secondary level. As a youth, he hoped for a career in the army driving tanks, or perhaps pursuing his other ambition, aviation. He belonged to a local flying club and did well in spite of a memorable incident that damaged an aircraft and brought down some power lines.

When the Great Patriotic War began, his age kept him out of the army. He attended the Caspian Naval College in Baku for a year until he was called upon to fight the Germans in their advance through the Caucasus. Kondratiev returned to school in Baku in 1944. Stalin, now confident of ultimate victory, decided to send most of the student officers drafted to fight the Germans back to their studies to make sure his future armed forces had adequate leadership. Graduating in the top five of his class in Baku, Kondratiev had the rare privilege of choosing his first assignment.[2]

He selected the submarine service, and in March of 1945 he found himself a lieutenant and the executive officer of a small coastal patrol submarine operating out of Vladivostok. Shortly before the conflict against Japan ended in August of 1945, Kondratiev traveled on a Victory-type cargo vessel to Cold Bay, Alaska, to participate in Project Hula. This was a cooperative venture to provide the Russians with surplus American-built destroyer-escorts to strengthen them against Japan in the closing days of the war. Kondratiev returned to the Soviet Union on board one of these vessels, intrigued by the American design but unimpressed with some aspects of American workmanship.[3]

Then, still a very junior officer, he drew one of the most unusual assignments in the Soviet Navy, helping fulfill a goal of Anastas Mikoyan, postwar deputy premier of the Soviet Union. Mikoyan sought a sturdy ship capable of multiple long-range missions and able to endure every kind of weather. As deputy premier, Mikoyan formulated national trade policy and regulated commerce and industry. His goal was to create a fishing vessel that could stay at sea in international waters for prolonged periods to locate and begin exploiting the best fishing grounds. It would also have an intelligence capability.

In addition to his role as navigator on submarine patrols into the middle and eastern Pacific from Vladivostok, Kondratiev collected information on the best types of vessels observed at sea doing this kind of work. However, in addition to the commercial criteria followed in identifying the ideal vessel, Kondratiev received a very special list of characteristics from his naval superiors for the intelligence mission. Among these was a requirement to ensure that it appeared to be only a fishing vessel, and that it be capable of refueling at sea.

As a result of these efforts, Kondratiev defined a basic 750-ton ship to initiate Soviet large-scale, long-range fishing. Powered by diesel engines, it would have one shaft and one propeller and a speed between 10 and 15 knots. Mikoyan had made a very pragmatic decision: The ship could gather intelligence while still securing food for the people of the Soviet Union. These dual-use ships, which entered service in the mid-1950s, were the direct ancestors of the ubiquitous Soviet trawlers that always appeared in strategic locations to collect information on NATO capabilities.[4]

These surveillance trawlers and the more sophisticated submarines made a worldwide Soviet naval presence possible. They provided the intelligence that was used to fashion a navy able to act effectively as an extension of Soviet state power. Early in the Cold War, the limited range of Soviet missiles and other seaborne weapons made precise geographical, oceanographic, and human intelligence critical if the navy hoped to apply significant force in case of war. Only ships could do this kind of work. Kondratiev helped create a mobile and flexible seagoing surveillance capability.

Following World War II, limited state resources made an off-the-shelf approach absolutely necessary. Given the already heavy burden on the Soviet domestic shipyards placed by warship orders, the trawlers had to come from facilities in friendly satellite nations. Experienced shipyard workers built these vessels rather swiftly from plans already on the drawing board.

The Soviet Navy took charge of equipping the trawlers with the surveillance gear. Once launched and properly fitted out, the ships would go to shipyards in Tallinn in the Baltic and to the Northern Fleet on the Kola Peninsula. There they would become sophisticated spy ships while preserving their outward appearance as fishing and cargo vessels.

As multi-purpose vessels, the trawlers selected by the navy spent more of their lives at sea and accomplishing a variety of different tasks. Over the last fifty years the roughly ten Northern Fleet surveillance trawlers completed about 400 long-distance cruises in the Atlantic Ocean. They journeyed to the east coast of the United States and into the Caribbean, the North Atlantic, and the Mediterranean.

While each cruise was potentially dangerous because of the need for the vessel to get close to the adversary's forces or bases, almost every nation conducted similar operations. Norway, for example, regularly conducts intelligence efforts against the Russians using similar dual-purpose fishing boats. The Norwegian surveillance ship *Marjata* has monitored the approaches to the Soviet Kola Peninsula submarine bases for more than thirty years, and at this writing the vessel remains on station. Soviet coast guard ships seized *Marjata* twice, citing espionage and a violation of the Russian twelve-mile limit.

At the height of the Cold War, the Soviet trawlers that Kondratiev had helped bring into service performed the same function as *Marjata* all over the world. The Northern Fleet surveillance ship *Lotlin* (*GS-319*), of the Okean class, once remained on station for 201 days, the longest mission of a career that included twenty-seven cruises lasting for a total of 2,316 days. In the summer of 1967, as she gathered intelligence along the North American east coast, *Lotlin* lost her propulsion, stopped dead in the water, and had to rig a sail to reach *Dauriya*, a Soviet North Fishing Enterprise tender more than 300 miles away. Since *Lotlin*'s task placed her in the Newfoundland Basin, the Gulf Stream waters helped make the voyage possible. Under sail she managed an average speed of two to three knots. Instead of returning home, the trawler received the necessary repairs and provisions and then returned to her observation station. Kondratiev had chosen well.

The relentless nature of the work requirements also made rest and recuperation stops necessary. In the Atlantic, Cuba provided the best location for the crew to get some rest. In the Mediterranean, Alexandria in Egypt, and the countries of Libya and Syria, regularly provided respite. The American-dominated Pacific Ocean presented more of a problem until the conclusion of the Vietnam War. After the fall of South Vietnam, the former American naval base at Cam Ranh Bay became the ideal spot for Soviet rest, repair, and replenishment. In 1979 the Soviets regularly stationed ten surface ships, eight submarines, a tender, sixteen missile planes, nine surveillance planes, and two or three military cargo planes at the former American facility.

Surveillance ships would occasionally work in concert with the submarine force. In 1970 the Northern Fleet trawlers participated in four anti-submarine warfare operations with Soviet submarines. The most successful operation occurred in the summer of 1970, when a Soviet nuclear submarine and two surveillance ships, *Ilmen* and *Krenometr,* operated against American SSBNs (strategic ballistic missile submarines) operating out of Holy Loch in Scotland.

Since the trawlers spent more time at sea than almost any other ship in the Soviet Navy, they frequently found themselves available and first to arrive in emergencies. Surveillance ships arrived first to help the *K-3* and *K-8* when they suffered fires in the Atlantic Ocean. When the Golf class *K-129* submarine sank in 1968 in the Pacific, a Soviet surveillance ship remained at the site of the disaster for two or three months retrieving debris that would occasionally surface from the wreck.

The surveillance ships would also find themselves doing odd jobs not typically in their line of work. In the autumn of 1972 the surveillance ship *Khariton Laptev* broke through some light ice in the Danish Strait to bring relief to the November class boat *K-38*. The ship transferred needed supplies to the submarine in a spacious *polinya*. As they concluded the transfer, the *polinya* began to ice over and a dense fog set in. As *K-38* submerged, her commander misjudged the distance between his boat and *Khariton Laptev*, tearing the trawler's hull as he descended. The crew quickly covered a four-foot-long crack in the hull with a tarpaulin secured with timbers and pumped the water out of the ship. Once they reached clear, ice-free water, the commander ordered the tarpaulin removed and the breach sealed with quick-dry cement mixed on board. In three minutes they had a repair that permitted them to remain at sea for three more months. Thus while the trawlers performed vital surveillance and intelligence work, they also became the all-purpose vessels of the Soviet Navy.

≈   ≈   ≈

WITH THIS EXPERIENCE and the work he did earlier on board Pacific-based submarines close to American shores, Gleb Kondratiev seemed naturally suited for intelligence work. Much of his early time on patrolling submarines involved selecting the best sites for launching missiles against the United States. The short range of Soviet submarine-launched missiles in the 1950s demanded both mathematical precision and detailed surveys of ideal at-sea launch sites close to both American coasts. As navigator, the job fell to him, but early on he exhibited a natural talent for it that his naval superiors noticed.

Kondratiev rose rapidly in rank, going from a junior officer to captain first rank and deputy chief of Northern Fleet Headquarters in just a decade. In 1967, at the age of forty-three, he achieved flag rank as the head of the intelligence service of the Northern Fleet. Giving the Americans a difficult time at sea became a profession, a hobby, and a pleasure. Providing Soviet submariners with intelligence they could put to good use became a passion.

For the Soviets, American submarine-launched nuclear missiles represented the greatest danger to national survival. Collecting practical intelligence on these vessels and their cargo became a constant occupation for Kondratiev's naval intelligence community.

In the late summer of 1970, Kondratiev hatched a plan to monitor a significant sea trial of the new American Poseidon submarine-launched ballistic missile. The launch would take place not from a test platform, but from an operational submarine. The Soviet Navy needed the data because they knew that this missile would eventually go to sea on some of the old and all of the newer American SSBNs.[5] Kondratiev dispatched the intelligence-gathering ship *Khariton Laptev* to the eastern coast of the United States in response to information that indicated the Americans would test the new missile from a recently commissioned SSBN home-ported at the Charleston, South Carolina, submarine base.

Kondratiev gave specific orders on how the mission was to be carried out. The *Laptev* was to take up station at coordinates best suited to careful and detailed measurement of the American submarine's characteristics, its course, depth, firing position, and acoustic signature. A record was to be made of all communications occurring on the transit to the launch site, and at the launch itself. The spy ship would also try to intercept and record as much of the launch and flight telemetry as possible. From the outset, Kondratiev made a Nelsonian demand that the *Khariton Laptev* perform its tasks "audaciously and confidently, avoiding or getting through obstacles that presumably would be created by the submarine's escort and companion ships."

This mission had importance far beyond the normal surveillance deployment. Familiarity or ignorance of this new missile and its launch platform could tip the balance of the Cold War. After a submerged launch, these weapons could easily reach most strategic targets in Russia. A successful mission by the *Laptev* would bring the Soviet Navy much needed data in their effort to imitate or counter the improved American capability. In this case, the observation vessel had to acquire evidence of the missile's capability and nature, even if it meant interference with American operations.

Khariton Laptev "casually" appeared off Charleston shortly after sunrise on August 3, 1970. For Soviet spy-trawlers, this long ago became just one part of a normal day's work. Like Russian submarines, the trawlers regularly plied the seas in proximity to locations of strategic significance to the United States, but just beyond coastal areas in international waters. On this particular morning, she took up station along the most likely exit route for the test ship, the USS *James Madison* (*SSBN-627*). The Soviet commander ordered his ship's twin diesels halted and the radar and acoustic surveillance devices activated. He hoped to start the day by picking up the sound signature of the *James Madison* as it emerged from Charleston. He did not have long to wait. Accompanied by the destroyer-escort USS *Calcaterra* (*DE-390*) and the scientific research ship USS *Observation Island* (*AG-154*), *James Madison* passed within 1,500 feet of the *Khariton Laptev*. The latter's presence presented the small task group with a *fait accompli*. They could not do much about Soviet surveillance because the *Laptev*'s position made her difficult to physically screen or move. Both sides snapped away with their sophisticated photographic equipment, the officers of the *Khariton Laptev* bringing back photographs precise enough to identify four officers and one rating observing the Soviets from their submarine's sail bridge as they passed in close proximity. The Russians also documented some members of the *Calcaterra*'s crew observing them as well as the research staff of the USS *Observation Island* gathered at the rails by the score, straining to see their adversary.

The *Laptev*'s commander felt the mission had begun well but also realized that he had to manage one variable very carefully. With his diesels idle during critical periods of data gathering, his ship would drift at the mercy of the current and the wind. The surveillance devices operated on their own source of power and did not need the engines running to gather the needed data. The helmsman's expert ship-handing skills kept the mission on track and the *Khariton Laptev* at a safe distance from the American SSBN and her escorts.

As the *Laptev* followed the submarine, the commander proceeded carefully because of the importance of this intelligence treasure. Information on American launch preparations, the launch itself, missile engine start-up once the Poseidon broke the surface, and the traces that were left floating on the ocean surface after the missile launch—these constituted intelligence treasures worth considerable risk for the Soviets.

The captain drilled his crew early in ship maneuvering as well as small boat handling and recovery operations, expecting the American escorts to attempt preventive measures when the Soviet mission became clear. He intended to take the *Laptev* through any obstacles created by the SSBN's escorts and to deploy his ship's motor launches to collect available debris as well as the membranes automatically discarded from the top of the missile silo during the launch.

Hovering 120 feet below the surface, USS *James Madison* launched the test weapon in a sudden upward rush of water from a calm sea. The missile broke the surface and seemed to pause for a moment in midair before its engines ignited, sending the weapon streaking down-range and out of sight. The guidance system put the missile into the proper trajectory to reach a target 2,800 miles down-range in the Atlantic, carrying telemetry instead of a warhead. This, the twenty-first in the Poseidon test series that began in August 1968, accomplished everything the United States Navy intended. It also permitted those under Kondratiev's command to accomplish their purpose. In a mad scramble that resulted in several near collisions, the *Laptev*'s crew pursued the missile silo membranes and any other significant artifacts of the launch bobbing in the water while their ship recorded the data passing between the missile and the American ships.

As the American escorts launched their own recovery boats, the Soviet crews went about their collection effort, all the while under a shower of metal objects dropped by low-flying American naval aircraft intent on damaging the small, swift boats and discouraging their occupants. This bizarre intelligence battle ended almost as soon as it began, as the *Khariton Laptev* successfully recovered its motorboats and their treasure while firing signal rockets to discourage low-flying planes.

Although the U.S. Navy press denied it, the treasure proved considerable. Not only had the *Laptev* recovered the membranes, but the small boats also picked up some of the telemetry buoys placed in the water by the USS *Observation Island* just before the launch. In spite of the dangerous close maneuvering required of the *Khariton Laptev* and the American vessels, Kondratiev's aggressive plan resulted in a considerable intelligence coup.

He fully expected the American media to deny that the Soviets had accomplished the collection of the missile launch debris, and the report appearing in the *Navy Times* of August 19 later confirmed his suspicions.[6] The navy reporter claimed that American motor launches recovered all of the debris from the launch, foiling the Soviet effort. Furthermore, neither the *New York Times* nor the *Washington Post* reported the incident at the time. That disappointed Kondratiev, who instructed the commander of the *Laptev* via radio to display all of his newly acquired launch artifacts openly on the ship's deck for the benefit of the U.S. Navy aerial photographers flying overhead. As was his habit, Kondratiev met the *Khariton Laptev* on its return to the Northern Fleet, examined the take, and sat down to share both a bottle of champagne and his professional satisfaction with the commander.

Yet not all was well for the Soviet Navy. Around the same time the *Khariton Laptev* was leaving Soviet waters for its mission, the Kola Bay Scientific Research Center was in the middle of a very ambitious project to record the acoustic signatures of all Soviet Northern Fleet submarines in similar oceanographic conditions to compare the results with the data obtained from American boats. In fact, the Research Center had demanded that acoustic signature measurements lead the list of the *Khariton Laptev*'s mission goals. The Research Center completed this project in September 1970, just as the *Khariton Laptev* returned from her appointment with USS *James Madison*.

The results proved disappointing. This critical comparison revealed beyond any doubt that Soviet submarines operated with much more noise than their American adversaries, placing them at a distinct acoustic and tactical disadvantage. The final data set provided by the *Laptev* made the disturbing conclusions inescapable.[7]

While this news may not have been surprising, it was profoundly disturbing and initiated intense discussions and disputes between the Soviet Navy and the shipbuilding industry regarding the acoustic characteristics of even the best Soviet submarines. Unfortunately for Kondratiev and his Northern Fleet intelligence team, the angry authorities reacted to the unwelcome news in time-honored Soviet tradition, by "killing the messenger." The *Laptev* mission brought this problem to the center of attention in the Soviet submarine community, which shot back that Kondratiev's team had "started the whole mess with their acoustic recordings." Bewildered submarine design and construction specialists began asking Kondratiev for a solution to the problem. His answer was to work harder: It was within their capability to achieve better results.

≈   ≈   ≈

DESPITE HAVING GATHERED acoustic signatures of various U.S. submarines, the Soviet Navy soon discovered that finding an American ballistic missile boat presented quite a problem. After submerging, an SSBN disappeared in every sense. She was constantly on the move, avoiding contact with the enemy, waiting to respond to a launch order from the national command authority.

In the peculiar Cold War conflict, which actually placed the respective submarine fleets on a war footing in time of peace, knowledge, in the form of gathered or stolen intelligence, emerged as the ultimate weapon. With both sides so careful about security, and espionage so dangerous and unpredictable, sheer proximity in the battle environment became the best way to understand your opposite number. Dangerous jousting on the surface and in the depths, done overtly or quietly, with subtlety and skill, offered a way to appreciate capabilities and to discover possible vulnerability.

Years before, science had demonstrated that hunting submarines with another submarine offered the best way to gather intelligence and learn. Thus Soviet and American submarine commanders followed one another all over the world's ocean during the half century of the Cold War. A study prepared for the Northern Fleet in 1965 reported that Soviet forces detected and trailed twenty-two American and British submarines patrolling the Norwegian Sea and the North Atlantic in that year. The Soviets classified 65 percent of the detected submarines as anti-submarine vessels with the other 35 percent outfitted to perform anti-ship and anti-aviation functions. In the 1970s, the Russians estimated that their operations involving the detection and trailing of American submarines took place geographically across roughly 40 percent of that 70 percent share of the Earth's surface covered with ocean.[8]

As passive as this activity sounds, it was actually dangerous work, as the following 1968 incident reveals. An American carrier task force built around the USS *Wasp* entered the Norwegian Sea.[9] When Soviet naval forces detected the approach of the *Wasp* task group, they sent submarines, surface vessels, and reconnaissance aircraft to monitor the activity. A Tu-16 "Badger" aircraft detected the task group almost immediately and began following and observing, photographing all the while. The plane's crew sent back a constant stream of reports despite efforts at communications jamming by the Americans and the activities of the carrier's combat air patrol to keep the Badger at a distance.

The Tu-16 pilot's efforts were soon countered by fighters from the carriers who flew so close that he had to maneuver while in low-level flight. Determined not to let the American aircraft interfere with his effort, the Soviet pilot took the Badger down and headed for the carrier. As the pilot brought his aircraft in very low, barely above the *Wasp*'s flight deck, the carrier air boss cleared a helicopter for takeoff. In a desperate maneuver to avoid a collision with the helicopter, the pilot let his wingtip touch the ocean surface. The Tu-16 cartwheeled, broke up, and sank. The task group commander immediately sent boats to pick up the survivors. Two of the six-man crew survived the crash, but even they died in spite of determined efforts by the *Wasp*'s doctors. They became another casualty of the intelligence wars. Kondratiev remembered as a "responsible and honest man" the task group commander who both tried to save the crew and took pains to return the Tu-16 casualties to the Soviet armed forces.

American submarines, for their part, regularly tracked Soviet boats, aided by the SOSUS network. As SOSUS developed over the next twenty years its effectiveness prompted intelligence officers like Gleb Kondratiev to recognize its success and deplore its existence. From his point of view, "This effective and permanently working net was a great pain in the neck for Soviet submariners, since the system would send messages to bases about detected submarines, then ASW aircraft would be able to keep tabs on the detected submarines. It was a great military treasure."

The Soviets could not prevent the installation of SOSUS, but they could interfere with its continued development by stealing SOSUS research buoys and chopping cables. NATO's "Fair Deal" exercises of September 1973 provides a case in point. The Soviets felt that the exercises, if successful, would enhance NATO's ability to monitor the passage of their submarines through the Iceland–Hebrides gap. As part of the exercise, the American cable layer USS *Neptune* (*ARC-2*), the scientific ship R/V *Chain* operating out of the Woods Hole Oceanographic Institution on Cape Cod in Massachusetts, and the German hydrographic ship *Meridian* seemed intent on exploring new detection capabilities, laying a length of transmission cable, and leaving buoys to monitor the bathymetry of the area, so important to the scientists who would draft the acoustic assumptions upon which the U.S. Navy would base SOSUS installation decisions.

Kondratiev sent *Khariton Laptev* to monitor "Fair Deal." After some time observing R/V *Chain* and the cable-laying activities of *Neptune*, the *Laptev*'s intelligence officers concluded that the American ship's mission included an examination of some SOSUS detection devices and the installation of new ones. As the small research fleet departed before the onset of severe autumn North Atlantic weather, *Khariton Laptev* managed to collect information on the NATO exercise and attempted to cut the newly installed cable.

Many Northern Fleet ships, including *Khariton Laptev*, had propellers that could cut through cable lines as they paid out over considerable distances from the stern of U.S. warships or cable-layers. Kondratiev viewed these cable-laying actions as an intrusion, and took audacious counteraction when he felt it was called for.

Even well-considered monitoring efforts could precipitate dangerous and politically explosive situations, and these were often resolved by the good sense of the naval commanders on site. As the United States and NATO began increasing the frequency of task group exercises in the North Atlantic and Norwegian Sea to test Soviet limits, to explore new tactics, and to provide experience for what would become the Maritime Strategy of the later years of the Cold War, dangerous encounters increased in frequency.[10]

OTHER SOVIET INTELLIGENCE
AND COUNTERINTELLIGENCE SYSTEMS

The public has become so accustomed to the present-day feats of satellites, spy planes, and deep-ocean acoustic methods in gathering intelligence that it sometimes forgets that the most useful information is usually obtained firsthand, on the scene, by a human observer.

For a firsthand example of such important intelligence gathering, we need to step back once again to one of the most important and unsung participants in the Cuban Missile Crisis, Captain Second Rank Vadim P. Orlov (retired).

Given that he came into the world on July 21, 1937, in Vladivostok, Vadim Orlov's life did not unfold as one might imagine. Sixty-five years later he vividly recalled making the very long trip by train from the Pacific coast to Moscow as the tide of World War II turned in favor of the Soviet Union because his family had to help his father prepare for a business trip to the United States. The eight-year-old Orlov soon found himself on an American passenger ship crossing the Atlantic in October of 1945. The Orlov family landed in New York and lived for a time in Washington, D.C., and San Francisco before returning to the east coast in 1947 when Vadim's father joined the Soviet diplomatic community in New York City. Orlov still remembers the contrast between life in the war-torn Soviet Union and that in the immediate postwar United States:

> My family, like many other Soviet families, suffered deprivations during World War II, so when we arrived in the U.S. life in America was so very different that it seemed like heaven compared to post-

war life in the USSR. . . . When we lived in San Francisco I went to
the Soviet embassy school. . . . My brother went to an American
kindergarten. When we lived in New York I went to a school with
350 Russian children of Soviet citizens—United Nations representatives, embassy employees, and employees of a joint Soviet–
American firm "Amtorg" that was in charge of dispatching lend-
lease American loads like food, tractors, machines, equipment, and
so on to the USSR. We had both Russian and American teachers.

I recall that our Soviet teachers were trying to teach us patriot-
ism towards our motherland and aversion towards the American
lifestyle. All kids were dreaming of becoming "pioneers"; we
would play Soviet games like soccer and make ribbons that said
"Aurora," the most famous Soviet cruiser that took part in the
October 1917 revolution, or "Soviet Union" for sailors' hats. A little
metal red star for a hat would be the most precious thing for us.

Orlov led this extraordinary life because although his father appeared
to work for Amtorg, he did not buy or sell in the world of business.
Rather, the senior Orlov traded in information as an agent for the GRU,
the Intelligence Directorate of the Soviet Ministry of Defense.[11] His affil-
iation with Amtorg, the company that represented the Soviet side in
many lend-lease and wartime commercial transactions, provided a
convenient cover for his clandestine intelligence activity. The family
lived in the Soviet diplomatic residence at 14 Riverside Drive in New
York City. Vadim walked through Central Park on his way to school, occasionally had fights with American boys in the normal course of a
rough and tumble urban youth, and went to a summer camp in Glen-
coe, New York, equipped with a swimming pool. Since his father the
GRU agent had a car, the family made frequent trips to view the beauty
of Niagara Falls. Compared to conditions in the Soviet Union, this felt
like heaven.

In spite of the economic contrasts, the Soviet youth living in the
United States demonstrated, like their occasional American playmates,
that they too lived in a larger world where kids made the rules and set
the expectations. Orlov and his younger brother went to the movies,
watched films about cowboys, and knew all the famous actors who

played their heroes. On one short journey to the Amtorg offices, where his mother worked as an accountant, Orlov turned around only to realize that his brother Victor had failed to emerge behind him from the crowded New York City Transit bus they had both used for transportation. Young Vadim told his mother and she called the police. He recalled years later:

> We found him only in the evening in the police station. The policemen laughed when they told us that little Victor came to them in the street and said, "I'm a citizen of the USSR and you should take me to the embassy, but I won't tell you anything and will be silent like a real Soviet partisan!"

With the Cold War intensifying after 1948, some of the Soviet embassy staff and Amtorg employees left the United States and the Soviet–American school in New York City closed.

Vadim Orlov decided on his career very early in life. He came from Vladivostok on the Pacific coast, cruised on the Atlantic Ocean, witnessed the heroism of sailors helping people survive a fire at sea, traveled to many places with his parents, and frequently received as gifts books about explorers and naval figures like Columbus, Magellan, Nelson, and the Russian admiral Nakhimov. His inclination toward swimming and diving in athletics and an early love of sailing made the choice almost obvious. Finishing English language school in Moscow in 1953, he entered the Frunze Naval College in Leningrad. After graduation in 1959 he joined an anti-submarine warfare surface ship with the Northern Fleet as navigator.

In a Cold War entering its most dangerous phase, Orlov lasted as a navigator for only two years. Walking away from that role had nothing to do with his ability. Indeed, he did an excellent job. Rather, his time on Riverside Drive, his familiarity with the United States, and his excellent American English made him far more valuable in another capacity: His superiors viewed him as uniquely suited for intelligence work. He became one of twenty-five young officers chosen for a special course at the Popov Academy in radio surveillance, what has since become known as signals intelligence or SIGINT. He would serve on board

Northern Fleet submarines performing a demanding balancing act between air, surface, and subsurface radio transmission, detection, and interpretation, providing his commander with intelligence that would hopefully contribute to success and survival. Many of his classmates at Popov found the curriculum too demanding and the responsibility too great a burden, and only half of them passed the three-month course.[12]

Orlov deployed thirteen times on patrols to the Atlantic Ocean, the Mediterranean Sea, South Africa, England, and the eastern coast of the United States on board submarines, eventually commanding a detachment of surveillance officers. Submarines with teams of surveillance officers on board regularly observed major NATO and American exercises and activities. He remembered well the first time the Soviet Navy assigned his group of surveillance officers to a highly significant project. He could not possibly forget. He was on one of the four Foxtrots that had attempted to run the U.S. blockade of Cuba in October 1962.

Unlike the rest of the crew, Orlov and his OSNAZ colleagues worked for the GRU. Through the GRU, the ministry engaged in espionage and foreign intelligence activity. OSNAZ detachments came from the GRU, but more often than not remained under the operational control of the fleet commands.

GRU had its own land surveillance centers as well as OSNAZ groups working on board civilian ships, commercial cargo ships, and tankers. GRU SIGINT officers often received orders on civilian ships as radio officers who could at any time cooperate with the navy by monitoring significant NATO exercises and maneuvers.

Signals intelligence had come of age in the Soviet Navy and in warfare at sea. During the Arab–Israeli War the radio surveillance centers remained on 24-hour alert. Instead of sleeping, they pulled in communications intelligence from the Mediterranean. As the Falklands War raged in 1982 and 1983, from halfway around the world Soviet radio surveillance captured signals from the American ships assisting the British. The SIGINT teams even worked out what kind of British naval forces took part in the war and the extent to which the Americans assisted, and informed the Soviet government of daily developments.

Since submarines offered a very potent covert surveillance platform, both the Soviets and the Americans used these vessels regularly to intercept radio traffic, record acoustic signatures, and visually track an adversary.[13] In one 1966 case, Orlov found himself on board a Romeo class diesel submarine sitting quietly in the approaches to the American fleet ballistic missile base in Holy Loch, Scotland.[14] The Northern Fleet command tasked his boat with monitoring American SSBN traffic to record communication, acoustic characteristics, and the regularity of deployments and returns. Hovering on the very edge of British territorial waters at 150 feet, the Soviet Romeo occasionally rose to periscope depth for a view of the vicinity and to extend its antennae to monitor the communications of the American submarine squadron. Soviet naval intelligence also had information that the British ballistic missile-firing nuclear submarine *Dreadnought* had tied up at Holy Loch and Moscow wanted confirmation.

Experiencing some initial success, the OSNAZ group detected USS *Ethan Allen* (*SSBN-608*) returning from a deterrent patrol. In succeeding days, the Romeo tracked American and British ballistic missile submarines as they left the base for a few hours to practice with a new underwater communication system. Orlov and his SIGINT team picked up coded transmissions designed to permit allied submarines to speak with one another while submerged and underway. He had never experienced this before and the Soviet Navy found it significant that the Americans had shared this advanced technology with their NATO allies.[15]

Regardless of its ability to hover and remain quietly submerged, in the late 1960s the United States and NATO had SOSUS, its own submarines, and the security system associated with a major base as tools to find a Soviet Romeo playing the surveillance game. On the fifth night of its activity near Holy Loch, and just inside British territorial waters, the Royal Navy decided that Orlov's listening platform had worn out its welcome.

Accustomed to occasional one or two plane overflights by Shackelton ASW aircraft, on this night the Royal Air Force treated the Soviet submariners to a squadron of twelve, all armed and ready to make them regret penetrating British waters. At the same time Orlov's people intercepted the message directing two British patrol ships to converge on their position, the latter reported with disturbing accuracy. The time to hide had passed. The boat's commander took the vessel down to 450 feet and began to move out of the area at four knots, hoping to mini-mize the noise generated by his propulsion system to make evasion possible.

Before two hours had passed British sonar detected two sets of rap-idly turning propellers. Two Royal Navy frigates had the Soviet boat on their sonar and began to track her, repeatedly foiling any attempt at evasion. The British reached the Romeo and remained on top of the So-viet boat for so long that the submarine's batteries spent their charge, forcing the Soviet commander to surface at roughly 0500. Listening to the intership communication as they broke the surface, Orlov realized that the British already knew the class and capabilities of their subma-rine. Upon opening the hatch and emerging onto the sail bridge, the Russians saw two British patrol ships close aboard and four Shackleton ASW aircraft overhead, still dropping sonobuoys. The senior British commander sent a brusque message in Russian to the Soviet boat in semaphore, "To the submarine commander. Maneuver to the north and don't submerge!" The Romeo immediately began a battery recharge as the Royal Navy provided a very close escort. The surface ships followed at a distance of about 1,800 feet, keeping both their sonar and radars ac-tive. At least two British ASW aircraft continued to cross the skies above.

After a five- to six-hour battery recharge, the Soviet boat submerged in spite of the British warning and tried to escape, but could not shake the Royal Navy. With batteries exhausted once again, she surfaced, and the Northern Fleet ordered the boat home. The commander complied immediately, proceeding on the surface. A Royal Navy frigate, two British aircraft, an American Neptune ASW plane, and a Norwegian Catalina patrol plane escorted the Romeo all the way to the Kola Bay en-trance. If nothing else, Orlov's report illuminated many aspects of Royal Navy ASW operational procedures.

≈   ≈   ≈

ORLOV'S FIRSTHAND VIEW of one individual waging a one-sided war against a technologically advanced opponent reflects the tone of the early, relatively unsophisticated days of Cold War intelligence gathering.

Nevertheless, the SOSUS network should have come as no surprise to the Soviet Union, which had itself experimented with noise detection for their coastal bases as early as 1927. World War II interfered with this experimentation and it was not until the mid-1950s that the naval engineering scientific research center produced the sonar surveillance system Volkhov. This system of anchored sonobuoys transmitted information by means of cable laid along the seabed. By 1994, the Soviets also produced a new sonar system called Dnestr, designed to work in both active and passive modes. But the American surveillance invasion went beyond SOSUS. While trailing Soviet submarines and recording the acoustic data, the U.S. Navy reportedly penetrated Soviet territorial waters to gather intelligence on a regular basis.

According to the CIA and Naval Intelligence reports, the Sea of Okhotsk, the Barents Sea, and the Baltic Sea were the optimal zones for this kind of secret mission. However, U.S. Naval Intelligence understood that such missions were risky, potentially making the world political situation more complex. That is why all the projects required official approval. One operation was to take place in the Sea of Okhotsk, which didn't have many Soviet submarines patrolling it. Rather it was filled with communication lines and isolated from the main coast commanding posts.

The operation was called "Ivy Bells."

The American submarine USS *Halibut* left Mare Island, California, en route to the Sea of Okhotsk in October of 1971 with special tapping devices and divers trained to operate at great depths. This team attached a tapping pod to the telephone cable in the narrowest part of Shelikhov Bay. The mission proved so successful that *Halibut* actually recorded several telephone conversations within a few days. Months later, improved eavesdropping technology replaced the old, enabling the submarine as well as remote surveillance sites to simultaneously collect information from dozens of telephone lines at a time. The submarine force installed the new system in the Sea of Okhotsk at the end of October 1972, just as USS *Seawolf* relieved USS *Halibut* to continue the critical intelligence gathering mission.

On the opposite coast the Soviets also had a vital communication link via cable between the factory producing Delta SSBNs, the missile testing site, and Northern Fleet headquarters. This line carried vital technical and strategic intelligence and thus became a prime candidate for tapping. USS *Parche* journeyed to the Barents Sea, inserted the surveillance pod, and eavesdropped on these communication lines for about two weeks. The submarine returned to the site five more times before 1984 to collect information from the pod. Every time she was escorted by another submarine acting as a decoy and screen in case the Soviets detected a submarine presence in the area. Commander Submarine Forces, Atlantic in Norfolk reasoned that if detection took place, the Soviets would expect one submarine, but not two.

For their part, the Soviet Navy did everything it could to prevent SOSUS detection of Delta submarines as they deployed toward the U.S. coast. Northern Fleet intelligence wanted to determine the nature and capability of the SOSUS arrays, so their submarines could approach the U.S. coast quietly and effectively. Indeed, Soviet naval leaders planned to damage SOSUS cables and create acoustic disturbances to inhibit the system's proper operation. The Soviets even created a special department of the GRU (naval intelligence) responsible for underwater surveillance. This department deliberately sought candidates with submarine experience from working-class and peasant families, as opposed to intelligentsia, who exhibited unwavering loyalty to the Soviet Communist Party. From the beginning, their activities remained so critical and clandestine that even fleet and squadron commanders knew nothing of their goals and tasks.

Ships and submarines were refurbished specially for the surveillance tasks. Their most distinguished feature was that they could tow special underwater vehicles with "aquanauts," as the underwater counterspies were called. These divers would visually explore the ocean floor and report the coordinates of the SOSUS cables to the submarine, who would then use the reconnaissance data to update their maps and further develop routes for other Soviet subs. In case of heightened international tensions they planned to destroy the cables, permitting Soviet submarines and ships to move undetected toward the U.S. coast.[16]

At the end of 1974 the fleet headquarters received information from the secret service that the Americans had compromised the Pacific Ocean Fleet's communication cable. Divers investigated the report by checking the cable in the narrowest part of Shelikhov Bay, the most obvious place for tapping the lines that connected the Pacific Ocean command post with the SSBN bases. This cable also connected Moscow with Petropavlovsk-Kamchatsky, the primary SSBN base in the east, and the missile-testing site "Kura" used by the Northern Fleet's submarines. Civil establishments also used the cable to connect to the continent.

Admiral Gleb P. Kondratiev describes it:

The Americans scrupulously prepared for intelligence operations to be held close to the Soviet naval bases in Kola Peninsula waters and Kamchatka approaches. The operations were headed by James Bradley, who ran the ASW department of the U.S. naval intelligence services. He sought and received permission from the President of the United States and the National Security Council, as well as other departments.

The first tapping pod was installed on a five-inch cable on the bottom of the Sea of Okhostk not far from the western shore of the Kamchatka Peninsula in the southern part of Shelikhov Bay. This cable connected Kamchatka with Moscow and with Vladivostok. The refurbished American submarine *Halibut* found the cable by searching the Sea of Okhostk for signs saying "Cable," or "Do Not Anchor." Discovering the cable area, they searched the sandy seabed and found the cable at a depth of 120 meters. *Halibut* installed the tapping pod—made by the NSA—along with a container with lithium batteries that could power the pod for up to two months. *Halibut* also later retrieved the pod and returned with it to San Francisco.

The Americans' first attempt to tap Soviet telephone lines was a success, and soon *Halibut* was sent back to the Sea of Okhostk with a second, more effective pod. This one was six meters long and one meter in diameter. It could operate for an entire year and was capable of tapping twenty different channels of communication—which, the Americans had learned from the first pod, was the amount of data carried by that particular cable.

For several years, *Halibut* continued to eavesdrop on Soviet telephone cables in the Sea of Okhostk, and even expanded operations to include the Kura site, also in the Sea of Okhostk, where cruise missiles launched from the Northern fleet areas would routinely fall. This allowed the Americans to recover missile fragments such as the thermo-visual tips for target designation and the altimeters that allowed Soviet cruise missiles to fly 20–50 meters above obstacles likes hills and mountains. *Halibut* was eventually succeeded by her replacement, the *Seawolf,* and another American submarine, the *Parche,* that conducted similar operations in the Barents Sea.

Through spies like Walker and Pelton, however, we eventually learned what the Americans were doing. Once we were aware of their operations, we started playing a "telephone game" with them, deliberately transmitting misleading information through the channels where we knew they were monitoring. When the Americans caught on and the game was no longer valuable, we retrieved the pods for examination. We also did our best to discourage American submarines from coming into our waters by using grenades to force them back out to sea. I returned from Germany and joined the GRU in the late 1970s, and personally witnessed two American nuclear submarines maneuvering at the approaches to the Kola Peninsula. Clearly, one was there to distract us in case the other one—the one that was actually doing the spying—got into trouble. To my knowledge, *Parche* went into the Barents Sea on secret missions seven different times.

When the Soviet secret service decided to play a "telephone game" with the U.S., they deliberately provided misinformation about Soviet missile subs, their "routes" and "patrol areas," "combat training," and "orders." Only the secret service officers accomplished the missions. After about five or six years of the operations it became more difficult to keep the telephone game secret. As a consequence, the Soviets decided to remove the pods (over time, the Americans installed a second pod) from the cable.

Because of the possible danger, the divers just disconnected each pod from the cable and attached it to the hoist hawser, then went back to the submarine, which moved away from the cable. The crane started to hoist the pod; fortunately, there was no explosion. By 6 A.M. the hoisting ship *Tavda* already had the two pods. One of them was five meters (sixteen feet) long and weighed about six tons; the second one was smaller. The pods were wrapped and sent to Moscow for further examination.

Among their feats during the Cold War, Soviet divers occasionally severed and recovered parts of SOSUS cable and were the first to find the sunken Soviet submarine *Komsomolets*. They played an important role in ocean research and in testing new diving equipment for working in deep water. Among their occasional humanitarian efforts was a tribute to the famous Soviet submariner, Mohammed Gadgiev, who died during World War II. Caucasian traditions required that his grave site contain a stone from the place where Gadgiev had died. The divers retrieved a stone from the seafloor where Gadgiev's submarine lay, and had it placed on the legendary submariner's monument in 1996.

8

IMPROVING THE BREED

The developments in submarines and submarine-launched missiles for both the United States and the Soviet Union had not occurred in a political vacuum during the early 1960s. The Cold War and its leading cast of characters drove these developments and continued to shape the evolution of undersea warfare over the next two and a half decades.

The increasing intensity of the Cold War after 1945 precipitated the greatest and most expensive arms race in history. The incredible Soviet scientific achievements in rockets and missilery and the swift Soviet progress in nuclear weapons stripped the United States of its customary sense of isolation, and for the first time forced it to maintain full-time professional forces in times of peace. In the past, it had relied on minimal regular forces, counting on having enough time to mobilize its population and industry in the event of war.

The threat of Soviet bombers merely hours—and Soviet missiles merely minutes—away transformed the American defense scheme. In the United States, General Curtis E. LeMay helped fashion the Strategic Air Command into the most powerful military force in history, and General Bernard Schriever, in four short years, fielded the Atlas ICBM; followed soon by the Titan and Minuteman systems.

The Soviet Union had not elected to build as big or as effective a bomber force, but its ICBMs carried larger warheads and were built in intimidating numbers. Ultimately they came to be more accurate than their American counterparts, and were protected in better, more "hardened" silos. The Soviet Union's introduction of diesel-powered guided missile and ballistic missile submarines posed a potent threat because they could strike inland Strategic Air Command bomber bases in as little as eight minutes.

It was essential to find a seaborne solution to offset this new Soviet advantage. In 1956, the American Chief of Naval Operations commissioned a special study called Project NOBSKA, chaired by Columbus Iselin of the Woods Hole Oceanographic Institution, and including Paul Nitze, Dr. Isidore Rabi, and Dr. Edward Teller, to look into this issue and other strategic and technical matters. The NOBSKA participants recommended that a fleet of submarines capable of launching ballistic missiles be formed to counter the Soviet numerical submarine advantage and to provide a virtually invulnerable weapon for a retaliatory strike. To the navy, the submarine-launched ballistic missile (SLBM) was the perfect mission, despite the obvious difficulties with the large size of nuclear warheads and the hazards of deploying a liquid-fueled ballistic missile aboard a submarine.

In 1955, the U.S. Navy set out to develop a sea-based missile in conjunction with the Army under the aegis of the liquid-fueled Jupiter intermediate-range ballistic missile (IRBM) project, establishing a Special Projects Office to handle the task. The Chief of Naval Operations at the time was Admiral Arleigh Burke, who had distinguished himself leading destroyer units in World War II. Burke had been a leader in the so-called "Revolt of the Admirals," as well as the bitter battle with the Air Force over the Consolidated B-36 bomber, and knew intuitively that the SLBM would convert the submarine from a tactical to a strategic weapon. He chose a naval aviator, Rear Admiral William F. "Red" Raborn, to head the Special Projects Office, saying later, "I did not want a technical expert because a technical expert would be too narrow-minded. I wanted an aviator because if this missile were successful, it would jeopardize the aviation branch. . . . I chose Red Raborn because he was a hard-working man."[1]

Raborn became the quintessential project manager, able to look into the future and gamble on his vision, delegating authority equally with responsibility, and inspiring his people to work as hard as he did, which was very hard indeed. Big, red-haired, barrel-chested, and swift with a joke, Raborn was able to get along with people under conditions of enormous stress. He was a natural with Congress because of his confidence and his candor. One of his most courageous aspects was his willingness to plan for the future based on technologies still in development.[2]

Fortune smiled on the navy, for it had equally talented, equally dedicated individuals working in the myriad disciplines necessary to create such a futuristic weapon, and it had a capable contractor, Lockheed Missiles and Space Systems Corporation. In the next few months the team made a number of crucial breakthroughs based upon scientific and technical recommendations made at the NOBSKA conference in 1956. On December 8, 1956, the secretary of defense approved the essential details of a two-stage solid-propellant nuclear missile with a 1,500-mile range, and Admiral Raborn gave it the name Polaris. It was to be operational by 1965.[3]

The arrival of *Sputnik* on October 4, 1957, lent urgency to the program, which was accelerated so that a 1,200-mile range weapon would be available by January 1, 1963. In essence, Admiral Burke traded a little range for a lot of time.

Both the missile and the submarine programs moved through their test phases swiftly, and on July 20, 1960—fifty-four months in advance of the first schedule, and thirty months in advance of the accelerated schedule—the first Polaris was launched from the submerged USS *George Washington*. On November 15, 1960, the *George Washington* sailed from Charleston, South Carolina, for the first Fleet Ballistic Missile (FBM) launch in history. Raborn was on board, and he celebrated the occasion with telegrams noting the success to the president and

congressional leaders. One message is memorable for its poetry—
Raborn notified President Eisenhower of the success with a message
saying POLARIS—FROM OUT OF THE DEEP TO TARGET. PERFECT.[4]
The implications were tremendous for friend and foe. In the United
States, it was now recognized that there was an indispensable strategic
triad consisting of bombers, ICBMs, and SLBMs. However, of all American weapons systems, the SSBN was quickly recognized by the Soviets
as the most elusive, constant, and dangerous.

Both nations continued to arm with nuclear weapons at an astonishing rate. Fortunately, if imponderably, the concept of mutually assured
destruction (MAD) was tacitly recognized. Both sides knew that no one
could win a nuclear war. Thus an uneasy peace existed throughout the
Cold War, even in spite of vicious peripheral wars, including the United
States in Vietnam, the Soviet Union in Afghanistan, and the litany of
wars in the Middle East. Incredibly, MAD led to peace, and even contributed, in the long run, to the ultimate dissolution of the Soviet Union.

The Cuban missile crisis of October 1962 had totally unforeseen
repercussions, starting with the beginning of the end of Premier Nikita
Khrushchev's reign as the leader of the Soviet Union. Khrushchev and
China's Mao Zedong had a fundamental disagreement over the conduct
of communist policy. Mao was much more radical, and openly con-
tested Khrushchev's position as the leader of world communism, despite the many concessions that the Soviet leader made to him.[5] Mao's
most radical position was his advocacy of a global nuclear war, one that
would kill hundreds of millions of people, but would see communism
emerge the winner over capitalism on an attrition basis: There were
simply more Chinese and Russians than there were Westerners. Having,
like Stalin, killed perhaps thirty to sixty million of his own people
through starvation and other means, Mao regarded Khrushchev as a
moral coward for not wishing to destroy capitalism once and for all in a
fiery nuclear holocaust.[6]

One very good reason that Khrushchev did not wish to embroil the
Soviet Union in a nuclear war was that despite all Western apprehen-
sions of a "missile gap," he did not have enough ICBMs to conduct such
a war, even with Russia's powerful ground and air forces. In Europe, a
Soviet army of some 175 divisions was opposed by only six United States

divisions and the relatively weak North Atlantic Treaty Organization (NATO) forces. It could easily have swept from the Fulda Gap in Germany through to the English Channel in a few weeks in a nonnuclear war. Yet this overwhelming conventional advantage was actually a liability, for Khrushchev believed (correctly) that the United States would be forced to resort to the use of all of its nuclear capability to stop such an invasion.

The "missile gap" did in fact exist, which John F. Kennedy exploited successfully and perhaps decisively in his presidential campaign, but only regarding conventional weapons missiles. By 1962, the United States actually had an enormous lead in nuclear weapons. With some 1,200 to 1,400 bombers in the Strategic Air Command, it could place up to 3,000 nuclear weapons on Soviet targets in a matter of hours. It also possessed no less than 183 Atlas and Titan ICBMs, plus 144 Polaris missiles, many of which were constantly on submarine patrol at sea. In contrast, even mustering all of its resources, the Soviet Union could only place about 300 nuclear weapons on the territory of the United States.[7] "Only" is such an absurd word in this context, for those 300 weapons were enough to destroy the country, but in the odd mentality of the time, "only 300 weapons" did not seem to be enough—especially when they would provoke a 3,000-weapon response.)

Because the nuclear missile submarine or SSBN was the newest and most potent element of the strategic triad for both the United States and the Soviet Union, it was subject to much urgent improvement. Both nations were well pleased with the success of their efforts, despite the difficulties and sometimes tragedies they had encountered, and both felt that improved submarines and missiles added measurably to their offensive and defensive capabilities.

And as the nuclear missile submarines improved, so too did the attack submarines whose mission it was to destroy them. Submarines have always been the best submarine hunters, but the advent of the nuclear submarine, with its long range and long time on station, opened up a new world of possibilities.

The image of World War I aerial dogfights is often used to describe the adversarial engagements of two modern submarines, hunter versus hunted, or even hunter versus hunter. But whereas World War I dogfights depended almost entirely on keen human eyes to find the enemy, the modern submarine depends upon a host of on-board electronic devices combined with assistance from surface vessels, aircraft, and even satellites to find and fix the opposition. There is a vast difference in the size, speed, mass, and medium of the submarine engagement as well, and the deep-ocean environment is vastly more hostile than the air.

That being said, Cold War oceans were filled with the tumult of submarine versus submarine encounters, any of which could have resulted in disaster, and some of which did result in collisions. To the United States and the Soviet Union, the threat of a ballistic missile submarine was so great that each one had to be identified, shadowed, and marked for instant destruction in the event of war. It was a demanding task, and required extraordinary equipment and crews in both navies.

Initially, all submarines were attack submarines, and shortly after World War II it was determined that the best counter to a submarine was another submarine. The advent of the nuclear ballistic missile submarine presented nuclear attack submarines (SSNs) with an additional and vitally important mission. Where previously attack submarines were intended, among other things, to destroy enemy warships and shipping, the modern SSN now had to prevent the destruction of the homeland by an SSBN ballistic missile submarine.

≈   ≈   ≈

IN THE PAST, the hauntingly brutal concept of mutual assured destruction had prevented war. With both sides possessing nuclear weapons in abundance, no one wished a nuclear exchange. Nuclear weapons also prevented extreme military measures, like any action by the Soviet army against NATO, because such an action would inevitably provoke a nuclear response. As a result, the United States and the Soviet Union stood like two huge nuclear sumo wrestlers, locked in an embrace that neither could break.

To maintain this absurd balance, both the Soviet Union and the United States created new and better nuclear weapons, and, to all appearances, both would continue to do so for the foreseeable future. The leaders and the populace of both sides had accepted this state of affairs, and eventually accepted the uneasy peace as the normal political situation. Fortunately for everyone but the leaders of the Communist Party, an entirely new situation developed as the result of the confluence of two totally different situations.

By the 1980s, the booming economy of the United States, spurred by the rapid growth in the power and applications of the computer, ushered in an era of entirely new weaponry, one that would enable a departure from the MAD philosophy of military action. This was a true Revolution in Military Affairs (RMA), one that caught the Soviet Union by surprise, and one that also surprised many in the West. Regardless, it revolutionized submarine warfare and increased its level of sophistication.

As the Cold War moved into its fourth decade, the confrontation below the surface of the World Ocean continued unabated. The geopolitical world began to change but Russia continued to control and exercise formidable nuclear forces, including a fleet of submarines of remarkable quality and efficiency, captained by men of great skill and daring. One of the best of these was Captain First Rank Anatoli I. Shevchenko, whose experiences under both Soviet and Russian regimes are worth recounting. He led daring operations that revealed true Soviet submarine capability and their dangerous operations against their American counterparts.

Born in 1941 during the eastern front Nazi nightmare, this redheaded Soviet submariner hailed from Odessa, one of the bustling Black Sea ports of the southern Ukraine. After spending two years as a sailor in the Black Sea Fleet, Shevchenko entered the Black Sea Naval College in Sevastopol, receiving his commission as a lieutenant in 1965. The school trained him in cruise missile technology and prepared him as a watch officer, capable of serving on any vessel in the Soviet Navy.

Like many of his future adversaries learning their trade at the U.S. Naval Academy in Annapolis, Maryland, this Soviet midshipman went on summer cruises while in school, visiting for a time with various fleet units to learn about surface and subsurface warfare as well as aviation. In 1963, the summer cruise took him and his Sevastopol classmates to Gadzhievo, near Polyarni, to visit the submarines of the Northern Fleet. He immediately decided to choose submarines as a career path.

Upon graduation, he joined the crew of a Northern Fleet Charlie 2 class nuclear submarine commanded by Captain Second Rank Valentin Savitsky, as the propulsion officer. After several years' experience in various capacities, including a year as assistant to the commander, he took the exams to qualify for command himself. With these behind him, he did a three-year tour as executive officer during which he made five combat patrols. In 1977, after passing a course for prospective commanding officers in Leningrad, he received his first command, a Victor 2. He took that boat and her crew to sea for the next five years.[8]

Shevchenko matured as a commander during years that witnessed the Soviet Navy coming of age. Gorshkov projected Soviet naval power on a global scale barely more than a decade after World War II, but the navy struggled to live up to the ambition. The submarine fleet Shevchenko joined had many new designs that could compete on an equal footing with American Sturgeon and Los Angeles class fast attack boats. His fleet now had a history, a reputation, and a generation of pioneers who had taken the Cold War to the Americans. For Shevchenko, command gave him the opportunity to test himself, to live up to the responsibility, to forge a family from the raw material of his crew. It also gave him the opportunity to stand out and add his name to the history of the Soviet Navy. As he recalled many years later, "I tried to do everything in a unique way. I wanted to command in a manner that would not occur to others. I wished to be a true original. I had to know my boat and the men, to make them both my ally, and to teach them to perceive the world as I saw it."

His first chance to test his crew and to display his truly contagious confidence came with a 1977 deployment with his Victor 2 in the Mediterranean Sea, which he already knew well.

On his transit toward Gibraltar he encountered an American Sturgeon class submarine attempting to trail him. Shevchenko, like many of his Soviet shipmates, viewed this most dangerous of undersea tactics very differently than his American and NATO counterparts. As happened so often during the Cold War, the two ships tested each other before Shevchenko ultimately slipped away. He knew that this cat-and-mouse game would reveal a submarine's technical capability, its tactics, and the level of competence of the commander. In many cases the submarines would come dangerously close, and collisions occurred with some regularity.

While Shevchenko expected the Americans occasionally to succeed in the game, he and his Soviet colleagues now felt confident that their submarines could meet the challenge, particularly in quiet operations. He viewed the submariner's world as that of the hunter—patient, deliberate, quiet, cerebral. Soviet and American submariners trailing each other to test skills and gather intelligence served as vital preparation for the shooting war that no one hoped would come.

Very early in his career as a commander, Shevchenko became one of the Soviet Navy's experts on Arctic operations. In this environment the hunt became even more difficult because the acoustics of the frigid ocean quickly betrayed the presence of one submarine to another. The absence of regular commercial traffic left the fish and mammal population and the ice itself as the only acoustic cover.

The forbidding ice was an unavoidable hazard in the Cold War because of the strategic importance of the Arctic, which provided the shortest trajectories for the intercontinental ballistic missiles available to both sides. By 1979, when Shevchenko made his first polar transit, both the Soviet Union and the United States could launch such missiles from submerged submarines.

Shevchenko knew that he would frequently find American submarines silently waiting for him along his path in the far north. A Los Angeles class submarine would hover in a neutrally buoyant state and acoustically collect operational and technical data on Soviet performance. It would then slide in behind the passing Russian to trail it. Shevchenko expected it and did not find it troubling. He would report all sonar contacts, all confirmed American contacts, and any indication that the adversary had successfully followed him. Sometimes he would pursue the American intruder to drive him out of the region, then return to the standard missile boat escort mission.

Rather than feeling compelled to play cat-and-mouse, Shevchenko regularly used active sonar to focus on any detected submarines, saying, "I used active only. If I detected a submarine I always assumed that the commander of that vessel had already detected me. Most of the submarines on both sides by that time had roughly equivalent detection capabilities. For me to assume that I might still mask my presence when I already had an American on my sonar was foolish."[9]

Shevchenko's first journey to the North Pole took place in 1979, after his command, the *K-513*, received an award as the best boat in his squadron from Deputy Defense Minister Marshal Kirill Moskalenko. *K-513* was then scheduled for maintenance, and he planned to go on leave. But a summons arrived from the headquarters of the deputy commander of the submarine flotilla, Rear Admiral Eugene Chernov, a man whom Shevchenko greatly admired for his confidence, competence, and style. Chernov possessed that special personality, self-discipline, and professional behavior known as "charisma." As a commander, he displayed the quick mind and combative personality that Shevchenko sought to emulate. Chernov, who was short, had to project size rather than physically display it. For Shevchenko, observing Chernov was a lesson in leadership, teaching him a commander's responsibility to educate his crew, to prepare them for every task, to make the essential decisions, and to take responsibility.

≈   ≈   ≈

IN THE SPRING OF 1979, the Northern Fleet commander Admiral of the Navy Georgi Egorov visited the *513*. He listened to Shevchenko's report on the status of his submarine, his crew, and the tests planned for his relatively new Victor 2, all in the presence of the new submarine squadron commander, Captain First Rank V. Anokhin. When the inspection concluded, the admiral asked Shevchenko if he had any questions. He would never presume to present the admiral with questions he had not cleared first through his chain of command, but he saw an opportunity and decided to take it. Based on the admiral's favorable estimate of the *513*, he asked Egorov to provide *513* with a newly developed narrow-band, low-frequency acoustic analysis system to improve the capabilities of the submarine.

Egorov ordered the head of the radio-technical department of the Northern Fleet, Captain First Rank Boris Novi, to provide *K-513* with the requested equipment. Novi quickly promised delivery and installation the very next week.

≈   ≈   ≈

IN PREPARING FOR THE POLAR TRANSIT, Captain Shevchenko went back to the very beginning, to the fundamentals of ship-handling and command.

His primary mission was to cruise under the Arctic ice and surface at the North Pole. In addition, he would add to their knowledge of the Arctic region so that nuclear submarines could operate more safely. He would open the operation by practicing cruises under the ice both solo and with other submarines. K-513's crew also studied the bathymetric conditions in the Arctic Ocean, to gather data on the features of the ice, to practice ways of establishing the submarine's exact location at any time and that of a patrolling partner, to take regular fathometer readings, and to lose no opportunity to carefully observe NATO naval forces.

Shevchenko scheduled his departure for August 1, 1979. K-513 would set out for the Arctic Ocean from Zapadnaya Litsa at a course and speed that would place her at the edge of the ice pack by August 24. Three days later the boat would begin a short-range practice cruise of twelve hours' duration in the company of the Charlie class submarine K-320, an ocean tug, and an icebreaker. Then K-320 would take its turn on August 28, practicing in the region for fifteen hours with the aid of K-513 and the two surface vessels. If the exercises proved successful, K-513 would then cruise under the ice into the Arctic Ocean via the deep canyons of the Franz-Victoria and Saint Anne's Troughs, approaching latitude 83°30' north. K-320 would accompany Shevchenko on this first leg to 83°30' and would then depart for home, leaving K-513 to complete the journey to the North Pole. If everything went according to plan, Shevchenko would surface at 90° north on September 1.

As their preparations approached completion, Gorshkov called the senior officers of the K-513 and K-320 to Moscow, along with Vice Admiral Rudolf Golosov, Shevchenko's superior, and Rear Admiral Chernov.

Shevchenko had never visited Gorshkov's inner sanctum before and was terribly nervous. When he met the Soviet Navy's most senior officer, Shevchenko reported on his preparations for the voyage. Both the presentation and the question session went well.

Shortly after 0900 on August 24, the *513*'s crew cast off the boat's lines and put to sea. The trip to the rendezvous point went smoothly and the presence of Rear Admiral Golosov on board as senior commander helped the crew focus on both their tasks and Shevchenko's orders. *K-513* met its companion vessels on August 27 at latitude 78°00' north, longitude 42°24' east, 143 miles away from the edge of the ice pack.

Shevchenko quickly implemented his cruise plan by submerging to 450 feet and proceeding north at 20 knots toward the edge of the polar ice. While in contact with the icebreaker *Dobrinya Nikitich* he explored the outer reaches of the Arctic ice cover at approximately 80° north latitude. His log reflects a close call that revealed the nature and power of the Arctic ice.

> 1905 hours, I arrived in the region where the submarine was supposed to practice and slowed down to 5 knots. According to our reconnaissance data there was no ice yet in sight. The sonar complex designed by Rubin showed a clear horizon. I brought *K-513* to periscope depth. I could see an empty horizon through the periscope; 1.87 nautical miles away on a bearing of 238° the radar showed a spot which presumably was a single iceberg.
>
> 1920 hours, Speed, 7 knots; submerged to 120 feet; I brought the submarine around to starboard and maneuvered toward the iceberg. My sonar picked up noises seemingly made by the iceberg; the detection resembled the sound made by the rising tide, a brook, or the sound of water poured from one glass to another.
>
> 1930 hours, I twice used low-power active sonar to measure the thickness of the iceberg at distance. There was no echo. Therefore, we assumed it didn't have a big draught. We were 1.6 nautical miles away. I used the mine detection sonar to control our distance as we approached the iceberg.
>
> 1934 hours, Our sonar screen showed the ice at a bearing of

219° at 1.1 nautical miles. I slowed to 3 knots to permit ice reconnaissance devices to work.

1944 hours, NOK-1 [the navigation ice detector] detected that
the nearest edge of the iceberg exhibited two oval ledges. I kept
the boat moving at 2.5 knots.

1945 hours, the device measuring ice thickness showed nothing, so I took *513* under the first ledge.

1947 hours, NOK-1 detected the second ice ledge at 10 to 15°
relative; the whole iceberg was drifting to starboard. Suddenly, the
sonar detected what was probably the right blade of my forward
dive planes brushing against the ice surface. *513* held its depth at
130 feet while the gyrocompass showed a drift to starboard. I
changed the rudder angle to move the stabilizers and propeller
away from the ice and took the boat down to 180 feet.

2004 hours. Course, depth, and speed unchanged. The stern
planes worked well. To discover the extent and effect of the damage sustained by our contact with the iceberg, I tested the dive
planes at 12 knots and carefully examined the attitude of the boat
at all times. The boat responded well. As a result, I made a decision to examine the outer hull and the dive planes when we arrived at the surface rendezvous.

Shevchenko did not surface until 0346 on August 28. He encountered
moderate waves at force one and foggy conditions that limited visibility
to one nautical mile. His crew immediately went topside to examine the
bow, finding the blade of the starboard dive plane a few degrees off with
a dent approximately one foot from its tip. The axle by which the dive
plane moved leaned over at a 15-degree angle and would not budge. It
had obviously brushed against the second ledge of the iceberg. The bow
and the outer hull showed no marks at all and the dive plane forward on
the port side worked very well. Given that a malfunctioning starboard
plane would have no impact on the boat at speeds up to 20 knots submerged, Shevchenko decided to continue the mission and report on the
damage when they returned to base. On August 28, the Northern Fleet
sent Shevchenko a report that *K-513* was proceeding north into a region

with a very high iceberg count, some with a draught of 210 feet. He decided to negotiate the ice field carefully, staying submerged well below the massive subsurface sections of the icebergs. He reached the edge of the ice pack at latitude 80°23' north.

That same day Shevchenko analyzed his progress so far, concluding that submarines en route to the Arctic via the Saint Anne's and Franz-Victoria Troughs should cruise for safety at or below 450 feet.

Careful acoustic analysis with new sonar equipment demonstrated that he could relate certain noises to the icebergs. Readings taken by the low-frequency acoustic analyzer revealed unique sounds when the boat moved at seven knots or less and remained relatively shallow at a depth of approximately 120 feet. Icebergs emerged clearly from the sonar at ranges of two or three nautical miles at a frequency of 5 kilohertz. He resolved to make sure the officers under his command studied this phenomenon carefully. While the active sonar permitted him to gauge the distance to these icebergs, it made sense to stay 450 feet down and rely on the NOK for further information. This instrument displayed the physical limits of the iceberg captured imperfectly by the active sonar. With it Shevchenko could see how easily the iceberg could have damaged his diving plane. He knew that he would remember his first encounter with the monstrous iceberg for the rest of his life.

On August 29 at 0100, K-320 and the 513 prepared for their joint run toward the Pole. As K-320 sat on the surface two miles away, both submarines tested every device on board, from communications to detection to navigation, to ensure a safe collaboration. They even submerged for a time to accept instructions from the Northern Fleet under different conditions to verify their ability to receive essential communication. Both submarines reported to the fleet that the exercise could begin.

At 0145 they began their voyage and both submarines began to dive. 513 descended almost immediately to 450 feet, leveling and adjusting trim at a speed of 12 knots.

All during the exercise the two boats constantly checked their course as well as their relative positions. In addition, Shevchenko had his navigation and control room personnel continually take readings for depth, sonar contacts with undersea formations, the configuration of the ice overhead, and the occasional *polinya*. For the next ninety-seven hours, the two crews learned, recorded data, and helped one another over a distance of 972 miles. At 0735 on August 30, *K-320* turned and set a course for home. Now on its own, *K-513* set its sights on the Pole, proceeding 450 feet down at 12 knots.

Surfacing presents one of the most daunting challenges of the polar experience for submariners. It requires common sense combined with the careful use of the precision data provided by advanced technology. Shevchenko intended to practice the surfacing maneuver as soon as a suitable location above presented itself. The need to practice became even more apparent as the overhead ice cover changed to a maximum thickness of up to 12 feet.

During the afternoon of August 31, Shevchenko decided to make the final run to the Pole. He began looking for a suitable *polinya* in a region of ice with a relatively smooth underside 1,500 feet long in order to practice surfacing. This would allow his communications gear to safely break the surface without damaging his rudder and dive planes.

His first surfacing exercise is recorded in his log as follows:

1317, course 0°, speed 12 knots, depth 450 feet; the mine detection device showed a plane ice zone, presumably a *polinya*. I slowed down to 3 knots; the ice-thickness measuring device was on, the officer observed the under ice surface through the periscope and over the television monitors.

1327, course 10°, depth 450 feet, speed 3 knots; I cruised under the center of an ice zone 4500 feet long with a relatively flat underside. The ice was 12 feet thick.

Shevchenko carefully maneuvered the boat to the center of the chosen area, approaching at a depth of 270 feet, completely level and parallel to the ice above. He stopped *K-513* and began to hover. The actual surfacing would take place without propulsion. He had to choose the correct speed of ascent by pumping water out of the submarine's ballast tanks, increasing positive buoyancy, and monitoring the rate of his rise. He would also adjust the angle of the boat slightly to protect his stern dive planes and his rudder from any collision with the underside of the ice. A slight down angle at the stern would place the bow slightly higher as the vessel rose to meet the surface ice.

He activated the training alarm, sending all of the relevant crewmen to their posts and focusing their attention on the next step in the exercise process. Shevchenko's log again picks up the story:

> 1336, depth 270 feet, deferent 0°. *513* in position for vertical surfacing. I kept the image of our target location on the television monitor.
>
> 1345, Resumed hovering at 255 feet. Initiated ascent via ballast release. The boat began to rise at 9 feet per minute. The vertical surfacing system worked perfectly. The huge ship responded well to each command from the diving officer Boris Dyachkov.
>
> 1359, depth 120 feet. Surfacing maneuver continued. As the boat came close to the ice, I slowed to 6 feet per minute. To protect the dive planes and the rudder I effected a 2° stern deferent (stern down) by pumping ballast water from the bow tanks to the stern.
>
> 1426, depth 45 feet. The stern deferent was 5°. The television complex clearly showed that the submarine was drifting with the current and with the ice. With a 1.2 feet per minute surfacing speed *513* touched ice projecting 15 feet below the surface with her bow. The contact immediately decreased the stern deferent to 3° and caused the boat to drift 30° to starboard with the under-ice current. The depth stabilizer was switched off and the television went white. To prevent the submarine from sliding along the underside of the ice, I pressed her to the ice by expelling 16 tons of ballast. The positive buoyancy pinned the boat to the underside of the ice and arrested the drift, avoiding damage to the stern dive planes, rudder, and the sail-mounted antennae. We proceeded to receive communication from base through the ice without any interference. Initially, errors in the signals received via the Marshrut radio-navigation system caused the navigators to make an 8-mile mistake in their estimation of the surfacing point location.

With this first exercise successfully completed, Shevchenko prepared the crew for the delicate diving process. Pulling away from the underside of the ice also required care. When the crew finished all of the planned activity near the surface, including a trash drop, Shevchenko ordered an increase in the ballast, and *K-513* successfully cleared the ice after spending twenty-nine minutes near the surface.

Due to temperature, pressure, and natural hydrodynamic forces, the boat began to descend quicker as depth increased. At about 150 feet the speed of descent increased to 30 to 36 feet per minute. Now timing became important. The diving officer had to pump water out of the trim tanks at about 300 feet, while the propulsion came on line to move the vessel forward. At that depth, the odds in favor of colliding with ice under the surface approached zero and the slowly increasing forward motion of the vessel would return maneuvering control to the helm. On board *K-513*, the propulsion officer, Captain Second Rank Vladimir Katomin, was responsible for performing this underwater ballet. At 430 feet, *K-513* resumed her course for the Pole.

For the rest of the journey to the Pole, the crew attentively observed the instrument readings and the television screens. Above them, there were occasional breaks in the ice, the size of a football field at most, on the surface. In addition, the underside of the floating ice displayed many ledges arranged like layers, some jutting out as much as thirty feet. At the North Pole, their fathometer showed a huge projection of the ice perpendicular to the surface down to 125 feet. Other areas had ice showing only a 6- to 8-foot draught underneath a smooth thick surface extending horizontally for 2,700 feet. Everywhere they looked the natural conditions awed them.

At 1832 on August 31, 1979, Shevchenko informed the crew that the navigator now placed them at the North Pole. The entire ship's complement received the news with cheering and excitement, for they had joined a rather exclusive Soviet and American club. Shevchenko congratulated his crew on their achievement and quickly set them to work finding a *polinya* so they could open their hatch at the top of the world.

He defined a search area of 360 degrees with the Pole as the center, and divided it into four quadrants. The boat then systematically surveyed each quadrant at 5 knots, looking for a suitable *polinya*. At 1815 the mine detector showed a distinct edge with a plane surface at a modest distance. Shevchenko set his course accordingly and felt almost instinctively that he had his *polinya*.

He carefully recorded the ascent and his achievement. He ordered his watch engineer Sergey Topchiev to stop the turbine and at his order the boat began its ascent. According to his log, at 1820 *K-513* rose to 180 feet; the boat's attitude and trim were checked. The periscope and instruments showed clear water above. The *polinya* was approximately 675 feet long and 300 feet wide.

≈   ≈   ≈

SHEVCHENKO LEVELED THE BOAT at 180 feet without propulsion, using his trim tank to adjust the ballast. The boat continued to rise at a rate of 12 to 15 feet per minute, and he kept the stern slightly lower than his bow, protecting his rudder, screws, and aft dive planes from the impact with the ice. He kept *513* in the center of the *polinya* by occasionally using his emergency slow-speed propulsion shaft driven by the turbine, making sure that neither the stern nor the dive planes came into contact with the ice.

By 1833, the boat reached 170 feet and continued to rise. With all of the reporting and ordering completed, everything became strangely quiet. Only the boatswain's voice, calling out the depth, broke the silence. In his memory, Shevchenko can still clearly hear the last call, ". . . depth, 12 feet; . . . the boat has stopped." Everyone felt the stern deferent suddenly disappear and the submarine commenced rocking gently on a clear surface. Smiling, Shevchenko turned to Admiral Golosov and asked permission to raise the periscope.

Nothing prepared him for this first glimpse of the polar region. As he recalls it:

> I didn't expect to see what I saw through the periscope! There was pure white and serene ice around the submarine. There was a wonderful rainbow stretched through the eastern part of the sky,

which was shining with all the colors as if it had multi-shade diamonds. It was gorgeous! Golosov went to the periscope.

A minute after, having opened the hatch, I was standing at the bridge. I really wanted the crewmen to see this beauty, and then to report to the commander-in-chief on the surfacing. Having prepared the machinery and devices for the stopover in the *polinya* and the communication means for the report to the base, the crewmen had a chance to admire the pure Arctic beauty, to feel the terrific ice silence, and to collect memories with their cameras. We had a meeting on the bow of the submarine and raised the Soviet and Naval Flag to the melody of the Soviet hymn. Then there were salute shots to commemorate the surfacing at the North Pole. The report on the surfacing of the *K-513* was sent at 1925. The men stayed on the upper deck for more than an hour. At 2000 the men of the second shift went to the upper deck. The sun was still above the horizon, but the area changed daytime colors for darker and deeper ones, all the while keeping the greatness of its silence.

As night descended, the crew took the flags down and the submarine began preparations to submerge. Shevchenko had the hatch closed at 2130 and immediately gave orders to dive the boat. At 120 feet the crew pumped water out of the trim tank to slow the speed of descent. Otherwise the effect of temperature and pressure in the depths would make the boat so negatively buoyant that the descent would proceed far too quickly. At 360 feet, Katomin, "the choreographer," once again brought main propulsion on line just in time. In those late summer days of 1979, *K-513* spent two hours and thirty-seven minutes on the surface at the top of the world.

At 450 feet, Shevchenko ordered the helm to make turns for 8 knots and then, handing the bridge over to his executive officer, he retired to the navigator's plot and laid in the course for their return trip. Later that evening he reported to Golosov on their probable time of arrival and extended an invitation for a midnight dinner to celebrate their conquest of the North Pole. A few hours later they turned for home; depth 450 feet, speed 12 knots.[10]

THE TIES THAT BIND

Anatoli Shevchenko built a solid naval career, including chases with American attack submarines, but that was only a glimpse of what lay in store for him when he conducted possibly the Soviet Navy's most audacious sting operation at sea, the large-scale operations Aport and Atrina of the mid-1980s.

Without complete secrecy, these plans would never have worked.[11] Complacency and routine on the part of the U.S. Navy would also play a critical role in this endeavor. Seemingly secure behind their constantly probing attack submarines, stealthy missile boats, powerful battle groups, and the SOSUS acoustic detection system, the U.S. Navy needed to feel in control of the GIUK gap, the North Atlantic, and the approaches to its own shores. As President Ronald Reagan preached the gospel of American military and naval strength arrayed against the "evil empire," Admiral of the Fleet of the Soviet Union Sergei G. Gorshkov prepared a secret exercise, a sting operation, that he hoped would quietly demonstrate Soviet naval capability and betray American practice and intention while leaving his old adversary none the wiser.

And now seemed the perfect time to do it. Gorshkov knew that his tenure as commander in chief of the Soviet Navy, initiated by Khrushchev in 1956, would conclude in December 1985. In his seventy-fifth year, this old destroyer sailor could not think of a better parting shot than asking his Northern Fleet submariners to lead the Americans and their NATO allies into a trap. Furthermore, the possibility of conducting a successful operation while Secretary Gorbachev prepared to meet Ronald Reagan in Geneva in November 1985, made it the perfect time to act on a plan conceived by one of the admiral's more promising and energetic subordinates. Reagan needed to know what the Soviet Navy could do, but not until the First Secretary of the Communist Party of the Soviet Union wanted him to know.

In his second year commanding the Thirty-third Division of the Northern Fleet, Captain First Rank Anatoli I. Shevchenko had his own memorable style and personal manner. An imposing figure of roughly six feet in height with a commanding presence, Shevchenko still has his penetrating stare and easy smile. As an operational commander, his personality quickly filled any room he entered with a determined manner, a preoccupation with significant detail, and a carefully applied sense of humor. Like an artist in the act of creation, he enjoyed the process of command; from the conceptual sketch, through the details and brush strokes, to the application of his unique style and signature to the finished product. This time his agile mind had concocted an operation that he felt sure would lead the Americans to betray themselves.[12]

After pulling strings to have his plan approved by higher authority, Shevchenko launched the preparations but kept everything to himself. Neither he nor his superiors informed the KGB or the GRU. None of the security services knew about the plan or the timing of the operation. Indeed, he employed a variety of stories to provide sufficient cover for the orders that arrived from Moscow instructing five submarines of the Victor 2 and Victor 3 classes to prepare for sea.[13] He wanted to demonstrate that the Soviet submarine force could acquire as much significant operational intelligence about the American fleet using ingenuity and sheer determination as the latter could about the Soviets with SOSUS and all of their other varied and vaunted ASW surveillance methods. Shevchenko also wanted to remind the Americans that Soviet submarines, some with missile capability, could still operate off the American coast, as they did in the early years of the Cold War, with nuclear warheads at the ready. Given the policies and the rhetoric of the Reagan administration and the increasing economic weakness of the Soviet Union, the geopolitical situation seemed to call for an operation that could give Gorbachev some authority at the conference table. Shevchenko and his fellow submariners did not like the First Secretary's inclination to redraw Soviet defense policy, but they understood the hard line coming out of Washington. They recognized that adversary all too well.

Just before he left for Cuban waters to take command of this secret operation, Shevchenko went to the head of Northern Fleet Security and presented for his signature the paperwork authorizing the operation. The plan carried the curious code name "Aport," a meaningless collection of letters selected deliberately to avoid betraying the essence of the plan. The submarines involved would leave for the Atlantic coast of the United States and Canada the next day. Rather than having an opportunity to complain about the lack of both information and prior consultation, the security officer found the document already approved by the most powerful flag officers in the Soviet Navy. Left with no choice, he signed on the dotted line. Shevchenko smiled and took all copies of the completed documents with him. He would leave no trail.

The only other officers briefed on this plan prepared their submarines and crews for immediate departure. Shevchenko himself set off for Cuba on board a Project 705 Lira-type nuclear attack submarine, the type NATO referred to as Alfas. The swift and deep-diving Alfa, very much like the one Captain Boris Kolyada took to sea, would transport Shevchenko and his operations staff to a position east of Fidel Castro's island at speeds approaching 45 knots submerged. There they would transfer to the Moma class hydrographic research vessel *Kolguyev*.[14] This scientific and intelligence-gathering surface vessel would enable Shevchenko to control the entire operation from the Caribbean Sea via satellite link.

Shevchenko designed Aport to present the U.S. Navy with a confusing, unexpected, and powerful Soviet submarine presence near the American coast. He gambled that this situation would force the NATO Atlantic command to respond immediately in ways that would reveal some SSBN patrol areas, the current tactical habits of fast attack submarines, the response time of ASW surveillance aircraft, and the extent of SOSUS capability and coverage. It helped considerably that the John Walker spy ring in the United States had already betrayed NATO sufficiently to give the Victors a fair chance to penetrate undetected into the North Atlantic.[15]

On the morning of May 29, 1985, the four submarines put to sea. Departing from West Litsa on the Kola Peninsula, they moved out into the Barents Sea and headed for the "corner," the name given to the North Cape, where the submarines began their turn south and west into the Norwegian Sea.[16] A fifth boat, the Victor 1 class *K-147*, left from Gremikha, the Northern Fleet base situated farthest to the east on the Kola, carrying a new on-board detector designed to search for submerged radioactive wake traces from the nuclear propulsion systems of American submarines. They all dropped down through the Iceland–Faeroes gap into the North Atlantic on their way to the Aport staging area Shevchenko had selected in the Newfoundland Basin off the Canadian coast.

Shevchenko knew that his Victors might not make it undetected through the American and NATO surveillance constantly focused on the choke points between Greenland, Iceland, and the United Kingdom. Neither would the presence of a lone Soviet hydrographic vessel in the Caribbean, placed there for his use as a command ship, go unnoticed at Atlantic Fleet Command in Norfolk. Of course, an operator of his experience knew all too well that you did not pin strategies on hope.

He had something else in mind. In this case, one has to look not at submarines, weapons, platforms, and sensors for the source of his confidence, but at the ocean itself. While the ocean environment might present regular dangers, it also provides the stealth that submarines need to succeed. If you look at a map of the northwestern Atlantic Ocean, examine carefully the coast of Maine and the Canadian Maritime provinces just to the north. Off that coast, to the east and north, lie the Newfoundland Grand Banks, one of the busiest fishing grounds in the world. Slightly farther to the east, the continental shelf ends and the bottom drops away into Shevchenko's chosen Newfoundland Basin. In this area the powerful Atlantic warm-water anomaly called the Gulf Stream turns east and north after its long journey from the Florida Straits, ready to become part of the North Atlantic Current before it proceeds across the ocean to the United Kingdom.

NATO scientists and ASW officers constantly sought better ways to examine the Gulf Stream because its warm waters profoundly affected the behavior of passing acoustic signals, whether generated by whales or by Victor class boats on their way to provoke the Americans into revealing valuable operational intelligence. Shevchenko hoped he might slip through the NATO surveillance network, but he did not worry too much. He knew the presence of the Victors would stir the NATO pot. When it did, he intended to hide his boats in the warm waters of the Gulf Stream. In this region, the ocean would provide physical and, even more importantly, intermittent acoustic cover. He would use the natural characteristics of the ocean, eternally reliable, to confuse the technology available to the Americans just long enough to win his prize.[17]

The operation began with a signal from Shevchenko on June 18. Beginning at a point barely west of the Newfoundland Grand Banks, two of the Victors began following one another, clockwise, in a gigantic circle, while two others did the same in a different but concentric circle moving counterclockwise. At the same time, four Tu-142M aircraft took off from the San Antonio air base in Cuba to join the operation by performing ASW sweeps of the Newfoundland Basin with sonobuoys and surveillance gear designed to detect American submarines and to intercept communications. Once the Soviet boats began their pattern running, the Americans reacted just as Shevchenko's plan had predicted. The Soviets observed at close range American and NATO ASW aircraft operating regular flights from Maine, the Canadian Maritimes, Bermuda, and the Azores at all hours of the day looking for the four Victors. In the meanwhile, the Russians looked for American submarines.

Gulf Stream waters populated by an increased number of Soviet submarines presented a terrible danger to the United States and a very perplexing problem for the U.S. Navy. While the boats clearly and often showed up on air, surface, and subsurface surveillance systems, they also disappeared with a disturbing regularity, often for many days without any indication of their activity or the timing of their return to base. Not unlike Tom Clancy's fictional Soviet commander, Marko Ramius in *The Hunt for Red October,* Shevchenko intended to use the Gulf Stream as intermittent cover; cover that would potentially permit him to move his boats from the Newfoundland Basin in the north as far south as the American submarine bases at Charleston, South Carolina, and King's Bay, Georgia. Ramius had a silent propulsion system, the dream of every submariner, and detailed undersea maps of the canyons of the Reykjanes Ridge, a mountain range projecting south and west of Iceland. Shevchenko's Victors could not operate with complete silence, but the warm waters of the Gulf Stream, an anomaly in the usually frigid North Atlantic, might hide their presence, almost on demand, for days or week at a time. Warm water temperatures would inhibit the detection capabilities of the passive sonar systems used by the Americans to track Soviet boats. For Shevchenko, that was enough.

Captain Peter Cressy, commanding officer of Patrol Wing Five based at the Naval Air Station in Brunswick, Maine, lost sleep because of Shevchenko's tactics. He found the increase in Soviet submarine activity disturbing and their regular tendency to disappear from his sonar absolutely maddening. Not a man to admit defeat and determined to discover the conditions that prevented his ASW patrol aircraft from regularly tracking Shevchenko's boats, he relentlessly exercised all technical and human means at his disposal for finding the Victors. This distinguished 1973 graduate of the U.S. Naval War College concluded that the dilemma had nothing to do with his aircraft, the ability of his aircrews, or the technology at his disposal. The ocean itself presented the problem; especially the most powerful dynamic force in the segment of ocean he patrolled, the Gulf Stream. As an ASW officer, he knew how easily the behavior of sound in seawater could change, and especially the critical role temperature played. He quickly asked one of his staff to produce the best Gulf Stream scientist the navy could find. In 1985, only two men fit that description: Henry Stommel of the Woods Hole Oceanographic Institution and Allan Robinson of Harvard University. Robinson quickly found himself in a car and on his way to Maine.

On hearing the problem of the lost Victors, this Massachusetts native, oceanographer, and physicist immediately realized he could help Cressy. Assisted by his postdoctoral colleagues and graduate students, Robinson had just finished formulating the first part of a computer modeling system designed to predict environmental change in the ocean. The first part of this "Harvard Ocean Prediction System," or HOPS, naturally—and in this case fortuitously—focused on one of Robinson's favorite Atlantic forces, the Gulf Stream. When Cressy and Robinson began to look for Shevchenko's Victors through the digital lens provided by HOPS, Patrol Wing Five detections via sonobuoy improved significantly. While not the ultimate answer to the acoustic fog generated by the Gulf Stream, Robinson's work helped predict the behavior of the stream in much the same way that an evening news show meteorologist would predict the week's weather. The process was not perfect, but it gave the hunters a better chance to flush their target with sonobuoys.[18]

As far as Shevchenko knew, his submarines had remained undetected throughout the operation, and only the *K-488* appeared on American surveillance devices in the vicinity of Iceland during the return voyage. Below the surface and frequently hidden in the temperature variations and the gyres of the Gulf Stream, *K-324* detected American SSBNs and fast attack submarines on three different occasions, maintaining a combined contact time of twenty-eight hours. Another of Shevchenko's sub captains reported that he had trailed an American SSBN for five days.[19]

In the hierarchy of targets for the Soviet submariners, only the SSBNs surpassed the American aircraft carriers in importance. Victors and all of the advanced Soviet boats existed to gather this kind of intelligence and every Soviet submarine commander lusted after the moment when he had the upper hand against an American ballistic missile submarine. Practical experience had already demonstrated that American SSBNs, operating in a patrol quiet mode at a very low speed, could remain so silent that a Victor would have to be within a mile of the American missile boat in order to be sure of detecting it. Shevchenko guessed that the SSBNs operated at one-tenth the noise level generated by the quietest Soviet submarines.[20] Shevchenko's efforts provided the Soviet Union with up-to-date intelligence on SSBN locations and operational areas, on attack submarine tactics and habits, and on the latest air search techniques employed by NATO and the United States. The operation concluded on July 1 and the boats involved returned safely to the Northern Fleet.

From Shevchenko's point of view, the operation succeeded beyond his expectations. The Americans had greater wealth, a larger navy, and amazing technical assets, at times making secret Soviet submarine missions nearly impossible. In response, he chose to gather intelligence with the best weapons available to him and on site, as a hunter might. With the Aport strategy Shevchenko flushed his quarry, and forced a reaction. As he directed operations from his ship in the Caribbean, the Victors sharply prodded the Americans and came prepared to observe and capitalize on the results. While more difficult, dangerous, and certainly less subtle than many of the methods employed by the Americans and NATO, the captain and the Soviet naval command considered the outcome and the lessons learned well worth the risk. They could move up and down the American Atlantic coast, keeping themselves concealed for much of the time. It became a first step in a much more ambitious application of a similar technique.

≈   ≈   ≈

APORT PROVIDED A PREFACE to a more elaborate plan; an effort to keep the Soviet Navy active, politically influential, and seemingly on par with NATO. Only weeks after the Reagan–Gorbachev summit in Reykjavik, Iceland, in October 1986, the new commander in chief of the navy, Gorshkov's successor, Admiral of the Fleet Vladimir Chernavin, decided that Captain Shevchenko needed to go to sea once again. Chernavin wanted to establish his reputation as a strong and aggressive leader, while giving the political leadership confidence in their ability to challenge the Americans in their own waters. This time, the techniques used in Aport, supplemented by lessons learned from the U-boat strategy employed with significant effect early in World War II by German Grand Admiral Karl Doenitz, gave birth to a more complicated hunt. Once again, Shevchenko would try to sting NATO. He would call this venture "Atrina."

He turned once again to five Victor class attack submarines. Using communication wavelengths more frequently employed by merchant vessels and ocean tugboats, all five boats carefully masked their communication with the Northern Fleet. They also tried to drown the acoustic signature generated by each submarine in a noisy sea. Given the traffic through the GIUK gap, both natural and man-made, they had their choice of using either inbound Soviet submarines or scores of noisy surface vessels as ponderous but relatively efficient cover. Each boat moved deliberately with the ship traffic through the Iceland–Faeroes region into the North Atlantic and then dispersed to predetermined locations scattered over that immense body of water.

Only the submarine commanders now taking up station in far-flung parts of the Atlantic received highly classified briefings on the operation. As with Aport, Shevchenko kept the number of informed men to a bare minimum, once again denying even the naval security services access to his plans. From the Soviet vantage point, Aport had worked flawlessly and Shevchenko had no reason to depart from a tried-and-true approach. Of all the boats chosen for the new operation, only one had experienced Aport. All five Victor 3's possessed the first Soviet operational, stern-deployed, towed sonar array that would enable them, like the Americans, to extend from a stern vertical stabilizer a very sensitive set of hydrophones towed well behind the noise made by the boats' own screws.

The Atrina strategy clearly followed the lessons that Aport had taught, namely, that NATO would obviously respond with all of its most critical assets if strategically important regions seemed threatened. Therefore, borrowing from Grand Admiral Doenitz's wolfpack technique of World War II, Shevchenko planned to stage smaller-scale versions of Aport at various strategically important areas in the Atlantic. With a critical mass of Soviet submarines gathering in any given region, NATO would respond aggressively, pursuing with both air and subsurface assets. The Soviet strategist planned to converge and then disperse at repeated but irregular intervals at various points in the Atlantic, revealing each time the nature of the NATO presence in the area.

The first convergence, for example, took place near the base used by the British and occasionally the Americans near the port of Hamilton in Bermuda. The Soviet boats came together, vectored at Shevchenko's command by satellite and aircraft communication, to a location in the Sargasso Sea, once again a warm-water area that played havoc with acoustic detection. When one or more of the boats had been detected, the others observed and often pursued the American fast attack submarines tracking individual Victors. This time Admiral Chernavin assisted Shevchenko with ASW surveillance aircraft not only from Cuba, but also from the Northern Fleet air bases on the Kola Peninsula.

NATO's swift and strong countermeasures only ended up serving the operation's strategic goals. According to Soviet sources, the American Atlantic Submarine Command, or "SubLant," dispatched six nuclear submarines in search of Shevchenko's group of five Victors, and the U.S. Atlantic Fleet used ASW surveillance aircraft and SURTASS ships of the Stalwart class to perform aerial and sonar sweeps.[21] Atrina repeatedly demonstrated the Soviet ability to explore NATO intentions and capabilities, while displaying the Northern Fleet's transatlantic reach. Along with the obviously important results of the sting operations, they needed to demonstrate for the Americans and NATO that the Soviet fleet could still operate at considerable distance, close to American shores, and in coordination. In spite of the geopolitical circumstances, Chernavin used Atrina to remind NATO that he had inherited and would use Gorshkov's formidable fleet in the interests of the Soviet Union.[22]

≈   ≈   ≈

AFTER THE PRECIPITOUS BREAKUP of the Soviet Union in 1991, Shevchenko witnessed the military services falling upon hard times. Senior officers in the former Soviet military had enjoyed many perks, from the important, such as good pay, housing, cars, vacations, and college educations for their children, to the trivial, such as hair styling for their wives and the occasional chance to travel to foreign countries. There was every incentive for young men (and, to a lesser degree, young women) to join the military services and make a career of it, notwithstanding the inherent dangers.

Things grew steadily worse after 1992, as all those benefits evaporated, to the ludicrous point that the United States Congress appropriated $25,000,000 to provide housing for former Soviet officers in an effort to stifle their growing discontent.

Maintaining an effective submarine fleet under such conditions was almost impossible, and depended almost entirely on experienced and dedicated officers like Shevchenko, who always looked for those men still in service who showed promise as future leaders and commanders. As everyone scrambled to make a living and care for their families, the former Soviet Navy had a very difficult time not only keeping those good officers still in the ranks, but also keeping them trained and challenged.

By 1994, as Shevchenko looked at the number of first and second rank captains within the submarine service, he realized that he had directly or indirectly educated many of them as submariners and leaders. Concerned that the Russian Navy would soon lose the remaining expertise within its ranks to take attack submarines to the far north, Shevchenko knew that he had to shape some of the young and talented commanders still driving Russian submarines in the same way that Chernov and Golosov had shaped him. The first of these would be Sergei Kuzmin, with whom he had first worked in 1987.

In 1994, Captain First Rank Kuzmin commanded the Victor 3 submarine *K-414*. When Shevchenko discovered that the high command wanted two of the Northern Fleet's submarines to make Arctic transits, he immediately thought of Kuzmin and the *414* as one possibility. And, Shevchenko decided, he would accompany him as senior commander, just as Admiral Golosov had done with him fifteen years before. There was little choice, as where the Northern Fleet once had five or six experienced Arctic commanders, now there were only two, Shevchenko and his former student, Mikhail Motsak.[23]

Shevchenko, looking out at the line of boats tied up to the pier for months and sometimes years on end, acutely felt the decline in readiness, in capability, and in purpose. These qualities were even more necessary than the boats themselves if the Russian Navy wanted to maintain excellence and retain talented people in the ranks. In June, Shevchenko and Kuzmin decided to conduct a training cruise in the deep-water zone of the Franz-Victoria–St. Anne's Trough. Given the fact that the forecast placed the edge of the pack ice on June 10 as far south as 76 north latitude, they had to assume rather severe conditions. *K-414* would require at least five days for training and exercises of the same type that Shevchenko had faced over a decade earlier on the way to the Franz-Victoria area. It included techniques for working with submarines in Arctic waters that he had mastered: diving, moving submerged through iceberg fields, avoiding the deep draughts of floating ice mountains, maintaining trim, hovering and approaching the underside of the ice, and coping with shifting ice movement and the Arctic currents.

But en route they encountered something new, something Shevchenko would rather have avoided. At 2345 on June 11, proceeding at eight knots, 450 feet down, the sonar detected a weak noise made by a turbine.

The boat's sonar specialists immediately identified the contact as an American Los Angeles class nuclear submarine, 3.5 nautical miles away. Shevchenko ordered a torpedo attack drill using the American as a target and, when completed, took evasive measures to avoid the intruder. At 2350, *414* slowed to five knots, while the American attack boat proceeded at eight knots, now 3.3 nautical miles away from *414*.

Shevchenko and Kuzmin trailed the American during the early minutes of June 12. As he continued to alter his course based on the stern course angles of the Los Angeles class boat, Shevchenko quickly realized that the American had deployed his towed array sonar and knew full well that *414* had picked up his trail. The American commander wanted to lure Shevchenko into following him and would, while choreographing the encounter, collect technical and operational data on Kuzmin's boat. At 0113 Kuzmin changed his course to approach the American boat from her starboard and altered his speed to keep a safe distance. Twelve minutes later the American also shifted to starboard at a distance of 2.3 nautical miles from *414*. Shevchenko continually checked the distance between the two boats, noticing that the American constantly tried to close the gap to a point that the experienced Russian felt might compromise both vessels, placing his boat in a potentially dangerous position. Given the possible intelligence to collect, Shevchenko concluded that the prize did not justify the risk the American took. Kuzmin maintained the cat-and-mouse game until the American submarine began to depart from the general course necessary for *414* to continue its mission.

≈   ≈   ≈

At 0400, *414* ascended to periscope depth to tell Northern Fleet command about the contact with the American submarine. Shevchenko and Kuzmin then submerged and proceeded to the edge of the Arctic ice.

After a short time back at the base near the end of June to replenish stocks and review the training effort, *K-414* finally set off for the North Pole on July 12. The wives, families, and girlfriends of the crewmembers managed to convince the commander of the ocean tug escort to give them a ride, so Kuzmin's crew had the opportunity to see their families up until the boat's actual departure from the waters near the base. Thirty days would pass before they would see one another again.

On July 17 at 0340, *K-414*'s sonar picked up the icebreaker *Captain Dranizin* with foreign tourists aboard 36.1 nautical miles away. The presence of the icebreaker did not surprise them, nor did the drifting ice. The Northern Fleet had already warned them about the ship and the increasing ice density along their course. Early that afternoon, with the edge of the ice pack so near, Kuzmin decided to make some practice dives under the ice before moving on to the Pole. He began the process at 1300, planned to finish by 1700 and then, without emerging from under the edge of the ice pack, move on toward 90° north.

By this point in the short history of the new Russian submarine force it had become routine to prepare four torpedoes for use in case they had to come to the surface without an available *polinya*. Shevchenko and Kuzmin wanted these weapons ready when they finished the dress rehearsal and proceeded to the North Pole. Until then they would make sure that sufficient detectable gaps existed in the ice above to permit an emergency surface if that became necessary.

At 1455, as the torpedo preparation proceeded, one of the weapons began to leak oxygen from an internal flask. Immediately the torpedo room sounded the alarm and Kuzmin took the boat to the surface. As he passed through 240 feet the torpedo room reported to control that the leaking weapon continued to expel oxygen from a safety valve. At that depth, Kuzmin leveled the boat to prepare for the slow surfacing process, keeping the hull of his submarine parallel to the ice cover above. He initiated an ascent that began at the rate of six feet per minute and accelerated. He also ordered the ventilators switched on to decrease the amount of the volatile gas in the torpedo room. One spark from any source, no matter how slight, would start a raging fire.

At 1536, *414* surfaced in a very tight opening in the frozen cover above them, blanketed by fog and surrounded by floating ice. The order immediately went out to ventilate compartment one, the forward torpedo room. It took ten minutes to bring the oxygen in the atmosphere down to a safe level from the 20.8 percent indicated by the instruments as the boat broke the surface. Upon closer examination, technicians determined that poor assembly procedures employed at the Northern Fleet's Torpedo Department had caused the casualty that nearly proved their undoing.

After further machinery and weapons testing, *414* submerged to 450 feet, assumed a six knot speed, and proceeded toward the Pole. Shevchenko decided to surface once or twice a day in ice breaks as they moved farther north to report to the Northern Fleet command on the few available *polinyas* and the general ice situation.

Unfortunately this already challenging voyage had one more disturbing surprise left. At 0028 on July 21 the propulsion compartment alarm went off and sent everyone to emergency stations. The reactor had "scrammed," shut down by the on-board computer upon detecting a dangerous situation. As a result, *414*'s two propulsion turbines and both electric generators had stopped. Only the batteries were left to supply power for the ship's systems, and battery power alone could only provide a meager four-knot speed—all of this with a twelve-foot-thick roof of ice overhead. Shevchenko had to find out what had caused the reactor's computer to detect a possibly fatal problem.

At 0036, with *414* moving at only 1.5 knots and trying to maintain depth, the engines finally came on line and the boat accelerated to 3.6 knots. They discovered the reason for the near catastrophe in the behavior of an inexperienced crewman. Recently assigned to Kuzmin's command because one of the crew's propulsion specialists fell ill, this new arrival did not pay sufficient attention to the evaporator in the reactor cooling system. Water invaded the main condenser and the reactor scrammed. The propulsion watch brought the starboard reactor back to life at 0042, and fourteen minutes later steam once again surged through the starboard turbo-generator. By 0100, *414* had her propulsion power back.

Looking back on this event, Shevchenko commented that for him the torpedo malfunction and the sobering reactor episode "proved the conclusion made by commander-in-chief Sergei Gorshkov when I was young—'There is no fatal and inevitable accident in the Navy! People themselves due to their own negligence and irresponsibility create the reasons for the results of accidents!' My naval experience verified this simple and true conclusion."[24]

K-414, under the command of Sergei Kuzmin, surfaced at the North Pole at 1800 on July 25, in a clear *polinya* 1,100 feet long and 900 feet wide. The beauty of the place had not changed since 1979. Shevchenko hoped that the Arctic's striking physical beauty and profound quiet would remain eternally unchanged as a reward to those who dared to journey that far north. The officers and crew raised the Russian flag and the flag of St. Andrew to the sound of the Russian anthem. They filmed the event and reported to the Northern Fleet that the flags had unfurled in the Arctic wind at 1817.

Back at their base on August 10, Shevchenko addressed the crew. He thanked them for their service, professionalism, and skill, calling them not Soviet but now Russian submarine pioneers in the far north. He felt he had managed, at least in part, to pass on the torch of his skill and experience in the polar region to the next generation of submariners.[25]

9

AN INSIDER'S VIEW
OF THE MYSTERY OF
THE KURSK

———————

Early on the morning of August 12, 2000, Captain First Rank Igor Kurdin, experienced Delta 4 SSBN commander and lately retired from the Russian Navy, sat in his vehicle and could see only cars in front and behind. On his way back from his dacha outside St. Petersburg, he did not feel rushed. His duties as executive director of the St. Petersburg Submariners' Club did not require his presence at the office, so he decided to arrive with the traffic and tried to enjoy the ride.[1]

Just as he resigned himself to a slow morning with minimal anxiety, his pager came alive. Cursing softly and pulling the device out of his pocket in the cramped car, Kurdin read the message from his fellow Club executive, retired Captain First Rank Igor Kozyr. He knew that Kozyr had the morning watch at the Club headquarters and could easily handle any normal business or emergency. He also knew that Kozyr would never page him unless it could not wait.[2] Upon calling his office he discovered that the Oscar 2 class nuclear missile submarine *Kursk* (*K-141*) had experienced an emergency at sea. Kurdin suddenly had a terrible sinking feeling. His hope for a relaxing morning had come to an abrupt end.

≈ ≈ ≈

BOTH THE UNITED STATES NAVY and the Soviet/Russian Navies have had far more experience than they would like with submarines sinking, and unfortunately it is all too rare that there is an opportunity to save some or all of the crew. Some submarine losses, such as that of the *Scorpion,* the *Thresher,* and the *K-429,* are so sudden and so cata-strophic that everyone knows the crew died almost instantly and were at least spared a long and agonizing ordeal.

The prospect of a successful rescue elicits the utmost attention from the public, who pull for both the rescuers and those to be rescued. One of the most well-known instances of this was the May 1939 rescue of some of the crewmen of the USS *Squalus.* The whole rescue endeavor was closely covered by newspapers, radios, and newsreels.

This famous rescue effort was the result of the intelligence, persist-ence, and dedication of two individuals. The more famous of these was Vice Admiral Charles B. Momsen, who developed a submarine escape device that was known as the "Momsen Lung." Less famous was Rear Ad-miral Allan R. McCann, who devised the diving bell used to rescue thirty-three crewmen from the *Squalus.* The submarine was sunk in 240 feet of water off Portsmouth, New Hampshire, and Momsen personally directed the rescue operations. (Both Momsen and McCann went on to distin-guished careers as submarine combat commanders in World War II.)

Another major rescue operation took place in October 1978 after a collision between the *S-178*, a Soviet Pacific Fleet diesel-powered submarine, and the trawler *RFS-13*. At the time, the Soviet submarine *S-178* was surfaced, cruising back home from exercises. The men were having dinner when suddenly the big fishing trawler, without her lights on, struck the submarine, washing the submarine's captain away (but later picking him up). The *S-178* sank in less than ten seconds.

In two hours, two rescue ships began arriving at the accident scene. Admiral Golosov supervised the rescue effort.

The survivors, twenty-two in all, waited for two days in the pitch-black of the sunken submarine, waiting for the rescue submarine to evacuate them. A Vladivostok repair and overhaul yard prepared the latter submarine.

On reaching the scene of the accident, the rescue submarine submerged to the depth of 115 feet, landing about 100 feet away from the sunken submarine.

Admiral Golosov had prepared a list of instructions, which were given to the surviving submariners through *S-178*'s rescue lock chamber. When the survivors acknowledged that they understood the instructions, the rescue submarine began evacuating submariners from the torpedo room. Outside the *S-178*, divers helped the crewmen to reach the rescue submarines, where they were placed for further decompression.

Some of the submariners were dreadfully stressed, having anticipated a slow death for more than two days. A few could not understand that they were being rescued and fought with the divers, trying to get to the surface as soon as possible. The temptation to see the light of day was overwhelming. The divers had to force them to comply because if they had risen too rapidly they would have been subject to the bends when nitrogen bubbles boiled up out of their blood. It was absolutely necessary that they spend enough time in the decompression chambers to accommodate to the change in pressures.

The experience with *S-178* was invaluable a few years later when Captain Suvorov's Charlie 1 class *K-429* flooded and sank off Kamchatka in the Pacific on June 24, 1983, although there were still some unforgivable mistakes made by the repair yard that endangered the lives of the crew. As the *K-429* settled on the bottom at 150 feet, the crew immediately shut down the reactor to avoid a nuclear accident. Captain Suvorov discovered that the emergency radio buoys could not ascend to the surface because the repair yard had spot-welded covers over the access points to avoid damage during the repair period. They also attached the wrong escape pod—they installed the one that the Charlie 1 class submarines possessed—so neither emergency system could assist the hard-pressed crew in any way.[3]

K-429 did not have compressed air to blow its ballast tanks and thus could not surface. Furthermore, most of the life-support equipment remained behind, taken off the boat when it went into preparation for overhaul at the yard.

Suvorov went forward with two petty officers to the forward torpedo tubes. He briefed them personally, going over the familiar drill on breathing techniques, and telling them that the observation vessel *MPK-122* would be on the surface, waiting to pick them up. The looks on their faces spoke volumes—they were frightened but they believed in him.

The two men climbed into the torpedo tubes, Suvorov gave each one a pat for good luck; the inner doors of the torpedo tube were locked closed, the outer doors were opened to flood the tube, and the two men began their long dark swim to the surface of the sea.

The observation vessel *MPK-122* picked up the two crewmen when they reached the surface. They had made the ascent safely, rising rapidly through the 150 feet of frigid water. The *MPK-122* notified Petropavlovsk and a salvage operation was soon in full swing.

Divers from Petropavlovsk began evacuating men from the stricken boat. Some emerged from the forward spaces through the torpedo tubes as the two petty officers had earlier, while men from the stern areas began escaping through the compartment seven hatch. They ascended to the surface unprotected by any recovery vehicle, using a "hydro-suit," a small oxygen flask, and the controlled breathing techniques taught in submarine school.

The Soviet salvage and rescue team took the added precaution of placing divers at the outer openings of the torpedo tubes and the compartment seven escape trunk hatch. Submarine salvage ships *SS-38* and *SS-83*, as well as two small boats for the diving specialists, held position just above the sunken submarine. Very few submariners believe they will ever have to make a free ascent escape, and facing such a reality causes considerable anxiety. The escaping crewman is locked into a torpedo tube (or crouches inside the escape trunk), and when the ice-cold water is let in from the outer hatch, even the most experienced submariner faces panic.

There had already been some errors; some men had left the submarine before the salvage ships had arrived and did not survive on the surface. One became tangled in a buoy cable as he passed through the escape trunk hatch, could not make the ascent, and drowned. Yet another crewman had a heart attack and died in the torpedo tube. But most of the crew left the submarine, were assisted by divers, and survived.

The story of the *K-429* captures the courage of the sailors who braved the sea, the callousness of the Red Navy bureaucracy, and the perils of submarine warfare. A total of 104 men would be saved, all thanks to Suvorov's dedication.

Sadly, in the most recent submarine tragedy, the *Kursk* would not have the good fortune afforded *K-429*.

≈   ≈   ≈

WHEN IGOR KURDIN ARRIVED at the St. Petersburg Submariners' Club that morning, he found fellow club member Igor Kozyr listening to a news report on the radio quoting official sources and saying that the Oscar 2 class nuclear missile submarine *Kursk* (*K-141*) grounded while at sea. The boat's reactors had ceased operating due to technical problems. Instinctively both Kozyr and Kurdin knew that something terrible had happened. Although the general public would not realize it, to experienced submariners who knew this vessel and many of her crew, grounding seemed highly unlikely. In addition, a reactor scram so critical that the on-board engineers could not bring the nuclear plant back on line suggested trouble far beyond the words of the official announcement. By the time Kurdin made it to headquarters the telegrams and e-mails began arriving. He expected this kind of traffic. The Club had long since become a center for submariners of many services and countries to share their experiences and concerns in an effort to achieve a true end to the tensions of the Cold War.[4]

Kurdin sat down to read an e-mail message from a concerned individual whom he had come to know well. The president of the National Association of French Submarine Veterans, Rear Admiral Jean-Marie Mathey, asked Kurdin, "as one submariner to another, what has happened to *Kursk*?" Both Kurdin and Kozyr wished they could reply. In spite of their central role in the community of Russian submariners, they knew almost nothing. As darkness descended on August 12, the Northern Fleet News Service reported that surface vessels had managed to establish communication with the stricken boat and that, if the weather permitted, the salvage vehicle *Kolokol* would try to supply *Kursk* with electricity and air when it arrived on the scene. The Northern Fleet repeated that it had no information on the fate of the crew. At the same time, Commander in Chief of the Navy, Admiral Vladimir Kuroyedov, announced that "salvage services were en route to the accident area. The situation is very difficult. The possibility exists that a serious collision occurred. . . . The chances that the situation will have a successful outcome are not high."[5]

Captain Kurdin and his shipmates at the Club knew the Oscar 2 class submarines almost as well as they knew many of the crew on board the *Kursk* itself. He recalled years before seeing the new submarine designs with their amazing hull forms taking shape at Severodvinsk, an industrial center created near Arkhangel'sk on the White Sea in 1936. The Soviet leadership had invested heavily in the city's industrial capacity with an eye toward creating the capability outside the Baltic Sea to build a blue-water navy capable of competing with the British and Americans. Standing at the shipyard pier during one visit, Kurdin recalled the curiosity raised by an odd, organic shape then under construction. Initiated in the late 1970s, the new submarines, nicknamed the Oscar 2 class by NATO, represented the latest generation of boats competing with the Americans for speed, quiet running, and depth capability. Similar submarines, under construction from about 1978, followed an improved Oscar class design officially called Project-949A or Antaeus.[6] *Kursk* joined the navy in 1994 as an Antaeus class boat.

Antaeus, the powerful wrestler of Greek mythology, lost his life to the wiser Hercules who realized that his opponent drew his strength from contact with the Earth. Hercules hoisted Antaeus into the air, interrupting his contact with the soil of his native land, and strangled the wrestler as his strength diminished. Given the possible fate of the *Kursk*, the submarine community did not fail to appreciate the irony of the class name.

Antaeus displaced twice the water volume of a Yankee class boat and carried twenty-four Granit cruise missiles and twenty-eight torpedoes.[7] The former carried jamming devices and a very sophisticated targeting system. Naval strategy called for Antaeus boats to operate in a pack, drawing their targeting data from satellites via the Zubatka or "whale-killer" towed antenna system. The submarine would carry eighteen universal, electric, smart U.S.ET-80[8] torpedoes and ten anti-ship torpedoes.

Submarines like *Kursk* joined the Soviet Navy to address the carrier battlegroup problem. The Americans combined their carriers and advanced aircraft with Aegis cruisers capable of detecting and targeting anything that might invade the group's battlespace. The Soviets believed that this surveillance zone extended out to 120 miles, with additional radar coverage to 350 miles, and then to 700 miles when supplemented by the airborne AWACS system. None of this took into account the sonar capability of the American and British fast attack submarines now operating more frequently with the battle groups. The naval college in Leningrad used these estimates in its course instruction, suggesting that effective action against an American nuclear aircraft carrier would require at least twenty-five torpedoes and fifteen cruise missiles. Kurdin recalled that any of his classmates destined for service against these carrier battlegroups qualified for the "suicide club."

When Antaeus appeared, this balance of power shifted considerably. The Soviets now seemed closer to equality with the Americans and their chances against the carriers seemed to improve. They also received encouragement from their attack submariners, who had already adopted more aggressive tactics in their Alfas, Sierras, and Victors.

Kurdin knew many of the men on board *K-141*, including the commander, Gennadi Lyachin. He remembered that the *Kursk* commander had begun his service as weapons officer on board the diesel sub *K-58*, after graduating from naval college in St. Petersburg. Kurdin attended this same college, took the same course of instruction for prospective submariners, and endured or enjoyed the same classes and parades with Lyachin for three years. After his first decade of service, Captain Second Rank Lyachin completed the course for prospective commanding officer and then assumed command of the Juliett class diesel submarine *B-304*.

In the decade-long military contraction that took place after the fall of the Soviet Union, scores of ships and men left the navy for the scrap heap and the unemployment lines, respectively. Only the most dedicated remained to face an uncertain future and bleak financial and professional prospects. Lyachin chose to remain. In 1991, he set aside his immediate desire for command, volunteered to serve as an executive officer on board one of the newer Antaeus boats, and immediately set about training a crew to man the *Kursk*.

Lyachin's crew successfully completed a course at the Obninsk educational center for the submariners before their appointment to *Kursk*. Lyachin himself passed all the required tests for certification on an Antaeus class submarine and quickly became the obvious choice to command *Kursk* after his crew not only completed a successful North Atlantic patrol in 1996 but also received acclaim as the best crew of their submarine detachment three years running. He had no trouble assuming command when the time came.

The devotion exhibited by Lyachin and his crew seems astonishing given the contrast with conditions in the former Soviet Navy. They must have lived on pride, self-satisfaction, and friendship, because they had little else available to them. A letter from *Kursk* sonar officer Sergei Loginov to his fiancée Natasha starkly illustrated the conditions in the submarine service as the century came to a close:

> I'm in the sea aboard my beloved one nuclear missile submarine
> *Kursk*. Unfortunately I have nothing closer than this submarine in
> Vidyaevo. I also have my one-room kennel where I sleep and if I'm
> lucky I might even have some food there. The crew is in the sea for
> the second time and the families are on the shore penniless. They
> keep promising to pay us, but when the submarine leaves the
> base they heave a sigh of relief. When the crew is in the sea there

are no problems. We swear, but getting a grip on ourselves to leave the base. I wonder how long the soul can take it and avoid becoming a beast with only the instinct to survive and eat, and remain a human-being with a conscience who is able to think, worry, love and hate? I'm so tired of this struggle of honesty with animal husbandry. . . . I learn culinary secrets. I make plain bland bread from water, flour, some salt and soda, when there is no real bread. Porridge, rice, buckwheat porridge and noodle soup is a luxury for me at the moment.[9]

Lyachin and Loginov hated the conditions but loved the boats. In spite of these conditions many junior officers sought to remain in the service and longed for assignment to an Antaeus boat. Kurdin and other veterans in the St. Petersburg Submariners' Club signed petitions for young men to the Northern Fleet command. Vadim Bubniv, for example, a young student soon to graduate from the naval college, appealed to the Submariners' Club for recommendations and Kurdin himself signed the petition to the personnel department of the Northern Fleet. Bubniv perished when the *Kursk* exploded. Many of Bubniv's fellow crewmen came from naval families well known to Kurdin and his shipmates. The *Kursk* crew also included the son of Kurdin's college friend Vladimir Mityaev, with whom he had worked in Gadzhievo. Club member Captain First Rank Vladimir Bagryanzev, a talented, sensitive, well-respected officer, joined the *Kursk* at the last moment, assigned as Lyachin's senior commander or tutor for the deployment. Like the others, he never returned.[10]

≈ ≈ ≈

IN THE OFFICES OF the St. Petersburg Submariners' Club, like people all over Russia and across the globe, they waited for further news. Kurdin hoped that the disturbing reports of August 12 formed part of a purposeful scheme that would reveal itself in time. Three months earlier, the press had reported that during the coming summer the Northern Fleet salvage force would stage exercises in the Barents Sea. The exercise script called for a submarine to come to rest on the seafloor so the salvage ship *Michael Rudnitsky* could rescue the crew.[11] Kurdin prayed that some minor unexpected event had complicated the rescue rehearsal. He recalled that sand occasionally found its way into the reactor cooling system during such exercises, causing the system to scram. Reflecting on this gave him some respite from darker thoughts inspired by the way the words of the official announcement played on his professional instincts, developed over twenty years living with submarines and the sea. He wanted the exercise scenario to emerge as truth, but felt strongly that something truly catastrophic had happened.

Club members also knew that these exercises occurred at a critical time for the new generation of Russia's naval leadership. Rumors had it that the current commander in chief of the Russian Navy, Admiral Kuroyedov, might move into President Putin's inner circle, and, with many of the older admirals retiring, some of the highest posts in the navy would soon come vacant. One of the Club's strongest supporters, Admiral Vyacheslav Popov, had overall command of the exercises in which *Kursk* participated, and could well become either head of the general headquarters of the Russian Navy or possibly succeed Kuroyedov as its commander in chief. The exercises tested both the candidates for naval leadership and Russia's ability to continue displaying its world influence through the power and reach of its navy.[12]

The international geophysical community provided part of the evidence that heightened Kurdin's concern. At 1132 Moscow time on August 12, American, Norwegian, and Russian geophysical laboratories reported a significant seismic disturbance. NATO countries with ships and submarines at sea heard the event on their sonar and acoustic detection devices. The scientific community, accustomed to reporting earthquakes, informed a number of international news agencies that an underwater explosion possessing the force of over 400 pounds of TNT took place followed roughly two minutes and fifteen seconds later by a similar event with a force equivalent to 1.7 tons of TNT. The disturbance originated in the Barents Sea off the northern coast of the Russian Federation at 69°38'north latitude and 37°18' east longitude. Since the shock waves from the explosion had to hit the bottom for seismic detection, the actual explosions had a slightly greater force. At 1145, ship sonar reported yet another explosion, this time with the force of approximately one half ton of TNT. Kurdin made a mental note that 1.7 tons of TNT would have roughly the same effect as the simultaneous detonation of three to five of the torpedoes carried by *Kursk*.

Kurdin and his colleagues at the Club did not want to speculate, even unofficially, with the fear that they might cause unnecessary anxiety among the crew's families or tension between the Club and the Russian naval authorities. Besides, at this stage they had so little verifiable information that conclusions about the situation seemed irresponsible. In their concern about the fate of their shipmates, they could not help speculating among themselves and occasionally sharing those speculations with close friends. Sharing the anxiety seemed to make it more bearable. Unfortunately the news that began leaking out to these retired professionals from their close friends still on active duty did nothing to reduce their concern. It had already come to the attention of the Russian naval high command that some of Kurdin's associates had openly shared their speculations about *Kursk*, and the swift official response did nothing to calm the officers at the Club. Kurdin received a fax from Northern Fleet headquarters instructing him to cease making "incompetent" comments about *Kursk* and to leave any speculation to the proper authorities. The brusque tone of the faxed note assumed that the Club had already played a part in whipping up emotions around the world by cooperating with the international news media.[13]

Kurdin and Kozyr soon realized that the high command perceived the Club as an uncontrolled source of information on *Kursk*. While the Club received a strong warning from the Northern Fleet, other sources of information did not receive the same treatment. Admiral Baltin, for example, suggested that another vessel had rammed *Kursk*. The historian Professor Dozenko openly offered as explanation an aggressive scenario with possibly explosive international ramifications. From his chair at the Naval Academy in St. Petersburg, Dozenko suggested,

> The commander of the American submarine USS *Memphis* considered the exercise torpedo shot of the *Kursk* as a real attack and returned fire. Perhaps the commander couldn't take the physiological pressure trailing the Russian submarines and ships, so he

completed the shot. It was also possible that after two minutes passed the American submarine launched a 3-torpedo volley.[14]

In the following days, lack of credible or verifiable information from the Northern Fleet or the Russian government fed the seemingly endless cascade of fantasy and fact delivered by journalists to a global audience. It seemed as if the absence of a strong official explanation led the media to frantically search for one of its own. As a result, the stories became more fantastic by the moment. In this atmosphere of disturbing uncertainty and speculation, the families and relatives of the crew began to make their way to Vidyaevo, north of Murmansk, to plead for more information and to wait for the return of their loved ones. In many cases these people did not have enough money to make the trip or did not know how to find the secret submarine base where their family members had boarded *Kursk*. Thus a regular flow of concerned and anxious people passed through the doors of the St. Petersburg Submariners' Club offices, asking for help and information. All of them continued to hope, bolstered by earlier cases in which crewmembers found a way to survive. Some recalled that twelve submariners on board Captain Boris Polyakov's *K-19* managed to survive that ship's nuclear accident in 1972. Many of those men had survived over three weeks in a stern compartment with limited air reserves and in complete darkness.

Inside the Club headquarters everyone continued to hope for the best until August 21, when the commander of the Northern Fleet, Admiral Popov, announced that all on board the submarine had perished. A flag officer held in high esteem by most Russian officers and ratings, Popov released a statement disturbingly devoid of any reason for the disaster. The same day he appealed to the relatives of the dead submariners:

There is no fault of the crew on what had happened. The circumstances were utterly catastrophic after the collision, and I'm sure the men didn't live for more than 3 minutes. I will do my best, and I'm going to strive for it all my life, to look into [the] eyes of a [*sic*] person who caused this tragedy. . . . Trying to rescue the men, we did everything we could and even more than that. Three thousand seamen of the Northern Fleet were in charge of rescuing the ship, but the circumstances were stronger than us. And even nowadays one tries to make sure that there isn't such an equality before fate aboard a submarine where either everyone wins or dies. It's a time of sorrow, but life still goes on. Bring up your children, your sons. And forgive me that I couldn't save your men.[15]

In spite of their respect for Popov, very few Russian submariners could permit this episode to pass without finding out what had happened. Kurdin urged people with the proper experience in Oscar 2 operations, nuclear matters, and salvage to come to the Club and share their views. He doubted that he could have kept them away had he wanted. In any case, the Club's primary purpose called for skills, knowledge, and experience to come together within its walls to address critical submarine issues and events, and this certainly qualified. Most of them doubted that the near future would bring any credible official explanation of the recent events.

≈   ≈   ≈

TWO VERSIONS OF THE TRAGEDY EMERGED as most likely from the almost constant discussion about the loss of the *Kursk*: a collision or an on-board explosion.

A collision with an American submarine or a boat from some other nation immediately raised unsettling domestic and international issues. *Kursk* had emerged from her base as part of a group involved in naval exercises. In common with the navies of other countries, the Russians never keep an exercise area secret. The danger to naval vessels and to commercial shipping demanded that the general region and the timing of the exercise appear publicly. The Russians usually did this through diplomatic channels and through publicly released "Notifications to Seafarers." Taking an unauthorized ship into an exercise area would invite disaster and possibly doom the vessel, for a Russian ship or submarine might shoot first and ask questions later.

The Russians also made a habit of releasing attack submarines in the exercise region to search for uninvited NATO intruders. If any appeared, the Russian submarine commanders had orders to trail them for intelligence purposes and then drive them out of the area. Kurdin and his colleagues openly asked whether the Northern Fleet exercise organizers had implemented these traditional precautions. If so, the likelihood of a foreign submarine ripe for a collision in the exercise area would decline. In the event a foreign submarine had eluded detection and appeared in the region, standard operating procedure would dictate both the tracking of the intruder by Russian forces and the cancellation or postponement by the operational commander of all exercises and experimental weapons tests. Did someone violate standard operating procedure?

If this scenario were true, the presence of American and British submarines adjacent to Russian territorial waters during the exercise did not strike the Club members as the best way to confirm international friendship and trust. Kurdin also recalled how some events came together in a disturbing chain that made many in Russia feel extremely uneasy:

> When USS *Memphis* arrived in Norway on 19 August for repairs, the head of the CIA unexpectedly visited Moscow, Presidents Vladimir Putin and Bill Clinton had secret negotiations, and $10 billion dollars of Russian debt was forgiven. This made a lot of people think that they were witnessing some cynical political deal.

Admiral Popov publicly responded with wit and anger to the lack of a detailed American explanation for the presence of *Memphis* in Norway undergoing repairs shortly after the loss of *Kursk:*

> What if I had sent 3 nuclear submarines with surveillance tasks to American shores and an American submarine sank due to strange reasons? And then one of the Russian submarines had arrived at some Cuban port for repairing and I had refused to show the damage to her bow? What kind of stories would American journalists print?

In spite of the presence of an American submarine in the area, something that Kurdin knew happened frequently during the Cold War, the evidence just did not justify a collision as the answer to the *Kursk* tragedy. In the days immediately after *Kursk* went to the bottom, Kurdin and his colleagues lamented the absence of official measures to inform the public and calm the situation.

Shortly after President Clinton offered an official apology for the presence of an American submarine in a restricted area, Kurdin recalled a comment made only months before by Valeri Aleksin, a leading Russian expert on incidents at sea. Reflecting on the dangerous deep-ocean games played by Russian and NATO submariners, Aleksin suggested that, "We walk on the razor's edge. This hunt will eventually end up in a disaster. I am sure today, too, that if such a practice doesn't stop, a disaster is inevitable."[16] Aleksin, who passed away in the summer of 2001, participated in composing the "Governmental Agreement between Russia and the U.S.A. on Preventing Accidents of Submarines Underwater Outside Territorial Waters," which addressed technical and legal issues concerning submarine operations.[17] At the time of the *Kursk* tragedy, this agreement, along with plans for international collaboration in the face of submarine accidents prepared after the loss of *Komsomolets*, had yet to be put into effect.[18]

A codified system of international cooperation might have helped answer critical questions in the early hours of the *Kursk* disaster and could well have brought assistance to bear much earlier. With such an agreement signed and in place, the Northern Fleet would have already known whether foreign salvage vehicles would fit on *Kursk*'s escape trunk. Nobody would have to wait to find out if the stricken boat's life-support system would work with techniques employed by non-Russian salvers. Most importantly, an infrastructure would already exist to effectively communicate with the salvage services of other countries. Submariners around the world found it difficult to understand why these documents had no signatures so many years after the conclusion of the Cold War. How many more would have to die on all sides before these agreements took effect?

In their brainstorming sessions in St. Petersburg, those gathered in the Submariners' Club discussed every conceivable scenario. What if an American submarine did approach *Kursk*? If he detected the American, the Russian commander would have to report the encounter immediately. Given the depth in the exercise area and the configuration of the ocean floor, the American would have his maneuvering range behind the Russian boat restricted to areas with depths of 135 to 240 feet if he wanted sufficient room to alter course and evade. As part of the exercise, *Kursk* had to approach the surface to communicate her readiness to perform the torpedo tests. Before doing so Captain Lyachin would have to change course and acoustically look behind his boat to ensure that no submarine lurked in his wake. Assuming the superiority of American submarine sonar, the American would have sufficient warning that his opposite number had started to ascend and would be checking for the presence of a possible hostile boat astern. The American would then have to react quickly and in a rather confined depth corridor.

Those working through this hypothetical process eliminated any head-on or tangential collision with an American attempting to reacquire *Kursk*. Besides, in the very limited maneuvering space, a head-on collision would have slowed or stopped both submarines, with the result that the American boat would have also suffered terribly. Given the explosions that accompanied the loss of *Kursk*, proximity alone would almost certainly have sent the American submarine to the bottom or inflicted some major degree of incapacity.

It then seemed possible that a tangential collision might explain the situation, but in the end, this scenario too lacked credibility. An expert on the Oscar 2 class, Captain First Rank Michael Volzhenski, became an early supporter of this scenario. He had participated in *Kursk*'s trials and had similar experience with other submarines of this class. His version suggested that,

> When *Kursk* started surfacing, the foreign submarine lost the acoustic contact with her and decided to establish it again, quickly maneuvering to an interception point. The American submarine commander accelerated the submarine up to 12–14 knots for 20 minutes at a depth of roughly 180 feet, a safe depth for this speed, and started following *Kursk*. But when he was choosing the

point at which he expected to reacquire, he didn't sufficiently consider possible maneuvers of *Kursk,* making collision a real possibility. Having reached the point of interception he slowed down
and came shallow, where he detected *Kursk* just completing her
[turning] maneuver, but now moving towards him. . . .

The commander of the American submarine formed the impression [that] *Kursk* was moving right. Since there was no time to
detect other aspects of *Kursk*'s movement, he instinctively gave an
order "left the helm" to avoid a collision. . . .

The American moved along a turning arc with her bow motion
moving into the turn forcing the stern to the right. At the beginning of the eluding maneuver there was a collision which shook
the submarine; the starboard horizontal stabilizer with blades of
the right horizontal and vertical control surfaces attached to it hit
the *Kursk*'s hull above the torpedo tube. . . .

In a second there was an explosion which shook the
submarine. . . .

In spite of this seemingly reasonable story, salvers found no evidence
of any stabilizer or rudder fragments or other parts of an American hull
near the explosion site. If a collision occurred, some evidence of the
American boat would surely remain in the debris trail scattered along
the path of events in those relatively shallow waters.

Left to explain this enormous tragedy with only news reports, official
fragments, rumors, and the collective experience of its members, the
Club moved to clarify the situation. Kurdin wished either to confirm the
possibility of a collision as real, or to dismiss this option and seek the
truth elsewhere.

Just before the *Kursk* retrieval operation began, and inspired by an-
nouncements from Presidents Putin and Bush regarding plans to col-
laborate against the threat of the international terrorism in the wake of
September 11, 2001, the St. Petersburg Submariners' Club sent letters to
the American president and the British prime minister, Tony Blair, asking them to reveal the location of the submarines USS *Memphis,* USS
Toledo, and HMS *Splendid* at the moment of the *Kursk* accident. Bypassing the normal diplomatic channels posed a risk in a Russia still

emerging from its Soviet past, but Kurdin received a reply that seemed to make the risk worth taking. Franklin C. Miller, special assistant to the president and Senior Director for Defense Policy and Arms Control, stated in his reply:

> President Bush has asked me to respond to your letter concerning the sinking of the submarine *Kursk*.
>
> As you may know, at the time of the tragedy, U.S. Secretary of Defense Cohen and the Chief of Naval Operations, Admiral Clark, corresponded directly with the Russian Minister of Defense and Fleet Admiral Kuroyedov. They offered both the assistance of the U.S. Department of Defense and their deepest condolences to the families, loved ones, and friends of those who perished on board the *Kursk*. They also provided strong assurance that no United States ship or submarine was involved in this unfortunate accident. Likewise Lord Robertson, the Secretary General of NATO, separately confirmed that no NATO assets were involved.[19]

In conversation with friends and contacts within the Russian Navy, Kurdin and his colleagues at the Submariners' Club set aside the collision scenario and slowly began to understand what must have happened. The surface forces involved in the exercises of August 12 last heard the voice of Captain Gennadi Lyachin the day before when he reported a successful torpedo launch to his flotilla commander.

"Thank you for the service!" replied the flotilla commander.

"We are serving the motherland!" replied Lyachin.

"You should add, and the flotilla commander," the admiral joked, obviously pleased with the results.

Since standard operating procedure demanded communication with the surface immediately after test shots, many Russian officers doubt the validity of the Northern Fleet report that they received news of a potential disaster while awaiting a report from Lyachin at 1645. They should have received at least two reports long before 1645. Both communications would have provided data permitting an analysis of the approaching weapons test.[20] Why would standard operating procedure change for *Kursk*?

Other departures from the norm seemed even more disturbing. Northern Fleet orders instructed *Kursk* to arrive on station by 0800 on August 12 to conduct additional torpedo tests and stage a mock submerged attack against a small task group built around the nuclear cruiser *Petr Velikiy,* Admiral Popov's flagship, and the ASW cruisers *Admiral Chabanenko* and *Admiral Kharlamov.*[21] The ships kept a considerable distance from one another, planning to listen for simulated torpedo shots made by other submarines while they passed through the exercise area. An air slug expelled from the torpedo tube provided the necessary detectable sound for the surface ship sonar during these ASW tests.[22]

Captain First Rank Michael Kolivushko, commander of *Admiral Chabanenko,* reported that his sonar picked up a radar signature at 1130. He then proceeded to put his crew through an attack drill against a submarine in accordance with the exercises. He assumed that the signature came from the *Kursk,* but never again detected that radar or any other sign from the submarine. Initially, Popov and Northern Fleet headquarters did not really worry about Lyachin's silence. Some technical malfunction or any number of other possible reasons could have explained the failure to conduct the scheduled torpedo launch. The task group left the exercise area and proceeded to Severomorsk, just over ninety miles away. En route, Popov finally ordered the fleet to find *Kursk* before transferring his flag via helicopter to the carrier *Admiral Kuznetsov,* and then cruising the site of the closing episodes of the submerged-attack exercise.

Given the task group's proximity to *Kursk's* last reported position before the explosion, it seemed odd at the time that the explosions that doomed the submarine did not illuminate the surface ship sonar. A Russian submariner at sea in a neighboring exercise area—about forty miles from the *Kursk*—later revealed that while rising from his seat, the shock of an underwater explosion many miles away caused him to stagger and fall to the deck. At first he thought his boat had collided with some submerged object.

Since the task group had come within ten or fifteen miles of *Kursk's* location, the sudden introduction of massive amounts of sound energy into the ocean at a position so near would have certainly illuminated the surface group's sonar. Since standing orders required the ship commanders to report any extraordinary circumstances to the exercise commander, Popov must have had some idea of the nature of the events taking place below the surface. Too many ships had come too close. They could not have missed the acoustic signature of this catastrophic event, and with it the location of the boat.

At the first sign of a submarine in distress, the naval authorities should have initiated a standard Northern Fleet salvage response, which would follow emergency measures already embedded in the exercise plans. Much later, members of the Submariners' Club managed to piece together the sequence of events after the Russian Navy began searching for *Kursk* on August 12:

- 1720 *Kursk* did not report via radio as scheduled at 1645 so the salvage ship *Michael Rudnitsky* began preparations to deploy.
- 1814 The Northern Fleet received orders authorizing the ships *Petr Velikiy* and salvage tug *SB-323* to make for the accident scene. *Petr Velikiy* received orders to the southern rim of the exercise site and *SB-323* proceeded to the accident area.
- 1852 Aircraft *IL-38* equipped with salvage equipment left for the accident area to make general observations.
- 1930 Admiral Popov returned from sea and appointed the head of the combat readiness department of the fleet, Vice Admiral Boyarkin, to lead the salvage operation.[23]
- 1932 The Northern Fleet asked submarine *K-328*, already in the torpedo test area, whether she monitored *Kursk* with her sonar at that time. Had she heard anything of significance? Her commanding officer replied in the negative. The practice torpedo retrieval vessel *TL-250* reported that she did not detect the scheduled *Kursk* torpedo launch.
- 2042 *Petr Velikiy* started dropping grenades into the ocean as a signal for *Kursk* to surface.
- 2045 *Petr Velikiy* arrived on the southern rim of the exercise area.
- 2050 *Petr Velikiy* started moving toward the stricken submarine's last reported position, gingerly probing the area, careful to avoid any possibility of a collision with a suddenly surfacing submarine.

- 2200 *Il-38* returned to base without spotting *Kursk.*
- 2300 The second scheduled opportunity for *Kursk* to communicate with the surface passed in silence. By 2320, the hospital at Severomorsk prepared its emergency room to serve the needs of a traumatized crew.
- 2330 The operational watch officer at the headquarters of the Northern Fleet salvage service reported no contact with the submarine and officially declared her down in the Barents Sea at a depth of 356 feet.
- 2337 *Petr Velikiy* reported detecting a detonation at coordinates 69°40.9' north latitude and 36°24.6' east longitude. The ship's commander made the report on his own, but had obviously not communicated the information in a timely manner or in response to a Northern Fleet inquiry.
- 2345 Salvage tug *SB-323* arrived and immediately went into a search pattern. Mother nature did not cooperate; the wind blew at force seven and visibility remained limited to ten miles. The ocean remained at sea state one, a condition of relative calm.
- 2355 Popov ordered the cruiser *Petr Velikiy* and the ASW ships *Admiral Chabanenko* and *Admiral Kharlamov* to assemble as a search group. Vice Admiral Boyarkin flew his flag on board *Petr Velikiy.*[24]

Around 0330 on August 13, the commander of *Petr Velikiy* informed his crew that they would conduct a search for a submarine presumed missing and in distress. He promised a vacation to any crewmember who found a white emergency marker buoy. If the *Kursk*'s commander had sufficient time and presence of mind to deploy the device when he lost control of the vessel and came to rest on the bottom, this should mark the position of the submarine. At about 0400 sonar on board *Petr Velikiy* detected *Kursk*. As Admiral Popov described it,

The sonar detected metal gnashing and some rumble. The ships started maneuvering in the area. Soon they found two buoys: one white and red and another one was greenish. They were both partially below the surface by about six to nine feet. The green buoy leaned over to one side. The cruiser approached the buoys but the crew could not pick them up. There were waves to force four. To avoid casualties the small boat launched to retrieve the buoys was recalled and hauled back on board. The sonic depth finder detected two bad anomalies that were sixty feet different from the sea depth in this region. The distance between the gaps was about a kilometer.[25]

At 0530 the salvage ship *Michael Rudnitsky* arrived at the area having received an order from the fleet commander to leave the base the night before after *Kursk* failed to broadcast the scheduled transmission.

For three days the crew found only debris, Fanta soft-drink bottles, and a few red condoms. At one point the chief of the salvage service Captain First Rank Alexander Teslenko reported finding green signal buoys, but they never publicly materialized and the media never saw them. The next day would offer far more drama.

On August 14 the navy made its first attempt to reach *Kursk.*

- 1530 Popov approved the deployment of the salvage submarine *Prize* (*AS-34*); the waves in the Barents Sea location reached sea state two.
- 1615 With *AS-34* in the water, the search group received an immediately identifiable signal from *Kursk*'s on-board MGS-30 sonar.
- 1748 *Prize* commander Captain Third Rank Maisak reported to the surface, ". . . course 90°; range 1,800 meters; signals coming from the MGS-30.[26] I am maneuvering towards it."

Maisak surfaced at 1834 and confirmed that he had found *Kursk.*[27]

The Russian Navy's reluctance to accept foreign assistance to reach possible survivors became one of the early disturbing mysteries surrounding the loss of *Kursk* and its crew. Two days after the official announcement of a missing vessel, the British naval attaché, Captain Geoffrey McCready, called Kurdin at the Submariners' Club with a desperate plea. The retired Delta 4 commander later recalled hearing McCready's voice almost leaping out of the telephone:

Guys, I can't understand what is going on! We want to offer our help to rescue the crew. As you know we have a deep-water vehicle *LR-5* that can dive 450 meters and it can take sixteen men aboard. Nobody wants to speak to us in the general headquarters. Maybe you could help us communicate with Northern Fleet command.[28]

The French and the Americans quickly made similar offers, with no response. The Russian admirals may have felt they had the situation well in hand, but how could they? Northern Fleet headquarters knew of the sale of the navy's deep-rescue vehicles to civilian organizations and companies at home and abroad. To make matters worse, many of the fleet's best deep divers left the navy to find steady, well-paid work in the business sector. They had families to support. The ability of the Russian Navy to rescue its own submariners had disappeared in a decade. The deep-submergence salvage vehicles *Bester* and *Prize,* still in the navy's possession, did not have rescue capability; their designers never envisioned the need for these craft to rescue a stranded crew.

The experienced divers who made their way to the Submariners' Club offices in St. Petersburg confirmed that only divers could secure a rescue or salvage vehicle to the escape trunk of the submarine, and only a pair of hands on site could attach the cables and hoses that would bring air, energy, and communication to the submarine. Deep-submergence, salvage, and rescue specialists insisted that *Kursk* should have had oxygen within twelve hours and twenty minutes of the navy declaring her down. Experts calculated that it would have taken twelve hours to get to the accident area. On the way, divers could have entered decompression chambers to acclimate their systems to the submarine's depth. Completely prepared, the divers could have put their hands on the hull 320 feet down in about twenty minutes, with air flowing to the boat only a few minutes later. Of course, this assumed upright and accessible escape trunks and air and communications ports not buried in silt or torn off by the violence of the events.

When *Prize* tried to secure itself to *Kursk*'s escape trunk, resting at a very awkward angle, the true magnitude of the disaster began to reveal itself. Captain Third Rank Andrew Sholokhov had just completed his tenth year as commander of *Prize* before transferring to a billet in St. Petersburg. When he heard of the accident he immediately volunteered his services. Within twenty-four hours he found himself on board *Prize* and face to face with the stricken *Kursk* on the bottom of the Barents Sea. He later reflected on the experience and a salvage and rescue process that he found unusual and awkward.

> It seemed that the organization was poor. There were three admirals aboard the salvage ship *Michael Rudnitsky*. They were professionals, specialists all, but they didn't understand much about our job. When the vehicle [*Prize*] was being retrieved it hit the ship. Immediately the sidescan sonar, the omni-directional sonar, and the compass went out of order. Later on the winch was damaged and its gear went out of order. The mechanic slept only for two hours because something always had to be repaired. . . . When we submerged for the first time we worked a bit more than for four hours. We tried to land on the escape trunk pad eight times. On the eighth time the vehicle managed to stay on the escape trunk landing pad for more than twenty minutes. The vehicle would hang above the submarine and frantically move its propellers [to push it toward] the pad. We had a special device that could catch the eyebolt of the hatch. [An] eyebolt is just a metal lug [attached to the pad on the submarine's hull]. Having caught it we started pulling the vehicle towards it, however we didn't manage to stick to the submarine for long. . . . It quickly became evident that rescue by this method would never take place. The attitude of the submarine on the bottom and the extensive damage made it impossible.[29]

After several unsuccessful attempts to attach *Prize* to the damaged pad, Sholokhov received an order from topside to examine the bow. Fortunately he had had the presence of mind to bring experienced Oscar 2 and Antaeus class submariners with him on the trip down to *Kursk* to make sure he could understand what he saw. As the *Prize* approached the bow, one of them made note of the compartments they were passing over, "One compartment . . . another one . . . the next one . . . "

Then Sholokhov said suddenly, "The submarine finished!" They stared through the port at a precipice at the bow composed of ruptured steel, adorned with crippled pipes and bent metal plates. After a moment of stunned silence another submariner voiced his shock and dismay, "It was as if compartment one was cut off or chopped off with a guillotine."[30]

Optimistic estimations by these experts gave any surviving crewmembers still sealed in the after compartments of the vessel until August 18 before their life-support systems failed. If one believed in miracles, the end might not come for them until August 21 or 22. The navy had run out of home-grown options. In the following days, the United States and Great Britain both offered Russia the use of their deep-sea rescue vessels, although the Russian government continued to insist it needed no outside help. Finally, on August 19, the Russian Navy relented and requested assistance from Great Britain and Norway. A Norwegian rescue ship set out from Norway on August 20 and arrived at the *Kursk*'s site the following day. But at that point, it was too late for the trapped submariners. In spite of best wishes from around the globe, no miracle occurred. They all died together, sharing the remaining air until it was exhausted.

≈   ≈   ≈

THE NEWS OF THE CREW'S DEATH shocked the world, and brought disturbing memories back to submariners. *K-19*, USS *Scorpion*, *Komsomolets*, USS *Thresher* . . . a crew won together or they all lost together. Only a few submariners have survived these disasters as the occasional exceptions to that relentless rule. In the midst of the suffering in Russia, Kurdin, Kozyr, and their shipmates at the St. Petersburg Submariners' Club noted that this case had a different quality about it.

The Club received only a small part of all the letters with words of sympathy and support for the families of *Kursk* submariners; but even those letters let us feel the tremendous power of the love of a million hearts that shared pain of loss with us. This was the new reality which manifested itself in spite of the potential ability of the politicians and naval commanders to hide the truth. Numerous internet sites filled with discussions of independent experts and veterans—submariners were the features of this new reality. The tragedy united all confessions and loyalties. . . . We saw American submariners praying for the Russian submariners and their families in Pearl Harbor together with the commander of the American Pacific Submarine Force, Rear Admiral Albert Konetzni on 28 August 2000.

On September 27, 2000, submariners from around the world gathered at Lancaster University in the United Kingdom to celebrate the centennial of the Royal Navy Submarine Force and gave a minute of silence to the memory of *Kursk* and her crew. Admiral Sir Michael Boyce, Chief of Naval Staff and First Sea Lord, led the sizable assembly in their tribute.[31] Weeks later, Captain Kurdin and other representatives of the Russian Submarine Force attended as honored guests the military ball held on the occasion of Veterans Day and the Centennial of the U.S. Submarine Force, invited by the U.S. Navy League in Santa Barbara, California. The ball opened with a prayer for those still on board *Kursk*.

Toe to toe, eye to eye, we have faced each other under the silent seas. Unseen, unnoticed, and unknown by most of our countrymen whom we were there to protect and defend. Once enemies, now only wary observers, and today only brothers. . . .

We hope the lessons to be learned from your death and ultimate sacrifice will be seized upon by all nations and especially by yours and be taken to heart by those who can correct the causes and can prevent it from happening again so that your death will not be in vain and may someday keep other brothers from the same fate.

Nevertheless, with honor and respect we shall keep your memory alive as we do our own that are Forever on Patrol. . . .[32]

Supported by submariners worldwide, the Russian submarine community, both retired and active service, worked to determine the cause

Shevchenko's Victor 2 poking up from under the ice during his first visit to the North Pole. *(Courtesy of Vice Admiral Anatoli I. Shevchenko)*

Shevchenko's Victor class submarine surfacing in a *polinya* near the North Pole in the mid-1980s. Note the relatively thin ice scattering on the deck of the boat. The existence of these areas of thin ice at the top of the world enabled submarines to surface safely. Shevchenko made many trips to the Pole during the latter half of his career. *(Courtesy of Vice Admiral Anatoli I. Shevchenko)*

Vice Admiral Anatoli Shevchenko was captured here on the bridge of his
Victor class boat at the North Pole in the mid-1980s. The Soviet naval ensign,
deployed from the aft portion of the sail, provides an historic backdrop.
(Courtesy of Vice Admiral Anatoli I. Shevchenko)

In this scene Shevchenko (center) enjoys with his officers some watermelon from warmer
climes in the officers mess on board their Victor 2. The boat is surfaced at the North Pole.
(Courtesy of Vice Admiral Anatoli I. Shevchenko)

A party from Shevchenko's Victor 3 attack submarine returns in a motorized launch from examining an iceberg not far from the North Pole. *(Courtesy of Vice Admiral Anatoli I. Shevchenko)*

Shevchenko's Victor 3 breaks through the ice in a *polinya*, surfacing into the sun at the top of the world. *(Courtesy of Vice Admiral Anatoli I. Shevchenko)*

Having penetrated the ice cover in a *polinya*, Shevchenko's crew checks for damage and examines the huge ice blocks resting on the deck.
(Courtesy of Vice Admiral Anatoli I. Shevchenko)

Captain First Rank Igor Kurdin's Delta SSBN in dry dock for repairs, sometime in the mid-1980s. The photo is taken from the bottom of the dry dock after the basin is drained to lift the boat out of the water. *(Courtesy of Captain First Rank Igor Kurdin)*

A Delta 4 SSBN at sea. Captain Igor Kurdin commanded a vessel of this type. During the latter stages of the Cold War this was the most powerful and capable Soviet strategic missile boat behind the Typhoon class. *(Courtesy of Captain First Rank Igor Kurdin)*

A pair of Northern Fleet Typhoon SSBNs tied up at the pier. This class of
Soviet SSBNs was the largest and most powerful of its kind ever built.
(Courtesy of Rear Admiral Oleg G. Chefonov)

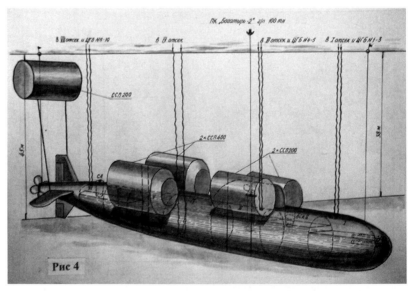

This diagram comes from the files of Captain First Rank Leonid I. Melodinski, a
salvage expert with the Soviet Navy. These techniques are not very different from
those used by the U.S. Navy to raise the USS *Squalus* before World War II. This
approach to the salvage and retrieval problem is still used with modern technical
variations by navies worldwide. Employing pontoons to assist in refloating stricken
submarines is a classic salvage technique that helped bring the *Kursk* to the surface
after her fatal explosions. *(Courtesy of Captain First Rank Leonid I. Melodinski)*

The ill-fated *Komsomolets, K-278*, at the pier just before its last voyage.
(Courtesy of Captain First Rank Boris G. Kolyada)

Soldiers stand honor guard at the
Northern Fleet memorial for the officers and crew
of *Komsomolets, K-278. (Courtesy of
Captain First Rank Boris G. Kolyada)*

This is a rare photo of Vladimir and Lev Chernavin seated together. These men were not related by family or marriage, but both became important individuals in the Soviet submarine force. Admiral Victor Chernavin, pictured left, succeeded Gorshkov as head of the Soviet Navy. Lev Chernavin spent his career with the Northern Fleet submarine force, an expert in diesel boat operations in the Atlantic Ocean and Mediterranean Sea. *(Courtesy of Rear Admiral Lev D. Chernavin)*

This is Rear Admiral Lev Chernavin leading a veterans' parade through the streets of St. Petersburg in the 1990s. In this Soviet naval city, celebrations affirming the value of naval service in the Soviet and post–Cold War era are a common occurrence. Rear Admiral Chernavin is now the officer in charge of the cruiser *Aurora*, the famed naval ship of the Bolshevik Revolution of 1917. The ship now serves as a historical museum. *(Courtesy of Rear Admiral Lev D. Chernavin)*

of the *Kursk*'s demise. Information on the actual sequence of events and technical data on the condition and the operation of the submarine remained hard to collect for months after the sinking. The Submariners' Club assembled what it considered credible evidence in an effort to explain the seafloor images that stunned Captain Sholokhov.[33]

- Lyachin had already extended his radio mast, suggesting that he wanted to communicate the progress of the exercise from a position at or near the surface.
- Seismic stations detected the two massive explosions. According to American sources made available to the Club, after the first explosion, sonar on board USS *Memphis* detected an attempt by the crew to increase speed and blow the main ballast tanks. It is likely that Lyachin ordered an emergency blow, which would put a full rise on the control surfaces, increase speed, and expel water from the main ballast tanks. The boat would begin to rise very quickly.
- Divers later found the remains of several of the officers and crewmen at their emergency stations, which confirms the crew reaction to the emergency and the nature of the orders given.

The Russian Navy ordered the oceanographic vessel *Academic Mstislav Keldish* to the salvage site along with her small charges, the deep submersibles *Mir 1* and *Mir-2*. Just as they had surveyed the wreck of RMS *Titanic* for Hollywood director James Cameron, the *Mir* twins would now take a very close look at *Kursk*. An anonymous participant in this effort passed details of the survey to the Russian journalist Marina Tokareva, who then made the information public in November and December of 2001. In addition to the necessary crew, the *Mir* submersibles transported experts from the Central Design and Construction Bureau "Rubin," responsible for the creation of the Antaeus class boats, and experts from the St. Petersburg firm of Gidropribor, the torpedo designers. In part, the *Mir* expedition report stated,

> . . . External features of the damage to compartment one appear like straight fractures of the pressure hull plating with sharp edges (without layers of plastic deformation), opening of the outer hull,

punctures of the rubber covering by edges of the damaged hull, high-pressure air cylinders broken in half, and severed pulleys of extendible devices.

These features confirm a devastating explosion. Presumably, the explosion took place either at the moment when the submarine touched the seafloor or when she was already lying on the seafloor for some time. Primary pressure hull damage occurred on the upper part of the sub, and high-pressure air cylinders and other components fell upon them, which confirms it. There are deep cracks with smooth surfaces, which could be created by the gases or water, in the keel area of the bow.

. . . Several fragments of the pressure hull . . . together with structures inside the hull built shows a deformation, which has edges of the crumpled plating of the outer hull as a contour. Inside the deformation, on the upper port side, there is a lock hatch for a 53-millimeter caliber (the visible part is 2.5 feet) torpedo tube, the back lid of the torpedo tube is bent inside the tube, the lock handle doesn't have any visible damage.

. . . The outer torpedo tube door (TA No. 4, the lower 65-millimeter caliber door on the port side) displays torn traction; two shields of the torpedo load hatch; signal rockets shooting device (that permits monitoring the torpedo motion from a surface ship; it was raised) were found within a 145×180 yard debris area at a distance of 50–80 yards from the screws.[34]

These observations confirmed what many experts and submarine veterans had already concluded. An explosion sent *Kursk* to the bottom and doomed its crew. Given the obvious location of the explosion, the likelihood that a torpedo chain-reaction explosion caused the disaster now grew with every minute of investigation. Doubtless, the state of the Russian economy and the declining defense budget would have to bear some of the blame. Regular overhauls, close examination, and routine system upgrades, as well as personnel training, would have significantly reduced the possibility of an explosion.

As the investigation progressed, based on close observation of the wreck, experts concluded that the explosion of a "practice" hydrogen peroxide torpedo in torpedo tube number four actually caused the disaster. The weapon's propulsion system contained 200 kilograms of kerosene, air compressed at 200 pounds per square inch, and about 1.5 tons of hydrogen peroxide, and required careful and regular maintenance. While capable of producing very high submerged speeds, this technology, with its roots in Hitler's Reichsmarine, had a history of capricious performance. Unfortunately, the highly unstable nature of the hydrogen peroxide made its use in submarines very dangerous in spite of its potential as a source of power independent of the atmosphere at the ocean surface. Known as the Walter System, after its inventor Helmuth Walter, the hydrogen peroxide proved expensive to install and maintain, and had a tendency to cause explosions. Used in the early Cold War British submarines *Excalibur* and *Explorer,* the latter ended its short operational career with the nickname "Exploder." In both the United States and Great Britain this form of propulsion quickly lost ground to the advent of reliable submarine nuclear power à la Rickover.[35]

Walter System torpedoes entered Soviet naval service in the 1970s and provided reliable service only because submarine commanders took the time and trouble both to maintain them carefully and to avoid any circumstance that would present a serious hazard to their boats. According to Kurdin,

> submariners didn't like these torpedoes, because, for instance,
> they required extraordinary attention. One of the first instructions
> in the use of this torpedo obliged the watch officer to count gas
> bubbles emerging from the hermetic seal on the outer torpedo
> casing. No wonder the commanders preferred to throw the re-
> serves of hydrogen peroxide overboard (the on-board torpedo
> weapons system had special outlets for that) when they first no-
> ticed this kind of "steaming."[36]

In the *Kursk* case, none of the experience and quality control needed to render this weapon safe to handle seemed available. During the opening stages of the investigation, a torpedo base officer in Vidyaevo from which *Kursk* received its "practice" torpedo claimed that the torpedo's technical documents included an official receipt signed by

Lyachin, but the official files for that weapon contained virtually none of the required inspection documents with certifying signatures. Furthermore, the ill-fated exercises in August 2000 would have provided Senior Lieutenant Ivanov-Pavlov with his first experience as torpedo weapons officer. Recently graduated with distinction from both the naval college and the educational center for submariners in Obninsk, he had very limited experience with this weapon. However, Northern Fleet command had assigned experienced torpedo officer Captain Third Rank Murat Baigarin as an acting chief of the torpedo department to provide guidance for the young lieutenant and others who lacked sufficient time at sea. Unusually, two representatives of the firm Dagdiesel, the engineer Mamed Gadzhiev[37] and the naval representative Lieutenant Arnold Borisov, also went to sea on the exercise. This appeared a bit curious since Dagdiesel did not produce these torpedoes, but rather a factory in Alma-ta, capital of Kazakhstan, an independent republic since 1991. Gadzhiev's mother testified that her son,

> was not supposed to go to the sea. There was no work for him there. He did everything he had to do on the shore. He found out that the torpedo batteries were too big, they weren't the right size.

His colleagues at Dagdiesel wondered why he went to sea at all. He actually had no vital on-board function to perform. Neither did Borisov. Divers eventually found Borisov's body not in the forward torpedo room engaged in some activity on the eve of the torpedo launch, but in the compartment four wardroom. The explosion probably took him by surprise in the middle of his lunch.[38]

≈　≈　≈

AFTER WEEKS OF OFFICIAL STATEMENTS, expert commentary, and informed rumor in circulation, a seemingly accurate picture of the *Kursk*'s last moments began to emerge. Poor maintenance and inexperienced personnel combined to permit critical oversights. The team in the forward torpedo room probably did not notice the onset of "steaming," or it might have commenced only after the torpedo went into the tube. When the torpedo showed signs of a critical malfunction, it took Lyachin and his on-board supervisor for the deployment, Captain Bagryanzev, only a matter of seconds to order both the defective torpedo expelled from the tube and an emergency surface. As the boat began to rise, Lyachin ordered his communication mast extended just before the first explosion. Later examination of the submarine's internal compartments and the position of crew remains indicated that many of the men had begun to move toward their appointed emergency stations. Unfortunately the torpedo propulsion system exploded too quickly, ripping open the outer doors of the torpedo tube and throwing the remains of the weapon overboard.[39] At the same time, the internal tube door imploded due to the explosion and the sea pressure and the torpedo room rapidly began to flood. Professor Dmitri Vlasov, an expert in this type of propulsion chemistry, provided an exclusive interview to the newspaper *Komsomolskaya Pravda* on November 28 and 29, 2000, offering a picture of the conditions in the forward torpedo room in the next few seconds.

> There was a horrendous uncontrolled mixture of hydrogen peroxide and kerosene, filling all of compartment one with fire. At the same time there was water coming from the torpedo tube or from what was left of the tube. The water gushed into the sub . . . but hydrogen peroxide and kerosene are lighter than water, so the mixture burned on top of the rising water. There was a burning layer from 1.54 tons of hydrogen peroxide and 331 pounds of kerosene.[40]

The acoustic character of the first explosion probably registered much like any detonation outside the submarine's hull. The force of the explosion rushed forward and out of the torpedo tube with its sound waves traveling in the near-surface acoustic propagation channels that are typical of the ocean in the Barents Sea area, permitting acoustic detection at great ranges.

Lyachin never had the opportunity to report the crisis on board his ship. Even if time had permitted, he would naturally hesitate to report a situation out of control because he might have informed not only the Northern Fleet but any NATO naval units in the area, including the Norwegian surveillance ship *Marietta,* lingering not far from the disaster site.

Meanwhile, the kerosene–hydrogen peroxide mixture floating on top of the seawater in the forward torpedo room burned at temperatures exceeding 3,600 degrees Fahrenheit. The torpedoes lying on the racks in proximity to the forward tubes could not withstand this heat. They exploded, shearing off the entire bow of the boat with an eruption akin to an earthquake. All of the men in the torpedo room died instantly and the rest of the crew went to the bottom as the boat sank quickly by the bow.

Sealed in the aft compartments, the few crewmembers who survived the explosions left a record in a letter penned by Captain Lieutenant Dmitri Kolesnikov. Salvers retrieved this testament once they entered the stern sections of the submarine. Apparently the survivors tried everything to conserve air and other vital resources, hoping for rescue. When this proved impossible, asphyxia closed the book on their naval careers.[41]

AFTERWORD

The Russian Navy, in cooperation with the Dutch salvage firms of Mammoet and Smit International, successfully raised the largest part of *Kursk*'s hull on October 7, 2001.[42] By October 15, the salvers delivered the boat to dock number 50 at the Northern Fleet shipbuilding facility in Roslyakovo. One week later, Lieutenant Gleb Lyachin, the son of *Kursk*'s commander, joined the Commander in Chief of the Navy Admiral Kuroyedov, the Northern Fleet commander Admiral Popov, the General Prosecutor of Russia Vladimir Ustinov, and investigators from the official court of inquiry to begin the investigation.

The court of inquiry had forty-two investigators and eleven forensic experts who examined everything from human remains to structural damage to the operational procedures employed both on the boat and by Northern Fleet command. Their efforts lasted from October 24, 2001, through February 18, 2002. During that time the forensic team identified the bodies of 115 men out of the 118 on board the submarine when she exploded. The last two sets of remains that were identified belonged to *Kursk* commander Captain Lyachin and his senior commander, Vladimir Bagryanzev. On February 28, the Minister of Industry, Science and Technology, Iliya Klebanov, confirmed that the navy planned to eliminate hydrogen peroxide torpedoes from its arsenal. Roughly three weeks later, on March 23, the navy laid Gennadi Lyachin and six of his crew to rest on the Avenue of Heroes in St. Petersburg cemetery.[43]

On April 25 the remains of *Kursk* left for the Nerpa shipbuilding facility to have the nuclear fuel unloaded and to begin the process of scrapping the vessel.

Exactly one month later, the new commander of the Northern Fleet Admiral Gennadi Suchkov began executing plans to raise select components of the forward torpedo room wreckage still on the Barents Sea floor in order to clarify the navy's understanding of the events that led to the boat's demise.[44] By the end of June the salvers recovered any remaining *Kursk* components that the Northern Fleet commanders found significant, such as select forward hull sections, torpedo-related equipment, and a 5-ton sonar fairing. The Russian Navy ordered the balance of the forward hull wreckage destroyed and that action took place on September 9, 2002.

On June 19 the official court of inquiry accepted the explosion of a hydrogen peroxide torpedo as the only credible explanation for the disaster. Stanislav Proshkin, general director of Gidropribor, which designed the 65-76-type hydrogen peroxide torpedo, objected to the conclusions of the court of inquiry. He continued to argue that some "external force" caused the explosion, but he could provide no convincing evidence.

General Prosecutor Vladimir Ustinov gave a press conference on July 26, announcing the end of the investigation and confirming that the court of inquiry had attributed the loss of the submarine to the explosion of a 65-76-A training torpedo in torpedo tube four. He asserted that the weapon detonated as a result of a hydrogen peroxide leakage. Uncontrolled hydrogen peroxide can spontaneously decompose into water and oxygen, in the process generating temperatures over 3,600 degrees Fahrenheit. Ustinov and the board of inquiry also reasoned that those submariners who survived the first two explosions perished from carbon monoxide within eight hours of the explosion. The submariners could not have left the boat on their own because the explosion crippled the bow compartments of the *Kursk* and denied them access to the rescue chamber attached to the forward escape trunk. They tried to use the rescue hatch in compartment nine but the lack of breathable air ended their effort to escape.

Although Ustinov argued that no direct link existed between senior naval officers, their actions at the time, and the loss of the boat, the story did not end there. An article entitled "Anti-state Secret," published in the official government newspaper *Rossiyskaya Gazeta* on August 29, 2002, revealed for the first time to the general public the most significant facts of the *Kursk* investigation: violations of naval exercise practice, the absence of reliable torpedo technology and personnel training, substandard rescue equipment, and the poorly executed rescue effort.

When many of the relatives of those who died on board *Kursk* demanded more information, the Putin government decided to give them access to the 130 volumes of *Kursk* investigation files. The General Military Prosecutor of Russia General-Lieutenant Alexander Savenkov took this unprecedented action on October 3, 2002. Some relatives, represented by a group of lawyers led by Boris Kuznetsov, vowed to look at the record more closely and to appeal the decision prohibiting legal action against the senior naval leadership.

The court of inquiry stated that the "training" hydrogen peroxide torpedo exploded in tube four aboard *Kursk* at 1128 on August 12, 2000. The crew had loaded the weapon that same morning. According to the court of inquiry,

> the explosion of fuel ingredients of the training torpedo in the torpedo tube 4 was caused by leakages of hydrogen peroxide PV-85 from torpedo oxidizer tank through leaking welds or sealing disks, and ignition took place when the chemical came into contact with non-metal materials in the torpedo tube.

Discussions held at the Institute of Science of Criminal Detection under the watchful eye of the Federal Security Service (FSB; formerly the KGB) drew an additional conclusion:

The epicenter of the explosion that took place aboard the submarine and caused initial damage aboard *Kursk,* was localized in the space where the training torpedo was placed. . . . The torpedo explosion was not caused by collision with any object that was outside the submarine or by a mine. However it's impossible to define correctly what caused [the] impulse for the torpedo explosion. . . .

In the end, expert opinion concluded that a thermal reaction caused the torpedo explosion when hydrogen peroxide leaked into the space between the torpedo tube and the torpedo. Torpedo or torpedo tube rust, or for that matter some ordinary lubricant in the tube, could start the thermal reaction by acting as a catalyst.[45]

Ustinov's office issued a press release on the second explosion that resonated well with the opinion of external experts, many of whom worked with and through the Submariners' Club:

A blast wave and scattering parts of both the torpedo and the torpedo tube initiated the explosion of torpedoes that were on torpedo racks in torpedo compartment one. Within two minutes other torpedoes detonated and passed the detonation impulse to other torpedoes on the racks.

Presumably four torpedoes detonated and destroyed the on-board arsenal, preventing an even more powerful explosion.

In the period between December 1993 and January 1994, the Arsenal Factory examined the training torpedo in question, upgraded its electric circuits, and installed a device to control the oxidizer system. The technicians replaced none of the rubber seals in contact with the hydrogen peroxide, nor did they notice that many of the replaceable parts in the torpedo had already exceeded their expected service life. *Kursk* received the training torpedo on August 3, 2000. It had never rested on the rack of any submarine nor had the Russian Navy ever tried the weapon with a test launch.

After the *Kursk* explosion, Northern Fleet torpedo specialists discovered that naval technicians had noted, on the same type of torpedoes, hydrogen peroxide leakage from both the torpedo oxidizer tanks and the flow control valves owing to defective seals. In other cases they found 5-millimeter craters in oxidizer tank welds. Other torpedoes had major rust problems. Astonishingly, the court of inquiry investigators stated that "the *Kursk* torpedoes didn't have any similar flaws." Given the failure of their record-keeping, would they know?

Bringing the poor training of the young torpedo room crew into the picture, the government investigators at last found the roots of the submarine's fate:

> the torpedo unit crewmen never had a chance to practice shooting the torpedoes since there weren't any special training facilities at the Vidyaevo base where the *Kursk* crew was stationed. Last time *Kursk* crewmen shot torpedoes was in 1998. At the end of July 2000 the *Kursk* was supposed to get maintained, but the maintenance was interrupted and was not completed.

The critical failure of maintenance and training programs disrupted careers, families, the life of a nation, and the story of a navy with a proud 300-year history. The manner in which the political and naval leadership fashions the future of Russia and the role it will play in world affairs may well mean that the *Kursk* disaster marks the end of the Soviet/Russian submarine force and the beginning of the Russian Federation's presence deep in the world oceans.

EPILOGUE

The tragedy of the Space Shuttle *Columbia* on February 1, 2003, is hauntingly similar to the tragedy of the *Kursk*. One has to pause and reflect that the conditions making such great technological breakthroughs achievable are, ironically enough, the same that make tragedies possible. Both achievements and tragedies ultimately are caused by brilliant individuals, brave crews, government sponsorship, aging bureaucracies, and ordinary human failures, all fueling, and fueled by, the desire to push beyond normal limits. The similarity in the two accidents and the variables that cause them are a stunning reminder that people, accidents, and governments are very much the same the world over.

The investigations into the loss of both *Kursk* and the *Columbia* have, to a remarkable degree, thoroughly explained the cause of those disasters and the kind of procedural and institutional failures that ended so many promising lives. Because such accidents can happen, one has to ask the question: Is the desire to live on the scientific and technological frontier worth the cost in human life? Almost certainly, the answer would be the same in both the Soviet/Russian submarine community and the NASA/astronaut community: Yes!

While some would debate that conclusion, few human beings would casually walk away from the promise and mystery that lie both in the deep ocean and in deep space. Curiosity about these things is too deeply embedded in the human experience. The people who built up the Soviet/Russian submarine force, as well as the people who manned it, responded to the call of both national service and life on the cutting edge of science and technology. They knew full well the price that kind of life might exact. The slow disintegration of the Soviet system only intensified their risk. The people who created and fly the Space Shuttle look proudly to their past scientific achievements, knowing all the while that their commitment might come at a high cost.

Put in perspective, the *Kursk* and *Columbia* episodes reveal more about people than machines, more about humanity than about warships or space vehicles. While the *Kursk* and its American counterparts exist to wage war, they also demonstrate the extent to which individual and national energy has served as a catalyst for awesome achievements in science and technology. The *Columbia*, while not a weapons system, represents similar national and individual vigor further energized over forty years ago by a young American president pointing at the Moon.

Unfortunately, most of what this book relates took place during the detestable Cold War. The American–Soviet standoff and the fear it inspired colored everything. Ever since the awesome roar of the first nuclear blast during World War II, many scientists and engineers openly wondered if working on weapons systems might actually violate their personal and professional ethics. They feared that national energies applied in this way around the globe might lead to its destruction rather than salvation. Science, they felt, should contribute to the latter, not the former. Many, including Albert Einstein himself, pleaded for sanity and restraint in a world that seemed bent on just the opposite.

In the post–Cold War world, this issue remains unresolved but still very fresh and compelling. Might human energy and determination serve a better purpose? Is it really true that the scientific and technical abilities enabled by the resources of the world's advanced nations cannot effectively address the AIDS pandemic or the hunger of African nations? Perhaps the lessons ultimately learned from *Kursk* and *Columbia* should go beyond a mere technical avoidance of a repetition—although this is certainly one desired outcome. Perhaps the time has come to redirect the energies and talents that drove the Cold War in an environment of fear and doubt toward new commitments requiring just as much energy, commitment, creativity, and talent. Division and fear led the great nations of the Cold War to build the submarines that fought in the darkness of the deep ocean and took American and Soviet naval personnel away from their families for months at a time, putting them and millions of innocent civilians in harm's way.

Nonetheless, their exploits in that forbidding environment constantly fascinate us; a fascination born of amazing technologies as well as the ocean's mysteries. Given the importance of the ocean to global prosperity, a healthy environment, and human survival, perhaps we should conclude *Rising Tide* with this question: What would happen if we asked the same talented people who conceived, designed, and manned *Kursk* or the American Los Angeles class attack submarines to protect the ocean environment on behalf of the world community? The answer to this question, given the story we have just told, obviously lies within our grasp. We have absolutely no doubt that the world's submariners could produce a future story about deep-ocean exploits that would truly take our breath away, while making sure that we would always have a healthy breath to take.

Appendix One

The History of the Russian Navy According to Gorshkov[1]

The highly unusual system of command that evolved in the Soviet Union occurred because the Soviet Navy was always a poor relation. Through 1937, the navy remained a poorly funded component of the Red Army. When aviation became an important factor, the Red Navy was moved to third place, and with the arrival of the intercontinental ballistic missile, the navy was allocated last place in the military lineup. This lack of regard for the value of the navy, with its concomitant inattention to naval detail, resulted in a command anomaly. In the other services, there was usually a rotation of commanders, which both afforded wider experience and avoided the possibility of anyone building a personal power base. Because no one, not even Stalin, really cared about the leadership of the Soviet Navy as they did about the Red Army or air force, it happened that in the Soviet era, only three men (Admirals N. G. Kuznetsov, Sergei G. Gorshkov, and V. N. Chernavin) controlled almost the entire period of the Red Navy's history. It is worth noting that both Kuznetsov and Gorshkov obtained their positions as a result of Stalin's favor toward each of them.

The most influential of the three, Gorshkov, was far more important than any combination of his U.S. counterparts, and it was he who directed the rise and fall of the modern Soviet surface navy. He also capitalized on the advent of nuclear weapons and the submarine-launched ballistic missile (SLBM) to revitalize the Soviet submarine force. His philosophy was immensely more threatening to the United States (and, as we will see, to the Soviet Union and the world's environment) than Soviet land armies and strategic rocket forces, for his iron control of the navy lapsed at its most critical juncture, the point where an individual Soviet submarine commander could launch a nuclear weapon.

Gorshkov's philosophy was also unsuccessful in another critical area, less obvious, but only marginally less hazardous. It failed in the design and construction of the nuclear submarines, missiles, and torpedoes that he deployed. Admiral Gorshkov demanded that a nuclear submarine fleet with a ballistic missile capability be launched at the earliest possible date, with a minimum regard for nuclear safety and no regard for human life. Even worse, he demanded the formal acceptance of these flawed weapons by the very naval commanders whom he knowingly sent to sea in fatally inadequate equipment.

To understand the long Cold War undersea contest between the United States and the Soviet Union (a war that goes on at a far lesser intensity with Russia today) one has to first understand Gorshkov and the ideas he imposed with such great success on the Soviet Navy, particularly upon the Soviet submarine force. We are fortunate that he put his ideas in writing in his book *Red Star Rising at Sea*, a compilation of articles that appeared in 1972 and 1973 in *Morskoi Sbornik*, the official journal of the Soviet Navy. In effect, *Red Star Rising at Sea* is to Gorshkov as *Mein Kampf* was to Adolf Hitler, in terms of it being both a revealing insight into the author's view of history and of the plans he had for the future. (This is not to imply that Gorshkov was in any way as evil as Hitler.) Gorshkov's writings were officially cleared for publication, and while this does not define them as Soviet policy, it does define them as at least acceptable to the leadership of the Soviet Union.

This appendix will provide a broad portrayal of the combined naval history of Russia and the USSR. It benefits immensely from having Gorshkov's interpretation of that history to illuminate the reasoning behind and the motivations for his future decisions as head of the Soviet Navy.

Mahan and Gorshkov

Russia made its "blue water" naval debut with the advent of Peter the Great's interest in the early 1700s, during the period that Alfred Thayer Mahan discusses in his seminal *The Influence of Sea Power on History, 1660–1783.*[2] It is interesting to compare England and Russia in terms of the principal conditions that Mahan states affect the seapower of nations, and then note Gorshkov's take on the matter.

In his famous book, Mahan says that the principal conditions affecting the seapower of nations are as follows:

1. Geographical position
2. Physical conformation, to include natural production (i.e., raw materials) and climate
3. Extent of territory
4. Number of population
5. Character of people
6. Character of government

In his analysis, Mahan naturally looks to England as the premier naval power of the era, due in no small part to its advantageous geographical position. As an island, it was not forced to maintain a large standing army for defense against a contiguous neighbor, and could therefore focus on its power at sea. England also had a good central position for strategic operations against any enemy that might arise, and that same position enabled it to control one of "the great thoroughfares of world traffic"—the English Channel.

Russia had almost the opposite situation, in that it was faced by enemies all around the perimeter of its borders, from Sweden in the north to Poland in the east to Turkey in the south to China in the west. It maintained a huge standing army, and had virtually no control of any of the vital "thoroughfares of world traffic."

It is interesting that Gorshkov takes a somewhat different point of view regarding geography. He notes that Russian maritime borders are almost twice that of the United States and fifteen times that of France. He calls upon Marx's writing, which says that to solve the problems of commerce, communications, and the fishing and maritime industries, men opened first the "individual littoral areas of the seas and the oceans."[3] By this statement, Gorshkov explains that Russia and the Soviet Union had in the past elected not to contest the world's oceans because its geography did not call for it. He then quotes Marx's commentary to the effect that prior to Peter the Great, no single great nation ever existed as Russia had, with her "shores and river mouths wrested away from her."

Mahan's second principal condition, regarding the physical conformation of a country and its natural production, finds England at a natural disadvantage, with its major cities not far from the coast, and subject to attack, as by the Dutch in 1667. England also lacked the natural productive capacity for food and for maritime requirements (wood, rope, sail). In contrast, Russia was difficult to invade by sea, and it was richly endowed with natural resources of every kind. Yet Gorshkov maintains that it was unable for many years to possess a strong navy because the development of armed forces is linked directly to the history of social-economic systems and those of Russia were then in the process of decay. In this regard he speaks most bitterly about Western European nations using their naval power for the accumulation of capital, stating that "they were used to seize colonies, for the enslavement of peoples of entire continents" and that a fierce struggle developed between rivals in this piratical role. The dawn of capitalism, he notes, was heralded by the discovery of gold and silver mines in America, by the eradication, enslavement, and burning alive of the natives in pits, the plundering of East India, and the transformation of Africa into a preserve for hunting blacks.[4] In essence, he declaims that Western navies were based on capitalist exploitation of the proletariat.

Mahan's third principal, the extent of territory, states that it is not the number of square miles of territory that is so important as the length of its coastline and the number of harbors available. England, of course, was dotted with excellent harbors, and more were available to her in her many colonies. Russia, on the other hand, had a tremendously long coastline but no access to a warm-water port, so that for many months of the year, the relatively few harbors were icebound. Because of these deficiencies, and despite the long tradition of the Russian Army resisting attempts to spend funds upon the Russian Navy, Gorshkov notes that Peter the Great's recognition of the need to obtain these outlets to the sea resulted in his building both a strong army and a strong navy. He quotes the great Tsar's comment: "Every potentate who has only ground forces has only one hand; yet whoever has a navy too, has both hands." Peter's actions, given in greater detail below, were, according to Gorshkov, the rebirth of the qualities of a seagoing people inherent in Russians since ancient times.

Mahan's fourth condition, the size of the population, was qualified in a manner similar to number three's qualification of the importance of the number of square miles of territory. Mahan states that the grand total of the population is not so important in terms of seapower as the total available for employment on shipboard and for the creation of naval material.

This was of course a key deficiency in Russia. Despite its huge population, relatively few were seagoing, and officers in particular often had to be imported from other nations. Gorshkov sidesteps this issue in an engaging way, quoting Fred Jane's statement that the Russian Navy can claim to be older than the English Navy, as one hundred years before Alfred built the first English naval ships, Russian ships were engaged in far-off sea battles. Gorshkov then buttresses this claim with further accounts of Russian naval combat taking place in the seventh century on the Black, Mediterranean, and Caspian Seas.

In his fifth condition, Mahan speaks about the national character of the people of a seagoing nation. He says that if seapower is going to be based on peaceful and extensive commerce, then aptitudes for commercial (as opposed to seagoing) pursuits must be a distinguishing feature of the population. Mahan notes that both the English and the Dutch were called in turn "a nation of shopkeepers," which, while intended as a jeer, was in fact a credit. Further, any "nation of shopkeepers" must have goods to sell and this in turn leads to industrialization, what Mahan describes as "the national characteristic most important to the development of sea power."[5] Industrialization promotes the development of healthy colonies to serve both as markets and sources of raw materials. He cites England's great success, and attributes it to two factors. First, the Englishman was willing to settle down and live in the new colony, without any "eager restlessness" to return. And second, he instinctively attempted to develop the resources of the colony in the broadest possible way.

This view is totally repugnant to Gorshkov, who systematically chastises Spain, Portugal, France, England, and Holland for their exploitation of colonies. He takes particular exception to England allowing its navy to directly enrich its officers and men through the prize system in which a share of the value of captured enemy merchantmen was distributed to all who took part. Gorshkov falls back on Marx again, citing his statement that trade dominance was directly related to the existence of a major industry. Marx points to Holland as an example of a dominant trade nation that fell from its position because it lacked major industries to back it up.[6]

Mahan's final condition, the character of government, compares England and France to England's great advantage, as it is an argument for the virtues of democracy in promoting the qualities of a seagoing people. Gorshkov's view is doctrinaire, for he says that a state will flourish or decline depending upon the condition of the social system, and, by implication, the Soviet social system was more progressive and had given impetus to military progress. Further, he posits that the quality of the armed forces depends in turn upon the qualities of the leaders of the fighting men, that is, the Soviet government.[7]

Gorshkov, far more than Mahan, pays repeated tribute to the virtues of "jointness," that is, the cooperation of the army and the navy, and goes so far as to say that an attack by Kutuzov forced Napoleon to abandon his planned invasion of England, and further, that the Battle of Trafalgar was not nearly so important as Napoleon's defeat in Russia in the Patriotic War of 1812.

In summary, Gorshkov states that despite foreign and domestic interference, the Russian Navy developed according to the needs of the Motherland, and has always been a vital part of Russia's defense, even though it has seldom received the credit it deserves.

THE HISTORICAL BACKGROUND

The origin of the word "Russia" is a matter of some debate. Some scholars believe that it derives from a geographic area west of the Dnieper River, and to support this there is a tributary to the Dnieper that is named "Ros." For the purposes of this book, however, another theory is more attractive, the long and often overlooked Russian fascination with the sea. In this theory, the Finnish name for Sweden was "Ruotsi." That name supposedly derives from "roosmenn," or men of the rowing way, who lived in what is today called Roslagen (Rowing-Law) in the coastal area of Swedish Uppland. They were, in short, Vikings, and the bravery, seamanship, and daring of the Vikings were emulated by Soviet submariners and their Russian navy successors.

The original Vikings came down the Dvina to the Dnieper on their customary raiding parties. It is said that a Viking by the name of Rurik established himself at Novgorod ("New City") and this became the first city of Rus, which later became Russia. As insight to the fundamental place a navy has in Russian history, one needs only to know that Rurik's successor, Oleg, first established Kiev on the Dnieper River. At the end of the ninth century, becoming annoyed with the way in which Greek traders treated him, Oleg sent an expedition of no less than 2,000 ships and 80,000 Vikings to Constantinople, the first, but far from the last, example of Russian employment of massive forces. When his ships found their way blocked into the harbor by a chain, Oleg beached his ships and had his men make huge wheels. He mounted the boats on the wheels and sailed on dry land into Constantinople's suburbs. This so terrified the Greeks that they immediately sued for peace, paying a ransom of six pounds of silver to each of Oleg's men.[8]

Gorshkov makes much of this incident as part of his long explanation of how the Russian Navy developed in the largest continental power on Earth. He believes that Russian naval development was systematically stymied in modern times by a combination of states led by England. Propaganda from these states exerted a psychological coercion on Russian leaders to misunderstand the role of the navy, and to underestimate its capabilities. The purported propaganda line was that Russia needed only a modest navy to protect its coastlines, and that it was not in any case a seagoing nation. He indignantly cites as an example President Richard Nixon's speech of August 4, 1970, in which the president stated: "That which the Soviet Union needs in the way of military preparation differs from what we need. The U.S.S.R. is a land power. . . . We, however, are primarily a sea power, and our needs are therefore different."[9]

This concerted and sustained action began, according to Gorshkov, after Peter the Great had created one of the strongest navies in the world. The great Tsar's efforts represented the extreme of "jointness," for to provide the basis for that navy, the Russian armies had to wrest territory from mighty Sweden, while already engaged in a protracted war with Turkey.

From 1700 to 1725, Sweden, then an incredibly powerful and belligerent nation led by the incomparable Charles XII, fought a bitter war with Russia, led by Peter I, later to be acclaimed "the Great." Both men were inexperienced in warfare to start and both became great leaders. Charles was only fifteen when he became king in 1697, and eighteen when a Russian–Polish–Danish alliance attacked Sweden. Peter was only seventeen when he at last seized control of the government in 1689. He immediately launched military campaigns, but more importantly spent the next eleven years introducing reforms and creating a conscript army. Perhaps the prototype of the "hands-on" manager, he labored incognito as Peter Mikhailov, a common workman in Dutch shipyards, learning the trade from the keel up. In contrast, Charles XII was a monomaniac warrior, always at war.

The long war with Russia was initiated when Charles began his campaign against Saxony by invading Poland in the spring of 1702. The Elector of Saxony, Augustus, was also king of the commonwealth of Poland, and Charles was determined to depose him. Peter welcomed the chance to confront Sweden in alliance with Poland and Denmark, even though he was at the time engaged in a bitter war with Turkey.

Charles had inflicted a humiliating defeat on Peter at the Battle of Narva in 1700, and was contemptuous of the Russian army. He turned his attentions elsewhere, delegating the Russian front to subordinates. It was a fatal error, for by 1703 the Russians had occupied the Neva Valley, where Peter would build his new capital, St. Petersburg. The willful Charles would not agree to peace terms, and in an attempt to settle the matter by his own leadership, pursued Peter's armies all the way to Poltava in the Ukraine. There the Swedish army was surrounded and destroyed on July 8, 1709.[10] Charles escaped to his ally, Turkey, only to be interned there for five years.

These were seasonal wars because the severe winters made it impossible to campaign. Peter had profitably used the "off time" building shipyards, melting church bells to cast cannon in his new arms factories, and establishing schools to train his growing armed forces. From 1703 on, Peter began to devise new ways to attack Charles' authority in the Baltic provinces. He saw that he could not match Sweden's conventional "blue ocean" warships in the near term, and instead began the manufacture of great numbers of small boats, propelled by oars and a single sail, seeking to defeat the larger ships by weight of numbers.

It was a brilliant insight, even though the ships had to be brought by intensive labor more than 600 miles from Voronezh on the Don, where they had been built at the base the Russians had used against the Turks. They sailed for the greatest distance on the Don and the Volga, but for the last long, hard miles, they were pulled overland by men and beasts through dense forests that had no roads.

Despite the difficulties, Peter's newly built ships with their newly trained sailors drove the veteran Swedish navy from Lakes Ladoga and Peipus in 1702. Peter adopted a *nom de guerre*, calling himself Rear Admiral Peter Aleexevich, and served under the man he had appointed as his naval commander in chief, the first Russian admiral, Fcodor Apraxin.

Apraxin had started his military career as a soldier, but his charismatic personality allowed him to argue with Peter over important matters, and at the same time maintain the goodwill of Peter's huge number of foreign mercenary sailors from any country in Europe.[11] He was the perfect counterpoint to Peter in the formation of a new navy literally being born in battle, for where Peter was impulsive, he was thoughtful, and where, in technical or personnel matters, Peter might be uncertain, he was decisive. While hundreds had lost their lives by opposing Peter on any subject, Apraxin maintained that in arguing with His Majesty as Rear Admiral Peter Aleexevich, he would never give way, but if Peter assumed his rank of Tsar, he knew his duty.

The following year, under Peter's direct leadership, the Russians captured the formidable Swedish fort at Nöteborg, built on a small island where it could control the juncture of Lake Ladoga with the Neva River. The Neva then followed a forty-five-mile fast-flowing course to the Gulf of Finland.

Peter quickly expanded his conquests, in part by hand-to-hand fighting when he again personally boarded Swedish ships, and by May 1703 had restored the province of Ingria to Russia, thus gaining access to the Baltic Sea. This was particularly sweet to him, for it had been taken by Sweden in the Peace Treaty of Stolbovo in 1617. The Swedish king Gustavus Adolphus described taking Ingria as "God's greatest good deed,"[12] for it bottled up the Russian nation, keeping it from the sea.

On May 16, 1703, Peter personally began the construction of St. Petersburg, the northernmost of the great cities of the world and the capital of Russia for more than two hundred years.[13]

It was built at terrible expense and at the cost of an estimated 250,000 lives, and can in that way be viewed as a metaphor for Soviet methods in the building of its fleet of nuclear submarines. From this time forward it was the Russian custom to fight their wars—or do their building—at great expense and with utter disregard for human life. The vast size of the country and the numberless citizens recklessly sacrificed to defend it kept it safe in many wars, even from foreign tyrants such as Napoleon and Hitler.

After the great victory at Poltava (the shuttle base site for U.S. bombers during World War II), Peter swiftly secured the vital Baltic coast area, occupying the important cities of Reval, Riga, Ebling, and Viborg in 1710. (Had Peter occupied Riga in 1703, he might never have built St. Petersburg, for it was an excellent port with facilities already in place.) For the first time in history, the Russian navy assumed a position of greater importance in combat operations than the Russian army. It now also had access to the shipbuilding resources of the Baltic countries, which were primary suppliers of timber, tar, flax, and hemp, commodities as valuable then as oil is today.[14]

These conquests provided the basis for the first Russian naval victory of consequence, the July 1714 Battle of Gangut (a corruption of the venue of the battle, Hangö Ud [Hangö Head]).

A Swedish fleet had appeared to threaten Peter's recent conquests, and he devised a plan by which he would create a diversion, taking eighteen sailing ships to Revel, while Apraxin's force of almost one hundred galleys and transports, carrying 24,000 troops, moved to conquer the Åland Islands and thus threaten Stockholm.

As things developed, the Swedish fleet trapped Apraxin's huge convoy, and Peter sailed to its rescue, assuming direction of the operation. A complex battle followed in which the Russian galleys sequentially swarmed around anchored Swedish ships before capturing them with powerful boarding parties. What remained of the Swedish battle fleet withdrew, and the Russians seized the Åland Islands.

The Battle of Gangut was the first major battle at sea won by the Russians, and it has been celebrated annually in the Russian and Soviet Navies ever since. Peter regarded it as fully equivalent to the victory at Poltava, and rewarded his sailors accordingly.

The later years of the great Northern War saw a long series of battles in which allies shifted sides rapidly for immediate advantage. England, so long Russia's ally, aligned itself with Sweden in 1719, and a force of thirty-three ships-of-the-line faced Peter and Apraxin. Remarkably, the Russians simply ignored the enemy and continued their small-boat raids on Sweden, including attacks on Stockholm itself. Finally, the Treaty of Nystadt was signed on August 30, 1721, ending the twenty-one-year war entirely in Russia's favor. Sweden surrendered to Russia the select areas of the Baltic provinces and hegemony in the north. The jubilant Russian people now bestowed upon Peter I the title of "Father of the Fatherland, Peter the Great and Emperor of all Russia." A special medal honoring the treaty was struck, and on its reverse side were the words: "The end of this war through such a peace was obtained by no one other than the Navy, for it was impossible to achieve anything by land."[15]

The scale of Peter's shipbuilding efforts was astounding, for while he purchased many vessels from abroad, his own shipyards turned out ships-of-the-line, transports, and galleys in great numbers. Today only those who sail the tall ships (or read Patrick O'Brian's Aubrey/Maturin novels) have any true understanding of the immense complexity and sophistication of such ships and of the skills necessary to sail them effectively. They were in fact intricate machines whose combination of rigging and sails had to be worked swiftly and correctly to survive, especially in the confined waters of the Baltic. Training the seamen to work these ships took time and effort, and many foreign sailors were employed. Unfortunately for Peter, there was never a sufficient pool of native Russian seamen qualified to go to sea.

Part of the problem was that he was fighting a two-front war. Charles XII had used his internment to persuade the Sultan of Turkey to attack the Russian armies in the south, which they did with great success. Peter had to agree at the Peace of Pruth to give up Azov and abolished his Black Sea fleet, which had grown to the incredible size of fifty-eight ships-of-the-line at a time when the vaunted Royal Navy possessed ninety-nine ships-of-the-line.[16]

After Peter the Great's death in 1725, the Russian navy went into a decline. The Tsarina Catherine did not have Peter's great interest in the navy, and their son, Peter II, virtually ended its existence by ordering it to stay in port unless he specifically ordered it to sea. The enforced idleness destroyed morale and prevented training. New ships were not built to replace losses and the existing Russian vessels, built of fir rather than stout English oak, deteriorated rapidly for lack of maintenance—a phenomenon being repeated in steel and titanium form today in the modern Russian Navy.

The one feeble pulse that kept the navy alive was the Russian army's requirement for ships to bring supplies on its many campaigns of the eighteenth century. Russia still possessed ships-of-the-line, but its admirals adhered to Peter the Great's doctrine that no attack should be made without possessing a superiority of at least one-third. As a result, Russia confronted, but did not engage, the Swedish navy in the first half of the eighteenth century. The situation changed dramatically when tiny Denmark became increasingly powerful and threatened to create a Scandinavian kingdom that would include Norway, Sweden, and Finland. Russia entered into an alliance with its old enemy Sweden that endured through the Seven Years War (1756–1763). That protracted conflict saw the Prussians under Frederick the Great allied with England against Austria, France, Sweden, and Russia. The Russian navy was again built up to provide ships to maintain a blockade and to transport men and supplies.

In 1761, the Russian Empress Elizabeth died, and her successor, Peter III, soon made peace with Frederick the Great, saving him from an apparently inevitable defeat. It was Peter III's misfortune to have as his Tsarina a German princess, Sophie Fredericke Auguste von Anhalt-Zerbst, who had him murdered by the Imperial Guards. She succeeded him to the throne, becoming the Empress Catherine the Great, who continued Peter the Great's policy of the Westernization of Russia.[17]

Catherine made a wise decision to allow matters in the north to subside, and concentrated her efforts against the Turks, resulting in a revival of the Russian navy in both the Black Sea and the Mediterranean.

Russia's enemy in the Seven Years War now proved to be its benefactor, as England opened its shipyards and even its naval officer corps to the service of the Russian navy. The latter were desperately needed, for experienced Russian naval officers were in short supply, and the English officers were tasked to run Russian naval operations in the Mediterranean.

There, according to Gorshkov, Admiral G. A. Spiridov wrote a brilliant page in history with his Baltic Fleet squadron, located in the Mediterranean for five years from 1769 to 1774. His mission was to threaten Turkey from the sea by supporting the uprising of the Balkan peoples enslaved by the Turks. The Empress Catherine told Spiridov that "All Europe is marveling at your feat, and is looking at you with expectation." In the course of the expedition, the Russian navy defeated the Turkish fleet in battles at Khios and Cesme and succeeded in blockading the Dardanelles (thus turning the tables on the Turks) while capturing twenty islands and several coastal cities.

Gorshkov cites the conduct of the Russian fleet in the Mediterranean Sea as an outstanding example of "autonomous operations by a large naval formation completely cut off from its home ports"[18]—an almost verbatim summary of his own goals with the Soviet fleet two hundred years later.

With his usual anti-capitalist vehemence, Gorshkov records that countries hostile to Russia, "above all England," still prevented the Russians from achieving complete freedom of passage from the Black Sea into the Mediterranean. He quite overlooks the immeasurable contribution the English made to Spiridov's success, perhaps because the English officers were quite candid in their assessment of the inferior quality of Russian officers, seamen, and ships. The writings of Rear Admiral John Elphinston, who, as a captain in the Royal Navy, served as a Russian flag officer, leave no doubt of his dislike of Spiridov nor of the low opinion the English had of their ally's capabilities.[19]

Elphinston had made his Mediterranean landfall on May 20, 1770, at Cape Matapan, site of a decisive victory of the Royal Navy over the Italian Navy in March 1941. As soon as the wind permitted, Elphinston, in the 80-gun flagship *Sviatoslav*, with two 66-gun ships and a frigate, rather precipitously attacked a larger Turkish force of fourteen ships-of-the-line. The enemy's numerical advantage threatened to overwhelm the Russian ships until they began firing explosive shells, a first in naval warfare, and both novel and effective enough to cause the Turks to flee. (Surprisingly, neither here nor elsewhere does Gorshkov elaborate on the many Russian tactical naval innovations.)

On July 5, 1770, Elphinston and Spiridov put aside their differences for sufficient time to launch another attack on the Turkish fleet. The heavy fighting spilled over into Tchesma Bay, where some two hundred Turkish ships were clustered. Almost all were destroyed by Russian cannon fire and fireships.

Gorshkov states that the combined actions of the Russian army in the north and the navy from the south forced the Turks to make a costly peace agreement, the Treaty of Jassy. It gave Russia the land between the Bug and Dnieper Rivers, and the right to free commercial navigation in the Black Sea and transit to the Mediterranean. Turkey was also forced to give the Crimea its independence. Catherine promptly established a puppet government and it later became part of Russia.

When the fourth Russo–Turk war broke out in 1787, Russia was unable to bring its Baltic fleet to the Mediterranean again because it was blocked by the Swedish fleet. This left Russian naval activity confined to its Black Sea fleet, which was outnumbered by the Turks by about fifty percent. The Russian deficiency in numbers was offset by the leadership of Commodore F. F. Ushakov, who, Gorshkov states, inflicted three decisive defeats on the Turkish fleet between 1790 and 1791—the sea battles of Kerch (1790), Tendra (1790), and Calicara (1791).

Ushakov distinguished himself further in the combined operations Russia conducted with England, Austria, and Turkey against France from 1797 to 1800. Commanding a squadron in the Mediterranean, Ushakov freed the Ionian Islands from French domination, and in 1799 captured the fortress of Corfu after a three-month siege. Gorshkov is quick to point out the political significance of the Russian naval victories, saying that naval power was the most important Russian foreign policy weapon, having drawn Italy, Sardinia, and even Tunisia into the Russian sphere of influence. Lord Nelson might have questioned the claim.

A true believer would ultimately decide from Gorshkov's writing that the Russian navy's operations in the Mediterranean had been something in the way of a massive compassionate relief mission to aid the Greeks and all others suffering under Turkish rule, an entirely defensive maneuver that helped its country fight off aggression from Sweden, France, Turkey, and England. In a similar way, he notes that the Russian fleet in the Mediterranean in the 1960s and 1970s was there only as a defensive response to the aggressive presence of the United States Sixth Fleet, which had as its basic mission "a surprise attack against the Soviet Union and the countries of the Socialist community." In contrast, the Soviet fleet in the Mediterranean was not there to threaten peace-loving people, nor to implement any expansionist desires, "which are alien to our Socialist state," but instead to nip aggression in the bud, promoting stability and the cause of peace. He characterizes the presence of the Sixth Fleet as a "clearly expansionary, antidemocratic, and policeman policy."[20]

What is perhaps most interesting in Gorshkov's historical account is that he ignores Russia's huge territorial expansion at the expense of Persia around the Caspian Sea, and other such acquisitions that thrust the Motherland into the Middle East. These were certainly expansionary, unquestionably anti-democratic, and Cossacks symbolized the policeman policy.

The Russian navy fell upon hard times again after Napoleon had finally met his Waterloo in 1812. Where Peter the Great had built 58 ships-of-the-line, 207 smaller sailing vessels, and 439 galleys for the Baltic fleet, by 1825 Russia possessed only five ships-of-the-line and ten frigates capable of putting to sea. Gorshkov quotes Admrial V. M. Golovnin's comment, "If rotten, poorly-equipped ships; elderly and ailing naval commanders, without knowledge and spirit at sea; inexperienced captains and officers; and farmers in the guise of seamen, formed into crews, can constitute a fleet, then we have a fleet."

Offsetting this dismal summary, Gorshkov takes obvious and justifiable delight in recounting the heroic exploits of Russian explorers who discovered numberless islands in the Pacific (including Kauai, whose king, Gorshkov tells us, became a Russian citizen). The Russian sailors explored Alaska and even established a fort near San Francisco in 1812. Their achievements, according to Gorshkov, demonstrate the love of the sea inherent in the Russian people.

Russia was caught, as she would be so often, behind the power curve of the Industrial Revolution when the Crimean War occurred in 1853–1856. Her navy, which had more personnel than any other navy in the world, and was second in the number of ships only to the Royal Navy, still consisted primarily of sailing vessels. The Crimean War was the first in which battles took place simultaneously all around the Russian perimeter, including the Black Sea, the Baltic, the White Sea, the Arctic Ocean, and the Pacific.

Combined, the French and British navies were larger at every point than the Russian, and were equipped with both excellent sailing vessels and steam-powered ships. The quality of their officers and seamen was very high compared to the Russian navy, particularly in modern equipment, for the Crimean War was the first in which large-scale use was made of steam-powered ships.

Oddly enough, the war had its first origins in a French dispute with Russia over the Holy Places in Palestine, specifically the key to the

Church of the Nativity in Jerusalem and the right to place a silver star on Christ's birthplace in Bethlehem. A series of misunderstandings and gunboat diplomatic errors escalated the tension until it became apparent that the real *causus belli* was the Russian determination to occupy Constantinople and thus control access to the Black Sea and the Anglo-French determination to prevent this.

After Russia occupied two provinces of the Ottoman empire, Turkey declared war on October 4, 1853. In the initial naval encounter, perhaps the last clash between squadrons of sailing vessels, the Russian fleet destroyed the Turkish fleet and coastal batteries in just three and one-half hours at the Battle of Sinope on November 30. Under the command of Admiral P. S. Nakhimov, the smaller Russian fleet used its smooth-bore explosive shells to wreak havoc on the wooden Turkish ships. Before the battle Nakhimov sent out a message paraphrasing Nelson, saying "Russia expects valiant deeds from the Black Sea Fleet, justification of that expectation depends on us." After the battle, he might well have sent out a message saying, "The day of the wooden ship is over."

While steam-powered vessels remained in the minority in the Russian navy, their presence was highlighted by the steam-frigate *Vladimir*'s capture of the Turkish armed steamship *Pervaz Bakhi*—another possible first in naval history.

That touch of modernity dimmed with the arrival of powerful Anglo-French forces on January 3, 1854, which was followed on March 28 by a British and French declaration of war on Russia. (One interesting by-product of this crisis is that Russia initiated the sale of Alaska to the United States for $7.2 million dollars in 1854, in the hope that a rapprochement engendered by the sale might result in the appearance of the American fleet in the Mediterranean to offset English power there. The Russian flag did not come down until the purchase was concluded in 1867.)

By September 13, 1854, a fleet of one hundred fifty Allied warships began landing operations in the Crimea, and a month later commenced the siege and naval bombardment of Sevastopol. The fort endured a year of punishment before surrendering on September 9, 1855, following the scuttling of the Russian Black Sea fleet. Admiral Nakhimov was killed during the siege. Casualties from all causes amounted to 252,000 for the Allies and 256,000 for the Russians.

The conflict was settled in the 1856 Treaty of Paris, with the effect that the Black Sea was neutralized, with Russia once again denied access to the Mediterranean through the Dardanelles, which were, as a sop, closed to all warships.[21] Russia had to cede the mouth of the Danube River and give up her Protectorate over the Danubian Principalities. The Russian fleet was prohibited from the Baltic again, but reappeared there by 1871.

Gorshkov disingenuously sums up Russian naval activity in the nineteenth century by saying that the Russian navy successfully executed its mission whenever opposed by Turkish forces, but was thwarted by superior Western power whenever it attempted to gain access to the Mediterranean.[22]

Many Russian naval officers were inventive, and in the Russo–Turkish war of 1877–1878, both the towed and the spar torpedoes were used. In January 1878 Stephan Osipovitch Makarov made history, not for the last time, by using two Whitehead torpedoes to destroy the Turkish dispatch boat *Intibakh*—the first successful wartime use of a self-propelled torpedo.[23]

Somewhat surprisingly, he omits mention of the June 1905 mutiny on the *Kniaz Potemkin Tavricheski,* the subject of Sergei Einstein's famous film *Potemkin*. Wistfully, he notes that every time Russia failed to develop and maintain its fleet at an appropriate level, it either lost battles or its peacetime policies failed to gain their objectives. His message is clear: The Soviet Union required a strong navy. It is again surprising that Gorshkov, who continually stresses the importance of the technological superiority of the enemy, does not mention that the inventive Russians led the world with their explosive shells, electrical and chemical-contact mines, and both spar and self-propelled torpedoes, all employed during this period.

The generally strident tone of Gorshkov's narrative when he discusses Western countries is noteworthy. When he writes briefly of the Russo–Turkish war, he laments the weakness of the Baltic fleet, attributing it to Tsarist officials who underestimated the importance of the navy, and consequently sacrificed the interests of the Balkan people to Great Britain and Austria. It is as if he fears that he cannot safely write a history of the Russian navy without constantly reassuring the die-hard communists in his audience that he is one of them. He was probably correct in this. One notable omission in his account is the twenty-year plan for naval expansion that the Russian government introduced in 1882. While, unlike Imperial Germany, Imperial Russia never intended to match the Royal Navy, it did wish to have a fleet that in alliance with another country—France in particular—would be capable of dealing with the British fleet.

THE ERA OF IMPERIALISM

Gorshkov pulls out all the stops when relating an especially bitter period in Russian naval history. He begins by quoting Lenin, who defined imperialism as the highest (and thus the last) stage of capitalism, and stated that it was completely developed by 1914. Gorshkov goes on to say that by 1914 the major capitalist powers had divided among themselves almost all the territory of the world, and had done so by the use of seapower. He particularly decries the pillaging of the Chinese people, first by Great Britain and France, and then by the "younger despoilers," the United States, Germany, and Japan.

The Spanish–American War again calls for a Lenin quote to the effect that "They [the Americans] plundered Cuba and the Philippines." Gorshkov calls the Spanish–American War "the first imperialist war for re-division of the world" and notes that the United States used local insurgent armies to do the bulk of the fighting—and take the bulk of the casualties.

Then, in a truly mendacious paragraph, he states that after the Spanish–American war, the United States entered a "prolonged period of un-restrained rearmament." It would be difficult to explain the total lack of American preparedness for World War I if Gorshkov was even partly correct. He cites Alfred Thayer Mahan as the "ideologue" who created the theory of seapower, and who was one of the greatest apologists of American imperialism.[24]

The Boxer Rebellion in China in 1900 required "all the major imperialist rivals" (Great Britain, Japan, the United States, Germany, France, and Russia) to send troops to attempt to grab the lion's share for itself. In a paragraph of almost sleight-of-hand slickness, Gorshkov doesn't mention anything about despoiling China when he notes that "after the occupation of Manchuria by Russia" the Far East policy of the United States, Japan, and Great Britain was to oust them from the regions they had seized and the annexation of those areas.

He then turns to an extensive discussion of the calamitous Russo–

Japanese war of 1904–1905. As background, he paints the earlier Japanese successes against China in the Sino–Japanese War of 1894–1895 as being based on Great Britain's support. He does give credit to the Japanese Navy for being able to support the Japanese Army in Korea and Manchuria.

In 1904, the Russian Navy was substantially larger than that of Japan's, possessing twenty battleships to Japan's six. However, the Russian fleet was widely scattered around its perimeter so that in its Far East fleets, it had seven battleships to Japan's six, but was outnumbered in cruisers and destroyers. (Oddly enough, the majority of the capital ships of both navies had been built in foreign shipyards.) The surprise ten-destroyer Japanese attack on Port Arthur on February 9, 1904, saw eighteen torpedoes (all equipped with net cutters) launched with only three hits. These hits were critical and decided the fate of the war, for they put the battleships *Retvisan* and *Tsarevitch* and the cruiser *Pallada* out of action. The Russian fleet was essentially defeated, and Japanese troops landed unchecked in Korea.

The attack presaged Pearl Harbor in its secrecy, brilliant execution, and the repeated charges that intelligence sources reporting Japanese intentions months in advance of the attack had been ignored. There was another similarity, for just as Admiral Nagumo declined to make a follow-up attack on Pearl Harbor because of his concern about the whereabouts of the United States carriers, so did Admiral Togo have to be concerned about the appearance of another Russian fleet.

On August 24, Tsar Nicholas II belatedly sent the Second Pacific Squadron from the Baltic. Had it been sent earlier, the Russians would have had such an overwhelming superiority that the Japanese probably would not have dared to attack.

Instead, Japan's superiority at sea combined with the efforts of a brave and efficient army to defeat Russia on land, with Port Arthur falling on January 2, 1905. The siege had lasted 329 days, and cost 28,000 Russian dead and almost three times that many Japanese. The large but demoralized Russian First Pacific Squadron then sailed for Vladivostok, where a unit of cruisers put to sea to meet it. Admiral Togo overtook the Russian fleet on August 10, then used superior gunnery to maul it, sending it high-tailing back to Port Arthur, where it would be attacked and all but one capital ship sunk by Japanese Army artillery shells. The one surviving ship, the *Sevastopol*, was scuttled.

On March 10, 1905, the long Battle of Mukden came to an end. Over half a million troops had been engaged, and Russia had some 90,000 casualties to 70,000 of the Japanese. The war was substantially over; only the intervention of the Russian Baltic Fleet could alter the situation.

The Second Pacific Squadron had not left the Baltic until October 15, 1904, under the command of Admiral Z. P. Rozhestvensky, who had made a name for himself commanding torpedo boats in the most recent Russo–Turkish war. On October 21–22, the squadron passed through a group of English fishing ships off the Dogger Bank, and in a mix-up of the first water, opened fire, destroying several of the sloops and damaging the Russian vessel *Aurora* with four hits—inadvertently the most effective Russian gunnery in some time. The Royal Navy, always ready for a fight, prepared to attack, but apologies and promises of compensation cooled the incident.

The Second Pacific Squadron then made an agonizingly long 222-day, 18,000-mile trip that caused tremendous wear and tear on both ships and men. Coaling was done from German ships under contract, the sweating men holding wads of cotton waste between their teeth to help them breathe.[25] Informed of the fall of Port Arthur as they were passing Madagascar, the fleet pressed on, short on coal, food, and fresh water, arriving in the Tsushima Straits on the night of May 26/27. There it was intercepted by Admiral Heihachiro Togo, commander of the combined Japanese fleet.

On paper, the fleets were evenly matched. The Russians had eight battleships and four other armored warships while the Japanese had four and eight, respectively. However, the Japanese were able to deploy forty cruisers, destroyers, and torpedo boats to the eighteen of the Russians.

But it was in firepower that the Japanese excelled, able to fire 360 rounds of artillery per minute, with a throw weight of 48,287 pounds. The Russians could fire only 134 rounds per minute, with a throw weight of just over 18,000 pounds. One advantage that the Russian Navy might have had was that it was equipped with armor-piercing shells rather than the high-explosive shells used by the Japanese. Unfortunately for the Russians, their shells were made of cast iron rather than steel, and broke up on contact. The shells, sabotaged by corruption or ineptitude, were perhaps symptomatic of the decay of the Russian system. Despite this, the ordinary sailors were confident that they would defeat the Japanese.

The long arduous trip, with its many stops for fuel, had been carefully monitored by the Japanese. As soon as the Russian fleet arrived in the waters near Japan, they shadowed it, and on May 27 Admiral Togo issued his Nelsonian exhortation, "The fate of our Empire hangs on this one action; you will all exert yourself and do your utmost."[26]

Togo had maneuvered around the Russian fleet, which was easy to track because its two hospital ships were operating with all lights on. The flag he used to order "Open Fire" was preserved and flown by the *Akagi* in the 1941 attack on Pearl Harbor.

The Japanese then executed the famous crossing the "T" maneuver to begin the Battle of Tsushima, one that ranks with Trafalgar and Midway in naval history. The Russian fleet, encumbered by its many auxiliary support ships, fought bravely at first, but the battle was essentially decided in the first thirty minutes by the superior skills, speed (the Japanese were averaging fifteen knots to the Russians' eight), and gunnery of the Japanese. Forty-two Russian ships were lost, including Admiral Rozhestvensky's flagship, the *Suvorov*. (Rozhestvensky was severely injured, but survived and spent time in a Japanese prisoner-of-war camp before being returned to Russia to face a court-martial.[27]) Two destroyers and the light cruiser Almaz reached Vladivostok, while six other ships were interned in neutral ports. One of these was the *Aurora*, which survives to this day in St. Petersburg. The Japanese lost only three torpedo boats. About 6,000 Russians were killed, while the Japanese suffered 600 casualties. One of the Japanese casualties was a young officer named Yamamoto Isoroku, who lost two fingers of his left hand, and who would become a primary figure in World War II.

Both governments were now weary of war, which had almost bankrupted Japan and brought revolution closer in Russia. They agreed to peace negotiations, led by President Theodore Roosevelt, which resulted in the Treaty of Portsmouth (New Hampshire). The treaty required Russia to remove its troops from Manchuria while permitting the Japanese to hold the Liaodong Peninsula and Korea.

There was public outrage in Russia that the "little yellow monkeys" of Japan could have defeated the Motherland and obtained so many important concessions. This had two political results: strengthening the military element in Japan's government, and forcing the Tsar, much against his will, to liberalize his government.[28]

It took Lenin to find a bright spot in the disaster, for he said that with the Russian Navy destroyed, the war was irrevocably lost, and the country was confronted with a complete military breakdown of the aristocracy.[29] Gorshkov then goes on to add that the real winners of the war were the imperialist nations, particularly the United States, Great Britain, and Germany. He then reveals his real message, that the lesson to be learned from the war was the need for warships of great cruising range, able to carry on "inter-theater maneuvers." This is exactly what he attempted to do with his submarine force, and if time and resources had permitted, he would have sought to do so with his surface forces.

World War I found Russia unprepared both militarily and politically. The adverse results of the Russo–Japanese War revealed how the Russian autocracy embodied in Tsar Nicholas II was incapable of making the necessary decisions for the present or the necessary provisions for the future. A huge rearmament program had been launched, at the instigation of and with the investment of France and Great Britain, in 1913, but it was programmed to require four years before reaching fruition. In August 1914, when war broke out, the Russian fleet was incapable of opposing the Germans in the Baltic. The Black Sea Fleet, while "imposing" in relation to the Turkish fleet, was obsolescent. Further, it was rendered impotent in the face of the arrival of the German cruisers *Goeben* and *Breslau*, which had brilliantly evaded the British fleet in the Mediterranean, to reinforce the Turkish fleet with two powerful modern ships and their well-trained crews. There was no fleet at all in the northern reaches of Russia, and the Pacific Fleet was no longer a credible force.[30]

While he covers most of the major naval actions, including a good analysis of the Battle of Jutland, Gorshkov is at his most incisive in writing of the German unrestricted submarine warfare that began in February 1917, and the enormous anti-submarine warfare efforts (ASW) that were necessary to contain it. He notes that in 1918 the Allies were employing 700,000 men, 5,000 ships, 2,000 aircraft, and a large number of dirigibles to combat German submarines. These numbers are high, but they do measure the scale of effort that was required—and they measure the importance Gorshkov imputes both to submarines and to ASW efforts.

It is only natural that he writes with some difficulty of the efforts of the Imperial Russian Navy during this period. On the one hand, he wishes to demonstrate the continuing effectiveness of naval forces, and states that the Baltic Fleet successfully prosecuted its mission of aiding the blockade of Germany. He does not mention that by early 1917 the Russian fleet had been built up to include 558 combat ships, a number of launches, and over 500 auxiliary transport vessels. Further, under construction were another 15 battleships, 14 cruisers, and 269 aircraft. The Imperial Russian Fleet employed 168,000 officers and men.

Nor does he mention that the February 17 abdication of Tsar Nicholas II destroyed the navy's remaining efficiency as the Provisional Government came to power. Riots broke out at once in the major Baltic ports, and many senior officers were killed, as the roots of the Russian Revolution took hold in the Russian Navy.

His way out is again through quoting Lenin on the relatively little known Moon Sound operation of October 12–20, 1917. Lenin asserts that the Central Powers (Germany and Austria) conspired with the Allies (Great Britain, France, and the United States) to create an imperialist plot to suppress the Russian Revolution by allowing the entire German fleet to proceed without interference against Russia in the Moon Sound operation. According to Lenin, the German aim was to attack and capture the Russian capital and, in doing so, uproot the revolutionary regime. Inasmuch as the Moon Sound Islands defend the entrance to the Gulf of Riga, this is perhaps too sweeping a claim.

The German landing operation on the Moon Sound Islands, under the command of Vice Admiral Eggard Schmidt, was on a very large scale. The admiral brought in more than 300 vessels carrying 25,000 assault troops. Although outnumbered in battleships by eleven to two, in cruisers by nine to three, and in other ships by 285 to thirty-three,[31] the smaller Russian force mounted strong resistance to the German squadron and, in Lenin's perhaps overgenerous view, prevented the Germans from stifling the Russian Revolution. They did capture the Moon Sound Islands, but they did not contain the Russian ships retreating from the Gulf of Riga. The Battle of Moon Sound was the last fought by the Russian fleet under the ensign of St. Andrew.[32]

Gorshkov concludes his article on the First World War by writing that it was decided on the ground, and that the Eastern Front was the most important in disrupting German plans. He omits mention here of the March 1918 Treaty of Brest Litovsk, which left the Western Allies in the lurch and forfeited huge amounts of Russian territory. Instead, he merely relates that the victory of the Great October Revolution in Russia and her revolutionary withdrawal from the war "activated the masses in

Germany." This resulted in the mutiny of sailors on board the German battleship *Markgraf* on October 28, 1918, when they refused to prepare for a final "death ride" sortie against the Royal Navy. (The *Markgraf* was damaged in the Battle of Jutland and later scuttled at Scapa Flow.) The mutiny was part of the series of events that led to the Kaiser's abdication and Germany's request for an armistice.

Gorshkov's view of the future may be found in his assessment of the German's unrestricted submarine campaign, which sank sixty-five percent of the British merchant marine before the Royal Navy got its act together with convoys and anti-submarine warfare craft. Gorshkov believes that Great Britain avoided catastrophe only because the German high command blundered in not building a submarine force of the necessary size, and not giving it the full support of its surface fleet. This is a key statement, for it underlies Gorshkov's philosophy with the Soviet submarine force—it had to be large, and it had to be fully supported by surface vessels.

Gorshkov does not really write without reservation of Russian naval history until after October 17, 1917, when "a new era in world history began . . . the first workers' and peasants' state in the world was born." The devotion of the Russian seamen to the proletarian cause made them, in Lenin's estimation, the leading detachment of the Revolution. (Gorshkov states that the Red Navy was born of the Red Revolution. He does not say that the birth was a mutiny, for it would not do to have the Red Navy's heritage rest on an action that is abhorred in all navies.)

After the Moon Sound operation, detachments of the now Red Baltic Fleet were ordered to ascend the Neva River and participate directly in the Revolution. In Petrograd, on October 25, 1917, Vladimir Lenin and his Bolshevik cohorts seized power. The expedition was highlighted at 2140 hours on November 7, 1917, when the *Aurora,* an armored cruiser, fired a shot that signaled the storming of the Winter Palace. The "bourgeois government" was captured by the sailors and imprisoned in the Petropavlovsk Fortress.

The new government brought the war to a close, and, in December 1917, an armistice was signed with Germany. By the Decree of the Council of People's Commissars on January 29, 1918, the Russian fleet was declared dissolved and the creation of the Workers' and Peasants' Red Fleet was proclaimed. Gorshkov notes piously that "the Red Navy, like the Red Army, by its mission, character, and socio-political essence, differed radically from the navies of the capitalist power, since it was an instrument to protect the independence of the Socialist state and the interests of the workers and was imbued with the spirit of proletarian internationalism, and friendship and brotherhood among peoples."[33]

In the Civil War that followed the October Revolution and in the Allied attempts at intervention, the newly created Red Navy played only a minor role, with many of the seamen being conscripted into Red Army units. Many ships were scuttled, and the most effective Red Navy actions were part of the riverine and lake operations. The most poignant event was the dissolution of the Black Sea Fleet, which, after having been seized by the intervention of the Western Allies, was returned to the defeated White Russian forces under Baron Peter Wrangle in 1921. He used the ships to evacuate 130,000 surviving members of the White Russian forces with their families to Bizerte, Tunisia, where they were interned by the French. The ships remained intact for almost ten years, and then were broken up for scrap.[34]

THE POST WORLD WAR I YEARS

Gorshkov plays strictly to his Communist friends in his coverage of the growth of the Red Navy during the period 1928 to 1941. In his view, every Western naval activity, including the several naval conferences that sought to set limits on naval armament, were imperialist plots designed to facilitate an attack on the Soviet Union. He notes a subplot to this activity, the efforts of the United States to gain world domination through naval supremacy.

He marks the May 1928 meeting of the USSR Revolutionary Military Council as being significant in the history of the Red Navy, for it laid down the first of two Five Year Plans for shipbuilding and determined that a harmonious yet diverse balance of surface, submarine, and naval air forces would be developed.[35]

The Red Navy did enter into a formidable construction program that would provide it with a sizeable surface force and the world's largest submarine fleet. The undersea force totaled 165 by September 1, 1939, and more than 200 by the time Hitler invaded the Soviet Union in June 1941. In a comparison of selected Soviet ships with their American counterparts, Gorshkov indicates the general qualitative superiority of the Red Navy. This is matched by the Soviet development of a new chapter in naval planning—the theory of the operational employment of naval forces. He hedges a bit, noting that this theory is not to be found in "official documents governing the employment of the Navy" but rather in the speeches of the Soviet Navy leadership, in the press, and in courses at the Naval Academy. In contrast to bourgeois naval science, the Soviets correctly determined the role of both naval aviation and amphibious operations. It also determined the correct employment of strategic and tactical forces, including long-range submarine operations. Then, without apparent embarrassment, he states that in practice not a single specially constructed landing ship was available to the Red Navy and that it lacked specialized naval aircraft.

THE GREAT PATRIOTIC WAR

Gorshkov makes a swift review of the Second World War in which the Western allies are painted only a little less harshly than Nazi Germany. He particularly resents any attempt to equate the battles of either El Alamein or Midway with the Battle of Stalingrad, and attributes Japan's surrender to the Soviet declaration of war and destruction of the Kwantung Army in August, 1945. He mentions the atomic bomb only in passing.

Inexplicably, in face of the facts, he denigrates the American submarine campaign against Japanese merchant shipping, stating that "American operations against Japanese communications were not distinguished by activity." And in a looping leap of Communist faith, he asserts that the reason Japan shifted to a strategic defense was not the actions of the American Navy, but rather the defeat of the German army at Stalingrad, which "convinced the Japanese military leaders of the hopelessness of the offensive strategy."

Buried underneath the political persiflage is his constant theme that the Red Navy is an integral and indispensable component of the Soviet armed forces.

THE SOVIET NAVY IN THE GREAT PATRIOTIC WAR

Admiral Gorshkov's comments on the Soviet Navy in the Great Patriotic War are surprising in two ways. He was, as we know, dedicated to the creation of a superb Soviet submarine fleet, but he minimizes the importance of submarine warfare in both the Atlantic and the Pacific. Rather than viewing submarines as the Western Allies do, as critically important elements of the war, he refers to them as being more or less secondary and entirely nondecisive when compared to the great land battles of the Red Army. The second surprise is that he makes almost no mention of the operation of the Red submarine fleet during World War II, although it was one of the largest submarine forces in the world, and certainly had the highest concentration of its forces in the smallest area, that of the Baltic Sea.

He instead emphasizes the importance of the Red Navy in acting as flank guards for Soviet land forces, and for its conduct of amphibious operations. His point of view in lauding the Soviet land operations is certainly understandable, for there is no denying that the Red Army met and defeated the German Army in the largest ground conflict in history. Yet his enthusiasm lets him veer into the ludicrous, stating that it was the Red Navy's operations that facilitated the destruction of the Japanese Kwantung Army by the Red Army. Further, he suggests that the Americans were actually delaying naval operations that impeded Japan's communications with the Kwantung Army, because they wanted to preserve that army for "an attack on the Soviet Union in case of a favorable development of events for Germany on the Soviet–German front."[36]

But putting aside the statements that Gorshkov is making for the benefit of his Communist peers, some facts emerge from his historical analysis. The first of these is that the Soviet Union needed to have a balanced fleet operating on all the oceans of the world. Second, and far less obvious, he stresses the importance of the submarine weapon over anti-submarine warfare efforts. The reason for this is not clear, unless it reflects an internal battle for resources within the post–World War II Red Navy.

In the concluding chapters of *Red Star Rising at Sea*, Admiral Gorshkov takes some parting shots at the use of naval force by capitalist nations as a means of "peacetime imperialism." He portrays the USSR as standing as an "immovable force" in the path of American imperialism. The American admiral D. L. McDonald characterized Gorshkov's writing as telling his Soviet naval officer students that "anything they can do, we can do better but of course, in our own humane way."[37]

Gorshkov cites the emergence of the Soviet Navy into the wide expanses of the ocean as a means of deterring aggression from the imperialist powers with "punishing retaliatory blows." But he also implies that the Red Navy now has an important peacetime mission of showing the flag in foreign ports, where Soviet seamen themselves become the best ambassadors.

Gorshkov concludes by making a strong case for a Soviet Navy with ships that can cruise for long ranges at high speed, aircraft with great operating ranges, and nuclear-powered submarines. The latter, with nuclear-tipped ballistic missiles, place the Red Navy in the forefront of strategic operations. He places less emphasis on the requirements of strategic defense, but notes the necessity of denying both U.S. submarines and aircraft carriers from areas from which attacks can be launched against the Soviet Union. Possibly as a sop to his army colleagues, he also lists cooperation in support of ground operations as being an important Red Navy function.

In this book and in his *The Sea Power of the State,* Admiral Gorshkov emerges as the modern Soviet Mahan, but with a vital difference. Gorshkov is not only a theorist but also the architect of the Soviet Navy, which, for a period in the late 1960s and 1970s, was the world's most modern naval force. As an admiral for more than thirty years, and commander in chief for almost twenty years, Gorshkov had a tenure not found in any service in any other country.

In addition to creating the new Red Navy, Gorshkov also saw that it acquired a true oceangoing capability, something the Soviet Navy had always lacked in the past. In doing this, he clearly defined the intent of the Red Navy to be a well-balanced force capable of contesting the control of the seas with the United States.

To achieve this, he had to forge ahead on many fronts, and he had to make life-or-death decisions about the types of ships to build. Conventionally powered surface ships did not present a major problem. But nuclear-powered submarines did. Admiral Gorshkov wanted to place a force of missile-launching nuclear submarines at sea to contest American power. To do that he had to make decisions regarding compromises in safety in the design and construction of those ships. In effect, he was balancing the value of the lives of his submariners against their value as an existing counterforce to the U.S. Polaris fleet.

He decided in favor of the nuclear submarine fleet, and against the lives of the submariners who manned them. It was a military decision, one that was consistent with the Russian tradition of sacrificing men on a wholesale basis for the good of the State.

Appendix Two

Soviet and American Submarines

Early Missile Submarines

Both the U.S. and the Soviet Navies were determined not to be marginalized by the role airpower had assumed in World War II and by the advent of missile technology and nuclear weapons. In the United States, the very heart and soul of the modern navy, the aircraft carrier, was threatened by the monopoly of the United States Air Force on nuclear weapons delivery. In both countries, all services were experimenting with missiles, and there began simultaneous interservice and international races for delivering nuclear warheads by means of missiles.

The first U.S. guided missiles derived directly from the Fieseler Fi 103 "buzz bomb" first used in combat by the Germans on June 13, 1944. These simple, pulse-jet-powered pilotless aircraft had a top speed of about 400 mph and a range of up to 230 miles. The American version, known as the Loon, was fired from the U.S. submarine *Cusk* on February 12, 1947. The *Carbanero* was also equipped to fire Loons, as was the USS *Norton Sound* (*AVM-1*). Loon technology was already dated, however, and it was superseded by the Chance Vought SSM-N-8 Regulus, which was powered by an Allison J33-14 engine. The Regulus was launched by two Aerojet JATO bottles, and was intended for use against large fixed targets, its accuracy being limited by its radio navigation system. It carried a 4,000-pound nuclear warhead. Four submarines (*Grayback, Growler*,[38] *Tunny*, and *Barbero*) were converted to carry Regulus missiles in large hangars. The great disadvantage of the Regulus was that it had to be removed from its hangar after the submarine surfaced, its wings spread out, its systems checked, and then fired. Nonetheless, the Regulus was used operationally on patrols in the Western Pacific.

It was succeeded by the entirely different Regulus II, which was larger, faster (Mach 2.0), longer ranged, and, more importantly, equipped with an inertial guidance system. It was just being incorporated into the fleet when the program was canceled, on the basis that the guided missile was now obsolete.

The Soviet Union made an earlier, more sustained, and technically more sophisticated missile effort, for it created diesel-powered boats with both guided and ballistic missiles. The following classes of Soviet and U.S. submarines represent major production developments during the Cold War era, and are not indicative of the current submarine fleet for either country.

EARLY SOVIET NON-NUCLEAR SUBMARINES

Whiskey Class

The Whiskey class submarines proved suitable as an early guided missile carrier, being equipped with versions of the Chelomey P-5 missile, which was known in NATO as the SS-N-3 "Shaddock." The Shaddock had a top speed of 600 mph in its later versions, and carried a 200-kiloton warhead. The first Whiskey converted to guided missile use carried one Shaddock. The next five were called "Twin Cylinder" because they were fitted with two Shaddocks with the canister/launcher located aft of the conning tower. Six Whiskey "Long-Bin" versions were built, each equipped with four missile tubes built into the conning tower and firing forward. The Long-Bin submarines apparently did not handle well and did not remain in service long. All of these submarines were extremely noisy underwater, thanks to the flow around the missile tubes.

Introduced into Service: 1950
Number Built: 236
Displacement: 1,350 tons submerged
Length: 249 feet
Primary Propulsion: Two 4,000 bhp diesel engines, two 2,500 bhp electric motors[39]
Speed: 17 knots on the surface, 13.5 knots submerged
Standard Depth: 656 feet
Typical Range: 13,500 nautical miles on the surface, 6,000 nautical miles submerged
Crew: 56
Armament: Six 21-inch torpedo tubes, four at the bow, two at the stern. Later models were outfitted with from one to four Shaddock missile launchers. Early models also carried a variety of deck guns, from a single .51 caliber gun on the conning tower to later twin 25mm or 57mm deck guns.

Juliett Class

In the 1960s, the Soviet Navy built another diesel-powered guided missile boat (Project 651, Juliett class) and went on to build several nuclear-powered missile boats, as will be seen later in the text. The Juliett class boats arrived long after the United States had abandoned (prematurely, as the Tomahawk would prove) the cruise missile. These boats were used until the early 1990s.

Introduced into Service: 1961
Number Built: 16
Displacement: 3,750 tons submerged
Length: 295 feet
Primary Propulsion: Two 7,000 bhp diesel engines, two 5,000 bhp electric motors
Speed: 16 knots on the surface, 14 knots submerged
Standard Depth: 1,310 feet

Typical Range: 9,000 nautical miles submerged
Crew: 80 (approx.)
Armament: Six 21-inch bow torpedo tubes, four 15.75-inch stern
    torpedo tubes, 4 Shaddock missiles

Zulu Class

The Soviet Union created the world's first ballistic missile submarine with its Project 611 (NATO code name "Zulu"). One was equipped with a single Scud missile. Five more were converted to carry two of the Scud missiles from launch tubes in the enlarged sail. The submarine *B-67* launched a missile on September 16, 1955. (The missile was the R-11FM missile designed by Sergei Korolev, using kerosene and nitric acid for fuel. The RF-11FM (Scud) missile was derived directly from German V-2 technology, and continued to haunt the world as it migrated down in the power chain to rogue nations of the Middle East.)

Introduced into Service: 1952
Number Built: 26
Displacement: 2,350 tons submerged
Length: 295 feet
Primary Propulsion: Two 6,000 bhp diesel engines, two 5,300 bhp
    electric motors
Speed: 18 knots on the surface, 16 knots submerged
Standard Depth: 656 feet
Typical Range: 20,000 nautical miles submerged
Crew: 70 (approx.)
Armament: Six 21-inch bow torpedo tubes, four 21-inch stern
    torpedo tubes

Golf Class

The success of the converted Zulu class submarines led to the first submarine designed from the outset to carry ballistic missiles, the Project 629 series of 1958. Called "Golf" by NATO, twenty-three boats were delivered to the Soviet Navy, and one was delivered in sections to Red China, starting submarine-launched ballistic missile (SLBM) development in that country. Various Golf boats were selected for experimental work, including testing new SLBMs and acting as communications ships.

Introduced into Service: 1958
Number Built: 23 (with one delivered in pieces to China)
Displacement: 2,700 tons submerged
Length: 328 feet
Primary Propulsion: Three 6,000 bhp diesel engines, three 5,300 bhp
    electric motors
Speed: 17 knots on the surface, 12 knots submerged
Standard Depth: 975 feet
Typical Range: 9,000 nautical miles submerged
Crew: 80 (approx.)
Armament: Six 21-inch bow torpedo tubes, four 21-inch stern tor-
    pedo tubes. Later models were converted to launch various
    SLBMs, including the SS-N-4, SS-N-5, SS-N-6, SS-N-8, and the
    SS-N-20.

THE SOVIET NAVY ENTERS THE EARLY NUCLEAR ERA

The Soviet nuclear program was led by a few key scientists, including Igor V. Kurchatov and Anatoliy Petrovich Aleksandrov, all under the kindly paternal political hand of Lavrenti Beria. A major submarine designer, B. M. Malinin, advocated nuclear submarines, as did one of his key protégés, Engineer Captain First Rank Vladimir N. Peregudov, who became the chief designer of the first series of Soviet nuclear submarines.[40]

So ambitious was the Soviet nuclear submarine program that lead units of three classes of nuclear submarines were commissioned between 1958 and 1960, with no less than twenty-six of all types being built by 1963. These were the Project 627 (NATO code name "November"), Project 658 (NATO code name "Hotel"), and Project 659 and 675 (NATO code name "Echo I" and "Echo II," respectively).

As all three classes were powered by two VI-A pressurized-water nuclear reactors, they were collectively known as HENs (Hotel, Echo, November) in NATO parlance.

November Class

Work began on Project 627 (November) in 1954 under the direction of Peregudov. The first ship was placed in commission on April 8, 1958, and twelve more were commissioned by the end of 1963. Although the Soviet Union had received espionage reports on the success of the USS *Albacore*'s hull design, the November class ships were built with a rather conventional hull.[41] The nuclear power plant powered two turbines delivering 17,500 shp.[42] The November class as a whole was ill-starred, thanks to production speed-ups, design insufficiencies, and a lack of quality control.

> Introduced into Service: 1958
> Number Built: 13
> Displacement: 5,300 tons submerged
> Length: 360 feet
> Primary Propulsion: Two pressurized-water nuclear reactors powering two steam turbines; total output approx. 35,000 shp
> Speed: 16 knots on the surface, 29 knots submerged
> Standard Depth: 985 feet
> Typical Range: 50,000–100,000 miles (est.)
> Crew: 80 (approx.)
> Armament: Eight 21-inch bow torpedo tubes

Hotel Class

Despite the Soviet predilection for long production runs, the Project 658 Hotel boats were caught in a shift in defense planning and only six were built. The Hotel was the world's first nuclear-powered ballistic missile submarine, with the first one completed in 1959, slightly ahead of the U.S. Polaris-carrying *George Washington*. The Hotel I carried three SS-N-4 SLBMs, the Hotel II carried three SS-N-5 SLBMs, and the Hotel III carried six SS-N-8 SLBMs. Hotel II's made their way to patrol off both the east and west coasts of the United States, presenting a dire threat to Strategic Air Command bomber bases, which were within an eight-minute flight of the SLBMs. The HEN nuclear power plant provided the two turbines with the ability to deliver 30,000 shp. The first of the Hotel class was the infamous *K-19*.

Introduced into Service: 1959

Number Built: 8

Displacement: 6,000 tons submerged

Length: 377 feet

Primary Propulsion: Two pressurized-water nuclear reactors powering two steam turbines; total output approx. 30,000 shp

Speed: 20 knots on the surface, 24 knots submerged

Standard Depth: 985 feet

Typical Range: 50,000–100,000 miles (est.)

Crew: 80 (approx.)

Armament: Six 21-inch M-57 bow torpedo tubes, two 15.75-inch
stern torpedo tubes. See preceding paragraph for information on
nuclear missiles carried by the various models.

Echo I and Echo II Class

The Echo I and Echo II class cruise missile submarines were also starcrossed, being powered by the very dangerous HEN reactor that caused
several accidents, and becoming involved in no less than four "midwater" collisions. Fortunately, no boats were lost as a result of these
mishaps, but reactor problems were so great that by 1989 all HEN-
reactor-powered boats were withdrawn from service.

Echo I Class:

Introduced into Service: 1960

Number Built: 5

Displacement: 5,500 tons submerged

Length: 374 feet

Primary Propulsion: Two pressurized-water nuclear reactors powering two steam turbines; total output approx. 25,000 shp

Speed: 20 knots on the surface, 25 knots submerged

Standard Depth: 985 feet

Typical Range: 50,000–100,000 miles (est.)

Crew: 75 (approx.)

Armament: Six 21-inch M-57 bow torpedo tubes, four 15.75-inch
stern torpedo tubes, six SS-N-3c SLCMs

Echo II Class:

Introduced into Service: 1960

Number Built: 29

Displacement: 6,000 tons submerged

Length: 377 feet

Primary Propulsion: Two pressurized-water nuclear reactors powering two steam turbines; total output approx. 30,000 shp

Speed: 20 knots on the surface, 23 knots submerged

Standard Depth: 975 feet

Typical Range: 50,000–100,000 miles (est.)

Crew: 90 (approx.)

Armament: Six 21-inch bow torpedo tubes, four 15.75-inch stern
torpedo tubes, and eight SS-N-3c SLCMs, or eight SS-N-3a anti-
ship SLCMs, or eight SS-N-12 anti-ship SLCMs

Follow-on Soviet Nuclear Submarines

The scale of the Soviet submarine effort was remarkable. Between 1967
and 1985 more than twenty classes of Soviet nuclear submarines, as
well as other classes of diesel-electric submarines, were built. In addition they also built several research and experimental submarines. The
following listing gives an indication of the scope of the effort:[43]

Class: Strategic Ballistic Missile Submarines (SSBN)

Year	Type	Number Built
1967	Yankee	34
	Yankee II (conversion)	(1)
1972	Delta I	18
1974	Delta II	4
1975	Delta III	14
1983	Typhoon	6
1985	Delta IV	6+

Class: Attack-Cruise Missile Submarines (SSGN/SSN)

Date	Type	Number Built
1967	Charlie I	11
1967	Yankee Notch (Conversion)	(2)
1967	Victor I Project 671	16

1967	Yankee (conversion)	(1)
	Yankee Notch (conversion)	(2)
1969	Alfa	7
1971	Papa	1
1972	Victor II	7
1978	Victor III	26
1982	Oscar I	2
1984	Sierra I/II	3
1986	Akula	5
1986	Oscar II	4+
1986	Mike	1

Yankee Class

The first Soviet submarine class to approach the standards of the Polaris submarines was Project 667, the Yankee class, the first of which was commissioned on May 30, 1967.

The eight years between the first Hotel and the first Yankee class allowed for some major changes in Soviet strategy. The Hotel class had stopped after only eight units were built, a reflection of the rise to prominence of the Strategic Rocket Forces that the bellicose Nikita Khrushchev had established in December 1959. This new service, as dramatic in its debut as the United States Air Force had been in September 1947, took over the first R-7 (SS-6) ICBMs as well as the medium-range missile units that formerly had been under the control of Long Range Aviation or reported directly to the Supreme High Command.[44]

The George Washington class (see p. 305) had to be matched, however, and the Central Design Bureau No. 18 responded with the Project 667, created by chief designer A. S. Kasatsiyer. Launch tube problems prompted the replacement of Kasatsiyer with S. N. Kovalev, who created the 667A Yankee class, the first in a long series of his successes. The Yankee's streamlined hull added speed, and the placement of the diving fins on the conning tower sail enhanced maneuverability.

The strategic effect of the Yankee class was dramatic. It enabled the Soviet Union to place SLBMs off the U.S. Atlantic and Pacific shorelines, which became an eight-minutes en route nuclear sword of Damocles hanging over U.S. cities and Strategic Air Command bases. Fortunately for the United States, the Yankee class boats were relatively noisy and could be easily tracked. The Yankee was armed with the D-5 missile system, which included sixteen R-27 missiles with a range of 1,440 miles. The R-27s could launch from a depth of 300 feet in four salvoes of four missiles each.[45] Accuracy was improved by the use of the Tobol inertial guidance system, enhanced by a package to use data from Soviet navigation satellites.

In an effort to reduce noise, the Yankee submarines had their outer pressure hull coated with a sound-reducing rubber compound, while the inner pressure hull was lined with rubber insulating material. All of the noise-producing mechanical systems were isolated from the hull with rubber padding.

As the Yankee class matured and replacements began to come on line, several were dedicated to special missions or experimental purposes. All of the Yankees were decommissioned by 1994.

Introduced into Service: 1967
Number Built: 34
Displacement: 9,600 tons submerged
Length: 426 feet
Primary Propulsion: Two pressurized-water nuclear reactors powering two steam turbines; total output approx. 45,000 shp
Speed: 18 knots on the surface, 26.5 knots submerged
Standard Depth: 1,312 feet
Typical Range: 50,000–100,000 miles (est.)
Crew: 120 (approx.)
Armament: Six 21-inch bow torpedo tubes, sixteen SS-N-6 SLBMs. The Yankee II class carried six torpedo tubes and 12 SS-N-17 SLBMs.

Delta Class

The Soviet Union was less conservative in its approach to nuclear reactors aboard submarines. In the United States Navy, the safety and reliability standards set by Admiral Hyman G. Rickover created a framework in which one reactor was deemed sufficient. The Soviets, however, chose to install two separate reactors on board their submarines. This increased the risk, but also greatly increased the available power.

This propensity to use more power combined with the natural Soviet tendency in all arms to evolution rather than revolution, and led to the development of Project 667B (Delta I) and 667BD (Delta II).

Only slightly larger than the Yankee class boats, and retaining the same forward (command center, quarters, torpedo tubes, sonar, etc.) and aft (propulsion) ends, the Delta I submarines featured a new center section that housed twelve R-29 missiles as part of the D-9 missile system.[46] The R-29, while still liquid fueled, had a range of 4,680 miles; the follow-on R-29D's used in the Delta II had a colossal 5,460-mile range. This provided entirely new basing opportunities for the Soviet Union and made the Deltas much more difficult to counter.

The reactors in the Delta I delivered 50,000 shp compared to 29,000 shp in the Yankee or to the 15,000 shp of the George Washington class.

The Soviet Navy built forty-three of the Delta class in a twenty-year period, and over time its missiles were modified from twelve SS-N-8's in the Delta I to sixteen SS-N-23's in the Delta IV. The subs grew in length as well, from 459 feet 4 inches for the Delta I to a mammoth 548 feet in the Delta IV, which displaced 15,500 tons submerged.

The Delta series was extremely important to Soviet naval morale, for they were clearly equal or superior in performance to their American counterparts. And even the SS-N-8 missile had a range of 4,200 miles, which meant that the Delta was a threat in its home waters of the Sea of Okhotsk and the Barents Sea.[47]

The final missile used on the Delta IV, the SS-N-23 "Skiff," had a 4,500-nautical-mile range while carry a MIRV'd (multiple independently targeted vehicle) bus that could place four 100-kiloton warheads on targets with an unforgiving accuracy.

Delta I Class:
    Introduced into Service: 1972
    Number Built: 18
    Displacement: 11,750 tons submerged
    Length: 459 feet
    Primary Propulsion: Two pressurized-water nuclear reactors powering two steam turbines; total output approx. 45,000 shp
    Speed: 18 knots on the surface, 25.5 knots submerged
    Standard Depth: 1,312 feet

Typical Range: 50,000–100,000 miles (est.)
Crew: 120 (approx.)
Armament: Six 21-inch bow torpedo tubes, twelve SS-N-8 SLBMs

Delta II Class:
 Introduced into Service: 1974
 Number Built: 4
 Displacement: 13,250 tons submerged
 Length: 510 feet
 Primary Propulsion: Two pressurized-water nuclear reactors power-
  ing two steam turbines; total output approx. 45,000 shp
 Speed: 11 knots on the surface, 24 knots submerged
 Standard Depth: 1,312 feet
 Typical Range: 50,000–100,000 miles (est.)
 Crew: 126 (approx.)
 Armament: Six 21-inch bow torpedo tubes, sixteen SS-N-8 SLBMs

Delta III Class:
 Introduced into Service: 1975
 Number Built: 14
 Displacement: 13,250 tons submerged
 Length: 510 feet
 Primary Propulsion: Two pressurized-water nuclear reactors power-
  ing two steam turbines; total output approx. 45,000 shp
 Speed: 17 knots on the surface, 24.5 knots submerged
 Standard Depth: 1,312 feet
 Typical Range: 50,000–100,000 miles, depending on power plant
  performance
 Crew: 130 (approx.)
 Armament: Six 21-inch bow torpedo tubes, sixteen SS-N-18 SLBMs

Delta IV Class:
 Introduced into Service: 1985
 Number Built: 6+
 Displacement: 13,550 tons submerged
 Length: 538 feet
 Primary Propulsion: Two pressurized-water nuclear reactors power-
  ing two steam turbines; total output approx. 45,000 shp
 Speed: 24 knots submerged

Standard Depth: 1,312 feet
Typical Range: 50,000–100,000 miles, depending on power plant
    performance
Crew: 130 (approx.)
Armament: Six 21-inch bow torpedo tubes, sixteen SS-N-18 SLBMs

Typhoon Class

The next major submarine class in the Soviet fleet was Project 941
(NATO code name "Typhoon") and, like the Yankee and the Delta, was
the design responsibility of S. N. Kovalev. The Typhoons were huge, with
a length of 560 feet 11 inches, and displaced an estimated 30,000 tons
submerged. Kovalev had used a unique catamaran configuration for
Project 941, using two separate Delta-type pressure hulls, each 27 feet
11 inches in diameter and connected to each other by passageways.
There were separate pressurized areas for the torpedo tubes, the command center in the sail, and a smaller one aft for the steering and control machinery. All three of these pressurized compartments were also
connected by passageways.

The missile compartment, consisting of two rows of ten missile
launching tubes each, was sandwiched between the two hulls. It contained the D-19 missile system, with its twenty 6,000-mile-range solid
fuel R-39 missiles. Each of these missiles carried a payload of ten 100-
kiloton warheads.

The two catamaran hulls were built of titanium and sheathed in a
huge outer steel shell, seventy-five feet in diameter, that covers them in
a hydrodynamic streamlined form. Built-in bow and stern thrusters
were used to help maneuver the enormous boat. Each of the hulls contained a pressurized water-moderated reactor of up to 50,000 shp each,
sufficient power to move the behemoth at 27 knots when submerged.

A total of six Typhoons were completed by 1989 (a seventh was broken up prior to completion) and were assigned to the Third Strategic
Submarine Flotilla of the Northern Fleet, based in Yagelnaya Bay.[48] The
range of their missiles permitted the Typhoons to operate under the
Arctic ice cap. If war came, they were to use their sheer bulk to force
their way through the ice and fire their missiles.

Russia found that the Typhoons were expensive to operate, and by

1999 the first of these craft, with all their sinister beauty, was consigned to salvage under the Co-operative Threat Reduction Program.[49]

Introduced into Service: 1980
Number Built: 6
Displacement: 25,000–30,000 tons submerged (est.)
Length: 561 feet
Primary Propulsion: Two pressurized-water nuclear reactors powering two steam turbines; total output approx. 45,000'80,000 shp
Speed: 25'27 knots submerged
Standard Depth: 1,312 feet
Typical Range: 50,000–100,000 miles, depending on power plant performance
Crew: 150 (approx.)
Armament: Six 21-inch and/or 25.5-inch bow torpedo tubes, twenty SS-N-20 SLBMs

SOVIET ATTACK SUBMARINES

Victor Class

The first Soviet attack submarines designed primarily for the anti-submarine role were the Project 671 Victor I, II, and III classes. They succeeded the November class and had a streamlined hull somewhat like that of the U.S. Navy's Albacore. Two 30,000 shp reactors were positioned side-by-side rather than end-to-end, as in the November class. Six torpedo tubes and eighteen torpedoes of varying types made up the offensive weaponry. The Victor II was longer at 345 feet, and employed the SS-N-16 missile system. Conceptually similar to the American SUB-ROC, this remarkable 35-mile-range homing torpedo was just over 21 feet long and 2 feet in diameter. Fired from a submerged submarine, it left the water to reach a speed of Mach 1.5 before its inertial guidance system signaled it to be paradropped back to the water so that its homing torpedo could find the submarine.

The Victor III was three feet longer than the Victor II and featured a passive/towed-array sonar. The last Victor was delivered in 1991, by which time the older Victors had already been designated for retirement.[50]

Victor I Class:
    Introduced into Service: 1968
    Number Built: 16
    Displacement: 5,100 tons submerged
    Length: 312 feet
    Primary Propulsion: Two pressurized-water nuclear reactors power-
        ing two steam turbines; total output approx. 30,000 shp
    Speed: 32.5 knots submerged
    Standard Depth: 1,312 feet
    Typical Range: 50,000–100,000 miles, depending on power plant
        performance
    Crew: 80 (approx.)
    Armament: Six 21-inch bow torpedo tubes, SS-N-14 ASW, SS-N-15
        ASW missiles

Victor II Class:
    Introduced into Service: 1972
    Number Built: 7
    Displacement: 5,900 tons submerged
    Length: 345 feet
    Primary Propulsion: Two pressurized-water nuclear reactors power-
        ing two steam turbines; total output approx. 30,000 shp
    Speed: 30.5 knots submerged
    Standard Depth: 1,312 feet
    Typical Range: 50,000–100,000 miles, depending on power plant
        performance
    Crew: 80 (approx.)
    Armament: Four 21-inch bow torpedo tubes, two 25.5-inch bow
        torpedo tubes, SS-N-15 ASW, SS-N-16 ASW missiles

Victor III Class:
    Introduced into Service: 1978
    Number Built: 25+
    Displacement: 6,000 tons submerged
    Length: 348 feet
    Primary Propulsion: Two pressurized-water nuclear reactors power-
        ing two steam turbines; total output approx. 30,000 shp
    Speed: 30 knots submerged

Standard Depth: 1,312 feet
Typical Range: Dictated by power plant performance
Crew: 80 (approx.)
Armament: Four 25.5-inch bow torpedo tubes, two 21-inch bow tor-
    pedo tubes, SS-N-15 ASW, SS-N-16 ASW missiles, SS-N-21 SLCMs

Oscar II/Antaeus Class

Initiated in the late 1970s, new submarines, nicknamed the "Oscar-2"
class by NATO, represented the latest generation of boats competing
with the Americans for speed, quiet running, and depth capability. Similar submarines, under construction from about 1978, followed an improved Oscar class design officially called Project-949A or Antaeus.

Antaeus displaced twice the water volume of a Yankee class boat and
carried 24 Granit cruise missiles and 28 torpedoes. The former carried
jamming devices and a very sophisticated targeting system. Naval strategy called for Antaeus boats to operate in a pack, drawing their targeting data from satellites via the Zubatka or "whale-killer" towed antenna
system. Each boat had eight torpedo tubes; four of the 533-millimeter
variety and four others at 650 millimeters. The submarine would carry
18 universal, electric, smart U.S.ET-80[51] torpedoes and 10 anti-ship torpedoes, of the long-range hydrogen peroxide 650-millimeter 65-76A[52]
type. Antaeus also employed a torpedo-missile similar to the American
SUBROC called Vodopad or "waterfall," which had a 50-kilometer range
and used the 533-millimeter tube for launch.[53]

Introduced into Service: 1986
Number Built: 4
Displacement: 16,000 tons submerged
Length: 512 feet
Primary Propulsion: Two pressurized-water nuclear reactors power-
    ing two steam turbines; total output approx. 90,000 shp
Speed: 30+ knots submerged
Standard Depth: 1,475 feet
Typical Range: Dictated by power plant performance
Crew: 107 (approx.)
Armament: Eight 21-inch or 25.5-inch bow torpedo tubes, SS-N-15
    ASW, SS-N-16 ASW missiles, SS-N-19 SCLM (anti-ship)

Sierra and Akula Classes

Two general classes of Soviet attack submarines were built in parallel, the Sierra and the Akula. Only four of the Sierra boats were built, in two classes, Sierra I and Sierra II. There were ten Akulas, with six Akula I's, three Improved Akula I's, and one Akula II. The latter two classes featured six additional external torpedo tubes. Both submarines had vastly improved noise characteristics over their Soviet predecessors, with the Akulas being especially successful in this regard.

Sierra Class:
   Introduced into Service: 1984
   Number Built: 3
   Displacement: 7,550 tons submerged
   Length: 351 feet
   Primary Propulsion: Two pressurized-water nuclear reactors powering two steam turbines; total output approx. 47,000–50,000 shp
   Speed: 35 knots submerged
   Standard Depth: 2,300 feet
   Typical Range: Dictated by power plant performance
   Crew: 60 (approx.)
   Armament: Four 25.5-inch bow torpedo tubes, two 21-inch bow torpedo tubes, SS-N-15 ASW, SS-N-16 ASW missiles. Later models may have carried the land-attack SS-N-21 SLCM.

Akula Class:
   Introduced into Service: 1984
   Number Built: 5+
   Displacement: 10,000 tons submerged
   Length: 370 feet
   Primary Propulsion: One pressurized-water nuclear reactor powering one steam turbine; total output approx. 43,000 shp
   Speed: 35 knots submerged
   Standard Depth: 1,475 feet
   Typical Range: Dictated by power plant performance
   Crew: 56 (approx.)
   Armament: Six 21-inch and/or 25.5-inch bow torpedo tubes, SS-N-15 ASW, SS-N-16 ASW missiles, SS-N-21 SLCM

Mike Class

These new boats, 354 feet long and 34.5 feet wide, displaced 8,500 tons submerged. With more than twice the Alfa crew at 64, a Mike could dive to 3,200 feet.

Introduced into Service: 1986
Number Built: 1
Displacement: 8,500 tons submerged
Length: 354 feet
Primary Propulsion: One pressurized-water nuclear reactor power-
    ing two steam turbines; total output approx. 43,000 shp
Speed: 37 knots submerged
Standard Depth: 3,280 feet
Typical Range: 50,000–100,000 miles, depending on power plant
    performance
Crew: 64
Armament: Six 21-inch and/or 25.5-inch bow torpedo tubes,
    SS-N-15 ASW

EARLY U.S. NUCLEAR AND MISSILE SUBMARINES

USS Nautilus *(SSN-571)*

The United States laid claim to the first nuclear-powered submarine ever launched with the *Nautilus* (*SSN-571*). Over the next quarter-century the first nuclear submarine of its kind sailed under the North Pole and eventually logged more than 300,000 miles on three different uranium fuel cores.

Introduced into Service: 1954
Displacement: 4,090 tons submerged
Length: 320 feet
Primary Propulsion: One pressurized-water nuclear reactor power-
    ing two steam turbines; total output approx. 13,200 shp
Speed: 18 knots on the surface, 23 knots submerged
Standard Depth: 700 feet

Typical Range: 50,000–100,000 miles, depending on power plant
   performance
Crew: 110
Armament: Six 21-inch bow torpedo tubes

Skate Class

After the *Nautilus* came the Skate class, of which four submarines were
built. The first two, *Skate* and *Sargo,* were equipped with the S3W pressurized-water nuclear reactor, while the second pair, *Swordfish* and
Seadragon, had S4W power plants. All produced 6,600 shp, and drove
two propellers. The Skate class's smaller hull and increased sonar capability revealed the U.S. Navy's determination to fashion the most effective ASW submarine. After all, in trials the submarine itself regularly
proved the best anti-submarine platform.

Introduced into Service: 1957
Number Built: 4
Displacement: 2,850 tons submerged
Length: 268 feet
Primary Propulsion: One pressurized-water nuclear reactor power-
   ing two steam turbines; total output approx. 6,600 shp
Speed: 15.5 knots on the surface, 20+ knots submerged
Standard Depth: 700 feet
Typical Range: 50,000–100,000 miles (est.)
Crew: 95
Armament: Six 21-inch bow torpedo tubes, two 21-inch stern
   torpedo tubes

Skipjack Class

The Skate class emerged just as *Albacore* proved the superiority of the
teardrop hull configuration. Thus the Navy's next step combined the
best of both worlds, the nuclear propulsion of *Nautilus* and *Skate* with
the *Albacore* hull. This equation produced the fastest submarine ever
built to that time: USS *Skipjack.* Six Skipjack boats, all using the S5W
pressurized-water reactor, exceeded 30 knots in submerged trials on

15,000 shp. Skipjack boats could travel at the same speed as surface groups, providing an enormous offensive and defensive advantage. Two of the Skipjacks were especially distinguished, one by a major technical advancement, and one by tragedy. By a twist of fate, both of these boats were named *Scorpion*.

Introduced into Service: 1958
Number Built: 6
Displacement: 3,500 tons submerged
Length: 252 feet
Primary Propulsion: one pressurized-water nuclear reactor powering one steam turbine; total output approx. 15,000 shp
Speed: 20 knots on the surface, 30+ knots submerged
Standard Depth: 700 feet
Typical Range: 50,000–100,000 miles (est.)
Crew: 95
Armament: Six 21-inch bow torpedo tubes

The major technical advancement came when the hull of *SSN-589*, the *Scorpion*, was selected to become the first Polaris-missile-carrying submarine, the *George Washington*, discussed on the next page. The tragedy came to the replacement submarine, which was given the same hull number, *SSN-589* (Ship, submarine-Nuclear-589), and the same name, *Scorpion*. The second *Scorpion* went to the bottom with all hands in May, 1968. Its shattered remains were found after months of search some 400 miles southwest of the Azores, on the ocean bottom at a depth of more than 10,000 feet. A close examination of the boat's remains by Dr. Robert Ballard's Deep Submergence Laboratory at the Woods Hole Oceanographic Institution and the Naval Sea Systems Command concluded that a second-order detonation in one of the Mark 46 torpedo batteries likely caused *Scorpion*'s demise by opening the torpedo tube to the ocean.

The final entry in this early list of U.S. nuclear submarines, the *SSRN-586*, the *Triton*, was the largest of the lot, 447 ½ feet long and displacing 7,780 tons submerged. Its size militated against its submerged speed, which was only 20 knots, but under the leadership of that great submariner and author, Captain Edward L. Beach, the *Triton* made the first submerged circumnavigation of the world, from February 16 to May 10, 1960. The *Triton* had steamed more than 36,000 miles in 83 hours and 10 minutes.[54]

COMPARATIVE DEVELOPMENT OF
THE MORE IMPORTANT SUBMARINE TYPES

George Washington Class

The George Washington class (SSBN) of Polaris-missile-carrying submarines had gone to sea in early 1960, some two years after the first of the Soviet Golf class (diesel-powered, but carrying ballistic missiles). The first two units of the Soviet Project 658 (Hotel class) nuclear-powered ballistic missile submarine were completed in 1959.

Both of the Soviet submarine types were primitive in the extreme when compared to the George Washington class, not least because they carried liquid-fueled missiles, which were inherently dangerous and difficult to service and launch. Their rush to service also resulted in inherent design flaws that caused many accidents and not a few casualties.

Introduced into Service: 1959
Number Built: 5
Displacement: 6,700 tons submerged
Length: 382 feet
Primary Propulsion: One pressurized-water nuclear reactor powering two steam turbines; total output approx. 15,000 shp
Speed: 20+ knots on the surface, 25+ knots submerged
Standard Depth: 700 feet
Typical Range: 50,000–100,000 miles (est.)
Crew: 135
Armament: Six 21-inch bow torpedo tubes, sixteen Polaris missile tubes

Ethan Allen Class

The United States continued its development of SLBM boats. Five Ethan Allen class boats followed the five George Washington class boats into service. These were not adaptations of the Skipjack class, as the George Washingtons had been, but were purpose built. Because they were expected to spend as long as sixty days cruising underwater, careful attention was paid to the design of the crew quarters. On May 6, 1962, the *Ethan Allen* launched a live SLBM that detonated on the Christmas Island test range, part of the larger Operation Dominic that tested IRBMs and bombs dropped from Boeing B-52's.

Introduced into Service: 1960
Number Built: 5
Displacement: 7,900 tons submerged
Length: 411 feet
Primary Propulsion: One pressurized-water nuclear reactor powering one steam turbine; total output approx. 15,000 shp
Speed: 20+ knots on the surface, 25+ knots submerged
Standard Depth: 1,300 feet
Typical Range: 50,000–100,000 miles (est.)
Crew: 135 (approx.)
Armament: Four 21-inch bow torpedo tubes, sixteen Polaris A-2 SLBMs, later refitted with Polaris A-3 missiles

Lafayette/Benjamin Franklin Class

Next was the Lafayette class, of which thirty-one were built between 1962 and 1967. (The first nineteen of these were externally similar to the Ethan Allen class; the last twelve carried a larger crew and were later officially designated as the Benjamin Franklin class.)

The boats were modified over time to accept improvements in the missiles available to them. The Polaris A-2 had a 1,500-mile range, whereas the A-3 was an eighty-five percent new design that had both greater range (2,855 nautical miles) and greater accuracy. The A-3 also carried three 200-kiloton MRV warheads.

Operational use had revealed that the requirements for shock mitigation in the missile launch tubes could be reduced. This allowed the diameter to increase from Polaris's 54 inches to 74 inches. The 34-foot-long Poseidon C-3 missile took full advantage of the diameter to create a 64,000-pound missile with a MIRV'd warhead, meaning that it was equipped with up to fourteen Mk 3 reentry bodies, each of which could be independently targeted. An independent analysis indicated that the Poseidon was eight times as effective as its Polaris antecedents.[55]

The Polaris submarines were progressively updated with the newer missiles. The George Washington and Ethan Allen classes received A-3's, and the Lafayette class received the A-3's followed by the Poseidon C-3's. During the period from 1978 to 1982, twelve of the Lafayette class were refitted with the larger three-stage Lockheed Martin Trident C-4, which carried eight 100-kiloton MIRVs. The Trident gave submarines the capability of striking Soviet targets from U.S. waters. The Trident's MIRVs had about twice the accuracy of the Poseidon missiles.

The series of improvements were not confined to the weapon systems, however. Electronic systems were upgraded or replaced, and the system of firing the missiles underwater changed from compressed-air ejection to the use of a rocket motor to produce a gas-steam mixture for ejection.

The submarines themselves were upgraded as well, and replaced by newer boats. As with the Soviet Navy, when these were replaced, some were converted to specialized duties, including that of attack submarines (SSN, with their missile tubes filled with concrete) to reconfigured vehicles capable of carrying up to sixty-six special operations personnel.

Introduced into Service: 1962
Number Built: 31
Displacement: 8,250 tons submerged
Length: 425 feet
Primary Propulsion: One pressurized-water nuclear reactor powering one steam turbine; total output approx. 15,000 shp
Speed: 20+ knots on the surface, 25+ knots submerged
Standard Depth: 1,300 feet
Typical Range: 50,000–100,000 miles (est.)
Crew: 143 (approx.)
Armament: Four 21-inch bow torpedo tubes, sixteen Polaris A-2 or A-3 missiles. Later models were equipped with Poseidon C-3 missiles.

Ohio Class

The most recent class of U.S. ballistic-missile-carrying submarines is the Ohio, which, despite a protracted building schedule, turned out to be a very effective weapon system. While only six feet shorter than the Soviet Typhoon class, the Ohio boats are much smaller in diameter, and have about half its submerged displacement. It carries a formidable armament package of twenty-four Trident C-4 or D-5 missiles.

The 130,000-pound Trident D-5 is much more capable than the C-4 it replaced, and was the first SLBM to have a "hard target" capability, that is, the ability to hit an ICBM missile silo. A typical range for the three-stage rocket D-5 is 4,000 nautical miles, although the payload can be reduced for a maximum range of 6,000 nautical miles.

Introduced into Service: 1979
Number Built: 10+
Displacement: 18,700 tons submerged
Length: 560 feet
Primary Propulsion: One pressurized-water nuclear reactor powering two steam turbines; total output approx. 60,000 shp
Speed: 20+ knots on the surface, 25+ knots submerged
Standard Depth: 1,000+ feet
Typical Range: 50,000'100,000 miles (dependent on power plant performance)
Crew: 155
Armament: Four 21-inch bow torpedo tubes, twenty-four Trident I and/or II missiles

NOTES

CHAPTER ONE: STALIN'S GRAND PLAN

1. http://www.geocities.com/SiliconValley/Circuit/1858/lampade.com.

2. Norman Polmar and Jurrien Noot, *Submarines of the Russian and Soviet Navies, 1718–1970.* Annapolis, Md.: Naval Institute Press, 1991, p. 1.

3. Brayton Harris. *The Navy Times Book of Submarines.* New York: Berkley Books, 1997, p. 27.

4. Norman Friedman, *U.S. Submarines Since 1945: An Illustrated Design History.* Annapolis, Md.: Naval Institute Press, 1995.

5. http: www.spartacus.schoolnet.co.uk/FWWwhitehead.htm.

6. Polmar and Noot, p. 7.

7. The Holland Torpedo Boat Company later became the Electric Boat Company, which John Jay Hopkins combined in 1952 with Canadair

and Electric Boat's Electro-Dynamic Division in Philadelphia to create General Dynamics. Half a century later, those two shipyards would be building nuclear submarines armed with ballistic missiles and tasked with deterring the Soviet Union.

8. Polmar and Noot, p. 18.

9. Polmar and Noot, p. 45.

10. <http://www.send.org/siberia/history.htm>.

11. V. E. Tarrant, *The U-boat Offensive, 1914–1945*. Annapolis, Md.: Naval Institute Press, 1989.

12. Eberhard Rössler, *Geschichte des deutschen Ubootbaus*. Munich: J. F. Lehmans Verlag, 1975.

13. Walter J. Boyne, *Clash of Titans: World War II at Sea*. New York: Simon & Schuster, 1995, p. 73.

14. Rössler.

15. Richard Hough, *The Longest Battle. The War at Sea 1939–1945*. New York: Quill, William Morrow, 1986, p. 37.

16. Kathleen Broome Williams, *Secret Weapon: U.S. High Frequency Direction Finding in the Battle of the Atlantic*. Annapolis, Md.: Naval Institute Press, 1996; Marc Milner, *North Atlantic Run: The Royal Canadian Navy and the Battle for the Convoys*. Annapolis, Md.: Naval Institute Press, 1985; David Syrett, *The Defeat of the German U-boats: The Battle of the Atlantic*. Columbus: University of South Carolina Press, 1994; W. J. R. Gardner, *Anti-Submarine Warfare*. Washington, D.C.: Brasseys, 1996; W. J. R. Gardner, *Decoding History: The Battle of the Atlantic and Ultra*. Annapolis, Md.: Naval Institute Press, 1999.

17. Boyne, p. 103.

18. Rössler.

19. Ibid.

20. Boyne, p. 115.

21. Rössler; Gary E. Weir, *Forged in War: The Naval Industrial Complex and American Submarine Construction, 1940–1961*. Washington, D.C.: Brasseys, 1998.

22. Rössler.

23. Gary E. Weir, *Building American Submarines 1914–1940*. Washington, D.C.: U.S. Naval Historical Center, 1991, Chapter 1.

24. Ibid.

25. E. W. Jolie, *A Brief History of U.S. Navy Torpedo Development*. Newport, R.I.: Naval Underwater Systems Center, 1978.

26. Ibid.

27. H. P. Willmott, *Empires in the Balance: Japanese and Allied Pacific Strategies to April 1942*. Annapolis, Md.: Naval Institute Press, 1982; H. P. Willmott, *The Barrier and the Javelin: Japanese and Allied Pacific Strategies February to June 1942*. Annapolis, Md.: Naval Institute Press, 1982.

28. Boyne, p. 312.

29. Rössler.

30. Yet it should be remembered that the first Japanese casualty of World War II occurred on the sortie of a midget submarine at Pearl Harbor. The boat was sunk by the USS *Ward* at about 6:40 A.M. on December 7, two hours before the air attack began. Discovered by the Hawaii Undersea Research Laboratory on August 28, 2002, the boat lies about three miles off Pearl Harbor in 1,200 feet of water. Its torpedoes were intact, and it is presumed that the crew remains are still on board. Gordon Prange, *At Dawn We Slept*. New York: Simon & Schuster, 1981.

31. U.S. Navy, Bureau of Medicine and Surgery, *History of the Medical Department of the United States Navy in World War II: The Statistics of Diseases and Injuries*. Vol. 3. Washington, D.C.: Government Printing Office, 1950.

32. Polmar and Noot, p. 66.

33. Polmar and Noot, p. 106.

34. Rene Francillion, *Japanese Aircraft of the Pacific War*. London: Putnam, 1979, p. 451.

35. Bryan Ranft and Geoffrey Till, *The Sea in Soviet Strategy*. Annapolis, Md.: Naval Institute Press, 1989, pp. 78–83.

36. Polmar and Noot, p. 140.

37. David Woodward, *The Russians at Sea, a History of the Russian Navy*. New York: Frederick A. Praeger, 1966, p. 228.

CHAPTER TWO: CRUISES AND TROUBLES

1. Norman Polmar and Jurrien Noot, *Submarines of the Russian and Soviet Navies, 1718–1970*. Annapolis, Md.: Naval Institute Press, 1991, p. 139.

2. There were many variations in the Type VII, but a typical submarine was 220 feet long, displaced 865 tons submerged, and had a surface speed of 17 knots and a submerged speed of 8 knots. Its rated diving

depth was 328 feet and it possessed a range of 6,500 nautical miles. Eberhard Rössler, *Geschichte des deutschen Ubootbaus*. Munich: J. F. Lehmans Verlag, 1975.

3. Polmar and Noot, p. 138.

4. Like so many German "miracle weapons," the Type XXI came too little and too late to affect the war. It did sire a revolution in submarine design, however. It was 251 feet long, displaced 1,819 tons submerged, and had a surface speed of 15.7 knots and a submerged speed of 17.2 knots, thanks to its two huge for the time 2,500-shp electric motors. Streamlined, it was also designed for mass production by the use of large numbers of subcontractors. Rössler.

5. Vladimir Shlpaentokh, *Public and Private Life of the Soviet People: Changing Values in Post-Stalin Russia*. New York/Oxford: Oxford University Press, 1989, p. 13; Gary E. Weir, *An Ocean in Common: American Naval Officers, Scientists, and the Ocean Environment*. College Station: Texas A&M University Press, 2001, Chapter 16.

6. Ibid., p. 215.

7. Norman Polmar, *The Naval Institute Guide to the Soviet Navy. Fifth Edition*. Annapolis, Md.: Naval Institute Press, 1991, p. 69.

8. Oral History with Rear Admiral Vladimir G. Lebedko by Dr. Gary E. Weir, St. Petersburg, February 16, 2002.

9. The term Whiskey class derives from the NATO code name. Called Project 613 in the Soviet Navy, some 236 Whiskey class submarines were built. With a 249-foot length and 1,350-ton submerged displacement, they had a top speed of 18.5 knots on the surface and 7 knots submerged. The maximum diving depth was 560 feet. A. S. Pavlov, *Warships of the U.S.S.R. and Russia 1945–1995*, translated by Gregory Tokar. Annapolis, Md.: Naval Institute Press, 1997.

10. Pavlov, pp. 70–74.

11. Vladimir G. Lebedko, "The Story of the USS *Gato* and the Soviet Hiroshima"; Oral History with Rear Admiral Vladimir G. Lebedko by Dr. Gary E. Weir, St. Petersburg, February 16, 2002.

12. This strait, which separates Bolshevik Island of the Severnaya Zemlya Islands from the mainland, connects the Laptev and Kara Seas.

13. Although Great Britain accepted a cease-fire proposed by the United Nations on November 6, soon followed by Israel and France, the U.N. Emergency Force (UNEF) did not arrive to enforce this agreement until November 15.

CHAPTER THREE: "UNDERWAY ON NUCLEAR POWER"

1. Francis Duncan, *Rickover: The Struggle for Excellence*. Annapolis, Md.: Naval Institute Press, 2001.

2. Brayton Harris, *The Navy Times Book of Submarines*. New York: Berkley Books, 1997, p. 354. James L. Mooney, editor, *Dictionary of American Naval Fighting Ships*. Washington, D.C.: U.S. Naval Historical Center, 1991 (hereafter cited as *DANFS*). See also: Richard Hewlett and Francis Duncan, *Nuclear Navy, 1946–1962*. Chicago: University of Chicago Press, 1974.

3. For the best personal and professional perspectives on Rickover, see the books by Richard Hewlett and Francis Duncan, and by Francis Duncan.

4. The one-off *Seawolf* was 338 feet long, displaced 4,287 pounds submerged, and had a speed of 20 knots underwater. *DANFS*.

5. Hewlett and Duncan.

6. Hewlett and Duncan, Chapters 7 and 8; Gary E. Weir, *Forged in War: The Naval Industrial Complex and American Submarine Construction, 1940–1961*. Washington, D.C.: Brasseys, 1998, Chapter 8.

7. The four Skate class nuclear boats were 268 feet long, displaced 2,850 tons submerged, and had a top speed of over 20 knots. *DANFS*.

8. The six Skipjack class nuclear boats were 252 feet long, displaced 3,500 tons submerged, and had a top speed of more than 30 knots. The Triton nuclear boat was 447 ½ feet long, with 7,780 tons submerged displacement, was a radar picket submarine, and was the largest submarine built to that time. *DANFS*.

9. <http://www.bellona.no/en/international/russia/navy/northern_fleet/report_2–1996/11084.html>.

10. Peter Huchthausen, *K-19 The Widow Maker*. Washington, D.C.: National Geographic, 2002, p. 66.

11. Vladimir S. Borisov, "First Soviet Nuclear Submarines," from an interview with Dr. Gary E. Weir, St. Petersburg, February 14, 2002.

12. <http://www.lostsubs.com/Soviet.htm> Russian and Soviet Peacetime Submarine Losses.

13. Sherry Sontag and Christopher Drew, *Blind Man's Bluff*. New York: HarperCollins, 1998, p. 407.

14. Huchthausen, p. 135.

15. Borisov, "First Soviet Nuclear Submarines."

CHAPTER FOUR: THE CUBAN MISSILE CRISIS

1. The NATO code name Foxtrot applied to Soviet Project 641 submarines. These were large (almost 300 feet long), with a submerged displacement of 2,484 tons. Three large diesels gave them a surface speed of 16 knots. A. S. Pavlov, *Warships of the U.S.S.R. and Russia 1945–1995*, translated by Gregory Tokar. Annapolis, Md.: Naval Institute Press, 1997.

2. Oral History with Captain First Rank Nikolai Shumkov by Dr. Gary E. Weir, Moscow, February 14, 2002. True knowledge of nuclear radiation and its effects varied greatly with time and nation. Very shortly after the Operation Crossroads atomic bomb tests held at Bikini Atoll in the Pacific in 1946, American naval personnel returned to the target vessels to examine the damage and take readings. Very few effective measures were taken to protect these people. The appreciation of the biological effect of radiation was still a new science. However, by 1961 the Soviets should have known that more substantive protection was needed with this kind of work.

3. http://www.cia.gov/csi/studies/vol46no1/article06.html.

4. On the issue of establishing a permanent submarine base in Cuba see also Oral History with Rear Admiral Vladimir G. Lebedko by Dr. Gary E. Weir, St. Petersburg, February 16, 2002.

5. The NATO code name Golf was given to Project 629 submarines, the world's first purpose-built ballistic missile submarine. Twenty-three Golfs were built for the Soviet Union. They were 328 feet long, displaced 2,700 tons submerged, and could make 17 knots on surface and 12 knots submerged. They carried three submarine-launched ballistic missiles (SLBM). Pavlov.

6. See Oral History with Captain First Rank Nikolai Shumkov by Dr. Gary E. Weir, Moscow, February 14, 2002.

7. Oral History with Rear Admiral Vladimir G. Lebedko by Dr. Gary E. Weir, St. Petersburg, February 16, 2002.

8. After the mission was over, only the chief of Naval Communications, Admiral Tolstolutski, took the time to apologize to the Foxtrot crews for the poor reporting instructions. Oral History with Captain First Rank Nikolai Shumkov by Dr. Gary E. Weir, Moscow, February 14, 2002.

9. Curtis A. Utz, *Cordon of Steel: The U.S. Navy and the Cuban Missile Crisis*. Washington, D.C.: Naval Historical Center, 1993, pp. 9–13.

10. See Chapter 6 and the sources provided by Rear Admiral Gleb Kondratiev on the trawler fleet.

11. When Anadyr failed, it took Orlov six months to get his luggage back after he returned to the Northern Fleet.

12. There is no American primary source material available to confirm or contradict Orlov's conclusion. He drew his own conclusions based upon the absence of prosecuting ASW aircraft or surface ships.

13. The NATO code name November was assigned to the fourteen Project 627A nuclear-powered attack submarines. At 363 feet 11 inches long, they displaced 5,300 tons submerged, and had a phenomenal submerged speed of 30 knots and could dive to 984 feet. The performance was amazing considering that the November class retained the classic long, conventional hull instead of the tear-drop hull. The November class had two V1-A pressurized-water nuclear reactors and two 17,500-shp turbines. Pavlov.

Chapter Five: An Uncertain Nuclear Beginning

1. Oral History with Captain First Rank Vladimir Borisov by Dr. Gary E. Weir, St. Petersburg, February 20, 2002.

2. Oral History with Captain First Rank Vladimir Borisov by Dr. Gary E. Weir, St. Petersburg, February 20, 2002.

3. Late Entry, Flag Plot, October 23, 1966; Naval Message from CO-MASWFORLANT to CTG 81.5 et al., October 24, 1966. U.S. Navy Operational Archives, Washington, D.C.

4. Rear Admiral Vladimir G. Lebedko, "The Story of the U.S. *Gato* and the Soviet Hiroshima."

5. Oral History with Captain First Rank Vladimir Borisov by Dr. Gary E. Weir, St. Petersburg, February 20, 2002; Borisov, "First Soviet Nuclear Submarines."

6. Oral History with Captain First Rank Vladimir Borisov by Dr. Gary E. Weir, St. Petersburg, February 20, 2002.

Chapter Six: Death in the Depths

1. Oral History with Rear Admiral Vladimir G. Lebedko by Dr. Gary E. Weir, St. Petersburg, February 16, 2002. This oral history is the most

authoritative source used in this chapter for the *K-19*–USS *Gato* encounter. Admiral Lebedko also provided supplementary material in an essay prepared for the author entitled "The Story of the USS *Gato* and the Soviet Hiroshima." Both the essay and the oral history are in the possession of the author.

2. Oral History with Rear Admiral Vladimir G. Lebedko by Dr. Gary E. Weir, St. Petersburg, February 16, 2002; Lebedko, "The Story of the USS *Gato* and the Soviet Hiroshima."

3. On the Thresher case see Francis Duncan, *Rickover and the Nuclear Navy: The Discipline of Technology.* Annapolis, Md.: Naval Institute Press, 1990; Richard Hewlett and Francis Duncan, *Nuclear Navy 1946–1962.* Chicago: University of Chicago Press, 1974.

4. Foxtrots were fitted with air conditioning systems between 1972 and 1974, just after Kolyada finished this Mediterranean deployment.

5. The Thresher (later Permit) class was originally designed to carry Regulus II cruise missiles but was redesigned as an attack submarine. It displaced 4,311 tons submerged and had a top speed of 27 knots.

6. The Sturgeon class boats were improved versions of the Thresher-Permit class, with a submerged displacement of 4,780 tons and a top speed of 28 knots.

7. Oral History with Captain First Rank Boris Kolyada by Dr. Gary E. Weir, St. Petersburg, February 17, 2002.

8. The Los Angeles class was the largest of all nuclear submarine classes, with sixty-two built. It displaced up to 7,177 tons submerged and had a top speed of about 33 knots.

9. Oral History with Captain First Rank Boris Kolyada by Dr. Gary E. Weir, St. Petersburg, February 17, 2002.

10. Peter Huchtahausen, Igor Kurdin, and R. Alan White, *Hostile Waters.* New York: St. Martins Press, 1997.

11. Only four Sierra class boats were built; they displaced as much as 8,500 tons submerged and had a top speed of over 33 knots. The crew was relatively small, only sixty-one in the Sierra II.

12. Kolyada, "The Last Cruise of the *K-278* (the *Komsomolets*)"; Oral History with Captain First Rank Boris Kolyada by Dr. Gary E. Weir, St. Petersburg, February 17, 2002.

13. This is a possibility. Kolyada and the Board of Inquiry also concluded that the mixture of water, seawater, various other fluids, lubricating oil, and the heat of the fire could easily have created clouds of

combustible chemicals like hydrogen as well as the oil vapor that ignited earlier, killing members of the crew. Hydrogen explosions as well as compressed air explosions combined to seal the fate of the boat. Oral History with Captain First Rank Boris Kolyada by Dr. Gary E. Weir, St. Petersburg, February 17, 2002.

14. Kolyada, "The Last Cruise of the *K-278* (the *Komsomolets*)"; Oral History with Captain First Rank Boris Kolyada by Dr. Gary E. Weir, St. Petersburg, February 17, 2002.

15. In the effort to discover what happened to the *278* boat, the Soviet Board of Inquiry concluded that hull damage sustained as the ship descended must have released the torpedoes in the tubes and these detonated on the bottom. These conclusions were supported by photos taken by the research vessel *R/V Keldish* in a later survey of the wreck. The hull was not torn apart by internal detonations, but explosions were felt by the survivors in the water. The force indicated weapons detonating, but the remains of the vessel did not show a level of damage that would be consistent with multiple internal weapons explosions. Oral History with Captain First Rank Boris Kolyada by Dr. Gary E. Weir, St. Petersburg, February 17, 2002.

16. The *Varyag* was a Russian ship that participated in the Russo-Japanese War in 1904–1905. The song tells the story of the *Varyag*'s crew, men who fought until the end and never asked for mercy.

17. Doctor Shabasov's comments are as Kolyada recalled them and as they appear in the official board of inquiry. Kolyada, "The Last Cruise of the *K-278* (the *Komsomolets*)."

18. The crew was placed under guard and in strict quarantine upon return to their base to prevent any knowledge of the event and its particulars from leaking to the general public. For a time Kolyada and his shipmates felt like prisoners. Oral History with Captain First Rank Boris Kolyada by Dr. Gary E. Weir, St. Petersburg, February 17, 2002.

19. In addressing the reasons for the disaster, Kolyada concluded that the Mike class needed more than the highly automated systems and the small crew of sixty-nine could provide. In the much smaller Alfa, this recipe worked. In a Mike it did not; you needed a larger crew to monitor compartments. The American Los Angeles class has a crew of 139, and both submarines have similar basic features (6,080/6,927 ton displacement; roughly 330 feet long and 30 feet wide). You also needed more reli-

able communication with central control and improved design and engineering features. In particular:

- The polyamide seals used in high-pressure air pipelines fused at a temperature of 392°F (200°C). They melted during the fire and air went to the compartments feeding the fire.
- There were many flammable materials in the compartments that prolonged the duration of fire, especially in the spaces aft.
- *278* did not have a sufficient supply of CFCs (gas used in cooling/refrigeration pipes and for fire extinguishing) on board; in any case, the CFCs did not prove efficient extinguishers. In addition, the central command center could not control the application of the CFCs.
- Many of the automated control devices were not reliable.
- There was no system of emergency air-integrity for the compartments.
- The space between compartments six and seven could not be made hermetic when the propeller shaft was moving.
- The boat did not have a reliable means of two-way communication; consequently the on-board command center did not have enough information on the situation in the stern compartments.
- The commander could not release via valve or some other safety measure the rising pressure in the compartments due to the fire.
- The main ballast tanks weren't equipped with Kingston valves so the submarine lost trim.
- There was no backup (reserve) way to blow the ballast tanks; a general lack of redundant control systems presented major problems.

CHAPTER SEVEN:
A VARIETY OF INTELLIGENCE GATHERING METHODS

1. E-mail communication with Rear Admiral Gleb Kondratiev via Mr. Iazamir Gotta, Moscow, June 25, 2002. Oral History with Rear Admiral Gleb Kondratiev by Dr. Gary E. Weir, Moscow, February 11, 2002. Kondratiev also provided supplementary material in an essay prepared for the author entitled "So What Was It: The Underwater War or Simply

Confrontation?" Both the essay and the oral history are in the possession of the author.

2. Oral History with Rear Admiral Gleb Kondratiev by Dr. Gary E. Weir, Moscow, February 11, 2002. This oral history is the most authoritative source used in this chapter for the life of Kondratiev, his submarine and intelligence experience, and the encounter with the USS *James Madison*. Kondratiev, "So What Was It: The Underwater War or Simply Confrontation?"

3. Richard Russell, *Project Hula: Secret Soviet–American Cooperation in the War Against Japan*. Washington, D.C.: U.S. Naval Historical Center, 1997.

4. Norman Polmar, *Guide to the Soviet Navy*. Annapolis, Md.: Naval Institute Press, 1986, pp. 334–335; Oral History with Rear Admiral Gleb Kondratiev by Dr. Gary E. Weir, Moscow, February 11, 2002.

5. SSBN is the American designation for a nuclear submarine capable of carrying and launching intercontinental ballistic missiles. The Soviets use PLARB for similar boats in their fleet. USS *James Madison* (*SSBN–627*) of the U.S. Navy's Lafayette class was one such vessel; she was commissioned on July 28, 1964.

6. "First Submerged Poseidon Firing Delayed, Hampered by Soviet Ship," *Navy Times*, August 19, 1970.

7. Ships similar in capability to the *Khariton Laptev* also recorded the signatures of American submarines as they emerged from their bases at Holy Loch, Scotland, and Rota in Spain. Oral History with Rear Admiral Gleb Kondratiev by Dr. Gary E. Weir, Moscow, February 11, 2002. Kondratiev, "So What Was It: The Underwater War or Simply Confrontation?"

8. This translates, according to Soviet statistics, into a 142-million-square-kilometer geographical surface out of a world ocean that covers 361 million square kilometers. Oral History with Rear Admiral Gleb Kondratiev by Dr. Gary E. Weir, Moscow, February 11, 2002. Kondratiev, "So What Was It: The Underwater War or Simply Confrontation?"

9. Michael Palmer, *Origins of the Maritime Strategy*. Annapolis, Md.: Naval Institute Press, 1990.

10. Palmer; David F. Winkler, *The Cold War at Sea: High Seas Confrontation Between the United States and the Soviet Union*. Annapolis, Md.: Naval Institute Press, 2000.

11. Oral History with Captain Second Rank Vadim Orlov by Iazamir Gotta, Irina Krivaya, and Dr. Gary E. Weir, Moscow, August–September

2002. This oral history is the most authoritative source used in this chapter. The author also consulted an essay prepared for him by Captain Second Rank Orlov entitled "The Story of a Radio Surveillance Officer." The oral history and the essay are in the possession of the author.

12. Oral History sessions with Captain Second Rank Vadim Orlov by Iazamir Gotta, Irina Krivaya, and Dr. Gary E. Weir, Moscow, August–September 2002. Orlov, "The Story of a Radio Surveillance Officer."

13. Oral History sessions with Captain Second Rank Vadim Orlov by Iazamir Gotta, Irina Krivaya, and Dr. Gary E. Weir, Moscow, August–September, 2002. Orlov, "The Story of a Radio Surveillance Officer." For the American side see John Craven, *The Silent War.* New York: Simon & Schuster, 2001; and Sherry Sontag and Christopher Drew, *Blind Man's Bluff.* New York: Public Affairs, 1998.

14. For details on the capability of the Romeo class diesels see A. S. Pavlov, *Warships of the USSR and Russia 1945–1995,* translated by Gregory Tokar. Annapolis, Md.: Naval Institute Press, 1997, p. 70. Very much like the battery capability given to the Tang class by the Americans to achieve the kind of speed displayed by the German Type XXI's at the end of World War II, this boat had an increased number of batteries that provided the capability of remaining submerged for 300 hours at very slow speed. The Romeo also had hovering capability. In many ways, it was the ideal pre-nuclear surveillance boat. These vessels came off the ways in the late 1950s, roughly the same time as the advent of the first Soviet nuclear boats, the November class.

15. It is not at all strange that this sharing should have taken place. After all, the three-star vice admiral who controlled all American submarines in the Atlantic (Commander Submarine Force Atlantic or ComSubLant) also commanded all NATO submarines in the Atlantic (as SACLant, Submarine Allied Commander, Atlantic). This is why ComSubLant is traditionally a vice admiral, while his counterpart in the Pacific is a two-star rear admiral.

16. By the 1970s the American SOSUS system was so extensive and sophisticated that this kind of countermeasure, executed in hostile conditions and in deep water in full acoustic view of American submarines, would have been impossible. In the oral history interviews with many of these officers, especially those active at senior levels before the mid-1980s, a confusion exists between SOSUS, its true nature and methods, cable tapping, and the use of air-deployed sonobuoys by American and

NATO forces. This confusion suggests that many of these senior Soviet officers did not understand SOSUS and how it worked.

CHAPTER EIGHT: IMPROVING THE BREED

1. Gary E. Weir, *Forged in War: The Naval Industrial Complex and American Submarine Construction, 1940–1961*. Washington, D.C.: Brasseys, 1998; Jeffrey G. Barlow, *Revolt of the Admirals*. Washington, D.C.: Brasseys, 1998; Walter J. Boyne, *Beyond the Horizons: The Lockheed Story*. New York: St. Martins Press, 1998, p. 278.

2. Weir, *Forged in War,* Chapter 9, provides the most complete discussion of the NOBSKA Summer Study's significance.

3. Weir, Chapter 9.

4. Norman Polmar, *The American Submarine*. Cambridge, U.K.: Patrick Stephens, 1981, p. 131; Weir, see Chapter 11, entitled "Brickbat 01," the navy's code designation for the highest development priority.

5. Interestingly enough, one of Mao's major criticisms of Khrushchev was his obvious enjoyment of his visits to the United States, which included receiving "star power" attention in Hollywood.

6. Norman Friedman, *The Fifty Year War: Conflict and Strategy in the Cold War*. Annapolis, Md.: Naval Institute Press, 2000, p.243.

7. Pavel Podvig, editor, *Russian Strategic Forces*. Cambridge, Mass.: MIT Press, 2001, p.7.

8. Oral History with Vice Admiral Anatoli I. Shevchenko by Dr. Gary E. Weir, Moscow, February 10, 2002.

9. Oral History with Vice Admiral Anatoli I. Shevchenko by Dr. Gary E. Weir, Moscow, February 10 and 13, 2002. In discussing this assertion with a few experienced American submariners who spent time at sea during this period, they universally questioned the assertion that the detection capabilities were roughly equivalent. In one case, a submarine officer who commanded an American fast attack submarine during this period read these pages and this quote, and when asked to comment on the possible equality of the sonars, he smiled and just said "B.S." While the continued presence of the Cold War adversarial feeling toward the Russians emerges from that comment, it could well be that Shevchenko and some of his able colleagues had learned to combine a skilled use of active and passive sonar to address a considerable Ameri-

can technical lead in passive detection. Some unclassified information exists on American passive capability, but very little has come out of the former Soviet Union.

10. Oral History with Vice Admiral Anatoli I. Shevchenko by Dr. Gary E. Weir, Moscow, February 10, 2002.

11. For his evaluation of the Aport and Atrina strategy and his insight into submarine operations, decision-making, and the significance of the Gulf Stream in the planning of Aport, which Admiral Shevchenko did not make clear in the original oral history, the author wishes to thank Vice Admiral George Emery, U.S.N. (Ret.), experienced submariner and former ComSubLant and ComSubACLant (Commander Submarine Allied Command Atlantic). E-mail correspondence between George Emery and Dr. Gary E. Weir, October–December 2002.

12. Oral History with Vice Admiral Anatoli I. Shevchenko by Dr. Gary E. Weir, Moscow, February 10 and 13, 2002. This oral history is the most authoritative source used in this chapter. The author also consulted an essay prepared for him by Vice Admiral Shevchenko entitled "The Arctic Cruises." The oral history and the essay are in the possession of the author.

13. The Soviet submarines of this period carrying the NATO designation "Victor" were powered by two nuclear reactors and displaced 4,108 tons on the surface and 6,085 submerged for the Victor 1, and 4,500 tons on the surface and 5,700 submerged for the Victor 2. They are capable of roughly 30 knots while submerged and carry a crew of approximately 80. While these boats employ torpedoes and mines, the Victor 3 can also use the SS-N-15, similar to the American SUBROC torpedo-tube-launched missile, and SS-N-16 missiles, which behaved like an ASW pattern search torpedo. The Victor 3 weighed in at roughly 600 tons more than Victor 2 and in the later Cold War represented one of the best attack submarines in the Soviet arsenal. Norman Polmar, *Guide to the Soviet Navy*. Annapolis, Md.: Naval Institute Press, 1986, pp. 144–145, 431; A. S. Pavlov, *Warships of the U.S.S.R. and Russia 1945–1995,* translated by Gregory Tokar. Annapolis, Md.: Naval Institute Press, 1997, pp. 52–53.

14. Polmar, *Guide to the Soviet Navy*, p. 343.

15. Oral History with Vice Admiral Anatoli I. Shevchenko by Dr. Gary E. Weir, Moscow, February 10 and 13, 2002; Shevchenko, "The Arctic Cruises." For Aport and Atrina, see also Admiral of the Fleet Victor N. Chernavin, "Atrina Operation," *Typhoon,* 25 (June 2000), pp. 34–35. Shevchenko insisted that the five submarines made it into the Atlantic

without SOSUS detecting them or any American or NATO submarine contacts. While this is possible, there are no unclassified American intelligence sources available to confirm his statement. Shevchenko also insisted that they knew the regions of SOSUS coverage and had experience working against the new American towed array sonar (SURTASS) ships of the Stalwart class. Betrayals by the spy John Walker may have helped the Russians here. Carefully crafted secondary sources on the Walker spy ring are hard to find. The sensation aroused by the discovery that John Walker and members of his family had betrayed some of the U.S. Navy's closest-guarded secrets over a period of nearly twenty years beginning in the late 1960s has inclined authors to emphasize the sensation over an unclassified analysis of the damage done by the Walker group. Some applicable but very general material relevant to the importance of SOSUS as a tool against Soviet submarines and the extent of Walker's knowledge can be found in Pete Early, *Family of Spies: Inside the John Walker Spy Ring*. New York: Bantam Books, 1988. Naturally the navy's internal estimate of the damage done by Walker is still classified.

16. All of the boats were Victor 3's save for *K-488*, a Victor 2.

17. For a discussion of the oceanographic aspects of the ocean, including the Gulf Stream, and the U.S. Navy's constant interest in them for reasons from the perspective of undersea warfare, see Gary E. Weir, *An Ocean in Common: American Naval Officers, Scientists, and the Ocean Environment*. College Station: Texas A&M University Press, 2001.

18. For HOPS, the Gulf Stream factor, and the possible solutions to the dilemma of increased Soviet deployments off the American and Canadian coasts, see Oral History with Allan Robinson by Dr. Gary E. Weir, Office of Naval Research/H. John Heinz III Center, Oral History Project, *Oceanography: The Making of a Science*, video tape 2 of 2, March 31, 2000, conducted at the Woods Hole Oceanographic Institution. U.S. Navy Operational Archive, U.S. Naval Historical Center, Washington, D.C.

19. There are no Soviet submarine patrol reports available to examine on this issue and therefore no documentation with the kind of detail an historian usually uses to confirm or deny these assertions. Of course, the U.S. Navy would never consider releasing this type of document either. Niktin could well have calculated a "combined" trailing time, piecing together intermittent contacts and trailing scenarios. Shevchenko's own estimate of the proximity to target required to acquire a submerged American SSBN would suggest, at the very least, that Niktin's reported

results would be very difficult to attain. However, that does not mean that he did not achieve this result. It just means that classified documents and their unavailability are often the bane of an historian's existence. Thus, there is a need for a qualifying footnote like this one.

20. Oral History with Vice Admiral Anatoli I. Shevchenko by Dr. Gary E. Weir, Moscow, February 10 and 13, 2002. This was Vice Admiral Shevchenko's estimate of the necessary assured detection range.

21. Oral History with Vice Admiral Anatoli I. Shevchenko by Dr. Gary E. Weir, Moscow, February 10 and 13, 2002; Shevchenko, "The Arctic Cruises." There are no unclassified sources that can confirm the assertion regarding the six American submarines detailed to track the Victors.

22. Robinson's Harvard Ocean Prediction System and the insights it made possible into the internal complexities of the North Atlantic made NATO action against a repeat of Aport more effective. However, the system did not, and obviously could not, change the nature of the Gulf Stream and the tactical possibilities it afforded the Soviets. Oral History with Allan Robinson by Dr. Gary E. Weir, Office of Naval Research/H.

23. Motsak has since achieved the rank of admiral and was recently made a Hero of Russia. Motsak was also head of the general naval headquarters when the submarine *Kursk* sank in 2000. Along with other senior officers, he was fired by Russian president Vladimir Putin as one of the those held responsible for the poor handling of the *Kursk* rescue and for the technological problems that caused the demise of that boat.

24. Oral History with Vice Admiral Anatoli I. Shevchenko by Dr. Gary E. Weir, Moscow, February 10 and 13, 2002. The quote appears in Shevchenko, "The Arctic Cruises."

25. Oral History with Vice Admiral Anatoli I. Shevchenko by Dr. Gary E. Weir, Moscow, February 10 and 13, 2002; Shevchenko, "The Arctic Cruises." Sergei Kuzmin became a Hero of Russia, a rear admiral, and commander of Shevchenko's 33rd squadron. He also went on to surface at the North Pole another nineteen times.

CHAPTER NINE:
AN INSIDER'S VIEW OF THE MYSTERY OF THE KURSK

1. The Submariners' Club was founded in Saint Petersburg in 1994. A group of officers from the third flotilla of the Northern Fleet, one of the strongest components of the Russian Navy, created the Club. Navigator

of the Yankee class boat *K-241* Eugene Aznabaev received the Club's first membership card. By the time of the *Kursk* tragedy the Club had members from twenty countries, including the United States, Brazil, Great Britain, Argentina, France, Switzerland, and Japan. Thus the Club became an independent source of expertise for the media, families, and fellow submariners on matters relating to the *Kursk*. Ex-submarine constructors and shipbuilders, salvers, and divers from the Club participated in the brainstorming that lasted for a year and a half in an effort to find out exactly what happened to the submarine.

2. Oral History with Captain First Rank Igor Kozyr by Dr. Gary E. Weir, St. Petersburg, February 19, 2002. This oral history and a short essay prepared by Captain Kozyr entitled "*Kursk* Follow-Up" are in the possession of the author.

3. Compiled from Melodinsky's recollections and a news story on *K-429* released in St. Petersburg by journalist Victor Tereshkin, August 23, 2000.

4. Oral History with Captain First Rank Igor Kozyr by Dr. Gary E. Weir, St. Petersburg, February 19, 2002; Kozyr, "*Kursk* Follow-Up."

5. Oral History with Captain First Rank Igor Kurdin by Dr. Gary E. Weir, St. Petersburg, February 19, 2002. This oral history is the most authoritative source used in this chapter. The author also consulted an essay prepared for him by Captain Kurdin entitled "The Mystery of the *Kursk*." The oral history and the essay are in the possession of the author.

6. For specifics on the Oscar 2 class and the Antaeus class boats, see A. S. Pavlov, *Warships of the U.S.S.R. and Russia 1945–1995*, translated by Gregory Tokar. Annapolis, Md.: Naval Institute Press, 1997, pp. 38–39.

7. Surface displacement, 15,100 tons; submerged displacement, 25,650 tons; length, 465 feet; 54-foot beam; height (from keel to the top of the conning tower), 55 feet.

8. The 533-millimeter torpedo U.S.ET-80 formed part of the naval arsenal since 1980. Search speed, 5 knots; maximum speed, 50 knots; motion range, 15 kilometers; weight of the warhead, 290 kilograms. The torpedo had silver-zinc batteries; however, the *Kursk* was equipped with a test torpedo with a cheaper battery system.

9. Kurdin, "The Mystery of the *Kursk*."

10. Oral History with Captain First Rank Igor Kurdin by Dr. Gary E. Weir, St. Petersburg, February 19, 2002; Kurdin, "The Mystery of the *Kursk*."

11. For details on *Michael Rudnitsky,* a Pioneer Moskvyy class salvage and rescue ship, see Norman Polmar, *Guide to the Soviet Navy.* Annapolis, Md.: Naval Institute Press, 1986, p. 283.

12. Oral History with Captain First Rank Igor Kurdin by Dr. Gary E. Weir, St. Petersburg, February 19, 2002; Kurdin, "The Mystery of the *Kursk*"; Oral History with Captain First Rank Igor Kozyr by Dr. Gary E. Weir, St. Petersburg, February 19, 2002.

13. Oral History with Captain First Rank Igor Kurdin by Dr. Gary E. Weir, St. Petersburg, February 19, 2002; Kurdin, "The Mystery of the *Kursk*"; Oral History with Captain First Rank Igor Kozyr by Dr. Gary E. Weir, St. Petersburg, February 19, 2002; letter from Vice Admiral M. Motsak to Igor K. Kurdin, St. Petersburg, August 21, 2000 (a copy of the letter courtesy of Captain Kurdin). Motsak took the trouble to state in the final line of his letter that he was writing to Kurdin as a private citizen and not as a representative of the Northern Fleet. Given Motsak's rank, Kurdin still took it as an official warning.

14. Kurdin, "The Mystery of the *Kursk.*"

15. Kurdin, "The Mystery of the *Kursk.*"

16. Sherry Sontag and Christopher Drew, *Blind Man's Bluff.* New York: Public Affairs, 1998, p. 268.

17. For a comprehensive discussion of the Cold War problem of incidents at sea, consult David F. Winkler, *Cold War at Sea: High Seas Confrontation Between the United States and the Soviet Union.* Annapolis, Md.: Naval Institute Press, 2000. It is difficult to discuss these matters in the open literature because of the level of secrecy maintained by all participants involved in the Cold War submarine confrontation.

18. See Chapter 6 for the loss of *Komsomolets* (*K-278*) in 1989.

19. Kurdin, "The Mystery of the *Kursk.*"

20. Kurdin, "The Mystery of the *Kursk.*"

21. Pavlov, pp. 108–110. Both ships were from the Udaloy class, Project 1155 (FREGAT).

22. In this case an air bubble is forced out of the torpedo tube at the moment of the torpedo shot. The coordinates of the submarine, the ship-target, and also the shot data are recorded. Oral History with Captain First Rank Igor Kurdin by Dr. Gary E. Weir, St. Petersburg, February 19, 2002; Kurdin, "The Mystery of the *Kursk.*"

23. After the removal of both Popov and Boyarkin, Northern Fleet chief of staff, Vice Admiral Mikhail Motsak took over the search and recovery effort and saw it through the raising of the hull and the official investigation.

24. Oral History with Captain First Rank Igor Kurdin by Dr. Gary E. Weir, St. Petersburg, February 19, 2002; Kurdin, "The Mystery of the *Kursk.*"

25. Kurdin, "The Mystery of the *Kursk.*"

26. This was one of the newer sonar sets on board *Kursk.*

27. Kurdin, "The Mystery of the *Kursk.*"

28. Oral History with Captain First Rank Igor Kurdin by Dr. Gary E. Weir, St. Petersburg, February 19, 2002; Kurdin, "The Mystery of the *Kursk.*"

29. Oral History with Captain First Rank Igor Kurdin by Dr. Gary E. Weir, St. Petersburg, February 19, 2002; Kurdin, "The Mystery of the *Kursk.*"

30. Kurdin, "The Mystery of the *Kursk.*"

31. Dr. Gary E. Weir was present at these events and heard Captain Kurdin's comments on the *Kursk* tragedy at the Royal Navy banquet in Lancaster.

32. This is part of the prayer offered on November 12, 2000, in Santa Barbara, California, and composed by MM2 (SS) Raymond (Rusty) W. Trent, Jr.

33. This would be their reasoning and evidence as of February 2002.

34. Oral History with Captain First Rank Igor Kurdin by Dr. Gary E. Weir, St. Petersburg, February 19, 2002.; Kurdin, "The Mystery of the *Kursk.*"

35. Gary E. Weir, *Forged in War.* Washington, D.C.: Brasseys, 1998, p. 74.

36. Oral History with Captain First Rank Igor Kurdin by Dr. Gary E. Weir, St. Petersburg, February 19, 2002; Kurdin, "The Mystery of the *Kursk.*"

37. Since Mamed Gadzhiev was Caucasian, some commentators publicly brought the Russian trouble in Chechnya into the discussion over the fate of the submarine.

38. Kurdin, "The Mystery of the *Kursk.*"

39. The *Mir-1* and *Mir-2* submersibles would find the remains of the weapon upon close examination of the bottom adjacent to the vessel.

40. Kurdin, "The Mystery of the *Kursk.*"

41. Oral History with Captain First Rank Igor Kurdin by Dr. Gary E. Weir, St. Petersburg, February 19, 2002; Kurdin, "The Mystery of the *Kursk.*"

42. The salvage operation would eventually cost the Russian govern-

ment approximately $65 million. The Norse Cutting and Abandonment Company removed the 66-foot bow section for the initial recovery. The Russian Navy recovered parts of the bow at a later date.

43. An essay entitled "*Kursk* Follow-Up" was prepared by Captain First Rank Igor Kozyr at the author's request to supplement internet and text publication sources used for information on the process of raising the submarine, investigating the events, and disposing of the hull. This essay is in the possession of the author. Internet-based reporting by the *Washington Post,* the Bellona Foundation, the BBC, and Strana.ru (the Official Russian News Service) also contributed to this final section, in addition to the text sources cited in the narrative and the oral histories conducted by the author.

44. President Putin removed Admiral Popov from command of the Northern Fleet. In addition, the Russian Defense Ministry's Press Service also released the following list of other officers dismissed or disciplined as a result of the *Kursk* sinking as of December 3, 2001: commander of the Northern Fleet's submarine flotilla Vice Admiral Oleg Burtsev; flotilla chief staff Rear Admiral Valery Filatov; divisional commander Rear Admiral Mikhail Kuznetsov; deputy divisional commander Captain (First Rank) Viktor Kobelev; department heads in the chief naval command Vice Admiral Nikolai Mikheyev, Rear Admiral Gennady Verich, and Rear Admiral Valery Panferov; Northern Fleet departmental commanders Vice Admiral Yury Boyarkin, Rear Admiral Vladimir Khandobin, Captain (First Rank) Alexander Teslenko, flotilla deputy commander Rear Admiral Farit Zinnatullin, and Northern Fleet unit commander Captain (First Rank) Ruben Karakhanov. Reported by Strana.ru.

45. There is special lubricant for hydrogen peroxide torpedoes formulated to avoid any catalytic reaction. Given the low level of maintenance in the submarine fleet at the time, another lubricant might have been used in this case, which would have acted as a catalyst for the hydrogen peroxide.

APPENDIX ONE:
THE HISTORY OF THE RUSSIAN NAVY ACCORDING TO GORSHKOV

1. This appendix offers a rather unvarnished version of naval history as seen through the eyes of the creator of the modern Soviet fleet. As

such it should be treated with care and critically evaluated as a political as well as a military-philosophical document.

2. Alfred Thayer Mahan. *The Influence of Sea Power upon History, 1660–1783.* New York: Hill & Wang, 1957.

3. Sergei Gorshkov. *Red Star Rising at Sea.* Annapolis, Md.: Naval Institute Press, 1974, p. 2.

4. Ibid., p. 6.

5. Mahan, p. 46.

6. Gorshkov, p. 6.

7. Ibid., p. 2.

8. From Medieval Russia, <http://xenohistorian.faithweb.com/russia/ru01.html>.

9. The *Washington Post,* August 5, 1970, p. 1.

10. Trevor Dupuy, Curt Johnson, and David L. Bongard, editors. *The Harper Encyclopedia of Military Biography.* New York: HarperCollins, 1992, pp. 151, 589.

11. David Woodward. *The Russians at Sea, a History of the Russian Navy.* New York: Frederick A. Praeger, 1966, p. 22.

12. Gorshkov, p. 14.

13. Robert K. Massie. *Peter the Great.* New York: Ballantine Books, 1980, pp. 338–366.

14. Woodward, p. 26.

15. Gorshkov, p. 15.

16. Woodward, p. 34.

17. <http://www.netsrq.com/~dbois/cath-gr.html>, from Microsoft Encarta.

18. Gorshkov, p. 17.

19. Woodward, pp. 43, 45.

20. Gorshkov, p. 20.

21. The Crimean War, <http://mars.acnet.wnec.edu/~grempel/courses/russia/lectures/19crimeanwar.html>.

22. Gorshkov, p. 29.

23. Norman Polmar and Jurrien Noot. *Submarines of the Russian and Soviet Navies, 1718-1990.* Annapolis, Md.: Naval Institute Press, 1990, p. 8.

24. Gorshkov, p. 30.

25. Woodward, p. 141.

26. Woodward, p. 147.

27. Woodward, p. 153.

28. <http://nmhm.washingtondc.museum/exhibits/mcgee/mcgee.html>.

29. Gorshkov, p. 35.

30. Gorshkov, p. 40.

31. Gorshkov, p. 46.

32. <http://www.neva.ru/EXPO96/book/chap11-4.html>.

33. Gorshkov, p. 55.

34. Woodward, p. 196.

35. Gorshkov, p. 67.

36. Gorshkov, p. 103.

37. Gorshkov, p. 120.

APPENDIX TWO:

SOVIET AND AMERICAN SUBMARINES

38. The *Grayback* and the *Growler* were large boats displacing 3,650 tons submerged, and were 322 feet long. The *Tunny* and *Barbero* were 312 feet long and displaced 2,400 tons submerged. *DANFS.*

39. bhp stands for "break horsepower," a term reflecting the instrument used in testing the engines to determine the power they could deliver.

40. Polmar and Noot, p. 162.

41. David Miller. *Submarines of the World.* St. Paul, Minn.: MBI Books, 2002, p. 350.

42. shp stands for "ship's horsepower," a standard measure of a ship's propulsion power or capability for its size and configuration.

43. Polmar and Noot, pp. 298–310.

44. A. S. Pavlov. *Warships of the U.S.S.R. and Russia 1945–1995,* translated by Gregory Tokar. Annapolis, Md.: Naval Institute Press, 1997, p. 5.

45. Podvig, p. 295.

46. Miller, p. 426.

47. Miller, p. 427.

48. Pavlov, p. 309.

49. Charles Krupnick. *Decommissioned Russian Nuclear Submarines and International Cooperation.* Jefferson, N.C./London: McFarland & Company, 2001, p. 156.

50. Miller, p. 356.

51. The 533-millimeter torpedo U.S.ET–80 formed part of the naval arsenal since 1980. Search speed, 5 knots; maximum speed, 50 knots; motion range, 15 kilometers; weight of the warhead, 290 kilograms. The torpedo had silver-zinc batteries; however, the *Kursk* was equipped with a test torpedo with a cheaper battery system.

52. The 65–76A class torpedo was used by the navy since 1976; speed, 50 knots; range, 50 kilometers; weight, 530 kilograms.

53. These measurements indicate the diameter or caliber of the torpedo tube.

54. Norman Polmar. *The American Submarine*. Cambridge, England: Patrick Stephens, 1981, p. 119.

55. Walter J. Boyne. *Beyond the Horizons: The Lockheed Story*. New York: St. Martins Press, 1998, p. 286.

BIBLIOGRAPHY

PRIMARY SOURCES (ARCHIVAL MATERIALS AND ORAL HISTORIES)

Oral Histories

Oral History with Captain First Rank Vladimir Borisov by Dr. Gary E. Weir, St. Petersburg, February 20, 2002.

Oral History with Rear Admiral Oleg Chefonov and Captain First Rank Igor Chefonov by Dr. Gary E. Weir, Moscow, February 12, 2002.

Oral History with Rear Admiral Lev Chernavin by Dr. Gary E. Weir, St. Petersburg, February 18, 2002.

Oral History with Captain First Rank Boris Kolyada by Dr. Gary E. Weir, St. Petersburg, February 17, 2002.

Oral History with Rear Admiral Gleb Kondratiev by Dr. Gary E. Weir, Moscow, February 11, 2002.

Oral History with Captain First Rank Igor Kozyr by Dr. Gary E. Weir, St. Petersburg, February 19, 2002.

Oral History with Captain First Rank Igor Kurdin by Dr. Gary E. Weir, St. Petersburg, February 19, 2002.

Oral History with Rear Admiral Vladimir G. Lebedko by Dr. Gary E. Weir, St. Petersburg, February 16, 2002.

Oral History with Captain Second Rank Vadim Orlov by Iazamir Gotta, Irina Krivaya, and Dr. Gary E. Weir, Moscow, August–September, 2002.

Oral History with Vice Admiral Anatoli I. Shevchenko by Dr. Gary E. Weir, Moscow, February 10 and 13, 2002.

Oral History with Captain First Rank Nikolai Shumkov by Dr. Gary E. Weir, Moscow, February 14, 2002.

Oral History with Allan Robinson by Dr. Gary E. Weir, Office of Naval Research/H. John Heinz III Center, Oral History Project, *Oceanography: The Making of a Science*, video tape 2 of 2, March 31, 2000, conducted at the Woods Hole Oceanographic Institution. U.S. Navy Operational Archive, U.S. Naval Historical Center, Washington, D.C.

Documents

Captain First Rank Vladimir S. Borisov. "First Soviet Nuclear Submarines" (personally prepared source essay).

Vice Admiral George Emery, USN (Ret.). E-mail correspondence with Dr. Gary E. Weir, October–December, 2002.

Captain First Rank Boris Kolyada. "The Last Cruise of the *K-278* (the *Komsomolets*)" (personally prepared source essay).

Rear Admiral Gleb Kondratiev. "So What Was It: The Underwater War or Simply Confrontation?" (personally prepared source essay).

Captain First Rank Igor Kozyr. "*Kursk* Follow-Up" (personally prepared source essay).

Captain First Rank Igor Kurdin. "The Mystery of the *Kursk*" (personally prepared source essay).

Rear Admiral Vladimir G. Lebedko. "The story of the USS *Gato* and the Soviet Hiroshima" (personally prepared source essay).

Captain Second Rank Vadim Orlov. "The Story of a Radio Surveillance Officer" (personally prepared source essay).

Vice Admiral Anatoli I. Shevchenko. "The Arctic Cruises" (personally prepared source essay).

Late Entry, Flag Plot, October 23, 1966; Naval Message from CO-

MASWFORLANT to CTG 81.5 et al., October 24, 1966. U.S. Navy Operational Archives, Washington, D.C.

Published

U.S. Navy, Bureau of Medicine and Surgery. *History of the Medical Department of the United States Navy in World War II: The Statistics of Diseases and Injuries.* Vol. 3. Washington, D.C.: Government Printing Office, 1950.

Sergei Gorshkov. *Red Star Rising at Sea.* Annapolis, Md.: Naval Institute Press, 1974.

SECONDARY SOURCES (BOOKS AND ARTICLES)

Jeffrey G. Barlow. *Revolt of the Admirals.* Washington, D.C.: Brasseys, 1998.

Walter J. Boyne. *Clash of Titans: World War II at Sea.* New York: Simon & Schuster, 1995.

_____. *Beyond the Horizons: The Lockheed Story.* New York: St. Martins Press, 1998.

Admiral of the Fleet Vladimir N. Chernavin. "Operation Atrina." *Typhoon*, 25 (June 2000), 34–35.

John Craven. *The Silent War.* New York: Simon & Schuster, 2001.

Francis Duncan. *Rickover: The Struggle for Excellence.* Annapolis, Md.: Naval Institute Press, 2001.

Trevor Dupuy, Curt Johnson, and David L. Bongard, editors. *The Harper Encyclopedia of Military Biography.* New York: HarperCollins, 1992.

Peter Early. *Family of Spies: Inside the John Walker Spy Ring.* New York: Bantam Books, 1988.

Rene Francillion. *Japanese Aircraft of the Pacific War.* London: Putnam, 1979.

Norman Friedman. *U.S. Submarines Since 1945: An Illustrated Design History.* Annapolis, Md.: Naval Institute Press, 1995.

_____. *The Fifty Year War: Conflict and Strategy in the Cold War.* Annapolis, Md.: Naval Institute Press, 2000.

W. J. R. Gardner. *Anti-Submarine Warfare.* Washington, D.C.: Brasseys, 1996.

_____. *Decoding History: The Battle of the Atlantic and Ultra.* Annapolis, Md.: Naval Institute Press, 1999.

Brayton Harris. *The Navy Times Book of Submarines.* New York: Berkley Books, 1997.

Richard Hewlett and Francis Duncan. *Nuclear Navy, 1946–1962.* Chicago: University of Chicago Press, 1974.

Richard Hough. *The Longest Battle. The War at Sea 1939–1945.* New York: Quill, William Morrow, 1986.

Peter Huchthausen. *K-19: The Widow Maker.* Washington, D.C.: National Geographic, 2002.

Peter Huchthausen, Igor Kurdin, and R. Alan White. *Hostile Waters.* New York: St. Martins Press, 1997.

E. W. Jolie. *A Brief History of U.S. Navy Torpedo Development.* Newport, R.I.: Naval Underwater Systems Center, 1978.

Charles Krupnick. *Decommissioned Russian Nuclear Submarines and International Cooperation.* Jefferson, N.C./London: McFarland & Company, 2001.

Andrew Lightbody and Joseph Poyer. *Submarines, Hunters/Killers & Boomers.* Lincolnwood, Ill.: Publications International, 1990.

Alfred Thayer Mahan. *The Influence of Sea Power upon History, 1660–1783.* New York: Hill & Wang, 1957.

Robert K. Massie. *Peter the Great.* New York: Ballantine Books, 1980.

David Miller. *Submarines of the World.* St. Paul, Minn.: MBI Books, 2002.

Marc Milner. *North Atlantic Run: The Royal Canadian Navy and the Battle for the Convoys.* Annapolis, Md.: Naval Institute Press, 1985.

James L. Mooney, editor. *Dictionary of American Naval Fighting Ships.* Washington, D.C.: U.S. Naval Historical Center, 1991.

Michael Palmer. *Origins of the Maritime Strategy.* Annapolis, Md.: Naval Institute Press, 1990.

A. S. Pavlov. *Warships of the U.S.S.R. and Russia 1945–1995,* translated by Gregory Tokar. Annapolis, Md.: Naval Institute Press, 1997.

Pavel Podvig, editor. *Russian Strategic Forces.* Cambridge, Mass.: MIT Press, 2001.

Norman Polmar. *The American Submarine.* Cambridge, England: Patrick Stephens, 1981.

_____. *Guide to the Soviet Navy.* Annapolis, Md.: Naval Institute Press, 1986.

_____. *The Naval Institute Guide to the Soviet Navy. Fifth Edition.* Annapolis, Md.: Naval Institute Press, 1991.

Norman Polmar and Thomas B. Allen. *Rickover.* New York: Simon & Schuster, 1982.

Norman Polmar and Jurrien Noot. *Submarines of the Russian and Soviet Navies, 1718–1970.* Annapolis, Md.: Naval Institute Press, 1991.

Gordon Prange. *At Dawn We Slept.* New York: Simon & Schuster, 1981.

Anthony Preston. *Submarine Warfare.* London: Brown Books, 1998.

Bryan Ranft and Geoffrey Till. *The Sea in Soviet Strategy.* Annapolis, Md.: Naval Institute Press, 1989.

Eberhard Rössler. *Geschichte des deutschen Ubootbaus.* Munich: J. F. Lehmans Verlag, 1975.

Richard Russell. *Project Hula: Secret Soviet–American Cooperation in the War Against Japan.* Washington, D.C.: U.S. Naval Historical Center, 1997.

Vladimir Shlpaentokh. *Public and Private Life of the Soviet People: Changing Values in Post-Stalin Russia.* New York/Oxford: Oxford University Press, 1989.

Sherry Sontag and Christopher Drew. *Blind Man's Bluff.* New York: Harper Collins, 1998.

David Syrett. *The Defeat of the German U-boats: The Battle of the Atlantic.* Columbia: University of South Carolina Press, 1994.

V. E. Tarrant. *The U-boat Offensive, 1914–1945.* Annapolis, Md.: Naval Institute Press, 1989.

Curtis A. Utz. *Cordon of Steel: The U.S. Navy and the Cuban Missile Crisis.* Washington, D.C.: U.S. Naval Historical Center, 1993.

Gary E. Weir. *Building American Submarines 1914–1940.* Washington, D.C.: U.S. Naval Historical Center, 1991.

_____. *Forged in War: The Naval Industrial Complex and American Submarine Construction, 1940–1961.* Washington, D.C.: Brasseys, 1998.

_____. *An Ocean in Common: American Naval Officers, Scientists, and the Ocean Environment.* College Station: Texas A&M University Press, 2001.

Kathleen Broome Williams. *Secret Weapon: U.S. High Frequency Direction Finding in the Battle of the Atlantic.* Annapolis, Md.: Naval Institute Press, 1996.

H. P. Willmott. *Empires in the Balance: Japanese and Allied Pacific Strategies to April 1942.* Annapolis, Md.: Naval Institute Press, 1982.

_____. *The Barrier and the Javelin: Japanese and Allied Pacific Strategies, February to June 1942.* Annapolis, Md.: Naval Institute Press, 1982.

David F. Winkler. *The Cold War at Sea: High Seas Confrontation between the United States and the Soviet Union.* Annapolis, Md.: Naval Institute Press, 2000.

David Woodward. *The Russians at Sea: A History of the Russian Navy.* New York: Frederick A. Praeger, 1966.

INDEX